BEYOND STRATEGIES

Cultural Dynamics in Asian Connections

Edited by

PRIYA SINGH
SUCHANDANA CHATTERJEE
ANITA SENGUPTA
ARPITA BASU ROY

Maulana Abul Kalam Azad Institute of Asian Studies
Kolkata

in association with

KNOWLEDGE WORLD

KW Publishers Pvt Ltd
New Delhi

2011 FPBA BEST PUBLISHERS AWARD (ENGLISH)

The **Maulana Abul Kalam Azad Institute of Asian Studies** (MAKAIAS) is an autonomous body under the Ministry of Culture, Government of India.

MAKAIAS is a centre for research and learning with a focus on social cultural, economic and political/administrative developments in Asia from the middle of the 19th Century onwards, with special emphasis on their links with India, and also on the life and works of Maulana Abul Kalam Azad.

ISBN 978-93-83649-04-4

Published in India by Kalpana Shukla

KNOWLEDGE WORLD

KW Publishers Pvt Ltd
4676/21, First Floor, Ansari Road, Daryaganj, New Delhi 110002
✆ +91.11.23263498/43528107 ✉ knowledgeworld@vsnl.net • www.kwpub.com

Printed and Bound in India

Contents

Commentaries

Research Notes

Film Review

List of Contributors

Shahmahmood Miakhel, Country Director for Afghanistan, United States Institute of Peace, Kabul, Afghanistan

Jael Silliman, Social Activist & Formerly Associate Professor, Women Studies, University of Iowa, United States of America

Raviprasad Narayanan, Assistant Research Fellow, Institute of International Relations and concurrently Assistant Professor, International Doctoral Program of Asia Pacific Studies at the National Chengchi University, Taipei, Taiwan

Sujata Ashwarya Cheema, Assistant Professor, Centre for West Asian Studies, Jamia Millia Islamia, New Delhi, India

Laura Yerekesheva, Deputy Director and Head of Department of Central and South Asian Studies, Institute of Oriental Studies, UNESCO Chair Coordinator, Almaty, Kazakhstan

Navras Jaat Aafreedi, Assistant Professor, Department of History and Civilization, Gautam Buddha University, Greater Noida, India

Rashmi Doraiswamy, Professor, (Central Asia) Academy of International Studies, Jamia Millia Islamia, New Delhi, India

Dilorom Karomat, Fellow, Maulana Abul Kalam Azad Institute of Asian Studies, Kolkata, India

Davlat Khudonazarov, Head, Focus Humanitarian Assistance Foundation, Moscow Representative Office, Moscow, Russia

Zalmay Wafamal, First Secretary (Political and Press), Embassy of Islamic Republic of Afghanistan, New Delhi, India

Sanaullah Tasal, Director, Baccha Khan Centre for Peace and Conflict Resolution, Kabul, Afghanistan

Sayed Mohammad Shah, Public Information Officer, United Nations Assistance Mission (UNAMA), Kabul, Afghanistan

Dmitry E. Nikolaev, Deputy Director, Research Centre "Analitik," Yekaterinburg, Russia

Aleksey Arapov, Senior Specialist, International Institute of Central Asian Studies, Samarkand, Uzbekistan

Chana Anzi, Cultural Attaché, Embassy of Israel, New Delhi, India

Preface

Strategic issues continue to be the crucial element for policy formulation be it at the local, regional, national and global level, yet, there are significant dimensions outside the hard core foreign policy framework that remain by and large unappreciated in policy-related literature. These dimensions envelop a rather wide range of actions/activities that essentially comprise what could be broadly referred to as constituting *cultural dynamics,* which entails looking *beyond* the radar of strategic relationships, particularly at socio-cultural engagements encompassing both institutions and communities that in turn involve a large number of citizens cutting across boundaries; reiterating and reemphasising a sense of belonging or (un)belonging.

Contemporary challenges in the local, regional, national and global sense raise crucial queries about cultural affinities and inclusive futures across the world in general and Asia in particular. This is an epoch where trans-cultural, trans-national and multicultural belonging are being tried and tested by way of environmental calamity, economic instability, insularity, notions of pluralistic and multicultural exhaustion, and war. A primary challenge lies in the contradiction of culture, in which belonging has become both an essential concern of conservation, tradition and survival; as well as one of hybridity, transgression, opportunity and conversion. In appreciation of the significance of responding to these encounters between the inclusiveness and exclusivity of cultures the Maulana Abul Kalam Azad Institute of Asian Studies convened an International Seminar on *Beyond Strategies: Cultural Dynamics in Asian Connections* in March 2013 in Kolkata, India. The seminar initiated debate and discussion, critical reflection and examination of emerging social and cultural identities that are formed at the crossroads of multiple and multi-sited belonging within the Asian expanse stretching from West Asia through Eurasia, South Asia to Southeast Asia. The aim of the seminar was to focus on a wide array of established as well as emerging cultural patterns which would facilitate in envisaging and contesting linkages across the Asian space along with their social, political and economic ramifications. The debates and discussions revolved around various themes in the realm of cultural studies encompassing gender, communication and film studies, as well as incorporating chronicles of the diaspora, perceptions of culture across borders, the interplay of cultural dynamics and developmental processes and the process of visualising new conceptions with the aim of transfiguring culture. The chapters in this volume incorporate an array of perceptions on the theme of cultural linkages in the Asian space as presented by the participants of the seminar. The writings in the volume has been categorised into essays, commentaries, research notes and a short film review.

Essays

Shah Mahmoud Miakhel's essay, *In the Afghan Diaspora: A Narrative* is an impression of his encounters as a member of the Afghan Diaspora in which he recounts his experiences as a refugee in Pakistan, his journey to the United States and his subsequent involvement in the process of reconstruction in contemporary Afghanistan in different capacities: as an associate of the government, a representative of the United Nations Assistance Mission of Afghanistan and as the Country Director of the United States Institute of Peace in Afghanistan. Jael Silliman's essay, *"A Diaspora of Hope:" The Baghdadi Jews of Calcutta (1970's-1965)* raises issues of identity, gender and what it signifies to live in diaspora and be part of a travelling community, in this case the Baghdadi Jews of Calcutta.

Raviprasad Narayan in his essay, *Culture and Foreign Policy: The Confucius Institutes and Advancing "Soft Power" with Chinese Characteristics* analyses from an Indian perspective the Confucius Institutes established by the Chinese government to promote the civilisational appeal of China, which appear to articulate China's ideational shift in the last three decades. Sujata Ashwarya Cheema in her essay, *Cultural Space between Iraq and Iran: Shi'i Identity, Traditional Connectivity and Social Exchange* examines the construction of a cultural space between Iran and Iraq created by the movement of the elites and worshipers to holy cities in the two countries/domains through centuries and analyses the factors that have sustained this space over time and also looks at elements that have caused it to shrink periodically. Laura Yerekesheva's essay, *The Net of Culture: Living in many cultures, defining own selfhood (Oralman Communities in Kazakhstan)* interprets the issue of culture-identity interplay in contemporary Kazakhstan as perceived through the prism of the net of cultures, that is, the sum of various types and forms of communities' selfhood and identity.

Navras Jaat Aafreedi's essay, *Between Indianness and Jewishness: The ambivalence of Indian Jews as reflected in Literature, Cinema and Art* explores how Indian Jewish writers and poets express in their prose and poetry the ambivalence they face and whether at all the pangs of marginalisation gets reflected in literature, cinema and art. Rashmi Doraiswamy in her essay, *Literature in the post-Soviet Central Asian space* examines some of the post-Soviet works by Central Asian as well as Russian writers as literature in the Eurasian space had to take up themes that concerned people in the new historical circumstances in the aftermath of the collapse of the Soviet Union which had led to a fragmentation of the cultural space. Dilorom Karomat in her essay, *Hip Hop music in Afghanistan, Tajikistan and Uzbekistan* studies the phenomena of Hip-Hop in the capitals Afghanistan, Tajikistan and Uzbekistan which she contends plays a crucial role in the process of developing musical culture as well provides motivation in building bridges between people of different countries and backgrounds.

Commentaries

Davlat Khudonazarov's commentary, *Cultural and Economic ties between the Indian Subcontinent and Central Asia: Past and Future* elaborates upon the history of shared culture between Central Asia and the Indian Subcontinent and the subsequent severing of connections since the collapse of the Soviet Union. Zalmay Wafamal's commentary, *Cultural Dynamics of Afghanistan: Religion and Pashtunwali* emphasises upon the success of the Afghan way of governance by striking a balance between religion and *Pashtunwali,* that is, the non-written ethical code of conduct of the Pashtuns in Afghanistan and Pashtun dwelling regions across the Durand Line.

Research Notes

Sanaullah Tasal's note on *Transforming the Culture of Conflict: Fostering Peace through Cultural Contribution in Contemporary Afghanistan* identifies the possible factors in the Afghan culture which could contribute to the transmutation of the culture of violence into a culture of peace. Sayed Mohammad Shah's note on *Gender Studies in Contemporary Afghanistan* deals with the position of women in contemporary Afghanistan in terms of the prevalent regressive cultural practices as well as the progress made within the legal framework. Dmitry E. Nikolaev's note on *Media's image management as a mechanism of expansion of cross-cultural interaction of India and China with*

Tajikistan briefly describes the core ideas which reflect a possible approach to dealing with media images based on the imaginings of China and India, as offered in the mainstream media of the Republic of Tajikistan. Aleksey Arapov's note on *The civilisational identification and consolidation of Central Asia in the cultural space of the Internet* contends with the new and varied formats of the internet that are now becoming one of the primary resources and tools for the consolidation of a new civilisation in Central Asia and its effective interaction with both, a modern Euro-American cultural world and the traditional worlds of Asia. Consequently this synthesis of the Eastern tradition and Western technology can create new and unexpected effects of cultural transformation.

Film Review

The solitary film review in this compilation is in the form of Chana Anzi's appraisal of *The Notion of Siege in Israeli Cinema: "Beaufort" a film by Joseph Cedar.* Anzi argues that the cinematic language of *Beaufort* reveals one of the intrinsic Israeli cultural notions which is not apparent in figurative understanding and analysis. It brings to the surface the embedded and probably impossible-to-get-rid-of "Siege" perception which is common among Israeli-Jews.

The compilation of essays, commentaries, research notes and film review is an attempt at presenting an inclusive volume based on the discussions and deliberations in a seminar which aimed at a critical understanding, analysis and appreciation of the cultural linkages in the Asian milieu as an important addition to the invasive strategic connects.

1. In the Afghan Diaspora: A Narrative

Shahmahmood Miakhel

The content of this paper is based on my personal experience as an Afghan escaping from tyranny and oppression of the communist regime first, then as a refugee in Pakistan, later on immigrating to the United States of America and returning to Afghanistan after the overthrow of the Taliban regime in 2001 and serving various capacities to rebuild Afghanistan. I consider myself as lucky but in general most other Afghans have been facing enormous problems. Every Afghan family lost their close family members, lived under very difficult conditions and each one can write a book about their life in the last thirty-five years. Most of these hardships and sufferings are beyond human tolerance but in Pashto language we have a saying that a man does not die from grievances (*Da Dard na Marg Nashta Day* ید هتشن گـرم من درد د) and another saying that a man is harder than stone when facing problems and softer than a flower when enjoying a good time which passes very quickly. (*Ensan da tegai na kalak day aw da gul na naram* ید کـلک من یږیت د ناسنا ید مرن من لگ د وا).

A Day Changed My Destiny

On Thursday, April 27, 1979, at one o'clock in the afternoon, I had an appointment with my brother-in-law, Eng. Mohammad Naim who was an air force officer in Shindand[1] air base in Farah Province, in Aryan Restaurant in Pul-e-Bagh Omemi area which was located in the north side of Kabul River close to the Ministry of Culture and Information. When Naim arrived, we left the restaurant to go to the Maiwand Jadah[2] (Maiwand Avenue). When we reached the Ministry of Culture and Information, we saw two girls near the building of the ministry who were running and crying but we did not know what was going on. We could not find a bus or taxi to take us to Maiwand Avenue and we decided to cross the river and walk.

Then, we returned to Pul-e-Bagh Omemi area to find a local bus to go out of the city either to Darul Aman area to my sister-in-law's house or to my hostel in Kabul University. When we reached Pul-e-Bagh Omemi, hundreds of people were waiting for buses and taxies and we walked towards Kabul Hotel in the southern side of Presidential Palace because we heard sounds of small arms. When we reached the west of Kabul hotel, about 200 people were standing and watching the military officers and soldiers positioning themselves in the southern side of the Presidential Palace. We saw my brother-in-law's cousin, Hedayatullah[3] who was a military officer in Balahisar and most likely working for the government intelligence agency, among the crowd and we asked him what was going on. He said that these treacherous people (leaders of the communist party who were arrested one night before) would be punished soon. We moved to the north side of Kabul hotel when we reached the main gate area which was just a couple of hundred metres from Pashtunistan Square, the military officers fired in the air towards the crowd to disburse them and we saw some police officers were killed or wounded and they were loading them into trucks. Later on we learnt that a quick reaction force of the Ministry of Interior had clashed with Military forces and they were killed in Pashtunistan Square.

During the evening, heavy fighting started near Darul Aman[4] Palace and we were listening to sounds of heavy artillery and machine guns all night. Next day, which was Friday morning, the sky of Kabul was very clear and we were on the top of the roof looking towards Darul Aman Palace when a reconnaissance plane came and then jet fighters arrived and bombed Qala-e-Tajbeg Palace in the outskirts of Darul Aman Mountains. We saw flames coming out due to heavy bombardment of the Palace. It was about 10 a.m. in the morning and a few minutes later, Kabul Radio announced that President Daud and his brother Sardar Mohammad Naim who were resisting till the last minute had met their fate; the Khalq Revolution attained victory and that all the forces should follow instruction of the revolutionary council through the Kabul Radio. After this news, Kabul became calm and dark days ahead covered the sky.

Moving to Another Unknown Destiny

After the coup of 1978, the PDPA regime, targeted arrest of senior government officials, religious and spiritual leaders, tribal and influential people, students and teachers. Those who were not members of PDPA were considered opponents of the government and would be referred to as agents of imperialists, reactionary, feudal and so on. Arrest and without trial execution of these people become common practice in most prisons of the country. In November 1978, unknown numbers of students from the hostel of Kabul University were arrested including my classmate, Mohammad Tahir from Lalpura district of Nangarhar province, and the fate of all those students are still unknown. Most of them likely killed in polygons[5] near the Pul-e-Charkhi prison.

My father, who was Director of ID cards department in Takhar province, was ideally a good target for them in the first batch of people to be arrested but he was saved by the Director of Zabt-e-Ahwalat (Intelligence Department, later on known as Khad) of Qataghan,[6] Gheyas Haqmal.[7] A few months later, my father was transferred to Nemroz province and after three months in Nemroz, he came to Kabul and told us that it was not possible to work with the regime and we should immigrate to Pakistan. In some parts of Kunar province, already some anti-regime activities had begun and we would receive news of resistance against the regime through media, friends and family members.

It was not an easy decision to immigrate to another country. The plan was that initially our family members should move to our district Khas Kunar and then it was easy to move to the mountains and onward to Pakistan. Our immediate family members were very large and my father had three wives, ten sons and two daughters at the time. I was the oldest among the siblings and just married at the age of twenty-one. Our family was a well-known spiritual family of Miagan or Sayyied in Kunar. We are descendants of Mia Ali Sahib. Mia Ali Sahib shrine is a well-known shrine in Afghanistan especially in the eastern region and people take mentally ill patients to the Shrine for treatment. My grandfather was a spiritual leader and a very influential person in our district. Also, most of our family members were working in the government. So, our family members were first targeted by the communist regime and we were very careful about our movements. Beside these problems, we were not a very rich family and had modest income and we did not know how to support our large family in another country. We moved to the Khas Kunar district with some of our family members and waited for my brother, Sultan Mahmood, who was a student of Agriculture High School in Mazar-e-Sharif to join us after his final exams.

When the local officials learnt that my father was in Khas Kunar in his house and had quit his job, they were suspicious about our activities and decided to arrest my father. My father knew, if he was arrested, he would be killed. Luckily, we were informed by some of our relatives working in the district headquarters that the district administrator was coming to our location. My father immediately decided to escape and we went to the nearby mountains to a village named Chan Chan. Khas Kunar district and especially our village, Mangwal, is very close to the mountains. The government did not have control in the treacherous mountain areas which was linked to Momand Tribal Areas and extended all the way to Momand Agency and Peshawar of Pakistan. It was the second time that my father escaped from arrest with his colleagues in the evening after several hours of fighting with the local militia.

Life in the Mountains and Momand Lashkar[8]

At the beginning, we were stationed in Badai village of Momand but it was too far away from the main route of the mountain and we were in a very isolated area. Living in the mountains was not easy. We would bring our necessary commodities such as flour, sugar and ghee from Gandab Area of Momand Agency which was about 18 hours walking from where we lived. After a week in Badai village, we moved to Bar Chan Chan Village which was located on the main route to Khas Kunar and we wanted to know about the activities of the government. When we left Khas Kunar, my father openly started an Armed Struggle (Jihad) against the government and encouraged people to rise up. He encouraged the Mohmand Tribes to support Jihad against the communist regime. Within a period of two months, a huge Lashkar, tribal irregular army, of Momand Tribes assembled and my father along with some other elders of Khas Kunar and Momand tribes was leading the Lashkar.

Later on, the tribes of border areas became supporters of the Mujahedin and allowed them to cross from their territory providing food and accommodation to the Mujahedin crossing these treacherous mountains inside Afghanistan to fight against the communist regime. For guerilla warfare, safe haven and external support, safe retreating space and local support among people is very important. Therefore, the Mujahedin were successful in fighting against the government and the border tribes supported them and provided safe passage back and forth. Due to government threats and Mujahedin activities, every day some families were leaving the government controlled areas and joining the Mujahedin or immigrating to Peshawar. In Khas Kunar, during the day time, the government militia and supporters would burn the houses of those who joined the rank and file of the Mujahedin or immigrated to Pakistan and during the nights, the Mujahedin would burn the houses of government militias and their supporters.

Moving to Peshawar from the Mountains

After spending four months in the mountains, my father's reputation and support among local people increased but at the same time, we were running out of money. We did not have enough money to support our family or feed 20-30 Mujahedin every day. I told my father that we would have no choice except to move to Peshawar, work there and get some assistance from the Mujahedin parties or government of Pakistan.

When we came to Peshawar, it was very difficult to find a house and we were only able to find two rooms for 400 rupees rent per month. There were no refugee camps at that time in Peshawar or surrounding areas. My younger brothers started to work in the local market for very minimal wages and I tried to find a job in one of the Mujahedin party or someplace else. My father and I met Gulbudin Hekmatyar and some other Mujahedin leaders. My father told Hekmatyar that Hezb-e-Islami provincial office appointed Mulla Sahaf as commander of Mujahedin in Khas Kunar and since he did not receive anything from his party, he did not want to be affiliated with Hezb-e-Islami anymore. Most of Hezb-e-Islami leadership was young and did not have experience to respect elders and former government officials from previous regimes. The structure of Hezb-e-Islami was the same as PDPA, with the only difference being one of ideology.

My father's friends in Jamiat-e-Islami took us to Professor Burhanudin Rabbani and he asked my father to work as his commander in Khas Kunar.[9] He promised to provide some military support. The director of administration of Jamiat-e-Islami, Mr. Abbas Mashfeq, who was my Dari Language teacher in Laghman province in 11 grade,[10] appointed me in the Political Committee of Payman-e-Itehad Islami[11] which was a four party alliance of Mujahedin parties at that time. Professor Rabbani was the head of political committee. Payman-e-Itehad Islami gave me sixteen rupees per day and Jamiat-e-Islami refugee committee prepared ration pass for our family. In the early days, the UN High Commissioner for Refugee Office (UNHCR) through the government of Pakistan would give one hundred and twenty rupees to each family member and some other commodities per month. At that time it was more than enough for our expenses. At that time, the government of Pakistan would not register refugees unless the family was affiliated with one of the Mujahedin groups. This trend had a huge negative impact later on because most Afghan intellectuals were not happy to be part of Peshawar based Mujahedin groups. Many of these intellectuals were obliged to leave Peshawar. Those who stayed in Peshawar lived under very difficult conditions and many of them who did not agree with the policy of Pakistan or Mujahedin, were killed in the 1980s and 1990s.

Working with Payman-e-Itehad Islami Afghanistan

In the summer of 1978, a group of Afghans known as Ulema lead by Moulavi Mohammad Nabi Mohammadi came to Peshawar to bring unity among these two Mujahedin groups and plan for future course of action against the communist regime. After consultation and pressure by party members of both groups, they made another alliance under the name of Harakat-e-Inqilab Islami Afghanistan (Islamic Movement of Afghanistan). In Mohammadia Mosque of Peshawar near Ashnaghari area, all party loyalists including Hekmatyar and Prof. Rabbani pledged allegiance to Moulavi Mohammad Nabi and elected him as leader of this new alliance.

After the Soviet invasion in the end of 1979, some leaders of Afghan refugees and Ulema organised a meeting in Peshawar and asked the Mujahedin leaders to unite and fight against the Soviet occupation. Many of these leaders would come to Payman-e-Itehad Islami Office and pressure the leaders to reach an agreement to have a united front. After a long negotiation and back-door lobbying by various foreign supporters of the Mujahedin, such as Pakistan, Arabs and Western Countries, they agreed to establish Itehad-e-Islami bara-e-Azadi Afghanistan (Islamic Unity for Liberation of Afghanistan). All six groups of the Mujahedin were members of this new alliance and each group introduced 7 members to the alliance as the ruling council. The ruling council would choose one person as its leader among themselves. Payman-e-Itehadi Islami merged into this new alliance and I was appointed in the refugee committee.

It is worth mentioning that more than 200 small and big groups of Afghans emerged by different names till 1982. My father with his colleagues also established a new group by the name of Wahdat-ul-Muslim of Afghanistan (Muslim Unity Party of Afghanistan). They selected Rahmat Shah Delawar[12] as leader, Haji Saifudin Momand[13] as his deputy and my father as Secretary General of this group. Moulana Qiyamudin Kashaf[14] was selected as head of Information Committee, Brigadier Abdul Rauf Safi[15] as head of military committee, Qazi Mirzaman as head of Justice Committee and Mahmadullah Khan a known prosecutor from Mazar was head of Refugee Committee. Most members of this new party had defected from Jamiat-e-Islami Afghanistan.

The moderate groups were:

1. National Liberation Front, lead by Professor Sebghatullah Muajdedi
2. Harakat-e-Inqilab-e-Islami Afghanistan (National Islamic Movement of Afghanistan) led by Moulavi Mohammad Nabi Mohammadi
3. National Islamic Front lead by Pir Sayed Ahmad Gilani

The moderate groups were led by a Supreme Council and did not choose one person as their leader. This alliance was also known as Ittehad-e-Segana (three-party alliance) and rented a huge office on Charsada Road.

The fundamentalist groups also kept the same name of The Unity of the Mujahedin of Afghanistan for this alliance. This alliance was also known as Ittehad-e-Haftgana (seven-party unity) They included:

4. Hezb-e-Islami lead by Gulbudin Hekmatyar
5. Hezb-e-Islami lead by Moulavi Mohammad Yunus Khalis
6. Jamiat-e-Islami lead by Professor Burhanudin Rabbani
7. The Unity of the Mujahedin for Liberation of Afghanistan lead by Professor Abdul Rab Rasool Sayaf

When the council of this new fundamentalist group of alliance chose Professor Sayaf as its leader, the leaders of Jamiat and both Hezb did not like this decision and blamed Sayaf for bribing each council member with 100,000 rupees and one brand new Corolla vehicle. This alliance did not function as well and later on Jamiat and both Hezb parties quit the alliance but Professor Sayaf kept the name of alliance and his party is still called by the name of Ittehad-e-Islami Mujahedin of Afghanistan. When Ittehad-e-islami Mujahedin of Afghanistan split into two alliances by the same name, deputy of Professor Mujadedi, Moulavi Mohammad Mir and Deputy of Harakat Moulavi Nasrullah Mansoor stayed with Professor Sayaf's and both of them were accepted as leader of the same groups. Also another member of Harakat named Moulavi Moazen also separated from Harakat and Professor Sayaf recognised him as leader of another faction of Harakat. Therefore, the fundamentalist alliance was called alliance of seven parties.

Life in a Refugee Camp

In spring 1981, our family decided to move to Kacha Gari camp near Peshawar city because it was newly established and most of our friends and people from our area had already moved there. It was also very difficult for us to pay rent for a big house in the city to accommodate all our family members. First we built a mud wall compound around 2,500 sq metres area in order to be protected from outside. Then my brothers and I built a couple of mud rooms by ourselves and pitched tents inside the compound. Living in tents was another experience; it was extremely cold in the winter and hot in the summer. Initially, there were two big problems in Kacha Gari Refugee Camp. One was lack of water and the second one was no electricity. There were no trees in the camp area and it is was extremely difficult especially for kids and women to stay in the tent during the day time in the very hot summers of Peshawar where the temperature would reach between 45-50° Celsius. The difficult part of the summer season was observing fast during the month of Ramadan. The days were long and the heat was high. Most people could not afford to buy ice from the local market, including us. Many children died in the summer of 1981 in Kacha Gari camp because of dehydration, including my two brothers from my second mother. In the north side of the camp, the refugees allocated a piece of land for graveyard and we buried the first body from our mosque, a person named Sher who was from Koz Kunar district of Nangarhar. Later on Kacha Gari Graveyard swelled to a thousand graves. Many refugees who had died in the city or martyred in Jihad inside Afghanistan, their relatives would bring them to Kacha Gari camp as well. My own brother, Sardar Mahmood, who was killed in Kacha Gari in 1990 by unknown people, was also buried in this graveyard along with many other relatives and friends. Later on you could see hundreds of green flags on the graves of those who become Shaheed during the war. Every morning, you could see many women going to the graveyard to pay respect to their martyrs, or relatives to pray and seek blessing from the Shaheed.

UNHCR and Afghan Commissionerate would bring some water by tankers but it was not enough and women, children and men would wait for hours in long queues. Some people started to dig wells but it was not easy because the water was 40-50 metres below the surface in rocky sands. Our brothers and I would pitch water every evening from a well outside of our compound and would reserve them in big buckets to use during the day. My brothers and I decided it would be better to dig a well inside our compound. We dug a well till 15 metres by ourselves but it was not possible to complete it so we paid a local person who knew how to dig the well, 20 rupees per metre. Paying a thousand rupees for having a well inside a compound was considered a luxury.

The number of Kacha Gari camp swelled very quickly and reached over thirty thousand people. People were organised around mosque structures and each mosque was known by people of the same area or tribes of Afghanistan. For example, our mosque was known as Kamawal Mosque because most people around the mosque were originally from Kama district of Nangarhar province and we were also originally from Kama district. My grandfather moved to Khas Kunar during the time of King Amanullah (1919-1929) because he became a disciple of Sarkano Mia Saib.[16] Some other camps were known by a specific tribe such as Abdur Rahim Zai mosque. There were around 61 mosques[17] in Kacha Gari. The Saudi Red Crescent established a BHU (Basic Health Unit) in the middle of the camp. In the beginning, there were no schools in the camp and most kids were only studying basic religious subjects in the mosques. My father admitted my younger brothers in Darul-ul-Hijra Madrasa close to the camp which was established by Hezb-e-Islami Khalis. Later on my father admitted one of my own brothers and two brothers from my second mother in Quran memorisation madrasa in the camp. Many of these madrasas were supported by Arabs and would give some stipend to the students as well. It was a trend that each family should have Hafiz or religious students in the house. My five brothers become Hafiz of Quran. UNHCR later on started some primary schools in the camp but the qualities of these schools were very low due to lack of qualified teachers, proper curriculum and teaching materials.

Since the Kacha Gari Camp was very close to Peshawar city on the main road to Jamrud and Khyber Pass, the government of Pakistan would try to bring more visiting dignitaries to Kacha Gari Refugee Camp. King Shah Fahid of Saudi Arabia, President Zia, Diego Cordovez and many others visited this camp. My father, who was known as Moder Saib,[18] would be selected by the refugees to speak on their behalf. Once, some cabinet ministers of Pakistan visited Kacha Gari camp, my father on behalf of refugees thanked them for their support to Afghan refugees but he mentioned that despite all their hospitality, it was not fair to treat refugees any differently from their own people because the refugees could spot the big electric poles inside the camp area but as they did not have electricity their children were dying from heat every day. Then, the government of Pakistan allowed the Afghan refugees to have electricity provided they paid the bills. My father commanded more respect among the refugees for this service. When Mr. Diego Cordovez, special representative of the UN who negotiated the Geneva Accord, came to Kacha Gari Camp after signing the agreement, my father spoke on behalf of refugees and told him, "it would be better that you would have come before signing of the agreement in order to include our concerns, but consultation with Afghan refugees after signing agreement doesn't make sense. This agreement cannot solve the Afghan problem which is returning of Afghan refugees to their country and ending war in Afghanistan." Mr. Cordovez again stood up and told my father that he was right that the Geneva agreement could not solve Afghan problems. But when he would have meetings with Afghan leaders, Pakistanis and Americans, everyone was saying that if the Soviet forces left Afghanistan, the Afghan problem would be solved. He said that the Geneva agreement was only for the withdrawal of the Soviet forces not for the other two problems that my father mentioned.

In terms of living conditions, Kacha Gari camp was much better than other camps in Peshawar area because it was very close to the city. Refugees had opportunity to work in Peshawar city and had some access to Pakistani schools for education. The Afghan Commissionerate divided the camp into five sections and each section had a camp commander who was responsible for distribution of assistance to the refugees. Each camp had several representatives of the Afghan refugees and each representative was called Malik of ration. These Maliks had links with the officials of Afghan Commissionerate and each one had tens of fake ration passes. I could say that corruption phenomena among Afghans started from distribution of these rations by Afghan Commissionerate and giving money and weapons to Afghan political parties with no accountability. The whole camp had one chief from the Afghan Commissionerate and called him Area Administrator.

Another Curve in My Life

The life of each person has many curves which changes his/her destiny to another direction. In 1982, my life curve changed when I met Professor David Edwards. As I was mentioned before, I was thinking to find another job independently from the Mujahedin parties. One day I was building mud rooms in our compound, a Japanese man visited the camp and came to our compound. This Japanese man named Kenzo Nakagawa had studied in Kabul University and later on I learnt that he was a missionary. He asked me if I could help to teach him Dari. I agreed and he told me that I should teach him

3 hours per week and he would pay me 15[19] (one and a half dollar) rupees per hour. Initially, he paid me 180 rupees per month. This amount was only enough to feed my second child, Zia[20] to buy milk for him. My second son Zia and daughter Abzamzam were born in Kacha Gari Camp in a tent. After a couple of months, Kenzo opened a school for Nomads on Bachagi road near Peshawar and asked me if I could teach them as well. I agreed and taught 10 hours per week Pashto and basic Math to those nomads and he would pay me 600 rupees plus transportation. At the same time, I started to teach the children of one of my father's friends, who promised to pay me 1,000 rupees per month in Gulbarg area of Peshawar. Ittehad-e-Islami Mujahedin Afghanistan also paid me around 1,800 rupees per month for a few months till it was disintegrated and I quit in summer 1982. In this way, I was the only one in the family to make enough money to support my family. My brother, Sardar, who got some basic medical training in ICRC hospital, opened a chemists shop in the camp and he was making some money as well.

In October 19982, one day, I was walking towards my father's friend's house to teach his children in Gulbarg area, I saw an American named John Kountze who was walking along the railway road and when I asked him where he was going, he told me that he wanted to go to Dabgari. I told him that he was going in the wrong direction and if he walked for a few minutes, there would be no houses and it would not be safe as well. John Kountze was an electronic engineer who spent a year in Kabul before 1978 and taught in the Engineering Faculty of Kabul. He was in Peshawar to pre-record Afghan music for the background of a documentary film. He was planning to go inside Afghanistan but his TV crew did not come to Peshawar for some reason. John asked me where I was going. I told him that I was teaching some children there and if he would like to have tea with us, it would be no problem. John accepted my offer and we had tea in our friend's house. He told me that he wanted to learn some Dari and whether I could help him during his stay. I agreed to teach him and he would pay me 100 rupees per hour. He paid me around 12,000 rupees which was a big amount at that time. He also asked me if I could help him to record some local Afghan music. Helping someone to record music in those days was almost impossible because of Jihad and the reaction of some Ulema and Mujahedin parties. Anyhow, I helped him and we visited Dabgari[21] area and met the famous Afghan singer, Shah Wali. He agreed to record some music in the hotel. I also contacted Abdur Rahman Or who was another well known singer and lived in Kacha Gari Camp. Mr. Or was a Moazen[22] in a mosque near our house. He agreed to record some music but said he did not have any instrument and team to play with him and that he would try to find a team in Dabgari.

In November 1982, when John was leaving for the United States, on the last day he asked me if I could visit him early in the morning for breakfast and he could introduce me to another American who would be in Peshawar for a long time and he may need an assistant. When I went early in the morning for breakfast, John introduced me to David Edwards who had recently arrived at Peshawar to conduct research for his PhD dissertation. When I met David Edwards, he told me that we should be in contact and we may work together. David rented a house on Sayed Jamaludin Afghani Road in the University Town. He told me that he would be in Peshawar for a couple of years and his wife, Holly Edwards, who was also working on her PhD dissertation, would arrive soon.

As David mentioned in his book, *Heroes of Age*, he was not sure in which direction his research might go because the government of Pakistan did not give him permission promptly to continue his research in a refugee camp. He asked me if I could visit him once or twice a week and he would give me some money because he was a student and did not have a lot of money. I agreed because I wanted to improve my English and wanted to be in contact with someone who could help me in English. Initially, David paid 300 rupees per month and I was visiting him more than once a week. He had a very good cook and fed us very well. David and I would talk about different topics such as history, tribal structure and the Sufi order. Honestly, I did not know what anthropology means at that time but I had interest in the above topics because of my personal interest and some family background. Later on, David would give me some interviews for transcription and translation. His wife would spend with me an hour to correct my translation which helped me a lot in my English writing. It is still not perfect but I can put together my thoughts on paper.

When David was interested to interview more people who had links with Mulla of Hadda, then he and I worked almost six days a week till June 1984. We interviewed tens of people in Peshawar and I transcribed most of the interviews and translated literally. Working with David enhanced my knowledge about Afghanistan's history, tribal structure and governance. Working with David shaped my career in the coming three decades of my life for the better.

Moving to the United States

After the Soviet withdrawal from Afghanistan, the trend of Jihad changed due to internal rivalries among the Mujahedin group. I was working for the Voice of America, Pashto and Dari languages as local reporter (1985-1990). Most of our reports were critical of the Mujahedin activities and the Kabul regime resisted fearlessly to stay in power for three more years after the Soviet forces withdrew. Most of the refugees were in despair about the future and many intellectuals were targeted by extremist groups and Arabs who lived in Pakistan and were active inside Afghanistan. Most of these groups were supported by ISI of Pakistan to keep alive resistance against the regime. Several of my close friends who had independent thinking about the future of Afghanistan such as Professor Majrooh, Dr. Ludin, Dr. Zakir, Aziz-ur-Rahman Ulfat and so many others were killed in Peshawar. I received threats and a theft occurred in my office, and was therefore advised by close friends to leave Peshawar. I went to the United States and applied for asylum in May 1990. Unfortunately one month later my brother, Sardar Mahmood, who was going home from his shop during the evening was killed. My other brother, Amir Mahmood along with my cousin Ajmal disappeared in Peshawar in 1987. Another of my cousins, Dr. Rohullah Omar who was a urologist also disappeared in Peshawar. But living as an immigrant in the US was not easy and I was worried about the education of my 7 children and so took the rest of my family to the US in 1997 and 1999.

Returning to Afghanistan after 2001

After overthrowing the Taliban regime in 2001, millions in the Afghan diaspora/refugees have returned to their country after decades of hardship in other countries with a hope to have a better future and stability in Afghanistan. It may take long to explain why these hopes are waning and now many Afghans are once again seeking to move to other countries for pursuing a better life. I returned to Afghanistan in 2002 in the hope of contributing to reconstruction, peace and stability in Afghanistan, supported Emergency Loya Jirga (ELJ), worked for UNAMA and conducted election for ELJ in four eastern provinces of Kunar, Nooristan, Laghman and Nangarhar. I was elected member of ELJ and wrote a book in Pashto language about ELJ and what went wrong because the decisions of ELJ had a negative impact on the future course of action. The decision of the delegates were undermined by the international community and the Afghan Interim government as warlords got more power and were appointed to senior positions in the central and local government. I decided to leave because I knew that the future course of action would not be good for peace and stability in Afghanistan but the new Interior Minister, Ali Ahmad Jalali, convinced me to join him and work with him as Senior Advisor/Deputy Minister of Interior till July 2005.

During my time in the interior ministry, we tried to build institutions and bring serious reforms in the police system and local governance but unfortunately with the cold shoulder of the international community and the lack of vision of the Afghan leadership, we were not able to improve governance. The International Community did not support the police and the actual support came in 2006 after four years of gap of security. This vacuum of security was filled by warlords, local strongmen, drug mafia, organised criminal networks and the Taliban. By the time more resources came, Afghanistan was in full swing of insurgency and in most cases more money become source of instability. Therefore, the most experienced technocrats and the Afghan diaspora who could deliver but did not want to be part of patronage mafia networks left the government. I joined the UN again and am now working with the US Institute of Peace hoping to bring positive changes from outside and still live in Afghanistan.

The future of Afghanistan depends on peaceful transition of power through democratic means in 2014 in order for Afghanistan to receive long-term support from the international community. If Afghan government, politicians and international community lose this last opportunity, Afghanistan may plunge into chaos once again like in 1992 after the collapse of the communist regime of Dr. Najibullah.

Notes

1. Shindand district used to be part of Farah province and later on became part of Herat Province.
2. Maiwand Jadah is a known avenue in Kabul which was located in the south side of Kabul river and most of the buses were going to the provinces from that area at that time.
3. After the coup, Hedayatullah was arrested and most likely killed because his family did not trace his whereabout since 1979.
4. Darul Aman and Qala-e-Tajbeg are two palaces in that area which were built by King Amanullah.
5. Polygons were the areas where the regime would kill people during nights.
6. The four North-eastern provinces of Afghanistan, Baghlan, Kunduz, Takhar and Badakhshan, are called Qataghan.

7. Gheyas Haqmal was pro-Hafizullah Amin and after Amin was killed, he was arrested in Pul-e-Charkhi and spent about 12 years in prison. When I was Deputy Minister of Interior (2003-2005), I appointed him as district governor in Chapa Dara of Kunar. In 2009, he was kidnapped by the Taliban in Khas Kunar and three months later after his abduction, he was killed by the Taliban.
8. Lashkar meaning irregular tribal army.
9. Ibid.
10. I was director of ID cards department in Laghman province between 1973 and 1976 and I studied 10 and 11 grades in Roshan High School in Laghman province.
11. National Liberation Front of Mujadedi, Harakat-e-Islami of Moulavi Mohammadi, Jamiat-e-Islami of Professor Rabbani and Hezb-e-Islami of Moulavi Khalis were members of this alliance.
12. Rahmat Shah Delawar was grandson of Ajab Khan Afridi who kidnapped the British Major's daughter Ms. Mollie Ellis from Kohat Cantonment in 1923 and killed his wife. Ajab Khan's family later on settled in Balkh Province of Afghanistan.
13. Haji Safudin was known Mujahedin Commander in Koz Kunar. In 1978, the district governor of Koz Konar, Hazrat Yunus, wanted to arrest him but instead he arrested the district governor, and took him to the mountain. He kept the governor for 14 months and then released him.
14. Moualana Qeyamudin Kashaf at present is head of Ulema Council of Afghanistan.
15. Brigadier Abdul Rauf Safi was Commander of Asmar Division in Kunar and deserted to the Mujahedin in 1980 after the Soviet Invasion.
16. Sarkano Mia Saib was originally of Kama district as well and he was disciple of Mulla of Hadda.
17. When David Edwards and I did research in Kacha Gari Camp between 1992-1994, we counted these mosques.
18. In Afghanistan people would be called by their Job titles as matter of respect. Since my father was director (Modir) in Afghanistan, people would call him Modir Saib. Saib is a term of respect.
19. One dollar was equal to 9-10 rupees at that time.
20. Zia completed his masters in Public Policy from George Mason University and works as Media Analyst.
21. Dabgari area is known for musicians and those who need musicians for weddings or other occasions, could hire from there.
22. The man who calls for people for prayers in a mosque.

2. "A Diaspora of Hope": The Baghdadi Jews of Calcutta (1780's-1965)

Jael Silliman

Introduction

In the eighteenth, nineteenth and twentieth centuries, the Baghdadi[1] Jewish diaspora stretched from Baghdad to Shanghai and westward to London. Throughout "Jewish Asia," small communities of Baghdadi Jews carried out their business ventures and community life in key financial and port cities. Calcutta became a significant point on this circuit. The Baghdadi Jews of Calcutta, always very small in number (at its largest in the 1940s numbering about 3,800 persons including 1,200 Jews from Burma), depended on other Jews in Basra, Rangoon, Bombay, Karachi, Jakarta, Singapore and Shanghai for religious, financial and social support. These scattered communities provided one another the business links as well as the religious resources they needed to sustain themselves. Not only goods and traders moved through this circuit. Women moved from one community to another in search of marriage partners, sons moved to expand businesses and extend trading reach and impact, and families moved to be part of wedding and bar mitzvah celebrations. Thus it was marriages, commercial news as well as businesses and family connections that welded the small communities of Baghdadi Jews into an important economic and cultural presence in the East.

This paper specifically examines the Baghdadi Jews of Calcutta as a diaspora community that thrived as a diaspora, perhaps even as a function of diaspora. I have argued that the Baghdadi Jews of Calcutta, unlike other Middle Eastern communities and the European Jewish diaspora, which is considered the quintessential diaspora, was a "diaspora of hope," as successive generations improved their standing in most realms of life through the two centuries in Calcutta and in their subsequent shift to the Western world.[2] In this paper I elaborate this argument that the Calcutta Jews, being at the nerve centre of the Empire (as Calcutta was the capital of British India), experienced many privileges that stemmed from processes of the Empire, which they were able to use to their advantage in India and in their relocation to other homelands in the mid-twentieth century.

The Baghdadi Jewish Economic and Political Muscle

The Baghdadi Jewish trading diaspora elaborated ancient and medieval mercantile routes that enabled them to flourish under colonial rule. Having pre-capitalist trading networks already in place the British provided the conditions for the expansion of these networks to new areas of the world. When the first Baghdadi Jewish settler, Shalome Cohen, arrived in Calcutta in the late eighteenth century, the British had identified Calcutta as an important commercial centre. The British East India Company whose trading domain included India, China, Persia, Basra and Baghdad allowed Jews free trade, used their help in its transactions and granted them British patronage.[3]

Calcutta's appeal for the British was enhanced by its connection to both river and ocean traffic. From 1853 onwards the British constructed a railroad to connect Calcutta with other strategic military and trading locations and established the key economic institutions to ensure commerce would flourish. In the mid-nineteenth century trade between Baghdad and India was dominated by Baghdadi Jewish merchants. In the first part of the nineteenth century they made large fortunes in the opium trade and in Calcutta's booming real estate market, and competed with other trading communities, especially the Armenians and the Parsis in this phase of mercantile capitalism. For example, David Joseph Ezra was one of the leading property owners of the city by the latter half of the nineteenth century. When opium was banned by the British in the early twentieth century, the Baghdadi Jews invested in export commodities such as cotton, indigo and jute products. They traded in silks and precious stones, and ventured into many other commercial enterprises. For example, several were active on the Stock Exchange and the wealthier Jews were largely urban landowners. There were a fair number of smaller Jewish tradesmen and businessmen. They also played important civic roles: Joseph Elias Ezra was Municipal Commissioner (1886-1896) and was Sheriff (1888-1889), the first Jewish Sheriff of Calcutta. Thereafter both his sons became Sheriff of the city.[4] David Ezra earned a knighthood and was director of the Reserve Bank, the Bengal Veterinary College and several other industrial organisations.[5] Thus the Baghdadi Jews prospered under colonial rule and played an important part in the economy as well as in civic and political spheres.

Ambivalent Identity as an Advantage in Colonial India

The Baghdadi Jews were neither Indian nor Western, Brown nor White, at once insiders and outsiders in the colonial structure of Calcutta that was highly delineated by both the British as well as by the class and caste hierarchy of India. They emphasised their foreign origin as they were always worried about assimilation, and they had a deep fear of inter-marriage.[6] The Jewish community chose to live in a very self-contained world in order to preserve their identity. They built the educational and social institutions that were necessary for them to live "apart" from those around them while keeping on very good terms with their neighbours. So the majority of Jews went to Jewish schools primarily. In the very compartmentalised society of India, where each community and caste lived in narrow social domains, the Jews fit in well and were not threatening to others. Other communities also married among one another and stayed within the confines of their own castes and communities. Thus their fear of assimilation and the maintaining of tight knit community structures did not work to their disadvantage. In fact this ambivalent status worked to their advantage in the colonial structure.

Anglicisation

It was only in the mid-nineteenth century that the more wealthy members of the community became anglicised and the community followed their lead. The Jewish schools were set up and run on British educational lines. By the twentieth century, the majority of the Baghdadi Jews born in India spoke English as their primary language at school and at home and they spoke in Arabic to the elders in the community, and Hindustani to their domestic staff and in the street. They read their prayers in Hebrew (much like Sanskrit) but did not understand the language. Like many other Indians, especially the upper classes, they listened to Western music, played the piano and were exposed to the West through books and movies. The wealthy and affluent, like their Indian counterparts, sent their sons to study in England, and some sent their daughters to finishing schools in Europe. The middle classes in the community, which constituted the majority, mimicked the mercantile elite and copied British tastes as best they could afford. Jewish homes had pseudo Western furnishings and décor: preferably heavy mahogany and teak *almirahs* or cupboards, carved tables and chairs and wood and glass china cabinets for their bric-a-brac. Many of the items they used were imported from England that was a common practice in India of that period.

This Anglo orientation was common among other minority communities and among many Indians. The Arab robes of their ancestors were abandoned in a couple of generations: the *dagla* gave way to the pant and shirt, and the flowing *wrappers* and head scarf worn by the women gave way to Western style dresses and hats for formal occasions. The Baghdadi Jews who danced to Western music were quite different from the much more conservative Baghdadi Jews of the nineteenth century who retained their Judeo-Arabic identity, spoke in Arabic, enjoyed *gana bajana* parties which featured Hindi and Urdu music which was much closer to their Arabic roots. The early settlers were much more Eastern in their orientation and had similar cultural practices as other communities in India. For example, they arranged marriages for their children, lived in large joint families and had very strict sexual mores for the women. By the twentieth century English was the main language of communication among the Jewish community, and their orientation was decidedly Western.

Though anglicisation had worked its way into the social culture of the community, the religious aspects and the ritual of the community remained conservatively Middle Eastern. The synagogues were a dominant social and community force from the nineteenth century onwards. Members of the community gravitated to the synagogue and its religious ceremonies. In the absence of a place for meeting, the synagogues were a point for social interaction and exchange, public meetings and the announcement of domestic occurrences. Baghdadi rituals and musical tunes were adhered to in worship. Jewish ritual events and festivals were eagerly anticipated social and ceremonial occasions.

Their food, too, remained Iraqi though they did draw on local vegetables and flavours that provided a distinct Indian twist to their preparations. For example, unlike traditional Baghdadi food the Calcutta Baghdadis added tamarind to flavour their food, and their food was spicier than the food they had eaten in Baghdad. While they mostly ate Iraqi preparations they also ate Indian and Western food. Their observance of festivals, rites, and rituals as well as the adherence to dietary laws and the distinctive foods they prepared set them apart. It all went towards their expression and maintenance of community identity and solidarity. Jewish community was thus deliberately marked and differentiated from others.

The Baghdadis lived in the "Grey" area of the City where other minority communities lived. The South was the "White" area where the British ruled from and were in residence, and the "Black" area to the North was where the local people lived. Thus, by geographic location too they were sandwiched between "Black" and "White" Calcutta. As they prospered, the more affluent moved into the South "White" area towards the late nineteenth and early twentieth century. Most Jews adopted colonial ideas about race and placed themselves in the upper echelons of the racial period that structured life in the colonies.

Sustaining Community across wide Geographical Spaces

The Baghdadi Jews were accepted and decidedly comfortable in Calcutta, and in the string of other port cities where they settled and travelled to for commercial reasons and to cement and sustain community across vast geographical spaces. However, they never identified or saw themselves as part of the lands where they lived. A Baghdadi Jew living in Calcutta had a very similar lifestyle to their counterparts living in Singapore or Shanghai which is why it was relatively easy for a bride to come from Djakarta or Shanghai to settle in Calcutta and vice versa. While in vastly different geographical locations, the members of the Baghdadi diaspora would be adhering to similar rituals and lifestyles. For example, their clothing styles across the diaspora would be similar, as would the food they ate with some local variations, as they would have to adapt to local produce. In fact the lifestyle in the port cities would have been much more similar to one another than they would have been to the hinterlands that the ports served.

Fearful of assimilation, the Baghdadis were extremely strict about intermarriage and lived in self-determined Jewish worlds. It was only the elite of the community who mixed beyond Jewish community confines. The very wealthy sent their children to England for school and college, and some of the upper and middle classes sent their children to receive professional training. A few Jews were trained in the professions though most men joined their family businesses or the Jewish firms. Religious Jews needed to join Jewish firms in order to observe the Sabbath that was hard to do in non-Jewish firms. Most Jews went to Jewish schools,[7] attended Jewish religious and social events, socialised in the Judaen Club[8] and worked for Jewish firms. Jewish charities that were established by the wealthy families took care of the needs of the poorer members of the community of whom there were many.[9] The Jewish charities provided the poor in the community with money during the festivals, clothing and other necessities and the schools helped poorer students with tuition fees, clothing, books and lunches.[10] The *Oseh Haised* (Doers of Good Deeds) was founded in the 1880s to ameliorate poverty in the community. These philanthropic efforts also helped to bind the community and give the community a strong sense of identity and purpose.

From the late 1920s Jewish women paved the way in terms of obtaining professional degrees. For example, Tabitha Solomon was among the early women in India to graduate from Calcutta Dental College, in 1928. Women like Miss Ramah Luddy went to study in London and returned to be the Headmistress of Jewish Girls School for decades and ensured it was a top-notch school providing middle-class Jewish girls with a very competitive education.[11] Women of more modest means took up teacher's training courses and taught in the Jewish Girls School, or worked as seamstresses for Jewish clients. Since acting and movies were not considered appropriate careers for the majority of Hindu and Muslim women, Jewish women in the late 1920s and 1930s also ventured into these fields, some of whom were chaperoned by their families to the studios.[12] This was the case for Miss Rachel Jonah whose screen name was Arati Devi. She acted in the late 1920s in silent film, her first being *Aparadhi*. There were several Baghdadi Jewish women who were in the Bollywood film industry that has been well documented. By the 1940s and the 1950s it was common for Jewish women to go to work and many Calcutta Jewish women, because of their familiarity with English and Western orientation, held very senior posts as secretaries and assistants to executives.[13] Women from elite families like Marie Mordecai (Dawsens) were actively involved in their family businesses.

Till the mid-twentieth century it was possible for Jews to identify primarily as Jews. They could live in India, identify as Jewish, be loyal British subjects, and not have these various allegiances be in conflict with one another. Jews were loyal to, but never considered themselves British—nor were they so regarded by the colonial powers. They clamoured unsuccessfully for European status, which the British never granted them. Over two centuries of colonial presence in Calcutta had a deep impact on the city and the numerous communities who lived there. By the mid-twentieth century the British presence was ubiquitous—embodied in street names, colonial monuments, stone mansions, and in the Indian English spoken there. British products flooded the market and British values and practices determined the way in which business was conducted, institutions run, sports played and social life structured.

Indian Independence

Most Baghdadi Jews steered clear of politics and were neutral in the Hindu Muslim riots that rocked Calcutta and the rest of the nation. Since the Baghdadi Jews came to India to expand British trading networks, when Independence came it represented a moment of crisis for them. They had only lived and flourished in India under British rule. With the world in turmoil during and after World War II, they were fearful of what an "Indian India" might look like. Despite what may have been their individual misgiving, as loyal citizens the Jewish Association of India sent messages of congratulation to Lord Mountbatten and Jawaharlal Nehru greeting Indian Independence and "offered heartfelt prayers for the future peace, progress and prosperity of the Indian Union."[14]

Independence meant that they had to redefine themselves as individuals and as a community in relation to the newly forming state. They were fluent in English and their knowledge of local languages were enough for business and domestic dealings but were not their primary language for communication. The horror of the holocaust was firmly imprinted on their minds as the Jewish community of Calcutta gave refuge to many European Jews who had to flee for their lives. The bloody Partition and the riots that accompanied it were also disconcerting. Questions of their ethnic and communal identity emerged in a more urgent way than they had in the past and the Jewish community was well aware that they could no longer define themselves in terms of their Jewishness alone. They had several choices they could assert. As a diasporic community their religious identity, economic status and connections to Jews elsewhere, along with their colour privilege and their ambiguous identity in India—neither white nor brown translated into their having more options regarding whether to stay on in India or relocate to other places than others in India.[15]

Those of the community who opted to stay in India thrived in the new India that was being forged. There were those who committed themselves fully to the Nationalist struggle like Hannah (her mother was a Jew who married a prominent Hindu lawyer) became the principal of Lady Irwin College and was active in national causes. She worked with the government on issues relating to women and children and represented India at many International conferences. Esther Abraham, screen name Pramila was the first Miss India (1947) and stayed on in India till she died recently in Mumbai despite the fact that her husband at that time emigrated to Pakistan. Ezra Mir (Edwyn Myers) was a documentary film maker and founded the Documentary Producers Association in 1956, and worked on over 700 documentary films. He was appointed the chief producer of the Ministry of Information's Films Division in 1956 and was awarded the *Padma Shri* in 1970. General Jack Jacob was one of the few Jews who sought a career in the army that he joined in 1942.[16] He later served in the Indian army and his Jewishness was no bar for him to rise to one of the most senior positions, Lieutenant General and then served as Governor in Goa and the Punjab. As is clear from the prestigious positions that Baghdadi Jews occupied in all walks of life during the Raj and after Independence, their being Jews was never a hindrance to their advancement. During the British Raj they were protected and favoured for political reasons. They never faced discrimination and were socially well accepted through the two and a half centuries in India.

Emigration and Community Dissolution

The increased possibilities for immigration to Australia, England and other Commonwealth countries in the 1950s and 1960s drew many members of the Baghdadi Jewish community abroad. It was mostly the younger members of the community who left to find prosperity abroad. In those days the West had enormous glamour and appeal as a place of opportunity and advancement. As they settled abroad they sent for their parents and other family members. The wealthy of the community were not sure of their economic future in India as the Nehru government was socialist in its leanings and talked about the nationalisation of key sectors of the economy, including the nationalisation of banks. The Jews were unsure of whether they would be allowed to take their money out of the country and were unsure what this would mean for their economic prospects. Thus many of them left too, and once they left their businesses were sold. Since they employed many members of the community, this meant that those they employed also looked abroad for job prospects. As they had skills that they gained in these Jewish enterprises they were able to use these skills to secure jobs in the West. The poor in the community were given support by the Israeli Government to emigrate to Israel and a few young Jews went there in accordance with their Zionist ideals.[17]

As there never were many Jews to start with, this immigration of so many members made it harder for those who remained to continue to live Jewish lives. There was concern about how younger members of the community could find Jewish marriage partners and observant Jews found it harder to continue other ritual functions such as circumcision and ritual slaughtering. As the community dwindled further in the late 1960s and 1970s some of the poorer Jews were helped by the Israeli Government to move to Israel where they had better economic opportunities. Once again their knowledge of English, their skin colour and their Western orientation was an advantage they carried with them to Israel. The darker Jews—the Bene Israel and the Cochin Jews—were more discriminated against when they first went to Israel than the Baghdadi Jews.

Those who left India for US, Canada, Australia and the UK primarily because of their familiarity with English and Western culture, and because they were observant Jews, were able to settle into their new lives. As there were other Sephardic Jews from the colonies who also shifted to the UK, Australia and Canada they grouped together with them to form their own synagogues and Sephardic services. They found themselves professional jobs and branched out into a wide range of professions. Thus the anglicisation that they underwent in India stood them in good stead and made their shift more seamless. Their being Jewish, too, also helped in their transition as they merged with Sephardic Jewish communities in their new locations. Though the first generation of Jews tended to stay together and lived Calcutta Jewish style lives where they moved, their children moved in broader spheres. Many of their children do not know Calcutta and do not have the same nostalgic connections of their parents and grandparents. Since their parents only identified with Jewish Calcutta, and had little knowledge or familiarity with India, the connections of their children to India are tenuous.

Remnants of Jewish Calcutta Today

Today only a handful of Jews remain in the city, but the community left out of choice not because they were compelled to do so. Once a few members left, their families followed making it increasingly difficult for them to live Jewish lives. The majority of those in Calcutta since the turn of the century are very elderly. There has not been any birth in the community since 1986 and the one before that occurred almost two decades earlier. The Nahoum confectionary that has been a landmark in the city for over a century is still a very popular shop and still Jewish owned and a Jewish institution in the city. The stately synagogues and schools that the community built and still support, the Jewish cemetery in Nakheldanga that is still maintained by community Trust funds, the Ezra hospital, the Gubbay and Ezra House in the zoo, the imposing buildings the Baghdadi Jews once owned and the streets that are still named after them, mark their material legacy. However, as the buildings and companies they established have changed names and hands, few realise that they were once Jewish owned and run. Similarly, the busy streets and the vendors that have encroached on the periphery and gates of the synagogues make it possible to miss the synagogues altogether that are in the busy commercial heart of the City.

Those who knew Calcutta when it had a thriving Jewish community, when they had Jewish friends, business partners, teachers, doctors and lawyers, are now ageing. Soon the Jewish presence will no longer be a living memory. It is the scholars from the community and other scholars in Calcutta and overseas that have documented the Jewish presence and their contributions that has ensured that the legacy of the Baghdadi Jews of Calcutta is firmly placed in the annals of Indian history

Concluding Comments

Though the Baghdadi Jews of Calcutta were a flourishing community for a little over two centuries, I would argue that they are an important diaspora to study. Not only did they play an important role in shaping the cultural and economic contours of Calcutta, they challenge and extend some of the contemporary discourses about diaspora and travel. In their move eastwards to Calcutta they were able to improve their economic situation, flourish as a Jewish community, and be very active and engaged in all aspects of life that they chose to be involved. This is why I argue that this was a "diaspora of hope," and all diasporic experiences cannot be framed in terms of overwhelming loss, exile and displacement. The Baghdadi Jewish diaspora experiences that I discuss demonstrate that diaspora narratives are very varied and can be as much about mobility and gain. Not only did the community prosper in India but they acquired professional and other skills that stood them in good stead. The community's exposure to the West was also beneficial in providing opportunities for women's educational, social and professional development. Through this diaspora experience in India and the Far East and then through its subsequent location to the West, members of this reconstituted diaspora continue to thrive. The quintessential diaspora experience—that is the European Jewish diaspora experience cannot be generalised to all Jewish communities.

The Baghdadi Jews of Calcutta were a "travelling community" as they shifted from the Middle East to India and while in India they were part of a larger community of Baghdadi Jews across Jewish Asia. There was a lot of travel back and forth by them. Thus they had the psychological tools and the networks to be able to live in diasporic spaces and they did so, even in their resettlings, very much in community. They formed strong community associations to support one another and bound themselves strongly to resist assimilation. The children and grandchildren of those who emigrated have merged into new communities/nations, so I would argue that the Baghdadi Jewish community that took root in Calcutta and lasted from the eighteenth century to the present will be no longer as the generation who left India passes away. Some of their ritual items, like the beautiful *sifrei torahs* are part of other Iraqi synagogues in the cities where they live such as London and Los Angeles, and other items are in the Diaspora Museum, Tel Aviv, and the Babylonian Jewry Heritage Centre in Or Yehuda, Israel. The scholarship on the Calcutta Jews and the significant contributions they have made to India in the colonial period and since Independence has ensured their place in history. This community speaks to India's plural tradition and underlines how minority communities like the Jews have enriched India.

Notes

1. While the Jews of Calcutta who came from the Middle East in the late eighteenth century are referred to as Baghdadi Jews, in fact this group of Jews came primarily from Iraq, Syria, Kurdistan and Yemen. They called themselves Baghdadi because they followed the liturgy of Baghdad and the majority came from Iraq.
2. For this paper I largely draw on my book *Jewish Portraits, Indian Frames: Women's Narratives From A Diaspora of Hope*, but updated the work and added a few more details to make the argument the paper puts forward.
3. Kaustav Chakrabarti, thesis "The Jewish World of Calcutta 1798-1948," p. 29, Dept. of History, Calcutta University, referencing the work of Dr. Zvi Yehuda, *The Jewish Community in Baghdad in the 18th Century*, op.cit., p. 14.
4. Kaustav Chakrabarti, thesis, p. 166, referencing the work of Louis Rabinowitz, *Far East Mission*, Eagle Press Limited, South Africa, 1952, ch. 30, p. 194.
5. Ibid, p. 166.
6. If a Jew married outside of the community the *kiddish* (last rites) was said for them.
7. It is interesting to note that the Jewish Girls School was always more educationally sound than the boys school. While the more wealthy of the community did send their girls to more prestigious schools, such as Loreto House, middle and upper middle class families

also sent their boys to the Anglican schools. For the most part the boys school was for poorer members of the community. Perhaps this was the case because parents were more strict about their girls having non-Jewish friends?

8. The Judaen Club was established in 1929 to provide cultural, social and recreational programmes for Jewish adults. It had a card room, a billiard room, a bar and a community meeting hall, at which events like dances, weddings and political meetings were held.
9. Ezekiel Musleah, *On the Banks of the Ganga; The Sojourn of the Jews in Calcutta*, Christopher Publishing House, Massachusetts, 1975, p. 311. He states that one quarter of the Jews relied on Jewish charities.
10. Kaustav Chakrabarti, doctoral thesis, p. 173.
11. The wealthy members of the community sent their children to the more elite Loreto College. As the Jewish Boys school was never very strong it catered mostly to the poorer boys of the community. Middle class and wealthy Jewish men went to Anglican schools across the city
12. In developing a digital project on the Calcutta Jews I have been collecting photos and documents from Calcutta Jews. This included pictures and information about Rachel Jonah (nee Sofaer) from her family in Israel. When the family business failed in Burma she came to Calcutta and started acting in movies to support her family. Her mother would accompany her to the studio to make sure she was in good standing. She died tragically in childbirth in 1948. Her work in the studios that she continued after marriage was quite apart from the Westernised life she lived with her husband and family in Agarpara where he worked.
13. This was the same for Anglo-Indian, Parsi and Armenian women all of whom were Westernised and English speaking
14. "Calcutta Jewry Welcomes Indian Independence," *Shema*, vol. 2, no. 4, September 1947, p. 6, in Kaustav Chakrabarti, thesis, p. 187.
15. During the five years after independence, each person living in India could make a decision to be British or Indian and accordingly get the necessary passport. Many Indians, several from India's minority communities, opted for British nationality. Australia extended the "privilege" of emigration to Anglo-Indians, Armenians, Jews and a few Parsis after the War in its White Australia Policy.
16. There were several Jewish boys who joined the war effort and enlisted in the British army.
17. While the majority of Indian Jews who emigrated to Israel were from Bombay, Poona and Cochin, there were a few from Calcutta to who went to Israel. This group of Jews became the core of Indian Jews who have multiplied in Israel. Today there are 100,000 Indian Jews in Israel while only 4,000 or so Jews live in India. To date, Bombay has the largest Jewish community today and functioning synagogues and Jewish ritual services. In Calcutta the ten men needed to conduct a service cannot be found so a formal service has not been conducted in the synagogues for over a decade.

Selected Bibliography

Chakrabarti, Kaustav. "The Jewish World of Calcutta 1798-1948." Thesis submitted for the degree of Doctor of Philosophy (Arts) in History, University of Calcutta, 2010.

Ezra, Esmond David. *Turning Back the Pages: A Chronicle of Calcutta Jewry.* Vols 1 and II. London: Brookside Press, 1986.

Hyman, Mavis. *Jews of the Raj.* London: Hyman Publishers, 1995.

Jacob, Jack. *Surrender at Dacca: the Birth of A Nation.* New Delhi: Manohar Publishers and Distributors, 1997.

Musleah, Ezekiel N. *On The Banks of the Ganga: The Sojourn of the Jews of Calcutta.* North Quincy, Ma: Christopher Publishing House, 1975.

Roland, Joan G. *Jews in British India: Identity in a Colonial Era*, Hanover, NH: University Press of New England, 1989.

Silliman, Jael. *Jewish Portraits, Indian Frames: Women's Narratives From a Diaspora of Hope."* Seagull Press, Calcutta, 2001.

Solomon, Sally. *Hooghly Tales.* London: David Ashley Publishing, 1998.

Timberg, Thomas A. "Indigenous and non-Indigenous Jews," in Nathan Katz (ed.) *Studies of Indian Jewish Identity.* New Delhi: Manohar Publishers and Distributors, 1995.

3. Culture and Foreign Policy: The Confucius Institutes and Advancing "Soft Power" with Chinese Characteristics

Raviprasad Narayanan

Introduction & Theoretical Approach

This paper attempts to craft a critical perspective to China's Confucius Institutes (CIs). By adopting a critical tone—at times severe—this paper strives to inject a counter-narrative that straddles two issues—China's CIs and India's "perspectival"[1] views and behaviour on the same. The criticality inherent in this paper flows from adopting a "critical discourse analysis" (CDA) approach. CDA with its multi-disciplinary characteristics enables the study and interpretations of power and power asymmetries, as also the manipulation and domination inherent in language that describes the "other."[2] In many ways the knowledge we have of the "other" is through the linguistic realisation of "texts and discourses" where the narrative element focuses on power relations and social constructions. It could be proffered that the challenge of deciphering China's soft power *vis-à-vis* the medium of the CIs encounters a methodological tightrope walking over adopting either an ideographic approach or a nomothetic approach.[3]

If one were to subscribe to the "constructivist" school and its derivatives, it logically flows that social constructionist methodologies also require "discourse" to be empirically dissected within its social and specific contexts—"the source of a people's reality."[4] In other words, "a discourse captures a particular way of talking about and understanding the world (or an aspect of the world)."[5] CDA is to be seen as both the "method" and "object." By teasing out the "structural" weaknesses in the bilateral relationship between China and India as a primary causal factor, the CDA applied in this draft paper attempts to reveal the real from the opaque and makes transparent issues that have the fog of uncertainty wrapped around them.

At the outset it has to be mentioned that the task of writing this paper was not made easy by the fact that there exist no official statements made by India on China's Confucius Institutes. Since both countries take extra pains to constantly reiterate their bilateral relations being guided by the "Five Principles of Peaceful Coexistence"[6] it could be surmised that official lack of comments adheres to diplomatic propriety.

Confucius Institutes: A Critical Appraisal

"What is soft power? It is the ability to get what you want through attraction rather than coercion or payments. It arises from the attractiveness of a country's culture, political ideals, and policies."[7]

In an age determined by the processes of globalisation nothing is more visible, alluring and powerful than that of global cultural exchange. The appeal of Hollywood, the *frisson* of Bollywood, the pulsating music of Korean Pop ("Gangnam style") and Canto Pop, Brazilian *telenovelas,* the many versions of Japanese "Manga," football fans doing a Mexican metachronal rhythm (wave)—the underlying message they all deliver is that they have been universally accepted transcending nation, language, race and faith. Into this global medley of cultural expressions one notices the rapid emergence of CIs as the "soft power" of Chinese foreign policy with its attendant *decisional* (institutional) and *distributional* (structural) perspectives.[8]

Undoubtedly, the promotion of CIs by China all over the world is by no means restricted to offering the opportunity to learn the Chinese language alone. They are windows to understanding Chinese culture and history to the uninitiated, preferably from a traditional lens. The learning of Chinese language and an appreciation of its unparalleled culture is in a nutshell the crux of the soft power projection that China has initiated to complement its already robust diplomatic presence. It has been stated that by the end of 2011, there were more than 400 CIs in 108 countries and more than 500 Confucius Classrooms with 600,000 registered students.[9] As a laudable initiative, the CIs have undertaken the "risk" in projecting an *idealistic* temperament to China's foreign policy complementing its otherwise "power" and "deal" oriented tendencies. As an opportunity for people around the world, the CIs are a welcome portal to learn "Chinese culture and its philosophical wisdom."[10]

The global appeal the CIs strive to aspire for is revealed by its very charter. The Constitution and By-Laws of the CIs states that:

> Confucius Institutes devote themselves to satisfying the demands of people from different countries and regions in the world who learn the Chinese language, to enhancing understanding of the Chinese language and culture by these peoples, to strengthening educational and cultural exchange and cooperation between China and other countries, to deepening friendly relationships with other nations, to promoting the development of multi-culturalism, and to construct a harmonious world.[11]

Locating the CIs from an Indian perspective necessitates the construction of a narrative with many strands each with its own form and content. The CIs to begin with could be seen as a positive force multiplier to China's ever expanding diplomatic objectives. Not only is China advertising "culture" as being a part of its overall foreign policy, but is more importantly positioning its culture as a *function* of its overall foreign policy and a *resource* too.[12] Their apparently limitless financial resources and state driven rapid expansion encourage notions of the CIs being a vehicle to promote propaganda. The former propaganda chief and politburo standing committee member Li Changchun has been quoted as having said that the CIs are "an important part of China's overseas propaganda set-up."[13] The CIs could also be seen as a rash endeavour promoting China for purely commercial reasons and as "Trojan Horses."[14]

To informed sections in India, the projection of Chinese "soft power" during the ongoing reform phase in force since 1979 is a stunning departure when contrasted with the political polemic that China espoused in the 1960s and 1970s. The violence and political irrationalism that passed for the Cultural Revolution in China had its impact even in a localised manner in India in the latter half of the 1960s.[15] Those events remain an anathema to the Indian political class at large but the memory of China's political intervention through editorials and ideological inspiration to the Naxalite leadership in seeking to violently overturn India's democratic process of governance still gnaws.

Staying the course of CDA, I argue that the CIs have internationalised China's residual nationalism. To a lively, colourful and immensely heterogeneous society like India, the terms "promoting the development of multiculturalism" and "construct a harmonious world" in the Constitution and By-Laws of the CIs would sound suspiciously hollow. A truly "multicultural" temperament should not only be reflected domestically (in the political and cultural spheres) but should in that case also involve the promotion of other languages of China (Cantonese, Shanghainese and even Tibetan) to the rest of the world! To add yet another layer of criticality, if the CIs want to promote a "harmonious world" do they not appear to be promoting contemporary official ideology under the guise of a civilisational tenet? Also, does it not sound hypocritical for a political culture that initiated an "Anti-Confucius" movement during the heydays of the Cultural Revolution to reify the "Confucian" in China and beyond by the medium of the CIs? Of course it can be argued that the political temperament of today is very different from what prevailed during the Cultural Revolution, but doubts remain. If the "Anti-Confucian" movement of 1973-1975 was used by the "Gang of Four" led by Mao Zedong's wife Jiang Qing to expel Deng Xiaoping a second time from positions of authority,[16] then only a very altruistic view would explain the establishment of the CIs as a version of official acknowledgement that the days of political absurdity are indeed in the past and the CIs that bear Confucius' name represent a glorious civilisation—a feature more important than the mere political.

To remain faithful to the critical tone adopted it ought to be stated that at the best of times Sino-Indian relations have exhibited a sense of disquiet and unease not easy to fathom. To put it succinctly, Asia's largest countries, China and India, share a complicated relationship. As nations with a sense of historical destiny—documented, invoked and invented—reflected in their civilisational spread, cultural attributes, geo-political/geo-economic aspirations and footprints, power capabilities and intentions, China and India perhaps pose a researchers dilemma by invoking analogous comparisons. At its very basic level, the holistic prism of enquiry the two countries face is of managing a relationship that for all purposes will always be less than ideal—and shall remain so. The existence of "foundational tensions" woven into their bilateral fabric inhibits realistic appraisal of the "other" leading to aspects of ennui in the relationship with inexplicably large perceptual gaps on both sides.

Confucius Institutes and India: A jinxed endeavour?

It is undoubtedly glaring that while the rest of the world plays host to hundreds of Confucius Institutes and Confucius classrooms, India does not have any to date![17] Other South Asian countries like Afghanistan,[18] Bangladesh,[19] Nepal,[20] Pakistan[21] and Sri Lanka[22] do have operational CIs, but not India. How does one look at this incongruity? One can look at it from several angles. From an extreme perspective, India's not granting permission for the establishment of Confucius Institutes could be interpreted as being reflective of the true nature of Sino-Indian relations—neither close nor hostile ... rather institutional wariness and suspicion The feverish reportage and unremitting coverage of the Depsang valley intrusion in Ladakh made by Chinese troops in April-May 2013 and the subsequent adroit management of the issue by both sides is for starters an illustration of the depth, intensity and entrenched attitudes prevailing on both sides. Looking at it from a moderate perspective, it could be interpreted that India is not comfortable with the setting up of Confucius Institutes since it exposes lacunae in India's own attempts at projecting its "soft power" capabilities. The starkly different positions the two countries occupy in the international hierarchy of power and influence is indicative of where India stands relative to China. The CIs also reveal a template of foreign policy decision making that seeks to integrate and channelise the efforts of various ministries, councils and bureaus into a purposeful endeavour that are seen as serving national interests by China. In contrast, India's attempts at projecting "soft" international flavour to its diplomatic initiatives are initiated by the Indian Council for Cultural Relations (ICCR), an autonomous body of the Government of India with a strong administrative component comprising exclusively Foreign Service officials. Other ministries in India that have strong international components (Commerce and Industry, Overseas Indian Affairs, Tourism, Civil Aviation, Shipping, Environment & Forests) do not appear to be coordinated with each other in projecting the country's image. It could of course be argued that India's political culture forces it to not replicate what its much larger and better organised and immensely resourced neighbour does, but does that excuse pretending a disconnect does not exist? When a country that advertises itself as seeking to benefit from its demographic dividend in the coming decades has a foreign policy decision-making mechanism that is anachronistic in its temperament and execution, isn't something amiss? From a perspective of total indifference it could be interpreted that India is unwilling to host Confucius Institutes—either within universities or independently—owing to the institutional memory of the brief boundary war fought in 1962 when India faced a drubbing. From a critical perspective, one could argue that institutions in India have developed a reflexive urge to stonewall, delay and whittle down any constructive proposal that has as its ideal closer people-to-people relations. Other South Asian countries—Pakistan, Bangladesh,

Maldives, Nepal and Sri Lanka—would attest to this reflexively obdurate position adopted by the Indian bureaucracy and elite policymakers. Needless to add, these are those South Asian countries whose bilateral ties with China have improved considerably in the past decade, while stagnating or recessing with India. Why CIs have not taken off in India like a "prairie fire" unlike, say, in the United States, is explained by the following two illustrations.

(a) Schools and the Chinese Language in India

Undeniably, there is growing demand in India for learning the Chinese language.[23] This comes about primarily since China has emerged as India's largest trading partner[24] and also because the Indian education system—as diverse as the country—is realising the need to introduce more foreign languages in its curriculum to complement existing emphasis on continental languages.

In 2010, Kapil Sibal, the Minister of Human Resource Development in India and Yuan Guiren, the Chinese Minister of Education, came to an agreement "to cooperate on Chinese teaching and learning, with the authorities providing support for teacher exchange, training and textbook development."[25] Recognisably, the Central Board for Secondary Education (CBSE) is India's apex body administering and setting the template for secondary education in most schools.[26] The CBSE had conducted a survey to gauge the response to the introduction of Chinese language and found that more than five hundred schools were willing to offer classes in Chinese. This level of interest expressed itself with the CBSE and the Chinese National Office for Teaching Chinese as a Foreign Language signing an MoU in 2012 that included China training more than 300 Indian teachers for six months in the Chinese language for 100 schools. All expenses related to the teachers being trained (travel, tuition and living expenses) will be borne by the Chinese government who will also give them instructional material and help in establishing teaching plans and evaluation standards. A point of concern however is the short duration for training in the language with the Chinese side emphasising two-year duration while the CBSE insisted on six months.[27] The Peking University and Beijing Foreign Languages University are expected to host the Indian teachers. It is beyond belief that the CBSE reasons that a language like Chinese can be learnt in six months and those who have undergone this training are capable of imparting this language to school students!

As a language, Mandarin has been introduced as an "optional" in the VI standard (middle school) in select schools. Whatever forms this cooperation assumes, it cannot be missed that the groundwork for understanding China by the next generation of Indians is being laid. India will only stand to benefit if its primary and secondary school system imparts an education that links "international education with inter-cultural learning."[28] The author believes that the imperfections in the method adopted by the CBSE to teach Chinese will generate demand for private "educational entrepreneurs" to teach the language. As for fees and infrastructure to teach Chinese, the lack of any relevant regulation or code will invite various "operators" into the fray, akin to the thousands of neigbourhood private "English medium schools" and "English convent education" we are familiar with.

At another level, it is believed that many prestigious private Indian schools are interested in introducing Chinese as an optional foreign language and in the next couple of years one can reasonably expect a positive outcome irrespective of the current state of inertia. In Mumbai alone, the elite Dhirubhai Ambani International School, the Arya Vidya Mandir, the Oberoi International School, the NSS Hillspring School as also a couple of nursery schools teach Mandarin.[29]

(b) Universities

A reading of the list of Confucius Institutes around the world reveals the names of two Indian universities—Jawaharlal Nehru University, New Delhi and Vellore Institute of Technology, Vellore—as hosting Confucius Institutes. Sadly, these are non-functional Confucius Institutes!

Jawaharlal Nehru University (JNU) is considered to be India's most prestigious university in the social sciences with an impressive alumni making up the who's who of India's academia, bureaucracy, media, politics and the social sector. The Confucius Institute to be set up in JNU was to have been a partnership with China's leading university, the Beijing University (BeiDa) but got stalled owing to "procedural differences." What these "procedural differences" were remains a matter of speculation, but one could surmise that since JNU has a world renowned School of Languages with a strong composition of experienced Chinese language teachers, a doubling of the same may have run into resistance. It is not known whether BeiDa was in favour of an institutionally reciprocal arrangement with an Indian language being taught at BeiDa and whether it was non-committal on that aspect. It has also not escaped the attention of scholars in India that the leading universities in the world—the Ivy League in the US, Oxford and Cambridge in UK, Tokyo and Kyoto universities in Japan, Seoul National University and Yonsei in Korea, the Ecole's in France and leading German universities have not associated themselves with CIs nor host any.[30] JNU by comparison is India's *primus inter pares* amongst universities and could perhaps have inferred that its academic links with China and successful long running Chinese language programme need not be conflated with the establishment of a CI.

Significantly, since true figures are not known, it is estimated that the Hanban supports the establishment of Confucius Institutes to the tune of around US$ 100,000 annually[31] for a specified duration. Indian universities supported by the Human Resources Development Ministry (which oversees Higher Education) and the University Grants Commission (apex body governing universities specialising in humanities) are loathe to accept foreign funding (institutional reflexivity!) and the prospect of funding from China—of all countries—must have encouraged bureaucratic inertia. The fact that the Hanban is directly funded by the Chinese state is bound to raise suspicion in India. To date even well-known educational initiatives from countries in the West (the DAAD of Germany for instance) do not have a very visible footprint within Indian universities and it is clear that there is an *insularity* with which Indian academia cocoons itself.

In the case of the Vellore Institute of Technology—a private institution teaching engineering and technology located 120 km west of Chennai—the difficulty in finding Mandarin teachers proved to be the spanner in the works. It is well known that Chinese from the mainland are not very enthusiastic about travelling to South Asia and perhaps the task of teaching Chinese in India appears daunting to most Chinese citizens.

It was also reported that Mumbai University had agreed to establish a CI with the Tianjin University of Technology being the partner institution.[32] At the time of writing this paper it appears there has been no formal agreement to establish a CI in Mumbai and the only document available is a report on the visit undertaken by several academicians from Mumbai to China from November 4 to November 10, 2011 on the website of Mumbai University that calls for the establishment of Confucius Chair/Institute at the University of Mumbai.[33]

Analyses

Joseph Nye Jr. would have been immensely thrilled to note that what he articulated—the need for the United States to complement its "hard power" with "soft power"—found a transfixed audience and robust institutional support from a system that micro-manages culture and the arts to suit a peculiar political template. For Joseph Nye Jr. the dominance of the United States and the theoretical extrapolation of soft power found practical application through the Marshall Plan that revived devastated Europe after the Second World War.

To China, the concept of "global governance" resonates from its appeal to integrate strong components of soft power within a multilateral setting. Articulations of a "harmonious world" are to perhaps soften the hard edges and monolithic form of the Westphalian state centric international system.[34] China's attempts at constructing an edifice that speaks of its soft power does not seem to have impressed sceptics(including the author!) especially in countries with well-established temperaments of democratic governance and active civil societies.[35] By focusing on the "traditional"—imparting language training and associated activities—the CIs have appeared to have adopted a safer frame for elaboration and explanation of Chinese culture. They also seem to be officially reiterating a stereotype with cultural presentations sticking to performances of Peking opera (and hence marginalising other variations like the Sichuan opera) and martial arts that seem politically neutral and shy away from experimentation. Presenting the "contemporary" would mean opening the frame of "soft power" more widely to accommodate "contestations" of various hues—something which the Party in Beijing would be wary of countenancing. Controversially, the CIs have been known to prevent discussions/exhibitions and talks on what China considers to be "sensitive"—namely Tibet and the Dalai Lama, Xinjiang, Taiwan, the Tiananmen Square massacre of June 1989 (Tiananmen Square "Incident" to the mandarins staying in nearby Zhongnanhai!) and the Falun Gong. Adding to the debate on the CIs and their not so subtle influence in promoting "self-censorship" are the bylaws of the CIs that state in their General Principles that:

> The Confucius Institutes shall abide by the laws and regulations of the countries in which they are located, respect local cultural and educational traditions and social customs, *and they shall not contravene concerning the laws and regulations of China.*[36] (Italics by author)

Interpreted, this by-law precludes any topic/theme deemed offensive and violating the spirit of the law in China! In other words, the CIs located outside provide space for the articulation of Chinese culture on exclusively Chinese determined terms—more appropriately Party (CCP) decided conditions. Internally, the party-state in China it appears wants to persuade people through its large propaganda machinery that the protection of Chinese culture from alien influences and the like lies in its promotion outside and consolidation within with nary a space for dissent.[37]

China and India need to walk a long road to understand each other. Their recognition of each other is through muddied lenses that need change. Initiatives like the CIs cannot be a one way street and there needs to be reciprocity in matters cultural and civilisational. India's soft power does not find audiences in China owing primarily to the abysmal lack of knowledge most Chinese have of India and whatever known is sadly dated. The author in his various interactions with people from all walks of life in China on several occasions was puzzled to notice that for most mainland Chinese, India exists as a stereotype. Only extremely well-informed segments of Chinese society (especially scholars working on strategic affairs in Beijing, Shanghai and Chengdu) could share some insights about India that were not dated but were rather unique. A primary reason behind this lacuna is that for most Chinese, an introduction to India is invariably through occidental literature or visuals that reinforce stereotypes. In tourism for instance, while half a million Indian tourists visit China each year—from January to May 2012 more than 245,000 Indian tourists had visited China—only 57,000 tourists from mainland China visited India during the same period. It is obvious that the two Asian giants need to seriously introspect why a perception gap exists between them.

It is the same in India with knowledge of China and its people, history, society and culture being very sketchy. Most Indians however are appreciative of China's tremendous economic performance and wish they could replicate it. For many entrepreneurs in India, a driving force is China's economic success in comparative terms and the inspiration it provides for India to transform its economy. The larger picture however remains bleak with contemporary understanding being dominated by the war of 1962. It could be posited that the sensationalism of the Indian media *vis-à -vis* bilateral relations with China are in themselves playing a role in the construction of a stereotype not flattering about China. In the realm of culture and its various expressions, the author firmly believes that as long as the major classics flowing from Chinese history and the writings of famous Chinese litterateurs like Lu Xun, Mo Yan and many others are not translated into the many Indian languages and similarly the writings of India's lively vernacular literary tradition (including English) translated into Chinese, the two countries and their people are not going to appreciate one another and the only prism of comparison will remain the material and bling! A pity indeed.

The future of CIs in India is worth watching. Practical issues regarding the financial viability of CIs are undoubtedly a consideration in countries like India where higher education still remains in many ways a privilege of few. Unless a self-sustaining financial model is established, the CIs after a quick start could end up being mired in financial paucity. There are also political aspects to be considered since the CIs reflect a particular temperament and will face scrutiny about their activities however sincere they may seem.[38]

To conclude, culture, political values and foreign policy are widely acclaimed to be three essential tools promoting a nation's soft power. These three tools have to work in unison and close synchronisation to have an appeal that goes beyond official levels and relates to the popular craving. Can China pull it off through the medium of the CIs will be a question that will keep us engaged for quite some time to come.

Notes

1. A philosophical view developed by Friedrich Nietzsche was that "all ideations take place from particular perspectives." Myriad possibilities exist conceptually from which flow interpretive truths and values. Since "truth" is created by integrating different vantage points together and hence separated from the vantage points there need not be any ethical or epistemological absolutes. Each perspective that emerges therefore need not be equally valid. See Linda L. Williams, *Nietzsche's Mirror: the world as will to power* (Lanham, MD: Rowman & Littlefield, 2001).
2. Stijn Joye, "News discourses on distant suffering: a Critical Discourse Analysis of the 2003 SARS outbreak," *Discourse & Society* (London), vol. 21, no. 5, p. 590.
3. Jack S. Levy, "Too Important to Leave to the Other: History and Political Science in the Study of International Relations," *International Security*, vol. 22, no. 1, Summer 1997, pp. 24-26.
4. Michael Vlahos, "Culture and Foreign Policy," *Foreign Policy*, no. 82, Spring 1991, p. 59.
5. Marianne Jørgensen and Louise J. Philips, *Discourse Analysis as Theory and Method* (London: Sage, 2002), p. 1.
6. The Five Principles for Peaceful Coexistence or *Panchsheel* (Five Virtues) stand for the mutual respect for each other's territorial integrity and sovereignty; mutual non-aggression; mutual non-interference in each other's internal affairs; equality and mutual

benefit, and peaceful coexistence. They were first enunciated in the preamble to the Agreement on Trade and Intercourse between Tibet Region of China and India signed in 1954.

7. Joseph S. Nye, Jr., *Soft Power—The Means to Success in World Politics* (New York: Public Affairs, 2004), p. x.
8. Sheng Ding and Robert A. Saunders, "Talking Up China: An Analysis of China's Rising Cultural Power and Global Promotion of the Chinese Language," *East Asia*, vol. 23, no. 2, Summer 2006, p. 5.
9. Qu Yingpu, Zhao Huanxin and Cheng Yingqi, "Confucius Institutes go beyond borders," *China Daily*, December 3, 2012. Available at: http://usa.chinadaily.com.cn/epaper/2012-12/03/content_15980161.htm (Retrieved on March 3, 2013).
10. Hongqin Zhao and Jianbin Huang, "China's policy of Chinese as a foreign language and the use of overseas Confucius Institutes," *Education Research for Policy and Practice* (Springer) vol. 9, p. 139.
11. "Constitution and By-Laws of the Confucius Institutes," Chapter 1, General Principles. Accessible at: http://english.hanban.org/node_7880.htm (Retrieved on October 23, 2012)
12. See Frode Liland, "Culture and Foreign Policy: An Introduction to Approaches and Theory," IFS (*Institutt for forsvarstudier*), Oslo, no. 1, 1993, p. 8 for an understanding of the many roles "culture" plays in the foreign policy of a nation. Available at: http://brage.bibsys.no/fhs/bitstream/URN:NBN:no-bibsys_brage_20800/1/INF0193.pdf (Retrieved on May 23, 2013).
13. "A message from Confucius—new ways of projecting soft power," *The Economist* (London), October 22, 2009. Available at: http://www.economist.com/node/14678507 (Retrieved on May 23, 2013).
14. James F. Paradise, "China and International Harmony: The Role of Confucius Institutes in Bolstering Beijing's Soft Power," *Asian Survey*, vol. 49, no. 4, July-August 2009, pp. 659-62.
15. The "Naxalites" in India who began their insurrection from the village of Naxalbari in West Bengal in 1967 were much enthused by the ideological support they received from China. The *People's Daily* of July 5, 1967 published an editorial stating: "A peal of spring thunder has crashed over the land of India … The Chinese people joyfully applaud this revolutionary storm of the Indian peasants in the Darjeeling area as do all Marxist-Leninists and revolutionary people of the whole world … Such trash as 'Gandhi-ism,' 'parliamentary road' and the like are opium used by the Indian ruling classes to paralyse the Indian people. Only by relying on violent revolution and taking the road of armed struggle can India be saved and the Indian people achieve complete liberation." Source: Marxists Internet Archive. Available at: http://www.marxists.org/subject/china/documents/peoples-daily/1967/07/05.htm (Retrieved on November 10, 2012).
16. A. James Gregor and Maria Hsia Chang, "Anti-Confucianism: Mao's Last Campaign," *Asian Survey*, vol. 19, no. 11, November 1979, p. 1074.
17. In comparison the United States hosted 81 Confucius Institutes and more than 300 Confucius Classrooms in 2012. See, Li Qikeng, "Confucius Institutes benefit US economy, culture," *Global Times* (Beijing) June 18, 2012. Available at: http://www.globaltimes.cn/content/715724.shtml (Retrieved on June 3, 2013).

18. In January 2008, Kabul University opened a Confucius Institute that was shut down in 2010 due to the deteriorating security situation and reopened in April 2013. See, "Confucius Institute reopens in Kabul," *China Daily*, April 8, 2013. Accessible at: http://www.chinadaily.com.cn/cndy/2013-04/08/content_16381699.htm (Retrieved on May 28, 2013).
19. North-South University, a private university based in Dhaka hosts a Confucius Institute that was inaugurated in February 2006.
20. Kathmandu University, hosts a Confucius Institute inaugurated in June 2007.
21. Despite its oft repeated "all weather friendship," Pakistan hosts only one Confucius Institute that is located within the precincts of the National University of Modern Languages, Islamabad and inaugurated in April 2005.
22. University of Kelaniya, in Sri Lanka hosts a Confucius Institute.
23. Abhishek Choudhari, "Portuguese axed, Mandarin included in CBSE curriculum," *Times of India* (New Delhi) September 21, 2012. Accessible at: http://articles.timesofindia.indiatimes.com/2012-09-21/news/34001700_1_cbse-curriculum-sadhana-parashar-board-of-secondary-education (Retrieved on October 23, 2012).
24. India is China's tenth largest trading partner with bilateral trade in 2011 reaching US$ 73.9 billion.
25. Luo Wangshu, "Indians to learn to speak Chinese," *China Daily* (Beijing) August 24, 2012. Accessible at: http://www.chinadaily.com.cn/world/2012-08/24/content_15704987.htm (Retrieved on October 18, 2012).
26. Other education boards in India include the Indian Certificate of Secondary Education (ICSE), National Institute of Open Schooling (NIOS) and respective State Boards of Education. The CBSE is considered to be the template for quality education. The ICSE is not common and is to be found mostly in elite public schools. The respective state boards differ in the quality of curriculum offered.
27. Ananth Krishnan, "China to train 300 Indian teachers in Mandarin," *The Hindu* (Chennai) August 25, 2012. Accessible at: http://www.thehindu.com/news/national/article3817554.ece (retrieved on October 16, 2012).
28. Nanzhao Zhou, "International education in systemic educational reforms: the Chinese case and lessons learned from an international perspective," *Education Research for Policy and Practice*, vol. 6, p. 159.
29. See Hemali Chappia, "With China's rise, Mumbai says 'Ni Hao' to Mandarin," *The Times of India*, October 14, 2012. Available at: http://articles.timesofindia.indiatimes.com/2012-10-14/india/34448273_1_mandarin-world-language-universal-language (Retrieved on February 6, 2013).
30. Don Starr, "Chinese Language Education in Europe: the Confucius Institutes," *European Journal of Education*, vol. 44, no. 1, March 2009, p. 73.
31. Ren Zhe, "The Confucius Institutes and China's soft power," *Institute of Developing Economies Discussion Paper No. 330* (IDE-JETRO) Japan, March 2012, p. 7.
32. "Confucius Institute to set up first branch in India," *Business Standard*, February 10, 2012. Available at: http://www.business-standard.com/article/management/confucius-institute-to-set-up-first-branch-in-india-112021000145_1.html (Retrieved on February

23, 2013).

33. See Report "University of Mumbai's Delegation To Universities in China," Mumbai University. Available at: http://www.mu.ac.in/uomuc.html (Retrieved on February 26, 2013).
34. Gerald Chan, Pak K. Lee, and Lai Ha-Chan, *China Engages Global Governance—A New World Order in the Making?* (New York, USA: Routledge, 2012). p. 37.
35. Gerald Chan, et al., ibid., p. 36.
36. See "Constitution and By-Laws of the Confucius Institutes," Chapter 1, General Principles, no. 6. Available at: http://english.hanban.org/node_7880.htm (Retrieved on February 12, 2013).
37. See Anne-Marie Brady (ed.), *China's Thought Management* (London: Routledge, 2012).
38. The imbroglio involving the CI in Stockholm University and demands that it be separated from the university following allegations of political interference by the Chinese Embassy are a case in point. Other places where CIs are seen as negatively influencing academic freedom include Australia, Canada, Israel, New Zealand, Poland and India. See Lionel M. Jensen, "Culture Industry, Power, and the Spectacle of China's 'Confucius Institutes'" in Timothy B. Weston and Lionel M. Jensen (eds.) *China—In and Beyond the Headlines* (Lanham, MD: Rowman & Littlefield, 2012) p. 293.

4. Cultural Space between Iran and Iraq: Shi'i Identity, Traditional Connectivity and Social Exchange

Sujata Ashwarya Cheema

The paper considers the creation, sustenance and limitations of the cultural space—the "fluid field of interaction"—between Iran and Iraq that transcends the extant political boundary between the two countries. It is an overarching space defined by sectarian identity, connectivity fostered through visitation rituals at the holy shrines, and socio-economic exchanges engendered by meeting of peoples from the two domains. The holy cities and centres of Shi'i learning in Iraq and Iran are frontiers of this space.

Iraq is considered the cradle of Shi'ism, as the territory has seen several formative years of Shi'i history. The Islamic conquest in the seventh century established Islam in Iraq. The fourth Caliph of the Muslims (*al-khulafa' ar-rashidun*, the four "rightly-guided caliphs") and the first imam of Shi'is,[1] Ali ibn Abu Talib (c. 601-61), moved the seat of Islam from Medina to Kufa in Iraq and was assassinated there in 661 AD. 'Ali's son, Hussein (626-80), who refused to accept the claim of Umayyad dynast, Yezid I (645-83), to the caliphate of Islam, was killed with his companions in a battle on the plains of Karbala about twenty years later in 680 AD. The partisans of 'Ali launched the Shi'i movement upon Hussein's death, spurred by the belief that right guidance could be had only through the "People of the House" (*ahl al-bayt*), the direct descendants of Prophet Muhammad, who possessed the necessary spiritual quality to transmit divine knowledge and exercise leadership of the Muslim community.[2]

Many of the twelve Shi'i imams[3] spent at least a part of their lives in Iraq. Naturally, Iraq has had a tradition of Shi'i seminary education since the early period of Islamic history. Iraq is home to the four most sacred Shi'i shrine cities, namely Najaf, Karbala, Kazimayn and Samarra. Najaf—one of Shi'i Islam's holiest cities—has the tomb of Ali, the first Shi'i imam. Karbala has the tomb of Imam Hussein, grandson of the Prophet Muhammad, by his daughter Fatima and Ali. The two Shi'i imams, Musa ibn Jafar al-Kadhim (745-99) and his grandson and successor Shi'i imam Muhammad at-Taqi (811-35) are buried in Kazimayn. Lastly, Samarra contains the mausoleums of Ali al-Hadi (c. 827-68) and Hasan al-Askari (846-74), the tenth and eleventh Shi'i imams, as well as the place from where the "Hidden Imam," Muhammad al-Mahdi (b. 869), the alleged young son of Aksari, went into occultation.

The above-mentioned shrine cities have been cultural-religious contact zones for Shi'is all over the world, especially, Iran and India. Together with Baghdad, the shrine cities of Iraq have also been centres of academic learning, one or the other rising in prominence at different periods in history. The Shi'ite majority of Iraq (where they are estimated to be 55 per cent of the population) is an outcome in large part of large-scale conversion of the southern tribes of the country during the course of the nineteenth century.

Until the adoption of Twelver Shi'ism[4] as the state religion of Persia by the Safavid dynasty in Iran from 1501, and the conversion of a majority of those who lived on the Iranian plateau to Shi'i Islam over the succeeding two centuries, Shi'ism had been one aspect of Islamic experience in Iran.[5] Pockets of Shi'i community existed in Tabaristan, Qom, Kashan, Avaj and Sabzevar and they were nourished from the academic and religious centres of Iraq. In many other areas the population of Shi'i and Sunni was mixed. The Shi'i under Safavids (1501-1722) underwent a transformation from "a persecuted minority to established dynasties and majorities."[6] Following an interlude of the Afghan invasion (Shi'i-Sunni compromise), the emergence of an independent hierarchical clergy beginning with the Qajar dynasty (1791-1921) reinforced the position of Shi'ism in Iranian social and cultural life. The Shahs in Iran actively promoted Iranian ulama through funds and stipends in Qom, Isfahan, and Iraq, because of the influence they exercised.[7]

As a result of significant state support, protection and funding, Persian Shi'ism exercised a profound influence in these centuries on many regions of the Arab East (Iraq, al-Hasa, Damascus, and Beirut), South Asia, and Central Asia.[8] The conversion of Persia to Shi'ism increasingly exposed Iraqi Shi'is to Persian influences through increase in religious traffic and movement of Persian students and ulama. Religious/academic centres in Persia/Iran also came into prominence, particularly the holy cities of Mashhad and Qom as well as Isfahan. Mashhad has the tomb of Imam Ali ar-Ridha (c. 765-818), the eighth Imam of the Shi'is Muslims, also known as a martyr. The city of Qom is the site of the shrine of Fatima Masume, sister of Imam Ali ar-Ridha, and more importantly, emerged as the centre of Shi'i religious scholarship with the decline of Najaf and Karbala. Isfahan was the main centre of ulama in Iran both under the Safavids and Qajars.[9]

Creation and Sustenance of Cultural Space

The fluid boundary between the domains of Iraq and Iran in pre-modern times facilitated criss-cross movement of elites and laity to the holy cities (shrines) for pilgrimage, visitations, religious studies, and corpse burial. Sustained contact between the Shi'is of the two domains/countries generated interstices of interaction that was reaffirmed by shared sectarian identity (among ethnically heterogeneous populations), common religious traditions, socio-economic exchanges at the holy sites, and development of Shi'i scholarship in academic centres in the holy cities. Najaf and Karbala in Iraq and Qom, Mashhad and Isfahan in Iran emerged as nerve centres of social, economic and cultural interactions.

Through several centuries Iranians (Persians) have come on pilgrimage to the holy Shi'i shrines of pilgrimage to the shrines of the Imams in Iraq. The act of pilgrimage—acknowledgement of the authority of the Imam as the leader of the community—helped to preserve Shi'i collective memory and identity as distinguished from Sunnis. Visitation to holy shrines in Iraq advanced on a massive scale, when the bulk of Iranians converted to Shi'ism under the Safavid rule. Contacts at the shrines stimulated religious devotion and sharpened sense of solidarity among the Shi'is. The transitional experience at the pilgrimage centres and the exhilaration of mass celebration broke barriers between peoples and reinforced the cultural space. In the late 19th century, ninety per cent of pilgrims to Iraq were Persians.[10]

The shrine cities were also spaces of robust economic activities generated by pilgrimage, which was the major source of income for local traders and businesses. An extensive marketing system thrived in the shrine cities that greatly improved the welfare of the merchants and clerics that lived off the pilgrim trade. The positive impact of pilgrim trade was felt even as far as Baghdad. Many religious and social services—attendants, khan owners, and mut'a marriage contractors—developed to cater to the pilgrims. Both foreign pilgrimage and internal visitations to the shrine cities bolstered the position of Shi'i Islam. While the former strengthened the socio-economic link of Najaf and Karbala with Iran, the latter was instrumental in forging linkages of the Iraqi Shi'is with the Iranians.

However, such interactions were not always smooth, especially when these cities were under mutually antagonistic dominions: Iraqi shrine cities were under the Ottoman rule (1533-1918) and the shrine cities of Qom, Mashad and others under the Persian empire/rule. Nevertheless, several treaties between the Persian rulers and the Ottomans guaranteed unimpeded access for Iranian pilgrims to the shrine cities. Particularly, the Treaty of Kordan (1746) signed between the Persians and Ottomans, guaranteed Iranians' unhindered access to Karbala and Najaf, and consequently prosperity for merchants, shopkeepers, and clerics who lived off the pilgrim trade.[11] Moreover, in the eighteenth century the shrine cities in Iraq paid no tribute to the government in Bagdad. In fact, during the two periods of Safavid occupation of Iraq (early 1730, 1740), Shi'i Persian merchants came to Iraq in large numbers, thus appropriating a considerable share of the commerce of Baghdad.

With the conversion of a large number of Iraqi tribes to Shi'ism during the nineteenth century, the cultural connectivity between the Shi'is of Iran and Iraq was reinforced. Although conversion to Shi'ism took place in Iraq throughout history, it was confined mainly to cities. Several reinforcing processes were, however, responsible for the conversion of the southern Iraqi tribes: (i) Wahhabi attack on Najaf and Karbala (1775-1795); (ii) Emergence of shrine cities as Iraq's major desert market towns; and (iii) Ottoman policy of tribal settlement.[12] The Wahhabi attack of Najaf and Karbala reinforced the sectarian identity of Shi'i ulama and increased their motivation to proselytise Arab tribes for security of the religion. Shi'i emissaries to the tribal areas promoted visitations to tombs of the Imams, cult of Shi'i saints, and the rituals connected with the commemoration of Ashura.[13] As the number of local believers increased, contributors and pilgrims strengthened the economy of Najaf and Karbala. The Ottoman attempts from 1831 to settle the nomadic population, expand agriculture, distribute title deeds to individuals and increase the collection of taxes in Iraq led to a feeling of injustice amongst tribesman. According to Juan Cole, "this mass conversion may have in part been a reproof from the tribes people to their Sunni Ottoman overlords, and a protest of their treatment by the latter."[14]

Karbala replaced Isfahan and Qom as the main centre of Shi'i scholarship in early eighteenth century. The Afghan occupation in 1722, displaced a large number of ulama, who migrated from Persia to Karbala, making the holy city a major centre of learning. The violent Ottoman occupation of

Karbala in 1843, Yitzhak Nakash has argued, forced Shi'i scholars to move to neighbouring Najaf, which gained a pre-eminent position as a Shi'i academic centre. Nakash further argues that the Qajars, alarmed at the violence in Karbala against Iranian people, succeeded in pressuring the Ottomans to grant Persians certain immunities.[15] With these developments religious hierarchy in Najaf came under the control of the Persian mujtahids. This attracted a bulk of students and charitable income from Iran and India. The flow of funds led to the establishment of more religious schools in Najaf, making them centres of educational, literary, and socio-political activities for students from both Iraq and Iran. As a result, Iranian Shi'i formed a substantial minority in Iraq and in the religious educational centres. Shi'i ulama from Iran often captured leadership places in the religious hierarchy of other shrine cities as well.[16]

Limitations on the "Cultural Space"

The creation of modern Iraq and Iran in the early twentieth century put an end to the centrality of Najaf and Karbala in the life of Shi'is in the two domains/countries. As a clearer border between the two countries came into existence, the movement of Iranian pilgrims, mujtahids and students to the shrine cities in Iraq was restricted. The restrictive policies of successive Iraqi governments and Iran's Pahlavi rulers eroded the long-established links of the shrine cities with Iran. With the advent of monarchy in Iraq in 1921, Sunni Arab minority gained precedence, pan-Arabism became the major nationalist trend, and governmental policies undermined the position of Persians in the country. The deportation of prominent Persian mujtahids and voluntary departure of students and settlers to Iran led to a sharp decline in the number of Persians residing in holy cities, and eventually undermined the fabric of Shi'i culture and society in Iraq.

Najaf and Karbala declined in importance and this trend continued even after the collapse of the monarchy in Iraq. Throughout the 1920s, the Pahlavi ruler sought to impose limit on pilgrimage and diverted Iranian resources from Najaf and Karbala to Mashhad, disrupting the linkages between Persians and the twin holy cities.[17] The Shi'i ulama expelled to Persia/Iran laid the foundations for the rise of the city of Qom as the centre of the Shi'i learning and authority at the expense of Najaf. Najaf lost its religious primacy to Qom and was not to regain it until the twenty-first century and the establishment of a Shi'i-majority government in Iraq after 2003.

In 1950s, *hawzas* (Shi'i religious seminaries) in Najaf and Karbala suffered further decline with the introduction of secular reforms. Simultaneous to the decrease in the number of students in Najaf, the Ba'ath government in Iraq started the persecution of Shi'is in the country. The Ba'ath government under Saddam Hussein also prevented movement of Iranian Shi'is for education and pilgrimage to the holy cities in Iraq. Throughout the 1970s, the Ba'athist regime stepped up the persecution of Shi'is in the South. Iraq witnessed a series of killings of Shi'i clerics. Baqir as-Sadr, a leading Shi'i religious leader, was executed in 1980 and personal funds of leading mujtahids were confiscated diminishing their ability to act as patrons and benefactors of students and lesser ulama.[18] These factors led to polarisation between the Shi'is in Iran and Iraq, reflected in the composition of the *hawzas* of holy cities. While Qom attracted students mainly from within Iran, the mixed student population of Najaf dropped with the declining movement of Iranians to Iraq. The Iran-Iraq war (1980-88) further polarised the Shi'i population of the two countries. Such developments led to the disruption of the inclusive cultural space between the two domains into "exclusive spaces" in Iran and Iraq. The rise of modern states that sharpened national identities reduced space for cultural interface, both at the level of religious elites and the laity. It was not until 2003, that this space was restored.

Post-2003 Restoration of Cultural Space

The end of Saddam Hussein's regime in 2003, followed by the election of a transitional government, brought the majority Shi'is to power (as opposed to Sunni Ottomans, monarchy and Ba'ath) for the first time in Iraq (or anywhere in the Arab world) and offers scope for resurgence and strengthening of the cultural space. Since then there has been a thaw in bitter relations between Iran and Iraq, as business and trade relations have increased.[19] There have been Iranian investments in Iraq's overwhelming Shi'i southern regions, especially in infrastructure construction and projects that enable pilgrimage.[20] Although Iranian pilgrims are the targets of Sunni extremists in Iraq,[21] their number has been in ascendance since the inauguration of the new political denomination in Iraq.

The surge in pilgrimages in recent times has once again reinforced the status of Karbala and Najaf as the focus of devotion for Shi'is. These factors have strengthened Shi'i affiliation and identity and have undermined the rigidity of formal political boundary between the two countries. Thus riding on the crest of a more open political environment generated by the existence of Shiʿi governments in both Iraq and Iran, the contacts between the Shiʿi population of the two countries have significantly increased. The "space" that had existed since Persians and subsequently marsh Arabs of Iraq converted to Shi'ism, until the events of the first half of the twentieth century caused a major disruption, appears to be on the mend.

Ever since the seat of Shiʿi religious learning shifted from Najaf to Qom, the latter has been the centre of Shi'i scholarship. A large number of contemporary mujtahids, many of whom are part of the political establishment in Iran, belong to the madrasas of Qom. In general, the mujtahids of Qom have been supportive of the marjaʿiyya (religious leadership) of Iraq, especially Ayatollah Sistani[22]—who has played a decisive role in reconciliation between Shi'i factions in Iraq in post-Baʿathist period—and his brand of quietist politics. Sistani does not subscribe to the idea of "rule of the jurist" (*vilayat-e faqih*), articulated by Ayatollah Khomeini (1902-89) and implemented in the Islamic Republic of Iran. Sistani represents the quietist school of thought within Shiʿism, and he has been reluctant to get directly involved in worldly affairs. He views Iran's theocracy as a departure from centuries of Shiʿi thought and does not advocate that clerics should be the final arbiter of state affairs.[23] Sistani's repugnance to the exercise of political power by the religious authorities is shared by many grand ayatollahs of Qom, such as, Yousef Sanei and Ali Montazeri, and their large circle of clerical fellow travellers. The "axis of cooperation," manifested in the support of the mujtahids of Qom for their counterparts in Najaf, has reinforced a sense of "collectiveness" at the level of the religious elites.

On the other hand—at the level of popular tradition—Najaf and Karbala have re-emerged as the centre of Shiʿi reverence and piety. With the resumption of pilgrimage (both internal and external) on a massive scale after the fall of the Baʿath regime in Iraq, Najaf and Karbala have once again become sites of collective celebration—a joint experience vital for preserving the collective Shiʿi memory and group identity as distinguished from that of the Sunnis—and sites of active Shiʿi-sation. This has reduced the ethnic differences that were sharpened in the last century as a consequence of the rise of nationalism.

Pilgrimage is once again developing an extensive network of marketing system in the shrine cities, and the contributions to mujtahids have resumed as a result of the relaxation in movement of the pilgrims and followers.

Charities and payment for religious services have also resumed and are now flourishing in the shrine cities. The intellectual tradition of Qom and the popular tradition in Najaf and Karbala manifested in pilgrimage and participation of the laity in other religious activities in recent times, fill up the cultural space with elements of high and popular culture. They exist together, develop networks of support among the Shi'is of the two countries and sustain the space from shrinking.

Surfacing Areas of Conflict

Dilemmas and contradictions in the contemporary cultural space could limit its expanse. The harmony of this space could be disrupted by the doctrinal differences between the religious leadership of Najaf on the one hand and Qom on the other, primarily over the question of the role of clerics in government. Khomeini's radical religious notion of direct clerical rule has been the source of underlying tensions within the clerical class for decades. While concurring doctrinal positions has brought the mujtahids of Najaf and Qom together, there is potential for conflict with the section of clerics who support the idea of *vilayat-e faqih* and are closely associated with the government in Iran.[24]

Further, successive Sunni governments in Iraq questioned the Arab origin of the Shi'is and associated Iraqi Shi'ism with Persian culture and Iranian history. In the post-2005 period, Iran's government is encouraging a greater Iranian presence in Iraq by supporting economic activities that control a segment of pilgrim business: renovating and maintaining Shi'i shrines in Iraq. This presence, though, on the one hand, has helped restore the cultural space (through movement of pilgrims, students and ulama), gives rise to factors that can limit this space. Iraqis feel that the pilgrimages present a small but important example of Iran's rising soft power in Iraq. This makes Iraqis increasingly resentful.[25] Iraqi Shi'is, who have shown a great degree of attachment to nationalist sentiments, at times strongly, assert their strong Arab identity. This creates problems and tensions between Shi'is of the two countries and impinges on their Shi'i identity.

Some Concluding Remarks

The change in the political complexion of Iraq has eliminated the barrier that separated the Shi'is of Iran and Iraq. Qom in Iran and Najaf and Karbala in Iraq together now constitute the triumvirate of Shi'i culture and power in the Middle East. The confluence between the extant intellectual tradition of

Qom and that of popular tradition in Najaf and Karbala has recreated the overarching Shi'i "cultural space" that had existed between the two countries. There is an axis of cooperation between the religious elites of Iraqi cities and Qom. At the popular level, the opening of the shrine cities of Iraq has had an emotional impact on the Iranians. Since 2003, thousands of Iranians have visited the two holy cities in Iraq and the Iraqis have once again begun to witness the prosperity generated by such visitations. The layers of connections established between the elites and laity sustain Shi'i identity strengthening the cultural space. However, shared sectarian identity does not always create a harmonious relationship. Doctrinal differences between the mujtahids of Iran and Iraq and the growing nationalist assertion among the Iraqi Shi'is vis-à-vis their Iranian counterparts help explain the factors that can limit expanse of the cultural space underpinned by adherence to Shi'ism.

Notes

1. Imamate, as opposed to the Sunni concept of Caliphate/Khilafat, is a doctrine of Shi'i Islam that spells out the basis of leadership of the Islamic community (*ummah*). The Shi'is believe that only the direct descendants of the family of Prophet Muhammad are his rightful successors. These are the imams or leaders (*amama*, Arabic for "in front of"), who by virtue of their ancestry have the divine knowledge and authority to lead the community of Muslims. They not only rule over the community justly but also interpret the divine law and its esoteric meaning, thus providing spiritual and moral guidance to the followers. For Sunni Muslims, the word "imam" is commonly used to mean a person who leads the prayer in the mosque. In Shi'ism, however, imams are those members of *ahl al-bayt* designated as the infallible by the preceding Imam. For Shi'is, Ali ibn abu Talib, the son-in-law and cousin of Prophet Muhammad, was the rightful successor of the latter, whom they consider as the first Imam. The Shi'is believe that Muhammad named Ali his immediate successor clearly during his lifetime. Hence, the Shi'is consider all other caliphs before Ali, as usurpers of the caliphate. In fact, the word "Shi'i" is derived from the phrase "Shiatu Ali," meaning partisans of Ali. See, Moojan Momen, *An Introduction to Shi'i Islam: The History and Doctrines of Twelve* (New York: Yale University Press, 1985); Abdulaziz Sachedina, *The Just Ruler in Shi'ite Islam: The Comprehensive Authority of the Jurist in Imamite Jurisprudence* (New York: Oxford University Press, 1998); Heinz Halm, *The Shi'ites: A Short History* (Princeton: Markus Wiener Pub., 2007).
2. Martin Kramer (ed.), *Shi'ism, Resistance and Revolution* (Boulder: Westview Press, 1987), p. 2.
3. Depending upon their belief on number of Imams, Shi'is in modern times are mainly divided into three branches, namely the Twelvers (*Ithna Asharriyya*), the Seveners (Ismailis) and the Fivers (Zaidis). The names of twelve imams held in belief by a majority Shi'is are: Ali ibn Abu Talib, Hasan ibn Ali, Hussein ibn Ali, Ali ibn Hussein,

Muhammad ibn Ali, Jafar ibn Muhammad, Musa ibn Jafar, Ali ibn Musa, Muhammad ibn Ali, Ali ibn Muhammad, Hasan ibn Ali and Muhammad ibn al-Hasan. For further understanding, see Sayyid Muhammad Hosayn Tabataba'i, *Shi'ite Islam* Seyyed Hossein Nasr (translator) (Selangor, Malaysia: Islamic Book Trust, 2010), pp. 43-55; John Obert Voll, *Islam: Continuity and Change in the Modern World* (Syracuse: Syracuse University Press, 1994), p. 18.

4. Within Shi'ism, various branches emerged over the issue of succession of imams, just as Shi'is and Sunnis had separated over succession to prophet Muhammad. With every succession dispute their emerged a different sect (*tariqa*). Each *tariqa* then followed its own dynastic line, and set of imams who were revered. When the imam died without an heir, his unborn successor was believed to have gone into concealment, i.e. the occultation. The Shi'i tariqa with a majority of adherents are the Twelvers or Imamis, who believe in the infallibility and spiritual guidance of imams. They also believe that the Twelfth Imam, who is in occulation, will appear at the "right time" to redeem the Muslims. The Twelvers are followed by the Zaidis and Ismailis. Zaidi doctrine of imamah does not presuppose the infallibility of the imam; they also do not believe in occultation. Ismailis get their name from their acceptance of Ismail ibn Jafar as the divinely appointed spiritual successor to Jafar al-Sadiq; they differ from the Twelvers, who accept Musa al-Kadhim, younger brother of Ismail, as the true imam. The Ismailis believe in occultation. See Tabataba'i, *Shi'ite Islam*; Ira Lapidus, *A History of Islamic Societies* (2nd ed.) (Cambridge & New York: Cambridge University Press, 2002).
5. Voll, *Islam, Continuity and Change in the Modern World*, p. 80.
6. Hamid Dabashi, Seyyed Hossein Nasr and Seyyed Vali Reza Nasr (eds.), *Expectation of the Millennium: Shi'ism in History* (Albany: State University of New York Press, 1989), p. 132.
7. Meir Litvak, *Shi'ite Scholars of Nineteenth Century Iraq: The "Ulama of Najaf and Karbala"* (Cambridge: Cambridge University Press, 1998), chs. 6, 9; Michael M. J. Fischer, *Iran: From Religious Dispute to Revolution* (Madison: The University of Wisconsin Press, 1980), p. 30.
8. Juan Cole, *Sacred Space and Holy War* (London: I. B. Tauris, 2004), p. 2.
9. Fischer, *Iran: From Religious Dispute to Revolution*, p. 30.
10. Yitzhak Nakash, *The Shi'is of Iraq* (Princeton: Princeton University Press, 2003), pp. 165, 167.
11. One long-lasting effect of Nadir Shah's Iraq campaign of the 1740s was the provisions in the peace treaty he finally concluded with the Ottomans that concerned Iranian pilgrims to the Iraqi shrine cities. While the Shah ceded these cities once more to the Ottomans in September 1746, he stipulated that Iranian pilgrims be able to visit the shrines and that "so long as these pilgrims carried no merchandise, the Governor and officials of Baghdad were not to levy any tax upon them." Moreover, in the eighteenth century the shrine cities paid no tribute to the government in Bagdad. Juan Cole, *Sacred Space and Holy War* (London: I. B. Tauris, 2004). p. 70.
12. Nakash, *The Shi'is of Iraq*, ch. 1.

13. *Ashura* is the tenth day of Islamic month of *muharram* when Shi'is observe the martyrdom of Husain ibn Ali, the grandson of Prophet Muhammad and the third Shi'i Imam, along with members of his family and close friends at the Battle of Karbala in the year 680 AD. The Shi'is often express public mourning by self-flagellation, crying and memorial service. The Sunnis abhor such display of grief.
14. Cole, *Sacred Space and Holy War*, p. 25.
15. Nakash, *The Shi'is of Iraq*, pp. 22-23.
16. For instance, Iranian officials dominated posts like the mayor of Najaf and the custodian of the shrine of Imam Husayn in Karbala until 1917. Nakash, *The Shi'is of Iraq*, pp. 22-23.
17. Nakash, *The Shi'is of Iraq*, p. 240.
18. Joyce Wiley, *The Islamic Movement of Iraqi Shias* (Boulder: Lynne Rienner Pub., 1992), p. 57.
19. Kenneth Katzman, "Iran-Iraq Relations," *Congressional Research Service*, August 13, 2010.
20. "Iran and Turkey battle for Iraq supremacy," *Business 360*, March 30, 2012, http://business.blogs.cnn.com/2012/03/30/iran-and-turkey-battle-for-iraq-supremacy/.
21. "Iraq's holy cities enjoy boom in religious tourism," *Al Arabiyya.net*, April 4, 2013, http://english.alarabiya.net/en/life-style/art-and-culture/2013/04/04/Iraq-s-holy-cities-enjoy-boom-in-religious-tourism.html
22. Ali al-Husayni al-Sistani (b.1930), an Iranian born Shi'i, is the highest-ranking religious scholar (marja) of Iraq and is the head of the *hawza* of Najaf.
23. The doctrine of *vilayat-e faqih* (governance of the religious jurist, preached in Qom) was formulated by Ayatollah Ruhollah Khomeini and served as the ideological underpinning of the 1979 Islamic Revolution in Iran. It grants absolute authority over all matters—religious, social, and political—to a person, who has earned the title of *mujtahid* or *Grand Ayatollah*—a person competent in interpreting the Islamic law (*sharia*) by legal reasoning (*ijtihad*). Although *vilayat-e faqih* was implemented in homogeneous Shi'i society in Iran, exporting the doctrine has proved much more difficult. The clerics of Najaf have always been skeptical about the doctrine, as they believe it contradicts the Shi'i tradition of thinking about political power, which does not envisage that clerics would exercise direct political power. In the medieval and early modern period, clerics were always outside the ruling system, praising the monarch for keeping to the faith or stood in opposition in case of deviation. Moreover, scholastic Shi'ism idealised that the laity would follow the single most learned and upright "object of emulation" (*marja at-taqlid*). However, there were always several contenders for the position; religious authority was thus multiple. Khomeini's innovation to the scholastic understanding of political power in Shi'ism lay in the fact that he declared monarchy to be incompatible with Islam and averred that till the coming of the Hidden Twelfth Imam, the clergy should lead the people by exercising political power. Khomeini especially taught the "guardianship of the jurisprudent," that supreme power would be in clerical hands, even if other formal structures of government are manned by lay people. The grand marja of Najaf, Abu al-Qasim al-Khoei (1899-1992), who is said to have been the most vocal critic of vilayat-e faqih, believed that the theory was an innovation "with no support in Shi'i theology or law." Grand Ayatollah Ali al-Sistani, who is originally from Iran, follows Khoei in rejecting the doctrine. According to Sheikh

Jalaleddine as-Saghir, Sistani's representative in Baghdad, the Ayatollah recommends a multi-sectarian government for Iraq, where people are the sole arbiter of government. See Hamid Algar, *Islam and revolution: writings and declarations of Imam Khomeini*, translated and annotated (Berkeley, California: Mizan Press, c. 1981); Vali Nasr, *The Shia Revival* (New York & London: W. W. Norton, 2006), p. 125; Yitzhak Nakash, *Reaching for Power: The Shi'a in the Modern Arab World* (Princeton: Princeton University Press, 2006), pp. 7-10; Yousif al-Kho'i, "Grand Ayatollah Abu al-Qasim al-Kho'i: Political Thought and Positions," in Faleh Abdul-Jabar," *Ayatollah, Sufis and Ideologues* (London: Saqi Books, 2002), ch. 14.

24. While some believe that the Iranian government has been working to ensure the primacy of clerics trained in Qom steeped in Islamic republic's ideology, over clerics trained in the relatively non-political "quietist" tradition of Najaf academies, others do not see an open rivalry emerging between Qom and Najaf, though there could be rival doctrines in the long-term. Robin B. Wright, *The Iran Primer: Power, Politics, and US Policy* (Washington: United States Institute Of Peace Press, 2010), p. 153; Nicholas Blanford, "Iran, Iraq, and two Shiite visions," *The Christian Science Monitor*, February 20, 2004, http://www.csmonitor.com/2004/0220/p01s02-woiq.html; Hamid Mavani, "Ayatullah Khomeini's Concept of Governance (*wilayat al-faqih*) and the Classical Shi'i Doctrine of Imamate," *Middle Eastern Studies*, vol. 47, issue 5, (2011), pp. 807-24.
25. Marisa Cochrane Sullivan, "Iran's Soft Power in Iraq," *Iran Tracker*, August 4, 2009, http://www.irantracker.org/analysis/iran's-soft-power-iraq.

5. The Net of Culture: Living in Many Cultures, Defining Own Selfhood (*Oralman* Communities in Kazakhstan)

Laura Yerekesheva

Methodology: Culture and Identity in a System Approach

Throughout the ages the question of "us and them," "we and others" highlighted the history and development of people, revealing one of the deepest problems of identity: how to deal with those who differ from you. In simplest terms, the concept of "we and others" is inevitably linked with the social environment and social context since the "other" always belongs to another cultural and social milieu, whether individually or collectively. However, to understand social structure one needs to take into account its cultural dimension and the meaning of culture in a broad sense.

The broad meaning of culture refers to all spheres of spiritual and material life of the people (at a religious, scientific, economic, political, agricultural, educational and military level) within the course of their immediate or prolonged time and space through interaction among themselves (on interpersonal, collective, societal levels), with the surrounding world as well as with the already existing patterns of culture. In this case, then, every aspect of such activity, including religious,[1] clearly bears a cultural dimension.

From the systemic analytical point of view, the broad understanding of culture is perceived as an inclusive general system (or certain framework) combining all other ones, i.e., cultural, social, personal and organic. Being the cumulative sum of knowledge and information elaborated by *all* systems during many thousand years of their existence, culture moulds them into the specific cultural codes, i.e., "genotypes" and then reacts back and influences all systems in the form of collective unconsciousness, cultural identity, collective memory and other mechanisms.

This structural position implies that all systems and their elements or units (such as religion, economy, politics, etc.) are culturally conditioned.

Identity is a cultural expression. It may be described as modes of functionality, certain expressions, ways of conveying culture's uniqueness and specificity. It is an essence and method, object and subject simultaneously. In other words, culture conveys its crucial messages through identity only and shapes the overall inclusive system. Once we presume the inclusive character of culture as embracing all other systems then identity too becomes an inevitable part of each of the systems. Hence identity bears systemic character and acquires various forms subject to the specificity of organic, personal, social and general cultural systems.

Thus, culture can embrace all its interdependent units, i.e., organic, personal, social and cultural. Identity too has the remarkable feature of being combined into a common personal, social and cultural identity that finally marks this or that person, group or nation. In other words, identity of one person always transforms into a broader identity—the cultural identity of a certain group to which this or another person belongs. Or we may say that personal identity always bears social and cultural features and has profound ties of bonding.

These ties between various types of identity (on personal and group levels) may create different outcomes, especially when it comes to assertion of identity under a wide umbrella or a net of culture. A net of culture as a cumulative sum of various forms and types of a certain group's cultural identities can be performed simultaneously along, both uniting and dividing lines. When personal, social and cultural identities are linked with each other and met altogether within certain spatial-temporary continuum, then the group solidarity paves a way towards assertion of the idea of a wide socio-cultural group identity, or the idea better known in political science as nationhood. However, when this group solidarity disintegrates due to the influence of another culture, then personal-social identities of a distinctive group tend to vary. The influence and impact of another cultural space can shape and modify the social identity of a given group. This happens due to the highest status of a culture as an all-embracing and inclusive system. As has been discussed above, this status gives culture a remarkable ability to shape, reshape and modify all other systems with their corresponding ways of expression, i.e., their identities.

This implies that the influence of another culture and cultural identity may have a significant consequence for the types and forms of a group's social identity. However, we cannot exclude at all the other influence, i.e., the ability of social identity of one group, which reflects one culture, to reshape another culture and its patterns. It may be said that this kind of feedback could be found in case of a very strong group solidarity imposing their will and patterns of their own culture in and over another cultural milieu. One may find this happening at the times of crucial transitions when the established cultural matrix is being changed or modified by the new evolving one. However, even in this case, the established cultural domain might restore its basic cultural features though not in full form. All radical transformations, revolutions and changes are the explicit samples of this process.

The interplay between culture and identities could be best illustrated by fluctuations in the border zones, i.e., those spatial-temporal continuums which imbibe and reflect various cultures. The case of *oralmans*—the native Kazakhs evolving as diasporas and irredentists and migrating to their motherland for a permanent living from other countries (as a rule, from neighbouring China, Mongolia, Russia, Central Asian countries)—is a bright example of these fluctuations. The case of the *oralmans* from Mongolia will be discussed below.

National and Cultural Identities: The Oralmans

The Kazakhs who historically lived in vast areas of the Eurasian continent, under conditions of various social and political transformations and the imposition of revised state borders throughout the nineteenth-twentieth centuries, presently are constituted as communities who are settled in various states of Central Asia, Russia, China, Mongolia and Turkey. In modern Kazakh, they are addressed as *oralmans* (returnees).

Oralman, according to Article 1 of the Republic of Kazakhstan Law on Migration is a person of native, or "titular" nationality who was expelled from the historical motherland and was deprived of citizenship due to mass political repression, illegal requisitions, violent collectivisation or other inhuman action and who, with his descendants, voluntarily moves to the Republic of Kazakhstan for permanent residence.[2] The state run migration policy of the Kazakhstan government of early 1990s to invite to and accommodate in Kazakhstan the Kazakhs living abroad (or *oralmans*) was aimed at increasing the overall number of the Kazakh population (which in 1989 formed only 48% of the total population) and more broadly—at asserting new national identity and nation-building process (i.e., "all those positive efforts undertaken to transform a state's population into a nation—to create a common national identity among the residents of the state."[3] Since the nature of links between the residents, population or groups on the one hand, and the state on the other hand, is subject to special characteristics of all actors involved, the issue of culture (as an overall inclusive system embracing social, personal and organic systems) and its modalities, i.e., identities, need to be addressed. In so far there is a state involved in the process of linking itself with the groups (i.e. in nation-building process), each individual case of national identity and nation-building process of a particular state should be addressed. However, the issue of national identity inevitably leads us to the aspect of cultural identity, the latter acquiring much broader meaning. In other words, national identity may be regarded as *a part* of a much broader concept of cultural identity, since culture does not confine itself to one particular state or one particular community only; in various degrees the more or less similar culture may be spread over different states. Consequently it means that broader cultural identity may embrace, though indirectly, various national identities as modalities of various states.

In so far as there are different group communities bound by different states' national frameworks, the overall cultural identity cannot be represented as a mere sum of some identities which participate in the formation of different national environments. Rather it could be seen as a net of culture(s), embracing its various elements/units and their respective identities which form certain "cultural hubs" spread over nation-states. Like Castell's net-based information society we may describe it as a net-based cultural society, mainly taking in view the fact that culture here transcends the space, i.e., nation-states, and while crossing borders, it forms a matrix of local cultural identities. Hence, the whole fabric of this or that culture is weaved with several sub-cultural patterns.

It is in this regard we may highlight the culture-oriented views of society which sees "the state as part and parcel of culture" and views the relationship between culture and the state from the standpoint of culture: "The state here is made to serve the needs of or contribute to the enrichment of the culture; it is never allowed to dictate terms to culture … ."

Since the culture-state relationship is featured by the prominence of culture, it is not surprising to witness a subsequent penetration of all elements of culture into the state structure with the result that cultural identity predominates over the state (national) one and alternative theories of the state emerge.[4] At the same time it should be emphasised here that local cultural dimension of a particular state actually gives shape to the overall content of culture.

The case of *oralmans* illustrates the cultural versus national identity issue. The Mongolian Kazakhs migrating to Kazakhstan within the broad net of culture have not simply changed their citizenship status. Though being under the same umbrella of a broad cultural identity (i.e., continuing to be ethnic Kazakhs with respective beliefs, traditions and identity), they have stopped their links with social groups as well as the state in Mongolia, and have started making new links in Kazakhstan. In other words, they have got involved in the same process on another soil, acquiring a new sub- cultural identity.

In Mongolia they became a part of Mongolian national identity, though constituting only 101,526 of the population[5] out of about 5 million population of Mongolia.[6] The Kazakhs of Mongolia are, numerically, an ethnic minority. Geographically they are concentrated mainly in one region, i.e., Bayan-Ulgei western *aimak* (region, oblast) of Mongolia which "alone accounts for more than 78,4% of the Kazakh population, thus, apart from being the most numerous, the Kazakhs are the only minority in Mongolia forming the majority of one *aimag*."[7] However, as it is noticed, they also live "in the industrial cities of Choibalson, Darkhan and Erdenetas as well as in the coal mining area of Nalaikh District, in Khoroo-4 ... which is 90 per cent Kazakh dominated area located near Ulaanbaatar."[8] This predominantly concentrated geographical location of the Kazakhs in one place (i.e. *Bayan-Ulgei aimak* which was specially demarcated for the Kazakhs in 1940) somewhat indicates strong group solidarity among the people. However, in a Mongolian environment the focus of the "we" among the Kazakhs *vis-à-vis* the "other" was not much highlighted. That may be explained by similar cultural traditions among the Kazakhs and the Mongols—referring to their shared nomadic civilisational heritage—providing them a ground for peaceful coexistence without major disturbances.

Thus the Kazakhs living in Mongolia with a Mongolian national identity as well as under the banner of a nation-state are the flag bearers of a broader cultural identity which linked them along ethnic lines with the other Kazakhs, living particularly, in Kazakhstan.

Living in Many Cultures

The crucial consequence of coming out of the net of culture as a constantly ongoing process embracing time and space is what Ashish Nandy has described as "simultaneously living in a number of cultures and even epochs." For developing societies especially this feature is almost forgotten or neglected.

For contemporary Kazakhstan, its historical past, Soviet legacy and the new independent experience are combined altogether in some cultural form or another which mould into everyday life, mentality, psychology and decision making and implementation processes taking place in the entire Central Asian region. In other words, for Kazakhstan, it is a huge task to understand and define its own culture and its own cultural selfhood that is derived from composite cultures and from various epochs and cultures associated with them. This explains partially why any attempt at modernisation inevitably goes hand in hand with traditional values, which ethnic groups tend to preserve. As a result a complex mosaic is formed where all "cultural layers" coexist with each other and mould the identity and psyche of communities and people. The rich historical background and radical changes associated with Soviet style modernisation along with contemporary nation-building process are crucial components of the process of attainment of cultural selfhood.

As far as everyday life is concerned, the traces of this cultural mix are visible everywhere, be it the perception of the "other" as seen through the lens of traditional economic modes of life, e.g., settled, nomadic, sedentary or through the lenses of tribal (*zhuz*) or regional affiliation, or through the lens of religious and primordial ethnic identities. Among the *oralmans* who are considered as new members of Kazakh society, some of their previous cultural layers were either unnoticed or were missing. Instead the more distant cultural features preserved in their cultural consciousness, memory and traditions were better highlighted and associated with the general cultural traditions among the Kazakhs. Though Kazakh communities, for example, in Mongolia and China also underwent the process of rapid modernisation throughout the twentieth century and associated with them dramatic social, economic and cultural changes, their experience was quite different. As a result, in their view, the links with the motherland were mainly along the ethnic primordial ties (like tribal and *zhuz* affiliation) and less along modernisation and social development. Therefore, they and the Kazakhstan government perceived that the same cultural system could be helpful for social and cultural adjustment.

However, the fact of being under the same umbrella or a net of culture (i.e., cultural identity of the Kazakhs) is not an adequate condition for smooth transition. In trying to make links with the state of their origin (i.e.,

Mongolia, China, etc.) or through the process of nation-building, they have already developed the sub cultural identity that allows them to participate in the life of this or that state. Their broad cultural identity goes hand-in-hand with various sub cultural identities—i.e., as citizens of Mongolia, and after migration—as nationals of Kazakhstan. Thus the problem of adjustment of *oralmans* in Kazakhstan cannot only be viewed in economic terms but also in cultural terms. It was not merely a change of citizenship, but of sub cultural affiliation. Since cultural and sub cultural identities are formulated over long periods of time, their transformation too takes time. This could be well illustrated by the difficult process of cultural adjustment of *oralmans* in independent Kazakhstan.

Cultural Adjustment: The Kazakhs from Mongolia

Regarding *oralman* migration the following facts must be highlighted: the Kazakh government aimed at attracting ethnic Kazakhs to balance the negative effects of immigration that took place in the country in early and middle 1990s, introduced presidential quotas and various judicial acts. Figures of the Migration Law, state programmes and decrees introduced in Kazakhstan since 1992 reveal that about 70,000-80,000 *oralmans* migrated to Kazakhstan.[9] Out of these figures about 100,000 people came to Kazakhstan from Mongolia. In 2000, the immigrants from Mongolia to Kazakhstan comprised only 2% as compared to 57% arriving from Russia, 19% from Uzbekistan, 5% from Kyrgyzstan.[10] From 1994 onwards, about 20,000 *oralmans* have migrated back to Mongolia. However, in the mid-2000s a second wave of migration to Kazakhstan occurred due to economic boom in the country. Other factors as climatic conditions and harsh winters in three consecutive years in mid 2000s in Mongolia accounted for the return of *oralmans* to Kazakhstan.[11]

The above discussion shows that the key issue in migration flows to Kazakhstan (including the second wave migration) is not only social and economic, but also the trend in cultural adjustments to the new space. It could be said that the successful integration of *oralman* communities into contemporary Kazakh society requires full scale adjustment—i.e., in language, culture and mentality. The linguistic adjustments offer a convenient way of life. The Soviet bilingual environment and the multicultural tradition may have modernised Kazakh society but it also became a challenge for *oralmans*, especially those emigrating from China. As for the Kazakhs from Mongolia, it was less pronounced since in socialist Mongolia the Russian language was taught in schools and the Mongolian language itself used the Cyrillic script. The other crucial factor was that not all the Kazakhs living in Kazakhstan know their mother tongue and that education and business activities (especially throughout the 1990s and even today) were conducted mostly in the Russian language, which has also added to the problems of adjustment.

The adherence of the *oralmans* to the established tradition and traditional ways of life encountered a lot of challenges in a new environment. The challenges were mostly visible in the lifestyle that they had to compromise with though it could be added that *oralmans* from Mongolia experienced lesser difficulties compared to other *oralmans*. According to the report, "to the great extent the so-called "first wave" of *oralmans*, repatriates from Mongolia have adjusted to the ways of local Kazakhs. In the first year of their arrival, these *oralmans* brought with them and used mostly handmade clothing, including winter wear. Now these *oralmans* have almost totally adopted modern, European style clothes."[12] The same could be referred to such lifestyle in the household items especially furniture: "Many *oralmans* do not buy furniture; instead they have an abundance of *korpe* (handmade patchwork blankets), pillows and rugs. Some of them live in yurts ... With their subsequent change in occupations, surroundings and the process of urbanisation this production of household items has all but stopped, especially among Mongolian Kazakhs ... One can say that over a ten-year period the culture of these *oralmans* (the Mongolian Kazakhs, for example) has been transformed."[13]

The crucial factor that has to be taken into account here is that the *oralmans* migrating to Kazakhstan usually come from the mono-ethnic rural areas, like Bayan-Ulgei *aimak* comprising of about 78% of all Kazakhs living in Mongolia. This factor implies preservation of traditional culture and consequently, a prolonged process of adaptation in a new environment.

During the interviews with the Kazakhs who came from Mongolia in the early 1990s,[14] it became evident that the adaptation process in Kazakhstan was more smooth compared to the people coming from the rural areas. The latter group was exposed to double pressure of transformation—cultural and social. To lessen this pressure, many of them tried to adjust themselves while preferring to live in suburban and rural areas, or to make some business in service sector such as catering and handicrafts for tourists exploiting the interest towards folklore and traditional cultural souvenir items. Some of them combine this existing interest in culture and tradition in order to live in yurts in the mountain suburban areas of Almaty, while doing business in food service that will bring them good business with the tourists. It should be added that this process of adaptation is more quick and vivid in urban areas than in rural areas.

It could be said that the process of bringing the *oralmans* to the mainstream of Kazakhstan society is a long process that requires not only state support and patronage but also patience from within the society itself.

Summary

The case of *oralmans*' cultural adjustment shows us that the broad net of culture is distorted in some spaces resulting in complications and cleavages especially where the sub cultural affiliation becomes more pronounced and profound. This makes adaptation and cultural adjustment far more complicated. It could be summed up that living in many cultures requires skilful management of all kinds of resources—material and human. Especially important is the ideological dimension. When the shifting ideological paradigms of "dominant-subordinate" cultures dictate the patterns of change in both domestic and external policies, the complexities are far more than would have been imagined. This also probably restricts the evolution of national ideology—a task which most nations set before themselves while searching for new prospects of independent statehood or development.

The issue of net of cultures is to be studied from the wider perspective of time and space especially where many cultures coexist and mingle with each other in such a way that disrupts the broad fabric of national identity. Cultural identity seems to get restricted by sub cultural affiliations.

Notes

1. From a methodological standpoint religion here denotes the realm of culture, notwithstanding various theoretical approaches both in sociology (Sorokin, Parsons, Giddens, Archer, Alexander) and anthropology (Geertz) that provide different understanding and definitions of culture. Whether from a viewpoint of ideational or sensitive cultures (e.g., Sorokin), a value-based approach to cultural and all other systems (e.g., Parsons), or from a view of cultural and socio-cultural systems and their cultural elaboration (Archer), all definitions of culture nevertheless consider religion as its substantial part. Religion (like culture in general) itself could be regarded through the institutional, relational and textual categories' lenses. In this case religion appears as a result of the human collective representations and institutions, of collective relationships, and of cognitive and mental activity. In other words it is a result of human's prolonged interaction (including an interaction with the cosmos and physical environment) and (as

Berger puts it) "a far projection of the human's self-externalisation ... Religion implies that the human order is projected into the totality of being. In other words, religion is an audacious attempt of the man to understand the whole universe as meaningful for him." Peter L. Berger, *The Sacred Canopy: Elements of a Sociological Theory of Religion* (Second Edition) (New York: Anchor Books, 1990), pp. 27-28. See M. S. Archer, *Culture and Agency: The Place of Culture in Social Theory* (Cambridge: Cambridge University Press, 1996) (Revised Edition); Peter L. Berger, *The Sacred Canopy: Elements of a Sociological Theory of Religion*. 2nd Edition. (New York: Anchor Books, 1990); Clifford Geertz, *The Interpretation of Cultures* (New York: Basic Books, 2000); T. Parsons T. *O sotsial'nyh sistemah* [On Social Systems/Translation from English] in V. F. Chesnokova and S. A. Belanovskiy, (ed) (Moscow: Akademicheskiy Proekt, 2002); P. Sorokin, *Sotsial'naya i kul'turnaya dinamika* [Social and Cultural Dynamics/Translation from English] (Sankt-Petersburg: RHGI, 2000).

2. L. G. Yerekesheva, "International Migration in Kazakhstan. An Analytical Report," in *International Migration in Central Asia: Challenges and Prospects* (Almaty: UNESCO, 2005), p. 70.
3. In this paper I do not broach on the debates about the term "nation-state". There should be proper analysis regarding various concepts, i.e., multinational, multiethnic or even civilisational state. On this see Ashis Nandy, *The Romance of the State and the Fate of Dissent in the Tropics* (New Delhi: Oxford University Press, 2010), pp. 1-14. Also see J. Broun and George J. McCall, "Introduction: Dilemmas of Nation-Building" in *International Social Science Journal*. vol. LIX, no. 2, June 2008, pp. 151-53.
4. According to Ashis Nandy, non-modern or postmodern concepts of state began to emerge in response to the crisis of the nation-state: "... while it is an open question what forms the postmodern state will take, there is little doubt that the dominant concept of the state will be drastically altered." Nandy, *The Romance* ... . p. 12.
5. Sharad K. Soni, "Kazakhstan-Mongolia Relations—Issues and Trends," in: G. M. Mir edited *Globalizing Eurasia. Potentials and Challenges* (Srinagar: University of Kashmir, Centre of Central Asian Studies, 2013), pp. 113-31.
6. According to other figures there are more than 1,40,000 Kazakhs in Mongolia which corresponds to about 5% of total population of the country. In Bayan-Ulgei *aimak* alone there live about 90,000 Kazaks belonging mainly to 2 major tribal communities such as *abak kerei* and *naiman*, whose economic activity is mainly cattle-breeding. See Karlygash Bukenova, *Po puti Chingiz Hana. Vstrechi s Mongolskimi Kazahami* [Going Along the Way of Chingiz Khan-Meetings with Mongolian Kazakhs], http://www.voxpopuli.kz/post/view/id/399.
7. Soni, "Kazakhstan-Mongolia Relations ..." p. 124.
8. Soni, "Kazakhstan-Mongolia Relations ..." p. 124.
9. According to Gulnara Mendikulova, there were about 703,000 *oralmany* who migrated to Kazakhstan. Gulnara Mendikulova, "Migrations in Central Asia-Problems and Prospects," in G. M. Mir edited *Globalizing Eurasia. Potentials and Challenges* (Srinagar: University of Kashmir, Centre of Central Asian Studies, 2013), pp. 274-75; Soni, op. cit, 2013, p. 127.

10. More on this see *Contemporary Demographic Situation in Kazakhstan* (Almaty: KISI, 2004), p. 102.
11. Figures are from the data presented by Peter Finke at the international conference on migration held in Almaty on November 30, 2004.
12. B. L. Tatibekov "Oralmans in Kazakhstan: Socio-Economic Status and Paths toward Integration into Kazakhstani Society," in *International Migration in Central Asia: Challenges and Prospects* (Almaty: UNESCO), 2005, p. 189.
13. Tatibekov, 2005, p. 189.
14. The interviews with the Kazakhs from Mongolia were conducted by the author in Almaty in 2013.

6. Between Indianness and Jewishness: The Ambivalence of Indian Jews as Reflected in Literature, Cinema and Art

Navras Jaat Aafreedi

The year 2013 is historic for Indian literature as well as Jewish literature for after a long period of fifty-two years, after Meera Mahadevan's *Apnā Ghar* (The Home of One's Own) (1961), the only other Hindi novel with a Jewish theme has appeared on the literary scene, in the form of Sheela Rohekar's *Miss Samuel: Ék Yahūdi Gāthā* (A Jewish Saga).

Acceptance rather than Equality

And the good news is that it comes across as more insightful with regard to the Jewish experience in India, than *Apnā Ghar*. It acknowledges the absence of anti-Semitism in India, but does not present a picture as rosy as one gets to see in *Apnā Ghar* and in the three English novels, namely, *The Walled City* (1997), *Book of Esther* (2002), and *Book of Rachel* (2006) and a collection of short stories, *Shalom India Housing Society* (2007) of the best known Indian Jewish writer, Esther David. Rohekar writes:

> India neither ever exiled the Jews nor persecuted them. They were never discriminated against for being Jewish. They got equal rights as citizens of India.
>
> But they were always seen as different and thus deprived of the joy of full integration in the Indian society. They were not insulted, but only seldom did they get honour and recognition. They were always seen as fellow human beings, but could never be included among "our own people."
>
> It is for this reason only that they remained rootless and could never muster enough courage to play any significant role in Indian politics and culture. And it is perhaps for this reason only that successive generations went to their graves with the unfulfilled desire of reaching the land they had set out from.
>
> According to their Jewish faith they had come to believe that as the chosen people they were destined to suffer. Seventeen to eighteen centuries

of financial and social hardships had left them broken until they got their own identity.

Today there are many among the Bene Israel who are keen on migrating to Israel ... in the hope of a change, sense of security and a miracle, for the brighter future of coming generations. But there are hundreds like the present author who believe that this country with the diversity of seasons, festivals, languages, customs and rituals, ascetics and holy men, cultures, is their motherland. Their identity is strongly connected with the land with which they have a deep bond spanning centuries. For such people India is their Israel.[1]

At another place in the same novel Rohekar writes:

Bene Israel ... outsiders ... with whom the common man of Ahmedabad was unfamiliar until the twentieth century and thought of them as Maharashtrians or converts to Christianity ... and on pulling down their pants in times of riots, Muslims.[2]

It is worth taking note here what Amartya Sen says: "If the inclusiveness of India made it easy for Christians, Jews, Parsis and other immigrants to settle in India to lead 'their own lives,' coming from places where they had been persecuted, the principle that is involved in this 'equity of toleration' is one of acceptance—of *swikriti*—rather than equality in any broader sense."[3] Rohekar's tone in *Miss Samuel: Ék Yahūdi Gāthā* is very different to the tone one finds in Meera Mahadevan's *Apnā Ghar*.

The Religion-Nation Dichotomy

Here is an excerpt from a dialogue between two Bene Israel characters that ensues as part of their argument on migration to Israel in *Apna Ghar*:

"There is no such nation in the world which could equal India in what it has given to the Jews. India has nourished us with affection for two millennia. No restrictions were ever imposed on the observance of our religion. We got land for our synagogues. We received such warmth that we started considering ourselves children of India. Now returning to Jerusalem is like turning our back towards our mother."

"But is it not bad to not return to one's mother?"

"Yes, of course! But can we forget what India has done for us. Everyone will have to admit that Jews have never been able to live in peace anywhere

> except India. Our religion was never defiled; on the contrary every deserving member of the community has been appropriately honoured."
>
> "I accept that."
>
> "As far as I know," Shulamith starts speaking, "We have been living here for two thousand years. Just think that in all of this long period we have never been persecuted or discriminated against and this is despite the fact that there is no commonality between our religion and Hinduism. ... It is necessary for Jews from Germany to return to Israel, for what happened there can happen again. But here? What never happened in more than two thousand years will never happen here. Is this one reason not enough for us to continue to stay in India?"[4]

Maybe it is the twenty years of diplomatic relations between India and Israel and the success of Esther David that emboldened Rohekar to write the way she did, unlike Mahadevan who published her *Apna Ghar* in 1961 at a time when there were no relations between the two states and it was to remain so for the next four decades.

Nathan Katz finds the "much lauded Hindu 'tolerance'" rooted in its hierarchical social structure. This is not the Western, liberal tolerance which "wishes to destroy (the individual) ... as a Jew and leave nothing in him but the man, the abstract and universal subject of the rights of man and the rights of the citizen." Hindu tolerance, on the contrary, embraces the person in particularity, as a member of a community, and not as a universalistic abstraction to which one is compelled to conform."[5]

The Marginality of Indian Jews

Both *Apnā Ghar* and *Miss Samuel: Ék Yahūdi Gāthā* give expression to the ambivalence the Bene Israel face with regard to their Indian identity which strongly bonds them to India and their Jewish identity which encourages them to migrate to Israel and take up Israeli citizenship. This ambivalence emanates out of their marginality in both Indian as well as Jewish society, given their peripheral positioning due to their function of possessing the elements and orientation of two cultures very different from each other, namely, Indian and Jewish, and at the same time being deprived of membership by both these cultures. Here marginality ought to be understood as partially belonging to both cultures rather than belonging completely to one. Its pathos can be clearly felt in what the Bene Israel writer Carmit Delman writes in her memoirs: "...

my only true allies were my brother and sisters, since my authenticity as a Jew was mistrusted by Jews, and as an Indian by Indians."[6]

Reflection of the Indian Jewish Ambivalence in Art

The US based Bene Israel painter, Siona Benjamin, particularly known for the eclectic mix of Jewish, Hindu and Muslim elements in her art, considers "the anxiety of finding home, both spiritually and physically, the perpetual preoccupation of her life and career."[7] "Benjamin's world is transcultural and transnational ... She comes to this multiplicity naturally, one might say," as Soltes points out.[8] He explains that "the matter of 'finding home' is for her less a matter of moving from one place to another than about becoming comfortable with being part of diverse cultures and traditions and drawing from them to create one's art ..."[9]

Autobiographical Writing

Esther David discusses this ambivalent situation in her autobiographical novel *Book of Esther*:

> The year before he died, Joshua often implored me to leave for Israel. He wanted me to make my *aliyah*—emigrate to the land of milk and honey. He was certain that I would be happy there and the children would have a bright future, and eventually find Jewish spouses.
>
> Israel is now a distant memory. There was a time when it was real. I tried to uproot myself from my surrogate motherland, and replant myself in the home of my ancestors. I tried to settle there, I could not. Yet, I liked it.[10]

The Acculturation of the Bene Israel

The millennia long stay of the Bene Israel Jews in countryside India in absolute isolation from the rest of the Jewish world resulted in their complete acculturation, which later made the Baghdadi Jews doubt the correctness of their religious observance when they came in their contact in the nineteenth century. We get a glimpse of the Indianisation of the Bene Israel in Esther David's *Book of Rachel* (2006):

> Rachel swept the floor, singing a *bhajan* to the child Moses floating in a basket on the river Nile. It was a popular Marathi song about the child Krishna. An unknown Jewish poet had changed the name from Krishna to

Moses, but the tune was similar to the one sung by Krishna devotees all over Maharashtra. Rachel preferred Marathi *bhajans* to the complicated Hebrew prayers. She knew their tunes and the occasions for which they were sung.[11]

At another place in the same novel David writes:

While rolling the matzos, one of the women would start humming a *kirtan* to the Prophet Moses, set to the tune of a popular Marathi *kirtan* about the birth of Krishna, which was picked up by the others. They sang about the parting of the sea and the Exodus, as the matzos were rolled, roasted, stacked, packed in wicker baskets, covered with cloth and divided equally.[12]

More than eighty per cent of the Indian Jews belong to the Bene Israel community. It is a well-known fact that before coming into contact with the British and before the first Jewish renaissance among them, attributed to a mid-eighteenth century Cochini Jewish agent of the Dutch East India Company, David Rahabi, the Bene Israel practice of Judaism was limited to the abstinence from work on the Jewish Sabbath, circumcision, the observance of Jewish dietary laws and festivals, and the recitation of *Shema*, the most important prayer of the Jews, on these and other important occasions. They did not even call themselves Jews, and instead preferred the term Bene Israel or "Children of Israel," though in the colloquial local language Marathi they came to be known as *Shanwar Telis* or "Saturday Oilpressers," because of their traditionally being oil pressers and abstaining from work on Saturdays.

The Transformation of the Bene Israel from a Rural to an Urban Community

The first major impact of the British rule in India on the Bene Israel was their transformation from a predominantly rural community to a predominantly urban one. From the mid-eighteenth century, when their population was not more than five thousand, the Bene Israel began migrating from the their villages in the Konkan to the towns of Pen, Panvel, and Thane, and then to Bombay, which was developing under the British and needed carpenters, masons, mechanics, and skilled tradesmen and artisans of all kinds. They built their first synagogue in Bombay in 1796 and called it *Sha'ar ha-Rahamim* (Gate of Mercy). By 1833, a third of their total population, two thousand of them had settled in Bombay. As the British East India Company sought to expand its regiments there, they got absorbed in those regiments in increasingly large numbers under the caste name of Israel to an extent that at one point of time about half of the Indian officer strength of the Bombay Army consisted of Bene Israel, as estimated. They benefited from the British policy of favouring the minorities who were too small to pose a political threat to British supremacy. They also took up skilled trades, became clerks in government service and with private firms, and eventually also found work in the mills of the Sassoons, Iraqi Jews. As Bombay developed into a bigger city, the size of the Bene Israel community in it also grew and they spread into several neighbourhoods of the city, where they established additional synagogues and prayer halls.

Religious Awakening among the Bene Israel

A second religious renaissance among the Bene Israel took place in the first decades of the nineteenth century, when in 1826 and 1833 they came to be acquainted with their Jewish heritage and were taught about Jewish ritual and ceremonials by Jews from Cochin. The efforts of Cochini Jews soon got augmented by those of the Arabic speaking Jews from West Asia, who came to be known as Baghdadis in the colloquial language. But the most important role in this religious revival was played by Christian missionaries, who strongly influenced the Bene Israel through their educational endeavours after the ban on missionary activity in India was lifted in 1813. The Bene Israel were taught Hebrew at the many schools established by the American Marathi Mission (Congregational) and the Free Church of Scotland. The missionaries translated books of the so-called Old Testament into Marathi and developed Hebrew grammars in Marathi to familiarise the Bene Israel with the religion and language of their ancestors, in the hope that the Bene Israel, already monotheists, could eventually be persuaded to accept Christ as the Messiah Jews have traditionally been waiting for. However, these missionary efforts only led the Bene Israel to try to hastily publish and translate from Hebrew into Marathi in the second half of the nineteenth century. The English language learnt from the missionaries enabled the Bene Israel to familiarise themselves with books of Jewish interest published in England and America, which only strengthened their sense of belonging to a larger Jewish community, gradually reducing their isolation and their dependence on other Jewish communities and missionaries in India for religious instruction and sustenance. "They had been Jewish in a particularly Indian way; now they adopted the beliefs, practices and concerns of Jewish communities elsewhere," as Joan Roland puts it.[13]

The Jewish Consciousness among the Bene Israel

It is suspected that voluntary caste associations developed in India in the late nineteenth century as a result of the British proclivity for naming and counting groups of people. The proliferation of caste associations promoted a caste consciousness which also influenced the Jews in India to form a number of organisations for communal improvement and to publish their own periodicals for the expression of their communal concerns. A number of organisations for communal improvement, such as the Bene Israel Association, the Bene Israel Benevolent Society, the Association for the Right Guidance of the People, and the Society for the Protection of the Jewish Religion, emerged by the end of the nineteenth century.

The ambivalence the Bene Israel faced, in spite of their undoubted loyalty to the British, as to how much they should identify with Indians culturally and politically while at the same time trying to maintain their Jewish identity was evident in their publications in Marathi, some with English columns, such as *Satya Prakash* (Light of Truth), *Friend of Israel*, *Lamp of Judaism*, *Israel Dharmadeep*, and the *Bene Israelite*, which they soon brought out driven by this new ethnic consciousness. The Bene Israel had assimilated in so many ways with the non-Jewish Indian population that when their quarrels were taken to court, local (sometimes Hindu, sometimes Muslim) law was applied to them, and they often suffered a great loss. However, they had been governed by the British law in two cases of adoption that had reached the High Court, which left the Bene Israel journal wondering whether the British law of inheritance was applicable to them. In 1895, *Israel Dharmadeep* noted that the community had been acquiring higher standards of modern civilisation and showing an increased interest in "higher education, literature, science and the fine arts, which was leading to better appointments and higher positions."[14] But the journal also noticed a distinct, if gradual drifting away of the community from the natives of the country among whom they had been living; "The time seems not far distant when ... [The Bene Israel] will entirely throw off their manners, customs, dress and language. We have too long mixed with and become, as it were, one with the gentiles. And today, we hear the voice saying, 'come out of her, oh my people, and be separate.'"[15] In order to strengthen Jewish identity, the periodicals tried to present portraits of outstanding Jewish, particularly Anglo-Jewish, personalities.

This sudden Jewish consciousness among the Bene Israel has been captured by Esther David in her *Book of Esther* in the following words:

> The Bene Israel Jews of India had suddenly become aware that they were connected to a larger Jewish community in Europe. More so, since they had been reading and listening to world news on the BBC about the gas chambers, concentration camps and the extermination of six million Jews by Hitler. They were horrified and afraid, and wanted to underplay their Jewishness or leave for Yerushalayem—Jerusalem—the promised land of their prophets. Perhaps on the eve of India's independence they may also have been disturbed by Mahatma Gandhi's views. Gandhi had advised that the Jews offer Satyagraha against Hitler ... The Bene Israel did not know where they stood and what should be their reaction when Hindu and Muslim riots erupted with the partition of India. There were harrowing tales of savage killings: stories of men taking a child by the feet and tearing its body in two down the middle. One story like this bred many more. When they fled their homeland and landed in India after the shipwreck, the Bene Israel had followed the dictum: mix with the people where you have found a new home. Keep your religion a secret. Let nobody know who you are.[16]

Ezekiel is known to have once said of himself, "I am not a Hindu, and my background makes me a natural outsider: circumstances and decisions relate me to India." He seeks to resolve this very feeling and sense of being an outsider in "Background Casually," a verse autobiography, first published in 1965, tracing what Ezekiel saw as the main stages of his life to date. The first section of the poem explores the main details of his situation and confronts the contradictions underlying it. The middle section of the poem deals with youth and manhood, along with references to the interlude of his stay abroad in London.

Return to home, however, forms the main theme of the middle section. Here again, the core of the spiritual difficulty the poet faces is highlighted in the persona of the poem. The Indian enveloped by a feeling of displacement, after a stay abroad, has the alternative of return to his Indian identity. This is the point where the Hindu presence is explicitly referred to. A major episode in the unfolding process of growth is provided by the encounter. "All Hindus are like that, my father used to say." A feeling of isolation descends upon the speaker, for the Hindus are "they," the aliens, in his own mental landscape, he himself being different, a Jew in terms of origin. In the concluding line of the second section there is again a reference to the origin: "My ancestors, among the castes, were aliens." There is a double aspect to the feeling of being an alien: the person, himself an alien, looks on others as aliens.[17]

When asked in 1979, whether the consciousness of being Jewish shaped his work at all, Ezekiel answered:

> It's a question that has really come to the foreground only in the last few years. I'm a little afraid of it. This is basically because, from the time I was seventeen, the attempt has been to become Indian, and that has meant responding to the Hindu tradition; the Jewish tended to be one among many other traditions.
>
> Now, I think that attempt of thirty years has been a failure. I see a great difference between a real Indian and my Indianness. A major Scottish poet recently said to me, at an international poetry festival, in Rotterdam, "You are not a real Indian," and my response was, "No, we've lived in India only two thousand years." A Jew can never be a "real" Indian or a "real" Chinaman. I'd say Parthasarthy and Ramanujan are real Indians.[18]

According to the eminent English critic Bruce King, "With him a post-colonial poetry started, which reflects the lives and identities that an increasing number of educated Indians knew or would seek. Being a Jew and raised as a secular rationalist by his scientist father made him an outsider to Hindu-Muslim culture; it is his very outsiderness, his marginality, which makes him a representative voice of the urbanised western educated Indian.[19]

It is this very outsiderness that Siona Benjamin refers to when she says, "I've always been an outsider in every possible sense. I've been an outsider being Jewish in Hindu and Muslim, India, but I've always felt that India has been the most inclusive and most multicultural country one could have been in. And I've always felt like an outsider being in America: I'm a Jew from India in mostly Ashkenazi America."[20]

Ezekiel, who won the prestigious Sahitya Akademi Award for his collection of poems titled *Latter Day Psalms*,[21] once divulged:

> Some among my friends—Alkazi, for example—found even my early poetry, written in London in 1949-1951, entirely Jewish. Through the years, Jewish and other readers have called my poetry Jewish. I've never known exactly what they mean. But of late I've found myself more deliberately turning to Jewish sources and themes as though some inner movement has required it.[22]

When asked whether his Latter Day Psalms manifested this, Ezekiel exclaimed:

> Yes, though first of all the idea is an accident, in response to an invitation, I travel to that poetry festival in Rotterdam ... taking no books with me, so as to give myself a chance to see and hear. I arrive at my hotel, am immediately struck by the total silence of the place. We're so accustomed to noise in India. I sleep for a few hours, get up, and it's too early for a meal. I need something to read. The only thing to read in the hotel room is the Gideon Bible ... I read something from the Old Testament. I turn to Job ... Still plenty of time for dinner, and I read the first Psalm.
>
> I think I realised suddenly that I had never accepted the Psalms, and crystallised into an answer to the first-one. Within ten minutes I'd written the first Latter Day Psalm and formed the idea of writing ten. I completed the Latter Day Psalms in Rotterdam (June'78). The tenth is a commentary on the other nine, written in modern English.[23]

When asked to comment on the charge that to get at the precise import of the psalms, they had to be read in conjunction with the old ones, and this compulsion relegated his psalms to the realm of second-hand poetry, Ezekiel retorted:

> In the *Latter Day Psalms* I have expressed my own view of the Old Testament Psalms. I do not claim that it is the view of "modern man." A commentary inevitably demands acquaintance with the original. So do references and allusions of all kinds. That does not make the poetry "second-hand." The "realities of life" are, in fact, confronted by denying or modifying earlier established views of those realities. I have described the Latter Day Psalms in the form of Psalms. My tenth psalm, in fact, is a commentary on the previous nine.
>
> That is the total form of the Latter Day Psalms, somewhat complex but, therefore, in my opinion, all the more interesting compared to many of my simple lyrics.[24]

Cochin Jewry

Cochin Jewry too borrowed heavily from Hinduism like the Bene Israel did. But they did so selectively and not blindly, educated and knowledgeable as they were about Jewish norms and standards unlike the Bene Israel. "Hindu practices were not uncritically and unconsciously incorporated into their *minhag*," writes Katz, "but were judiciously weighed against the standard of Jewish law (*Halacha*) before being accepted and Judaised. The one exception to this rule of judicious accommodation was the Jews' caste like social structure in which they contravened, even defied, *halakhic* standards."[25]

The Portrayal of Jews in Indian Cinema

The only film to give a glimpse of the ambivalence faced by Indian Jews between the choice of staying in India and that of migrating to Israel is the Malayalam film *Gramophone* (2003), whose story revolves around Gregory who stayed back in Cochin while most of the members of his community migrated to Israel. Although he did so out of choice and not as a consequence of a lack of opportunity, yet after some time he starts thinking of moving to Israel in search of a suitable marriage partner for his granddaughter. *Gramophone* is one of the only two films with Indian Jewish characters, the other being the English language film *Mr. & Mrs. Iyer* (2002), which had just one minor Jewish character.

The Baghdadi Community

The situation was far less ambivalent for the Baghdadis for they had never Indianised to any degree even after decades of having settled in India and now stood even more firmly in the British camp as it seemed wiser to them to identify with the rulers than with the ruled, aware as they were of British racism against Indians. They "may have identified with British ways, but they did not see themselves as—nor did the British accept them as—Britishers. However, they did not see themselves as 'the colonised' either and did not experience the kind of hatred or low self-esteem that is, according to the analysis of scholars such as Fanon and Memmi, part of the colonised psyche," writes Jael Silliman.[26] According to her:

> The ambivalent position of Baghdadi Jews in the colonial structure worked to their advantage. They were neither Indian nor Western, Brown nor White, but sandwiched between the two, at once insiders and outsiders. They partnered both European and Indian commercial interests ... The Baghdadi Jews' relationship with India was complicated. They played an exploitative role as outsiders in the economic colonisation of India, while

> facilitating the colonial project from the inside. They were loyal to, but never considered themselves, British—nor were they so regarded by the colonial powers. They clamoured unsuccessfully for European status, which the British never granted them. ... Neither British nor Indian, the Baghdadi Jews clung tenaciously to their Jewish identity. While their political allegiances changed over time, their commitment to Judaism as both cultural and religious practice was central to their sense of who they were.[27]

At a time when the British-Indian relationship was that of superior-inferior, the identification of the Baghdadi community with the Europeans resulted in a social rift between them and the Bene Israel. The doubts expressed by the Baghdadis about the purity of descent and religious observance of the Bene Israel also contributed to the weakening of the Jewish fraternal ties. Perhaps it was the increasing rejection by their coreligionists, the Baghdadis, which led the Bene Israel to strengthen ties with the Jews abroad and engage with the Zionist movement.

The cultural and religious autonomy that the Jews had come to enjoy under the caste system acceptable to Hindus in the pre-modern period, served them well also in the post-colonial period. Encouraged by the British, they underwent a transformation from a caste-like designation to an ethnic identification.

In the years just before the Second World War, certain British attitudes proved to be disappointing for the Jews of India, namely, the British refusal to recognise the Bene Israel as a special minority for recruitment to the services and their refusal to include the Baghdadis on the European electoral rolls. It made the Indian Jews fear about safeguarding their interests. Attraction to the Holy Land and uncertainty about postcolonial India led the Indian Jews to migrate en masse to Israel.

It was the onset of the Second World War that posed before the Baghdadi Jews for the first time the troubling question of identity. Silliman quotes Sally Solomon to illustrate this ambivalent sense of identity that the independence of India forced the Baghdadi Jews to come to terms with:

> ... Are we English? Are we Indian? I did not feel either of these; just thought of myself as Jewish—not so much in a religious sense as belonging to a group identified by its religion. I dressed like the English, spoke their language, embraced some of their ways of life; but neither they nor I would consider I

> belonged. The same applied to being Indian, but in different areas. I did not adopt their dress, speak their language even reasonably well, yet I belonged more, felt like India was my native place.[28]

Silliman narrates how her Indian identity was once challenged by an Indian friend of hers:

> I had reached my mid-thirties so sure of my Indianness that it came as a rude shock when a progressive Indian friend challenged my identity. We were at an indigenous women's meeting on a reservation in Montana, listening to Native Americans as they outlined their priorities for political and social action. During one session I doodled an intricate Indian design, and a colleague complimented me on its beauty. When she said, "Indians are so artistic," my friend interjected: "But Jael is not really Indian." Her callous remark pained me, and I responded sharply: "Since when have you joined the Jan Sangh?" We both knew what it meant. The Jan Sangh is the Hindu chauvinist party that advocates a Hindu India. It gives voice to Hindu nationalist sentiments and is known for its anti-minority political rhetoric. Although my friend immediately backed off and shamefacedly mumbled an apology of sorts, her remark stayed with me as a symbol of a larger phenomenon, the attempts underway to remake India into a Hindu nation. From the inclusive rhetoric of the anti-colonial leaders after Indian independence and through the 1950s and 1960s, India has experienced a decisive shift to the Hindutva politics that have found expression in the Bharatiya Janata Party (BJP). Not only in the charged communal environment within India, but also among many Indians living in the United States, a narrow view of who is Indian keeps gaining ground.[29]

Interestingly, the very political outfit, the Bharatiya Janata Party that Silliman refers to above was joined in 1991 by her paternal grand uncle Lt. Gen. J. F. R. Jacob, one of the most famous Indian Jews. He is largely credited for India's victory in the 1971 India-Pakistan War that resulted in the birth of Bangladesh. He recounts in his autobiography how he came to join the BJP:

> In 1991, I was approached by Professor Manohar Sondhi to join the BJP. I considered the offer for some time, and after some three months agreed to join to advise in the fields of defence and foreign affairs. At that time the

> BJP was just beginning to develop its personality as a party, claiming to be a "party with a difference." That difference, I feel, with the passage of time began eroding.[30]

We will come to know only upon its release in June 2013, whether Silliman's maiden novel, *The Man with Many Hats*, reflects the ambivalence the Baghdadi Jews faced in India. It comes across as an autobiographical novel in which the protagonist Rachel seems to be the author herself. This would not be the first ever novel to depict the Baghdadi Jewish life in Kolkata, as there has already been one to do so, Gay Courter's *Flowers in the Blood* (1990), but it would certainly be the first to be produced by a member of Kolkata's Baghdadi community.

The Survival of Indian Jews?

The main issue that confronts the Jews that remain in India today is that of the very survival of their community with their dwindling numbers. With perhaps only five thousand Jews remaining in India, if the Jews that have emerged as a result of the two Judaising movements are not included, and seventy to eighty thousand Indian Jews now settled in Israel, their institutions in India are struggling to sustain themselves. Synagogues and prayer halls are gradually closing or finding their membership shrinking. The apprehension of the Jewish life coming to an end was very poignantly expressed by the Bene Israel historian Benjamin J. Israel:

> This will be a loss to India, if not to world Jewry. However insignificant a part the Bene Israel played in the general life of India, by their very existence in sizeable numbers on the West coast, they have constituted a Jewish presence in India which in its small way has enriched its multifaceted culture. More important, they have provided living evidence that, in at least one country in the world, Jews can exist with pride and honour and without any need for self-consciousness or protective withdrawal into a self-created ghetto.[31]

Notes

1. Sheela Rohekar, *Miss Samuel: Ék Yahūdī Gāthā* (New Delhi: Bhartiya Jnanpith, 2013), pp. 179-80. (The present author's translation.)
2. Ibid., p. 157 (The present author's translation).
3. Amartya Sen, *The Argumentative Indian: Writings on Indian Culture, History and Identity*

(England: Penguin Books, 2005), p. 35.
4. Meera Mahadevan, *Apna Ghar* (Delhi: Akshar Prakashan Pvt. Ltd., 1961), pp. 44-45. (The present author's translation.)
5. Nathan Katz and Ellen S. Goldberg, *Kashrut, Caste and Kabbalah: The Religious Life of the Jews of Cochin* (New Delhi: Manohar, 2007), p. 15
6. Carmit Delman, *Burnt Bread and Chutney: Growing Up Between Cultures—A Memoir of an Indian Jewish Girl* (New York: One World– Balantine Books, 2002), p. xxii.
7. Menachem Wecker, "Siona Benjamin: An artist who paints from the East," *My Jewish Learning*, http://www.myjewishlearning.com/culture/2/Art/History_and_Theory/Jewish_Painters/siona_benjamin.shtml (Accessed on May 30, 2013).
8. Ori Z. Soltes, "Finding Home: The Transcultural Worlds of Siona Benjamin," *Feminist Studies* 38, no. 3, Fall 2012, p. 689
9. Ibid., p. 693.
10. Esther David, *Book of Esther*, Viking—Penguin Books, New Delhi, 2002, pp. 370-71.
11. Esther David, *Book of Rachel*, Viking—Penguin Books, New Delhi, 2006, p. 13
12. Ibid., p. 49.
13. Joan G. Roland, "Indian Jewish Identity of the Bene Israel during the British Raj," in Nathan Katz (ed.), *Studies of Indian Jewish Identity* (Delhi: Manohar, 2004), p. 121.
14. Cited in Joan Roland, *The Jewish Communities of India: Identity in a Colonial Era*, Second Edition (New Brunswick, USA and London, UK: Transaction Publishers, 1998), p. 38.
15. Ibid.
16. Esther David, *Book of Esther* (New Delhi: Viking—Penguin Books, 2002), pp. 198-99.
17. Digish Mehta, "A Search for a Perspective: Nissim Ezekiel's Background, Casually," in K. Ayyappa Paniker (ed.), *Indian English Literature Since Independence*, Golden Jubilee Volume (New Delhi: The Indian Association for English Studies, 1991), pp. 140-41.
18. Devendra Kohli (ed.), *Indian Writers at Work* (Delhi: New World Literature Series: 43, B. R. Publishing Corporation, 1991), pp. 2-3.
19. King, op. cit., p. 92.
20. Lisa Traiger, "Siona Benjamin: Bridging Cultures", *Baltimore Jewish Times*, April 19, 2013, http://www.jewishtimes.com/index.php/jewishtimes/news/jt/local_news/siona_benjamin_bridging_cultures/ [Accessed on May 30, 2013].
21. Navras Jaat Aafreedi, "Hindustān kā Yahūdī Adab ("India's Jewish Literature"), in *Imkān*, November 2003, pp. 81-85 (Urdu).
22. Kohli, op. cit., p. 3.
23. Ibid., pp. 3-4.
24. Ranavir Rangra, *Interview with Indian Writers* (Delhi: New World Literature Series: 43, B. R. Publishing Corporation, 1992), pp. 250-51.
25. Katz, op. cit., p. 14
26. Jael Silliman, *Jewish Portraits, Indian Frames: Women's Narratives from a Diaspora of Hope*, University Press of New England in arrangement with Seagull Books, Calcutta, 2001, p. 172.
27. Ibid., p. 18
28. Silliman, op. cit., p. 175.

29. Ibid., p. 167.
30. Lt. Gen. J. F. R. Jacob, *An Odyssey in War and Peace: An Autobiography*, Roli Books, New Delhi, 2011, p. 147.
31. Benjamin J. Israel, *The Jews of India*, Second Edition, Mosaic Books, 1998, p. 60.

7. Literature in the post-Soviet Central Asian Space

Rashmi Doraiswamy

The fall of the Soviet Union led to the formation of fifteen independent countries. The transition from the supranational identity to what Brubaker calls "nationalising regimes" had its impact on culture as well. The Soviet Union was multinodal in culture, even if in the political realm Moscow served as the "centre." The republics, during the course of seventy years had participated in the creation of the supranational Soviet identity through culture by traversing, paradoxically the "national" route, even if this route had evolved from a top-down movement where the State had taken decisions on aesthetic form as well as content. The point that is missed in the Cold War rhetoric of valourising dissident or émigré Russian literature is that there were many "critical insiders" who had learnt to negotiate the paths laid down by official ideology and wander off into thickets or create clearings for themselves. These critical insiders had devised a wide-range of discourses to talk about and critique the problems of their societies, while continuing as members of the various professional associations and even being Party members and functionaries. Although the framework of socialist realism existed, there was a large spectrum of styles, techniques, formal innovations and themes and issues being taken up. Aesopian language, science-fiction, undercurrents of modernism all laced the works of a wide variety of multicultural, multilingual writers. Socialist realism was not always a straitjacket. Censorship and self-censorship existed, but the tradition of literature being the conscience keeper of the nation and the people was too deeply ingrained from the nineteenth century onwards, to be stifled by any official ideology. During perestroika and glasnost the three writers who produced the books that came to be called "The 3 Ps of Perestroika"—*Plakha* by Chingiz Aitmatov, *Pechalny Detektiv* by Astafiev and *Pozhar* by Rasputin—not by Moscow or Leningrad-based writers but by writers from Kyrgyzstan and Siberia. The problems of drug trafficking, generational issues, the erosion and loss of moral values among the youth, alcoholism, uprootment of people for developmental projects, the scientific-technological revolution and the havoc it was creating in Nature—all these themes were dealt with in these works, without really offering optimistic endings or positive heroes, the staple requirements of socialist realism. The periphery was so only geographically and politically to a "centre" that was Moscow; the periphery was "writing" back. In fact, it was writing back in a way that the binary opposition really was not applicable at all. If the works become emblematic for a time, then at least in the realm of culture the periphery had become central. The Soviet identity had actually become a tangible entity: these works were deeply embedded in local cultures and issues, but spoke to a pan-Soviet audience, and had a resonance. Even if they were designated as "periphery" it must be emphasised that there was intense cultural interaction not only between the "centre" and "periphery" but also between "peripheries." Many forums, platforms and publications existed under the Soviet Union for such interactions.

Transition and New Relations

The collapse of the USSR accelerated the pace of some of the processes that had begun in the 1980s and gave rise to new ones. The transition was painful, full of shocks and manifold in nature: from command to socialist economy, from socialism to capitalism (which included the processes of globalisation), desovietisation and derussification. All these were to have a deep impact on the cultural sphere. From a supranational Soviet identity where there was a paradoxical investment in the national, as well as an overarching identity as Soviet citizens, the fifteen successor states of the Soviet Union were willy-nilly forced to make the "national," at least in their political rhetoric, as the central argument. The setting up national political and cultural icons that pre-date the Soviet period, are part of the repertoire of "new" national identities. There is a curious duality in this enterprise. On the one hand, new icons are being found; on the other, the Soviet system of having such icons at all continues to exist. Nikolai Verevochkin, a writer who lives in Kazakhstan, poignantly describes his "position" as an "insider" in terms of his emotion, but an "outsider" in terms of his ethnicity in the new Kazakhstan: "I was born in Kazakhstan. This was my motherland. I did not want to leave it. Russia is good in everything, but it does not have these mountains. Nevertheless I forgave Russia this one deficiency and loved her too, a country where I have no one. A crack that slowly tore apart a unified country, passed through me. The people of my generation are people with a crack in their hearts."[1] He further points out that "The former Republics of the Soviet Union are, quite understandably, taken up with their own identity and return to roots. But this does not mean that there was no such effort during the Soviet period. It is just that the process has gained a clear, well-expressed direction. Members of other ethnic groups, as is natural, are adapting to the titular groups. … The more the merging, the less the problems. If you remain there is one way out: adapt to the new rules and solve your problems with these rules."[2]

Both Verevochkin and Evgeny Abdullaev, a writer from Uzbekistan, refer to the fluidity of identities, political and ethnic, in the post-Soviet space, that are redefining notions of what constitutes "centre" and what constitutes "periphery," not just between Russia and the now independent Central Asian countries, but also with the larger world outside. They are also underscoring the fact that the Soviet period too had its own quests for political identities, and that the shift from socialism to a post-socialist political scenario is a very nuanced, difficult and complex one. Writing on the political scenario of the twenty-first century, Abdullaev states: "In politics we are undergoing a transition from the neoliberal model to the neoconservative one. Party politics is on the wane, the number of non-state actors on the political field is getting reduced. The Western vector is getting weak and there are attempts to get back lost positions in former zones of Soviet influence—in the Near East, in the countries of the Third World, but most importantly in the post-Soviet space. With the alignment of "vertical power," political and symbolic relations between Moscow and the near abroad regions are being restored. In this the neoliberal rhetoric is not being changed in entirety, it fits into the general neoconservative mainstream. An eclectic weave appears, combining differing, formerly irreconcilable ideological positions."[3]

The cultural ties between the former republics of the Soviet Union have refused to wither away and Russian language has remained one of the significant components of these "ties." According to Aleksei Ustimenko, a Tashkent based writer, "(Russian) language has stayed and will continue to do so. It will be a pity if it only exists as an economic factor. There are schools which teach in Russian, as before. Courses that teach Russian are also overflowing. … A good number of Russian newspapers and journals are still published. I do not want to mention the number, since they are obviously so many."[4]

Nikolai Verevochkin succinctly sums up the distinction between the paradoxical attitudes to "Russia" and "Russian," both popular and official: "It is very easy to be branded a democrat—spit in the direction of Russia and you are a democrat. The temptation is great. In Kazakhstan the multivector policy was followed. Not losing one's old neighbours, they wound up with new ones. A decision in the spirit of Solomon. Here they did not start fighting with Russian language. Every citizen of Kazakhstan must know Kazakh, Russian and English. This cannot be faulted. … As Abai said, a man is man as many times as the number of languages he knows. Kazakhstan, in general, went through what was for many others a terrible period of disintegration, honourably."[5]

Literature's role as the conscience-keeper of the nation also underwent a sea-change. Conscience-keeping went beyond the immediacy of politics. During perestroika, the literature of conscience-keeping (that was more philosophical in nature), and of political engagement (that addressed immediate social issues)—both flourished. After the fall of the Soviet Union, the literary process was fragmented into different political groupings. Consumerism and neoliberalism, towards the end of the twentieth century, pushed political engagement of the pre-Soviet and Soviet kinds, away from the arts. "High" literature had to abdicate its place of dominance in the post-Soviet cultural space; popular literature, aimed at a lower common denominator of taste, took over. To a question by Natalya Igrunova if there are any "national projects" in literature as there were in cinema, for example, *Nomad*, Mikhail Zemskov replied there weren't any in the commercial sense—"… because literature cannot attract the kind of mass audience that cinema can … Ideologically there are many, of course, particularly in the literary works in Kazakh language. And these relate primarily to history."[6]

Evgeny Abdullaev characterised the literature of the new century as being "Without the influx of young names. Without politics. Without aesthetics. Without the West. Without Brodsky."[7] The literary field in Central Asia, however, is not entirely bleak. Russian literature in the pre-Soviet period and even more emphatically in the post-Soviet period was deeply linked to the culture of "thick journals." It was in these journals that the best work of the period was published; it was also through these journals that the State exercised its censorship. "Thick journals" continue to thrive in the post-Soviet space, even though the political and technological scenarios have changed. The journal *Druzhba Narodov* (*Friendship of Peoples*), for instance, which was founded in 1939 by the Union of Writers at the suggestion of Maxim Gorky, still continues to publish writers from the ex-Soviet Republics. This journal leads; there are others, however, such as *Oktyabr*, *Arion* and *Novaya Yunost* that are also publishing works in Russian (written in the language or translated) by writers outside the Russian Federation but from within the CIS. In the Central Asian countries, too, there is evidence of literary activity. Abdullaev notes that in literature "First of all, new groups, movements, associations are disappearing and the boundaries between the existing groups are getting eroded. (This is not surprising: periods when literary groups rapidly multiplied in Russian history always coincided with periods of political turmoil.) The literary journals and almanacs are not increasing in numbers; these efforts are fizzling out as are the attempts to bring out literary journals in glossy format. The standing of old 'thick journals' has been strengthened but with the least—as never before—political engagement. Despite the resource crunches, these journals have managed to retain the neoliberal outlook of the nineties ... In these 'thick journals' the moderate 'pochvenniki,'[8] the statists and the radical-conservatives get published; but what is important is the literary level of the text."[9]

Uzbekistan's Zvezda *Vostoka* still continues to be published, despite several identity make-overs through the decades. It was started in 1932 under the name of *Sovetskaya Literatura Narodov Srednei Azii*, and got its name as the "Star of the East" in 1946. In its long life this journal has published works by leading writers of the Soviet Union such as Mikhail Bulgakov, Evtushenko, Bella Akhmadulina, Isaac Babel and others. Its "Golden Age," however, was the period from 1991 to 1996 when it reached a circulation of 250 million copies and published not only the work of twentieth-century writers from abroad, but also writers from Riga, Moscow, St. Petersburg, as well as the literature of Uzbekistan, particularly the poets of the "Fergana School." The journal was widely recognised as being among the best in the post-Soviet space. The decade that followed saw a downward slide and in 2006 it was shut down. Publication resumed in 2007 and in 2009 there were changes once again. It assumed a "dual" face, that of *Zvezda Vostoka* and *Shark Olduzi*. The other publication of interest to come out of Uzbekistan is *Maliy Sholkoviy Put*, bringing together many of the writers of the "Tashkent School" such as S. Yanyshev, V. Muratkhanov and S. Aflatuni (the pen-name of Evgeny Abdullaev). The first issue was published in 1999 and five issues were brought out till 2004. According to Alexander Pravikov, "The most important themes of the Tashkent School, apart from the elegiac motifs of loss, are their comprehension of their position of in-between-ness, of being on the border, or of bringing together two sides of the world."[10] Kazakhstan, too, has its own "thick journals": *Prostor*, *Niva*, *Musaget*, *Amanat*.

The Soviet cultural icon, Chingiz Aitmatov, continued to write in the 1990s. While he continued to take up global and "Soviet" themes during the 1990s, his last novel before his death *When the Mountains Fall*, is set in Kyrgyzstan. Andrei Volos from Tajikistan, who now lives in Moscow, in his novel *Hurramabad*, which is a collection of short stories of the fictional "City of Happiness" deals with the "small" histories of "small people" in Civil War ridden, post-Soviet Tajikistan. The book won the Anti-Booker Award in 1998. Novelist and dramatist Mikhail Zemskov, winner of the Russian Prize for his collection of short stories *Almatinskiye Istorii*, is from Kazakhstan. Talip Ibraimov, from Kyrgyzstan won the Russian Prize in 2006, while Alexei Tork, won it in 2009. Sukhbat Aflatuni (aka Evgeny Abdullaev)j has been awarded the Prize of the journal *Oktyabr* (2004, 2006), of *Voprosy Literatury* (2009), the first laureate of the Russian Award. His works have been published in Uzbekistan, Russia, South Korea and the USA. All this is evidence of the fact that the post-Soviet space for writers continues to be multinodal and one that is quite vibrant, with works by older and younger authors from Central Asia being published and awarded. The post-Soviet space, at least culturally, is still a space that allows mobility, and a space where the centre-periphery equations are continuously being redefined, if not subverted. According to Abdullaev, the lists of poets published in Russian in the "thick journals" is very telling in this respect: "The number of poets from other Russian cities has grown. If in the 1997 list of poets there are only three poets who are not from the 'capital' (6%), then in 2009 there are already fifteen, more than a quarter of the list. If in the first list there is only one poet from the 'Near Abroad,' then in the 2009 list there are five. Thus the 'thick journals' have become less 'Moscow centric,' and more open to authors from, relatively speaking, the Russian provinces and the former Republics."[11]

In Focus: Aleksei Tork

Alexei Tork is the pen-name of Alisher Niyazov. Born in 1970 in Tajikistan, Tork has worked in the mass media and been a correspondent in Kyrgyzstan and Kazakhstan. He has covered the conflicts in Tajikistan and southern Kyrgyzstan. The first story he published was *Pension* in the prestigious journal, *Druzhba Narodov*. This was produced as a play by the Moscow Art Theatre. Since then Tork has published several short stories, novellas and essays. He now lives in Bishkek and works as a freelance journalist and writer. He identifies himself as an "Uzbek, living in two homes, in Tajikistan and

Kyrgyzstan, and writing in the Russian language."[12] This paper analyses one of his short stories, *Lukhtak*.[13]

The border is an important theme of Tork's story *Lukhtak* that deals with the life of a Russian woman, the daughter of a well-known specialist on the Pamirs, who was abducted in 1916 by Afghans and is married off to an Afghan after she is made to convert. She has children, grandchildren and dies after a long life in a small town that, as the author says, neither the Russians nor the Mujahedeen's were interested in. She is called Lukhtak (a doll) and is the eldest wife of Sheikh Mavlon. She is constantly tested by Mavlon's other wives and by the villagers as to whether she remembers her past life, but she gives no clue as to the workings of her mind:

> Then, when grandchildren grew up and gifted Mavlon with great grandchildren, the war began. Russians brought it. They did not reach Kishmien, a mountain village that did not interest either the Russians or the Mujahidin. Only once a local field commander, Zarif, visited the village. He was wounded in his shoulder and wanted to relieve his pain with sacred water. His people brought with them a captive Russian soldier. ... He was lying in the van in-between the legs of the mujahedeen. The soldiers were patiently waiting for Zarif and were playing cards, placing them on the back of the Russian. Great grandsons and great granddaughters of Mavlon were running around the car and were throwing pebbles at the soldier. ... Marziya came out of the gates and started to call her grandchildren. Other mujahidin who were from Kishmien, shouted with laugh: "Hey, Apa, look at the Russian, he is your compatriot, give him some water." Marziya went inside the house and came back bringing a ladle of water.
>
> At that time commander Zarif and Sheikh Mavlon came out of the gate. Mavlon saw how his wife was giving the soldier water to drink. The captive soldier took two drops and asked the old woman about something. Marziya looked at him with silence. Then she took the ladle and went inside the house. The mujahedeens were disappointed. The old woman did not show any feelings from the meeting with her compatriots either by word, or by gesture.[14]

When the other wives start washing the body for the last rites, they discover that she had worn the cross in a tuft of hair. There is thus a conundrum: no one knew Marziya's real Russian name, no one had seen her talking or bonding with Russians, or craving for things Russian, this woman who seemed to have lost all memory of her past life and her own name in the trauma of abduction. Sheikh Mavlon, her husband, is caught in a dilemma:

> There can be absolutely no question, the old man said, about her being buried in the family graveyard. Marziya was not a Muslim and she should be buried as far as possible from Kishmien, in some scrub manure wasteland. It should be like this. But Mavlon did not like it: Marziya had been his wife for eighty years. The law of beliefs and the virtue of the spouse were fighting in him.
>
> He thought about it and found the only way out. Marziya would go back to where she had come from. She would return to her motherland, to her beliefs, which she had kept all these years consciously or without realising it. ... He would take her dead body to the other bank that very night ..., he would persuade the Russian border guards, offer good money for their efforts.

So the body is sent to Dushanbe where it was "taken by tractor to the local Orthodox graveyard. Unrecognised—and these are mainly Russians, old men and old women—in Dushanbe, they are buried in trenches on the remote eastern part of the graveyard, with a distance of one metre. There are number plates above, so that if relatives turn up, they could find out the dead body. On the whole, the old woman ended up there, where the Afghanis were shy to lay her, on the wasteland, with a number-plate."[15] In contrast, the body of the high-ranking Russian official who has died in France, is being brought back to his homeland with much fanfare. It is the Tajik narrator who, caught up in the problems of his day-to-day life, manages to trace the name of this unknown woman: Anastasia Zaitseva.

The short story foregrounds the theme of memory and its loss. "She is not Lukhtak, but we are. We are without a face, without memory," decides the narrator, wondering why the Russians had not searched for her in 1916 (Were they afraid to anger the British, their allies?) and why no one was interested in her eighty years later. Did Marziya really forget herself as Anastasia, or was her amnesia a survival tactic? Did she forget her cross that she had plaited into her hair, or had she continued to believe in her Orthodox faith? Is religion the only identity that matters, when a woman has lived docilely in the country of her abduction, following all its rules? Was Sheikh Mavlon being compassionate or cruel when he dispatched off Anastasia/Marziya's body to her "homeland," a homeland she had been cut off from for nearly seventy years of her life?

Her only transgression in her long years of marriage was in embroidering birds that were unknown to the Afghans around her. Nigora, Mavlon's second wife complains to her husband about the birds and that she is not a Muslim by faith.

> Mavlon listened with annoyance. Nigora was his favourite wife. He only felt towards Marziya a feeling of duty entrusted to him by his father. He explained to Nigora, that depriving Marziya her Muslim name would lead to her being denounced and beaten to death with stones.
>
> What would I say to the Ulemas? That my wife embroiders unknown birds? That she prays without faith? Who apart from God would take a risk to judge about this?'
>
> Just to be on the safe side, he called Marziya and told her about his conversation with Nigora.
>
> Marziya got frightened. "My motherland is your house and my children," she said. "I was told … that I was brought to Kishimen by Abdrahman-bek, But I remember only a hard saddle, which caused my abdomen to burn, and pain in my temple. Later sometimes I saw a snowy field in my dream, heard somebody's laugh, and somebody's voice calling out to me to put on mittens. That's all … ."
>
> Mavlon left her and never referred to that topic again.[16]

Tork's work thus deals with the borderland, literally and figuratively. Through the metaphor of the borderland, Aleksei Tork raises questions of identity and otherness. The notions of selfhood keep changing as do the notions of otherness. In dealing with the borderland he looks at the intercommunity relations between the various groups in this borderlands, as well as the relations with the neighbours. All this is seen through the life of ordinary people, who bear the brunt of large historical events. Memory and forgetting and the selectiveness of both processes are also important concerns of his work. Tork is linking himself to literature in Russian in the post-Soviet space that deals with the "small man" with humour, with a strong sense of *skaz* (a personalised form of narration), with "positive heroes" of the present, who are folkloric and realistic at the same time. In an interview Tork has stated: "Now a lot is being said about how the internet will finish off literature, will kill it … . It is true that it will kill it. And beat it. Literature (I am referring to contemporary literature) will die from the lack of ideas, the absence of ethicality, the absence of commitment, that which was manifested in Russian literature of the twenty-first century."[17]

Notes

1. Nikolai Verevochkin, Roundtable: "Razmykaniye Prostranstvo. Peredelkinskiye Vstrechi—2007," *Druzhba Narodov*, no. 4, 2008. Internet version: http://magazines.russ.ru/druzhba/2008/4/ra14.html. (All quotations from texts whose references are in Russian, have been translated into English by me—RD.)
2. Ibid.
3. Evgeny Abdullaev, "Ekstensivnaya Literatura 2000-kh," in *Noviy Mir*, no. 7, 2010, Internet version, http://magazines.russ.ru/novyi_mi/2010/7/ab15.html
4. Aleksander Ustimenko, Roundtable: "RazmykaniyeProstranstvo. Peredelkinskiye Vstrechi—2007," *Druzhba Narodov*, no. 4, 2008. Internet version: http://magazines.russ.ru/druzhba/2008/4/ra14.html
5. Ibid.
6. Ibid.
7. Evgeny Abdullaev, op. cit.
8. "Pochvenniki" were the members of a movement of Russian social thought, to which Slavophiles like F. M. Dostoevsky, A. A. Grigoriev, N. N. Strakhov belonged. They wrote in the journals *Vremya* and *Epokha* and believed that the educated classes should come closer, on a religious-ethical basis, to the people (the soil: *pochva*).
9. Evgeny Abdullaev, op cit.
10. Aleksander Pravikov, "Maliy Sholkoviy Put." Almanakh Poezii', in *Znamiya*, no. 10, 2002. Internet Version: http://magazines.russ.ru/znamia/2002/10/pravik.html
11. Evgeny Abdullaev, op. cit.
12. Olga Lebedushkina "Aleksei Tork: Ya Pishu Dlya Svoei Uchitel'nitsy Aleksandry Avzadrovny," *Chetvyortaya Kniga. Idei. Sudby. Vremena*, http://ps.1september.ru/article.php?ID=200702232.
13. *Lukhtak*, Alksei Tork in *Druzhba Narodov*, no. 4, 2007. Internet version: http://magazines.russ.ru/druzhba/2007/4/to4.html
14. *Lukhtak*, Aleksei Tork, Translated from the original Russian into English by Tanya Kalyan for a forthcoming publication.
15. Ibid.
16. Ibid.
17. Aleksei Tork: Ya Pishu Dlya Svoei Uchitelnitsy Alexandry Avzadrovn, *Chetvyortaya Kniga. Idei. Sudby. Vremena*, Olga Lebedushkina, http://ps.1september.ru/article.php?ID=200702232.

8. Hip Hop Music in Afghanistan, Tajikistan and Uzbekistan

Dilorom Karomat

Popular music is one of the main bases of soft power in the global network. Socially conscious musicians today not only sing at open stages, rallies, demonstrations and on picket lines, but typically have professional websites and post videos on *YouTube* and other popular internet sites. Almost 90% of all the youth of the region are learning about new forms of music through the internet. Rock and *hip hop*[1] (Afg. Dari *Guftor* and Afg. Uzbek *Gaplama*) are upcoming genres of music that are very popular among the youth and the immigrant community of the five Central Asian countries and Afghanistan. Moreover, Rap and Hip Hop are filled with local traditional values along with American ones. In the post-Taliban period when music came to symbolise freedom in Afghanistan, these songs became very important for the young generation, who were influenced by Western popular musicals. Several modern singers of the region have found this genre the most comprehensible form for the expression of their ideas.

In an era of rapid globalisation the process of "salutary influence of music" has become complicated. In the beginning of the twentieth century the music of Central Asian countries and Afghanistan had an advanced system which consisted of the national monody style of professional music with an oral tradition and folklore and its own types of composition, genres, etc. By the middle of the century it was enriched by the Western-style polyphonic, which also possessed its own forms, genres and kinds/methods of performance So, till the end of the twentieth century, new methods, art values, aesthetics, etc., which came to the music of Central Asia and Afghanistan through Russian and Western musical traditions were adopted/assimilated and acquired new qualities. All these achievements were sidelined when youngsters became involved with genres of popular music. Thereafter the omnipresence of genres of popular music, their popularity among the young generation and the necessity of development of popular music according to *national* values became evident.

Rap/Hip Hop under Censorship and Their Role for Identity

In the 21st century, popular music is still censored[2] and repressed all over the world. This shows not only the political weight and the mobilising capacities of popular music, but also how authorities react to them. For example, in Uzbekistan, a round table was organised by *Uzbeknavo,* the state association of singers dedicated to Rap/Hip Hop, a few years ago. Authorities in Uzbekistan have tried to set up a council of Rap artists and tried officially to establish the aims of rap music. A number of important tasks were put before the singers. At the round table the participants were informed about the necessity to "take into account the Uzbek mentality" and "correspond to the interests of society." There was also focus on increasing the level and perfection of the quality of the text and music of pop songs. The singers were requested to clean up their lyrics, delete swear words and slang, remove anything offensive—and replace them with more patriotic tunes about the Motherland and upbeat themes like loyalty, kindness, and love of one's family.[3] Many famous musicians and Rappers welcomed the creation of the council.

There are many well-known instances where governments have lived in fear of effects of popular music, censored its sounds and imprisoned its creators.[4] Rap-performer Dorob Dorobov (Dorob Yans) was detained in Moscow on the basis that in his song *Karor mak* (Be not silent) he incites the people of Tajikistan for revolution and offends the President of the Republic Emomalii Rahmon. The rapper declares that he did not intend to offend anybody and only "let the people know that at presidential elections, it will be necessary to make a right choice" (the next elections in Tajikistan are planned for fall of 2013).[5] On the other hand, the Rap song of Master Ismail (M. One) in Russian "*Raxmon, davay do svidaniya Master Ismail*" (Rahmon, let's say goodbye to Master Ismail)[6] was not banned (at least its internet versions) and the rapper was not imprisoned. It is well known that Rap is a radical way of musical expression and a kind of protest against injustice in society. This rap about suffering, corruption and other injustice in society by the peoples of the country with the main message: "*moya strana tiho plachet i jdyo, / Jdyot, kogda yeyo spasyot narod ...*" (My country silently cries and waits ... (She) waits when her citizens will rescue her ...) is a political Rap. As we can see some rock groups and singers have openly expressed political messages in their music and most of them use swear words and slang, which are not supported by censors. In Tajikistan, as well as in Afghanistan, Rap and Hip Hop music have more freedom and are not excessively censored.[7] Underground rappers have used them more than official ones. For example, in Tajikistan, well-known poets and language specialists are neutral to Rap/Hip Hop movement among youngsters. The only thing, they want is an improvement of the language and poetry.[8] However, among young people Rap music and the use of swear words and slang often have quite different meanings: it indicates that one is a cool guy.

In the history of popular music, Rap and Hip Hop cannot be divorced from that of social, cultural and political movements. Music is always produced within a social context, and always has a potency of expression that reaches far and wide. Also governmental structures do not support the songs whose ideas and views propagate intolerance of one nationality by the other and contain elements of separatism. Thus, the court banned all dissemination (including by internet) of the Uzbek-language song "*Osh City Uzbek Mahala*" ("Osh is an Uzbek Quarter"),[9] which became increasingly popular in the city of Osh, where violent ethnic clashes claimed hundreds of lives in 2010. The song was transmitted among locals mainly via mobile phones, allegedly insulting the Kyrgyz community. Also criticised (singer were exiled) was Akram's anti-Kyrgyz song (*gangsta-rap*) from 2010: "Akrom: *Iflosligini ko'rvotti dunyo* (the whole world is seeing how dirty ...) for promoting separatism and inciting hatred between Kyrgyz and Uzbek people. Allegedly in response to the provocative messages in Uzbek rap songs, similar songs have been released by Kyrgyz artists.[10] Such examples show that music's affective power can be used for stability in society as well as for violence and politics. As we see, in such cases political rap, unlike many other types of hip-hop music, is used to portray a specific political message and usually within a given political context and time, when (and for what) it is composed.

On the other hand musical styles that accompany social and political change are part of a musical continuum. Rap and hip-hop singers of the region understand the mentality of their listeners. The singer of Uzbek group "*Radius 21*" Shahzod (late), for example, has not used rapping as such but artistic reading of poetry (as it was traditionally established in the twentieth century in Uzbekistan).[11] Rap singers also try to use melodious refrains, popular melodies of the past as well as joint songs with other singers (Aziz Aliev feat Mr. Slan *Olisdan* (from far).[12] All these efforts not only draw the attention of more listeners, but by using popular melodies of the past they are using the power of music to recall (a traditional Afghani [dari] folksong "*Bia Ke Berim Ba Mazar*" in Afghan Rap by DJ Besho[13]).

People sing and play and they use music to connect with fellow migrants or refugees in political landscapes. Songs serve as a bridge between the past and present by associating nostalgia with the wish for change or also to smooth out the transition to a new life and a new identity as individuals and groups assimilate into another culture.[14] Thus, music "regularly provides an arena for negotiating and playing out local, national, regional and even global identities."[15] Musical activities among youngsters, for example, migrants from Afghanistan in European countries and America, shows how they try to be like local young people and at the same time try to keep their national identity.[16] Many Rap singers of Afghanistan have started their Rap/Hip-hop activity overseas, when they were in their teens. Nowadays they tour the world and their concerts not only show the level of pop music in Afghanistan, but also bring unity to the World Afghan community. In this respect we can mention the attachment of ethnic Tajiks and Uzbeks of Afghanistan with the culture and history of Central Asian Republics—Tajikistan and Uzbekistan. Ethnic communities of Afghanistan not only listen to songs composed in the Central Asian Republics, invite singers,[17] but also compose songs in which they use (remix) songs of singers from Tajikistan and Uzbekistan. The song *Dunya*[18] can be mentioned here as an example. The remix was done by Youssufu (Yusuf Uzbek, the ethnic Uzbek from Balkh, DJ Balkh),[19] by using Yulduz Usmanova's (Uzbekistan, exiled to Turkey) popular song *Dunyo*. His songs are not only "critical" (political), but also patriotic (even pan-uzbek)[20] and dedicated to cultural values of Afghan Uzbeks. Among his songs is one named "*Ozbegim*" which will be discussed later. The political situation of Uzbeks in Afghanistan, as well as Tajiks, changed radically when the United States led a coalition to overthrow the Pashtun-dominated Taliban government. Feelings of nationhood are gaining strength everywhere in the region. Afghan singer and composer Farid Rastagar,[21] who recently returned from living in Germany and has a recording studio in Kabul, has argued:

Rap is needed here. We need to bring changes in all parts of life including music.[22]

Rap/Hip-Hop: Yesterday and Today

In the beginning, many people found this to be amusing. They said—this isn't a song because this man isn't singing, he is talking. But slowly, this American genre,[23] found its way into hearts of Afghan people, as well as to the hearts of the young generation of all five Central Asian Republics. Afghan Rap singers who started their activity in Western countries have been referred to above. Here we would like to draw attention to the difference between Rap/Hip-hop, which *came* to Central Asian countries and *were brought* to Afghanistan. Thus, Central Asian Rap/Hip-hop was establishing itself when in Afghanistan along with process of establishing, was present the ideology or power which was supporting development and interest in it.

Rap/Hip-hop came to Central Asia in the mid-1990s of the twentieth century through copying the singers of Russian popular music. Nathan Hamm in "Thematical zones" of *Registannet* posted interesting facts about Uzbek Hip-Hop on January 26, 2006:

> Back when I was in Uzbekistan, I ran into a teen who was *really* into hip-hop. I knew plenty of other guys who were huge fans of Eminem in particular. (And I knew them because another volunteer sent them to me, since I'm a male and all, to translate the delightful lyrics.) However, as far as I saw it, the hip-hop scene was still in the womb. My Uzbek instructor asked me if I knew the song "Qora Bumer" in class the other day. I didn't, but I did manage to track it down a long with a lot of other Uzbek rap. (Well, rap as it were. It's a lot different than what I like and … sound like pop to me.) … "Qora Bumer," which, I discovered, is a translation of a Russian song … The other stuff by the group that does the song, Radius 21, sounds better to me …[24]

Some Myrthe comments to him on January 27, 2006:

> Guessing from the title, "Qora Bumer" is the Uzbek version of "Chyorniy Bumer," a Russian song that was a big hit in Armenia as well, and I suppose all over the FSU. A song that gets really annoying when you hear it too often—it gets stuck in your head and refuses to leave (guess what: I'll probably have "Chyorniy Bumer" running through my head now for the rest of the day!). As far as I know, there is no Armenian version of the song.[25]

His comment about Armenian version of the song is very interesting, because in You Tube one can find several versions of Sergey Parkhomenko's[26] Rap song *Chyorniy Bumer* (Black BMW) in Georgian, Bashkir-Tatar, Uzbek and in Turkmen.[27] The intonations of the Russian song is obviously changed with changing the languages. Moreover, the words of the song not only translated into other language (he is simply looking guy, but all girls like him, when he goes out in his Black BMW), but also adjusted to local mentality. Thus, in Uzbek version the singer says that he is orphan from *Eski shahar* (old city) and has brought up himself by earning his bread in *Chorsu Bazar* (market in old city, Tashkent), now he has his own respect and authority and his black BMW which runs like bird. The popularity of this pop song is not only because it is sticks in the head, but also in new values (black BMW), etc., which were "cool" for the young generation of post-socialist countries.

Many local Rap/Hip-Hop singers of Central Asian countries not only sang Rap/Hip-Hop in Russian mixed with English, but felt that they need be more professional (or be with professionals) and so, moved to Moscow (Mr. Slan form Uzbekistan,[28] Master Ismail from Tajikistan[29]). Only, in the beginning of the twenty-first century the local singers have started talking/rapping in native languages. Master Ismail has claimed as a first who start Rap/Hip-hop in Tajik language. His first album in Tajik language became popular with Rap song *Tojik Bacha* (Tajik boy).[30] For the first time in the history of Uzbekistan Mr. Slan launched a radio show "Hip-Hop Education" on the radio "*Sesame*" in 1999. A year later his authorised projects like "Hip-Hop education" "Underground" and "Volcano" continued in radio "*Hamroh.*" From 2000 to 2003, "Hip-Hop education" and "Underground" of Mr. Slan (he came back in 2006) became one of the highly rated radio shows for youngsters. In 2011 Ruslan Saliev, known as Mr. Slan, editor of Radio Terra, was appointed by the government to serve on the new Council of Rap Music Performers.[31] Rap and Hip-Hop singers of Uzbekistan also have a lot of sites dedicated to this kind of music.[32] Moreover, the *Shark Attack Rap festival of 2003* (three days marathon *"Open Air")* and *Tashkent Hip-Hop festival* were organised few years before and even had a *Tashkent Hip-Hop Awards* ceremony.[33] There were plans for organising the *Tashkent Hip-Hop festival-2* at 2011 in Uzbekistan, but unfortunately official information about the festival was not published.

Hollywood and Bollywood films, travelling, study and work of young the generation in European, South Asian[34] countries and America has played one of the important roles for establishment of national Rap/Hip-Hop songs in the region and in increasing their popularity. For example, only in Tajikistan (according to Master Ismail) there are about 380 Rap groups divided into local zones: Dushanbe Rap, Pamir Rap, etc.[35] As we mentioned above, many Afghan pop singers come back from overseas to Kabul.[36] Among them is the first internationally known formal Afghan Hip-Hop artist Bejan Zafarmal (nicknamed DJ Besho),[37] Farid Rastagar (mentioned above), Farhad Darya[38] and others.[39] Dj Besho Kunduzi in one of his Afghan Raps is talking in Dari:

> Bachaho-i Afghon hama pareshon … DJ Besho omad … Ki oward musiqi-i nav dar Afghoniston/ Musiqi-i mo az musiqi-i oyanda … musiqi-i man memonad dar oyanda …[40]

Dj Besho often sings songs composed by Farhad Darya. For many years Farhad Darya supported young Afghan musicians and composed new songs for newcomer talents along with his team. His music is a result of changes in popular musical culture of Afghanistan. A lot of rap singers are growing today and singing and talking in Pashto, Dari and Uzbek languages. For contemporary Afghanistan diversity becomes the challenge for peace and brighter future and interest for promoting the concept of multiple identities and a common heritage for the country. The new issues concerning assimilation of regional traditions into modern and the activities of fusion musicians try to bring the new and free "breath" into development of musical culture. Rap singers of Afghanistan seem be very active in posting and rating their new songs on You Tube and in other internet sites. They organise and run Award ceremonies like *Annual Ariana Awards* (7th run last year in India) and priority is always given to patriotic songs dedicated to Afghanistan. Female musicians face several kinds of difficulties and dangers in present-day Afghanistan. They must practice music under cover and be careful to protect their names,[41] or, like Sosan Firooz,[42] the first Afghan female rapper, be carefully protected by their families. Recently in the *Express Tribune* she told AFP in an interview in the office of a local company that is helping to record her first album:

> My raps are about the sufferings of women in my country, the pains of the war that we have endured and the atrocities of the war … If rap singing is a way to tell your miseries, Afghans have a lot to say … That's why I chose to be a rapper."[43]

Thematic of Rap/Hip-Hop Songs

The governments of Central Asian countries have declared the revelation of national values as a top-priority task of culture in last decade. These aims are realised in several ways. One of the important thematic for the Rap music of the region is when musicians through music (mainly songs) express joy and bitterness of life, patriotism and love to mother and motherland. If in Uzbekistan Rappers officially were asked to sing about Motherland and family values, then in Tajikistan and Afghanistan (countries which suffered from war) this thematic became a necessity. Here we would like to mention only few songs (mainly dedicated to Motherland, unity and nationalhood), which can easily be viewed on *You Tube*.

The song of Uzbek Rap singer Shoxrux (Shahrukh) named *Vatanim* (My Motherland)[44] one of the official songs, fulfilled the values and ambitions of Independent Uzbekistan. His official video film starts with words of Amir Temur:

> Biz kim? Mulki Turon, Amiri Turkistonmiz!/Biz kim? Millatlarning eng ulug'i va eng qadimi Turkning bosh bo'g'inimiz![45]

After several official shots of old and modern Uzbekistan, its flag and globe at *Mustaqillik Maidoni* (Independence square) and under sounds of musical instrument *tar*[46] appears the Shoxrux (in hip-hop style) rapping about his Motherland, where he roamed without any trouble ... Then suddenly he appears in formal black dress singing Refrain (main accent is on the Motherland):

> *Vatanim maning tanho ghururim maning,/Vatanim maning jannat makonim maning.*[47]

Again he raps that he has traveled near and far, but he felt by heart the importance of his Motherland, the sweet words told by father, the dialogues with grandfathers and their *nasihat-s* (advices) ... So, he has always been in a rush to come back to Motherland ...

The Tajik Rap singer Mr. Ismail in his *Vatan* (Motherland)[48] is touching on different feelings. He remembered that they are children of the 1990s, the children of civil war (*go'dakoni jang*) in Tajikistan, he is rapping about the school where he is studied, how they don't know what is internet, etc., and did not even learn any lyrics of poet Rudaki ... In Refrain he is singing:

(chorus) Dar yodi man hamesha hast Vatan/(Mr.Ismail's Rapping) To vaqti ki dilakam mezanad ... (chorus) Dar yodi man hamesha hast Vatan/ (Rapping) Yagonai tu Tojikistoni man[49]

As culmination in his song are the words:

Yak Vatan Dorum, Yak modar dorum, Yak millat dorum, Yak Khudo dorum ...[50]

Mr. Ismail is talking about migration of Tajiks and the necessity of unity. The Afghan Rapper Dj, Besho, llke Mr. Ismail, also saw the face of war in childhood.

The thematic of people in exile, with broken life and heart is more widely sung by Rap singers of Afghanistan. One such song is DJ Besho's *Kabuljon* (2009).[51] This song starts with an old Afghani song which recalls the past, and in video we see the ruined house where the rapper found some old photos and nostalgic melody became Refrain of the Rap song. DL Besho is rapping about how they passed through difficulties and were forced to go on exile to alien countries like Pakistan, Iran, America, Germany; when he recalls all this his eyes fill up with tears. He is praying "Hey, Ali! Help us!" and later "Alleluia to God, that new morning has come to Afghanistan! (*Shukri Hudo, subh omad dar Afghoniston)* and at the end is Praying for Peace in Pashtu ...

In this song DJ Besho is touching on two thematics, one is Mother and second is "no place like motherland." In this respect important role is played by historical and cultural unity of poetical tradition (Persian and Turkic) of Uzbekistan, Tajikistan and Afghanistan. This unity or traditions of expression are present in the songs of Rap singers of the region, particularly, when they appeal to Motherland ("*obi-havo-i Vatan nest dar ro'i Jahon*"—there is no place (weather and water) like Motherland in the whole world. And, secondly, when they rap about Mother, they are saying[52] thanks to her and asking to forgive their sins.[53] That is the Mother who is crying for their dead sons and always praying for Peace.

Most of the music is aimed at helping the people of Afghanistan and bringing unity to his native country. DJ Besho reached the top of popularity with the Rap song *Gap* [54] In *Gap*, singer DJ Besho, in very simple talking language, raps in a staccato hip-hop style and delivers the message with lyrics such as:

Bagu ey, Vatana ki Obod mekuna, o jonon?
Amriko? Pokiston? Urusiya ya Arabiston?
... Khud mo Obod me kunem Vatana
Khudi mo parvarish metyem Chamana
Moh nakunem tu nakuni o nakuna ....
Khay ki mekunah,hah?
Gorbachyov? Usomo? Obama? Sarkozi?/Ne ... ne ...
... Megam Mo chu hamaki Afghon astem ...
Shukur Musulmon astem
... Yaki rah Pushtun gufta/Digah ro Tojik megan,
Yaki ra Hazarah gi/Digah ra Ouzbek megan[55]

As we can see, here, music has played a political role for propaganda of the key ideas of the establishment. The future of Afghanistan depends upon the ability of its national and local leaders to unite ethnic groups and organise the favourable conditions for cultural development. Most of educated Afghan people understand that without cultural development the country cannot achieve economic development and cannot get political stability. In this respect the traditional Islamic values have played an important role. Modern singers of the region have showed their attachment to values of Islam. For example, DJ Besho has Rap songs where he is has used quotations from the Qur'an.[56] This fact also can help to win the attention of more listeners from different social groups.

Post-Taliban Afghanistan has gone through many changes and modernisation. Sosan Firooz[57] (mentioned above) is the first Afghan (hazara) female rapper.[58] She is breaking traditional rules for women.[59] Her debut track is "*Our Neighbors,*"[60] about life as a refugee in Iran and Pakistan. With lyrics such as, "Listen to my story! Listen to my pain and suffering!" Firooz sings about repression of women, her hopes for a peaceful Afghanistan. In her song she gave the message to Afghans: Stay in your homeland. Those who leave, she sings, will only get jobs washing dishes or working at a car wash. "They will miss their homeland," she raps in a staccato style, part rap and part hip-hop. "They will want to kiss the dust of their homeland." "What is the result of Afghans being refugees in Iran and Pakistan?" she raps in Dari, one of Afghanistan's two main languages. "Half of them are addicts and the other half are terrorists!"[61]

Along with raising the feelings of self-respect these songs are raising the feeling of pride in their own historical past and national identity. These feelings come in two ways: supported by government and from the bottom of the ethnic groups as a call for be stronger. The Rap songs of Uzbek singer Shoxrux and Ethnic Uzbek from Afghanistan Youssufu have been composed in the last few years and similarly named—"*Oz'begim*" (My Uzbeks).[62] Both songs praise the similar values of Uzbeks (*qo'lini ko'ksiga qo'ygan*; *akhloq-u-oqibat*; hospitality, kindness, good qualities), similar feeling of greatness (recalling the names of great sons like Ibn Sina, Naqshband, Ulughbek, Navai, etc.) and the most important the air of Temur and Temurids (if in Shoxrux's song the Taj Mahal is used as a supporting video image, then in Youssufu song is comes in the text). The difference is in main message. The Shoxrux's song is about Uzbeks (he is rapping in formal dress), who make him proud, and Motherland extending to Bukhara, Samarkand and Khiva. The main message of DJ Balkh (Youssufu) is very simple—don't be afraid of busters and learn more from history about greatness of Uzbeks, who were in the frontline of Spirituality (Religion—al-Bukhari etc.) and Knowledge. Youssufu also appeals to one Turkestan (*Ye ... hammamiz Turkestonlikmiz ...)*. Musically the Refrain of Shoxrux's *O'zbegim* is like a slogan, while Youssufu's Refrain is more simple using the folk melody. The video visualisation of both songs aimed to show the great culture of Uzbeks. In this kind of songs we can see how musicians try to use the power of music and lyrics to inspire, touch, influence, uplift, heal and transform society and also play out local, national and regional identities.

Conclusion

Rap/Hip-Hop music is becoming one of the important genres and way of expression for bringing people together and propagating national values, necessary to build a peaceful society. Unlike other musical genres Rap/Hip-Hop cover all kinds of thematic, and also assimilate different genres and styles of musical expression. It is also enriched by local musical traditions. It is a very interesting movement, especially among youngsters, which requires greater investigation.

Notes

1. *Hip-hop* as music and culture was formed during the 1970s in America, but in Asian countries became popular after 1990s. Hip-hop music, also called rap music, is a music genre consisting of a stylised rhythmic music that commonly accompanies rapping, a rhythmic and rhyming speech that is chanted. Hip-hop's inspiration differs depending

on each culture, but looped, stripped-down drum machine rhythms are usually used. For more information: http://en.wikipedia.org/wiki/Hip_hop_music

2. Uzbek rappers advised to sing about love for homeland, at http://www.uznews.net/news_single.php?lng=en&sub=&cid=33&nid=16668 (accessed March 3, 2011); Catherine A. Fitzpatrick "Uzbek Government Censors Rap Music," at http://www.eurasianet.org/node/63340, (accessed April 21, 2011).
3. The government weeded out underground Uzbek rapper Akrom's "*Povod Bermiman* (uzbek rap 2011)" (I am not giving the motive) that can be found on *YouTube* at http://youtu.be/4yKHtCsJipo (published on January 4, 2011). The lyrics describe a young man cruising around in his car, then stepping on the gas to escape the police, then sticking his hand out of the window to give the cops the finger, bragging that he has to stay in shape by taunting the authorities. The video description was removed, only the song remains.
4. *Populiarnyh v Turmenii pevtcov vypustili iz tiurmy,* at http://lenta.ru/news/2013/02/26/release/ (accessed February 26, 2013).
5. *Tadjikskogo repera zaderzjali "za oskorbleniye prezidenta"* at http://lenta.ru/news/2013/05/06/dorob/, (accessed May 6, 2013).
6. At http://youtu.be/wNIRLc6SrCM, published on November 13, 2012.
7. Listen toTajik rap. Master Ismail – Batle – at http://youtu.be/3vlC3o7GVno; (uploaded on May 5, 2010), http://youtu.be/3vlC3o7GVno
8. Interview of "WolF's De Pamir" about Taj.rap by Safina Tv channel, http://youtu.be/Z1APveNyY-k, (uploaded on February 7, 2012).
9. The court did not name the author, but said that he was citizen of Kirgizstan and now citizen of Russia.
10. *Kyrgyzstan: Court bans rap song for "hate speech,"* at http://www.freemuse.org/sw48402.asp (accessed July 27, 2012).
11. Radius 21 va Nigora - Shekspir (Official HD Clip) at http://youtu.be/9cvBfJpCGV0 (published on June 28, 2013).
12. AZIZ ALIYEV feat MR SLAN OLISDAN at http://youtu.be/wtV3z4g4MpI (uploaded on March 19, 2009).
13. Afghan rap DJ Besho at http://youtu.be/UKHpLdRvmTI (uploaded on April 27, 2007).
14. See John Baily "So near, so Far: Kabul's Music in Exile," Ethnomusicology Forum, vol. 14, no. 2, 2005.
15. Laudam Nooshen (ed.), *Music and the Play of Power in the Middle East, North Africa and Central Asia*, Ashgat, 2009, p. 19.
16. John Baily, "So near, so Far: Kabul's Music in Exile," Ethnomusicology Forum, vol. 14, no. 2, 2005.
17. Many ethnic Tajiks of Afghanistan are settled in Republic of Tajikistan and have established strong business relations. The second largest ethnic group in Afghanistan always was close to Tajiks of Central Asian Republic. For example, in YouTube can be seen the concerts of female pop singer from Tajikistan Manija Davlatova at http://www.youtube.com/watch?v=F87dvxluSoE&feature=share&list=RD18uvLchi_aHv0 ; http://youtu.be/R3lr3vzml9U; http://www.youtube.com/watch?v=UMCfGmxIZPI&feature=share&list=PL7E4770A2B0E0F655 and http://youtu.be/uvLchi_aHv0 etc.

18. At YouTube and in his official site named *Mr.Afg._Uz ft Yulduz Uzmanova dunya remix; listen at* http://youtu.be/BlD92vrUtKs.
19. Youssufu is political Rapper, he started Rapping in Uzbek language 12 years. Nowadays he lives in Austria, because of his political songs. Youssufu Rap can be heard on https://soundcloud.com/mr-afg-uz.
20. In one his *Gaplama* 2012 is given: *O'zbek bo'lib o'zbekliginga g'urur qilmasang, o'zingni san hech qachon erkak sanama* [If you are not proud that you are Uzbek, never think about yourself as a man].
21. Farid Rastagar (born March 26, 1963) is from Panjshir, a singer, music arranger, and composer. He is one of the 1980s era singers who rose to popularity as Afghanistan's pop music was reaching its zenith of maturity. His early albums became highly successful due to the keen detail he gave to the background music all of which he arranged, composed and sang himself. Source: http://en.wikipedia.org/wiki/Farid_Rastagar
22. Sosan Firooz: First Afghan female rapper at http://tribune.com.pk/story/449452/sosan-firooz-first-afghan-female-rapper/, (accessed October 10, 2012)
23. Hip-hop as music and culture formed during the 1970s when block parties became increasingly popular in New York City, particularly among African American youth residing in the Bronx. Block parties incorporated DJs who played popular genres of music, especially funk and soul music. Due to the positive reception, DJs began isolating the percussive breaks of popular songs.
24. Uzbek Hip-hop at http://registan.net/2006/01/26/uzbek-hip-hop/, posted on January 26, 2006.
25. Ibid.
26. Sergey Vasilyevich Parkhomenko is a Russian-Belarusian rapper. Seryoga's popularity soared with the "Чёрный Бумер" (Chyorniy Bumer, meaning Black Beemer). The "Чёрный Бумер" music video was shot in the summer of 2004 by Ukrainian director Vladimir Yakimenko (Pistolet Film) and premiered on September 15, 2004 in Kiev. This song and video were immediately nominated for the MTV Russian Music Awards in the categories "best hip-hop project of the year" and "best debut of the year." By the end of 2004, "Чёрный Бумер" became the top hit on MTV's music charts for Russia.
27. Uzbek "Qora Bumer" at http://youtu.be/JiGngGLuYoI (uploaded on December 10, 2006) other one at http://youtu.be/Kzk87aIsHfU (uploaded February 16, 2012); Bashkir-Tatar "Kara bumer" at http://youtu.be/bPS36pSfvO8 (Uploaded on November 10, 2011); Turkmen "Gara BMW" at http://youtu.be/zLP48U5ilfc (uploaded on February 1, 2013: Bashkir-Tatar "Kara bumer" at http://youtu.be/bPS36pSfvO8 (Uploaded on November 10, 2011).
28. Mr. Slan at http://ru.wikipedia.org/wiki/Mr._Slan
29. Interview with M. One (Master Ismail) by Huseniyon production at http://youtu.be/Iu3OznlqwIg (published on July 17, 2012); *HIP-HOP v Serdce Dushanbe* (Hip-Hop in the Heart of Dushanbe) by Huseniyon production at http://youtu.be/3dVT_69UXc4, (Published on July 17, 2012).
30. DJ ISMAIL "Tojik Bacha" [Official video 2013] HD at http://youtu.be/rtR2R7Zgoxk (published on March 29, 2013).

31. Catherine A. Fitzpatrick, "Uzbek Government Censors Rap Music" at http://www.eurasianet.org/node/63340, (accessed on April 21, 2011).
32. Hip-Hop in Uzbekistan at http://uzhiphop.ru; the official site of Flash Jam (Tashkent) group at http://www.fj.by.ru; Hip-hop in South-west of Uzbekistan (Bukhara) at http://www.streetlevel.sitecity.ru; Termez at http://www.rft.freenet.uz; Site of singer Shohruh (Tashkent) at http://www.shoxrux.com; Infornation about Rap in Uzbekistan at http://rapzone.uz - информационный портал рэпа в Узбекистане (г.Ташкент):site Underground Records at http://www.ur-pro.com/ etc.
33. Tashkent Hip-Hop Awards 2010 at http://clublife.pro/clauses/455-tashkent-hip-hop-awards-2010-in-club-zhara.html
34. Hip-hop spread into all regions, including Russia, Japan, Philippines, Canada, China, Korea, India and Vietnam. In East Asian countries hip-hop music has fused with local popular music to form different styles such as K-pop (Korean), C-pop (Chinese) and J-pop (Japan).
35. Pamir Rap at http://pm-rap.my1.ru/; Ma'ruf from D-Town Clan (Deshanbe) at http://mrshady.narod.ru/aboutme.html; The official site of Tajik Rap at http://tajik-rap.ru/index.html etc.
36. Obama, Afghanistan and Gangster Rap in Central Asia at http://easterncampaign.com/2009/12/02/obama-afghanistan-and-gangster-rap-in-central-asia/
37. DJ Besho grew up in Kabul in communist era, but in 1990s his family shifted to Germany. There he has a group of 18 musicians in Wiesbaden, not far from Frankfurt-on-Main. Besho can speak fluently in American slang. More information at http://www.facebook.com/pages/farhad-darya/64705581122?v=info#!/pages/Dj-besho/306525046059756?fref=ts;
38. Farhad "Darya" Nasher (b. September 22, 1962, from Kunduz, Afghanistan) is an Afghan singer and composer, as well as a highly acclaimed music producer, and Goodwill and Peace Ambassador for Afghanistan to the United Nations. Widely popular, he has earned affection for not only his music but also patriotism. He has a fan base that stretches from his native Afghanistan to Central Asia, Pakistan and extending to the West among the Afghans. Farhad sings in various languages including: Pashto, Dari Persian, Uzbek, English and Urdu. For more information see: at http://en.wikipedia.org/wiki/Farhad_Nasher; www.farhaddarya.info; www.daryasworld.com; www.farhaddarya.info/bio.html; www.facebook.com/pages/farhad-darya/64705581122?v=info etc.; BBC Studio 7 with Farhad Darya & Haroon Yousufi, AfghanMusicCHannel1at http://youtu.be/lSIqGNrOdok
39. List of Afghan Rap & Hip-Hop Artists can be seen in site *Afghan Rap and Hip-hop* at http://afghanhiphop.com/music/
40. Translation (main): All Afghan youth are restless … DJ Beshi has come … and brought the new music in Afghanistan…Our music is music of future … My music will live in future… YouTube at http://youtu.be/UKHpLdRvmTI
41. A report about Nazir Khara's music school in Kabul (supported by Americans), was published in *San Francisco Chronicle*. According to the article, Nazir Khara is well aware that teaching women music could mean a death sentence for them or himself, since "many Afghan men believe a woman's voice should not be heard by men, and some conservative clerics believe it is a crime against Islam for women to sing or perform music." Source: at

http://www.freemuse.org/sw24048.asp, dated January 15, 2008.

42. *Sosan Firooz: First Afghan female rapper*, published October 10, 2012 at http://tribune.com.pk/story/449452/sosan-firooz-first-afghan-female-rapper/ ; Her song in Youtube at http://youtu.be/1Gwi7SNiTx0
43. "First Afghan female rapper seeks reason with rhymes," at http://tribune.com.pk/story/488450/first-afghan-female-rapper-seeks-reason-with-rhymes/ (published on January 3, 2013).
44. SHOXRUX—VATANIM 2011 at http://youtu.be/Nr9XOcTeO4U (Uploaded on August 30, 2011), also http://www.shoxrux.co
45. Who are we? Turanian, Amir of Turkistan! Who are we? [We are] greatest and oldest between nations, the main branch of the Turks!
46. Tar (lute) is the type of string instrument played with plectrum; Tar is a Persian long-necked instrument, shared by many cultures and countries like Iran, Afghanistan, Armenia, Georgia, Kurdistan, Republic of Azerbaijan, and other areas near the Caucasus region and Central Asia.
47. My Motherland is only my pride, My Motherland is my Heaven-land.
48. Master Ismail—Vatani man 2013, at http://youtu.be/gZKBWNl_kvI, (published on July 22, 2013).
49. My country is always in my remembering, till my heart is beating; My country is always ... You are only one my Tajikistan.
50. I have one country, one Mother, one Nationality, one God!
51. Afghani DJ Besho Behzan Kabul Jan at http://youtu.be/10lZlIYrWug (uploaded on February 9, 2009).
52. Youssufu—Mother & Ona—Afghan Uzbek Rap at http://youtu.be/xFUqau0khoc (published on May 21, 2013).
53. Bek "Ona" at http://youtu.be/oNEnHj14mCI (uploaded on June 8, 2009).
54. GAP. Composer, Lyricist: Farhad Darya, Artist: DJ Besho, Produced by: Darya Management, Haroon Kargha, to see the lyrics: http://www.darya-management.net/besho/index.htm; YouTube link http://youtu.be/DtOqS8IPLeI
55. The English translation (completed by me): Tell me who will care for Motherland?/ America? Pakistan? Russia or Arabiya? ... We yourself will care for Motherland,/We yourself will care for Flower-garden, If we don't do it, you don't , he don't .... Then who will, hah? /Gorbachyov? Osama? Obama? Sarkozy? No... No... I tell that we all are Afghans... Thanks to God are Muslims... One of [us] are named Pashtun, other one calls Tajik, / one more Hazara, other one named Uzbek ...
56. Afghan rap DJ Besho, YouTube link http://youtu.be/UKHpLdRvmTI
57. *Sosan Firooz: First Afghan female rapper,* published October 10, 2012, at http://tribune.com.pk/story/449452/sosan-firooz-first-afghan-female-rapper/; her's guftor can be watched at http://youtu.be/1Gwi7SNiTx0
58. The first Afghan female rapper (BBC, Dari), YouTube at https://www.youtube.com/watch?v=qJ3eG8xUByk; Dari Afghan Female Rap Singer (News.com on dari), posted in YouTube, at https://www.youtube.com/watch?v=dNcghoFrLUk ; Afghan Female Rapper (News,com in Pashtu), Youtube, at https://www.youtube.com/watch?v=-XW9b4amCXo.

59. Artists in Afghanistan don't enjoy the same perks and privileges as their peers do elsewhere in the world. Firooz lives with her family in a mud brick house in a poor neighborhood in north Kabul. She uses an old desktop computer to write her music and recently received an electronic keyboard as a gift from one of her supporters. She doesn't even have the money to make CDs or a more elaborate music video. Source: *Sosan Firooz: First Afghan female rapper* Published: October 10, 2012, at http://tribune.com.pk/story/449452/sosan-firooz-first-afghan-female-rapper/
60. https://www.youtube.com/watch?v=1Gwi7SNiTx0
61. *Sosan Firooz: First Afghan female rapper,* published October 10, 2012, at http://tribune.com.pk/story/449452/sosan-firooz-first-afghan-female-rapper/
62. Shoxrux—O'zbegim [Official Video] [Uzbek Rap] at http://youtu.be/K-tX_So6olc (uploaded on January 5, 2010); Youssufu (uzbegim) new album dunya 2012 (afg uzbek rap) at http://youtu.be/83UXvJCF-0Y, published on March 25, 2012.

9. Cultural and Economic Ties between the Indian Subcontinent and Central Asia: Past and Future

Davlat Khudonazarov

Following the breakup of the USSR, the political map of Central Asia changed completely. The titular republics of the Soviet Union gained autonomy and independence overnight. This experience of independence from an authoritarian regime is similar to India's experience of independence from British colonial control. So both Central Asia and India have a commonality in terms of their experiences of independence. They also have a shared history. From the beginning of the thirteenth century, since the time of the Delhi Sultanate and up to the middle of the nineteenth century and the last days of the Mongol Empire, this region of Asia was a unified cultural space. An important unifying factor was the Persian language, which became widely spoken after the conquest of India by Babur. While this dynasty was primarily Turkic, the language of the nobility was Persian. Persian writers in Mughal courts like Amir Khusrau Dehlavi and Mirza Abdul Qadir Bedil are also respected as national poets in Iran, Tajikistan and Afghanistan. The shared culture comes not only from a shared language, but also from the universality of ideas which spanned from the Indian Ocean to the Chorasmian steppe. A striking example of such common classical ideas can be seen in the poetry of the Indian poet Kabir and the works of Tajik/Persian poet Rumi, though the language is different.

A key factor in this history of shared culture is the proximity of both regions. The northernmost territory of India coincides with a small portion of southern Tajikistan. This region of Tajikistan is the Pamirs, also called the "Roof of the World" by the daring Scottish explorer John Wood in 1838. The resident population here is very similar to the residents living in the north of the Indian subcontinent. It is in this region that remnants of ancient languages and of pre-Islamic, ancient Aryan/Indo-Iranian culture are visible. The culture of the Pamiri people of this region could be considered ethnographically closest to the northernmost part of India and the easternmost part of the

Persian world. The northernmost border of the Indian subcontinent merges with the mighty Hindu Kush and Pamir mountain ranges. The narrow Wakhan Corridor in Afghanistan demarcates the Pamirs from Hindustan.

It is this territorial stretch of high mountain ranges that has been considered to be a strategic gateway by the Russians and the British during various phases of geopolitical rivalry. While the former considered it a gateway to Central Asia, the latter considered it to be a gateway to Russian Turkestan. These two competing empires were engaged in a geopolitical game that essentially curtailed all connectivity and exchange between India and Central Asia, restricting its prospects as a unified cultural and economic space. At the end of the 1920s, Soviet Union lowered the Iron Curtain on its borders, cutting off the people-to-people exchanges. Only certain antiques or jewelry that are seen in Tajikistan, were at one time available in Northern India, and this reminds my generation of the long-lost ties between India and Central Asia that became pawns of the two competing empires, recalled by historians and political scientists as the "Great Game." To my mind, both countries should try to restore their historical participation in the southern Silk Road. However, the reality is that such restoration attempts are fraught with numerous and perhaps insurmountable obstacles.

Returning to my original argument, I wish to emphasise that more than twenty years have passed since the fall of the Soviet Union and the connections between the Central Asian states and India have not been restored to the level that one could have hoped for. There are several reasons for this failure of which the following are the most important:

(1) The complicated geopolitical situation in the northern part of the Indian subcontinent.
(2) The long-drawn protracted war in Afghanistan
(3) The activity of radical Islamist groups in the region.
(4) The weak national economies of the Central Asian countries.

It is the last point into which I would like to delve a bit deeper. It is closely related to the erosion of traditional culture in Tajikistan and to the challenging situation of the labour migrants I work with on a daily basis in Russia. I would like to point out that I am neither a social scientist nor an anthropologist, but a cinematographer who began his career during the Soviet period. For the last 17 years I have worked in Russia with my fellow Tajiks, initially with refugees from the Tajik Civil War and later with labour migrants. Trying to alleviate some of their problems is itself a difficult task. What I will do here is to best convey my emotions and narrate the concerns of those Tajiks that worry me the most.

In the wake of Soviet dissolution, people of the sovereign republics were confronted with a precarious socio-economic situation. Over the course of 70 years, the factors of production and labour-management relations (i.e., the extraction of raw materials, the creation of components for manufacturing machines, the sources of energy, employment of the work force, etc.) were all part of central management. Most of these production units, although located thousands of kilometres from each other, were interdependent. The newly independent countries which were rich because of natural resources were able to find a solution from the recession through the sale of hydrocarbon resources and rare and precious metals. However, several of post-Soviet states remained unable to come up with self-sustaining growth measures and their economics lacked resilience and the ability to produce globally or regionally competitive products.

In Central Asia, this crisis situation was most pronounced and long-lasting in Tajikistan and Kyrgyzstan. These two mountainous republics, poor in hydrocarbon resources, greatly depended upon the centralised Soviet state budget for subsistence. With their limited transportation infrastructure, they were unable to traverse the mountain ranges of Tien Shen, Pamirs and the Hindu Kush and the trade barrier between China and India proved insurmountable. The few natural resources in these countries were too expensive and to extract them was difficult because of the mountainous terrain.

The situation in Tajikistan was worsened by a five-year civil war (1992-1995), in which tens of thousands of people died and hundreds of thousands became refugees. The populations in the mountainous regions were living from hand to mouth and were saved from starvation only through the help of international humanitarian organisations. While the war continued, the Tajik people found solace in only one path: that stability would return after the Civil War. In 1997, the war officially ended, but they were not able to return to their original life. Instead, economic disaster cropped up, that manifested itself in unemployment. Beginning in 1996, the Tajiks left their homeland to live with fellow Tajik refugees in Russia in order to find work. The economic crisis which occurred in Russia at the end of 1998 made the search for employment difficult. However, at the end of 1999, the price of oil reached 24 dollars per barrel, which amounted to a 2.6 per cent price increase in one year. From that point onward (up to 2008), the price of oil continued to increase and jobs were in plenty in Russia. By the end of 2011, the Russian economy reached pre-crisis levels, climbing from the status of the eleventh biggest economy in the world in 2007 to the ninth largest, according to World Bank figures. In fact, as of early 2012, in terms of consumers' buying power, Russia has become the sixth largest economy on a global scale.

Labour migration from Tajikistan to Russia, regardless of the inhuman conditions it has put workers in, began to sharply increase in accordance with the relative boom in Russian economy. By 2008, one in four households in Tajikistan had a family member who worked abroad. The Tajik government currently estimates that 900,000 Tajik nationals are currently working legally in Russia; however human rights activists claim that for every legal worker, there are at least two people who are working illegally.

This labour migration is fuelled by high levels of unemployment in the home country. Migrants typically find work abroad in the hope of sending money back to their families in the form of remittances. According to 2012 estimates by the National Bank of Tajikistan, 45.4 per cent of Tajikistan's official GDP comes from remittances, with the real number approaching 50 per cent when non-bank transfers are taken into account. From World Bank rankings, Tajikistan is currently the most remittance dependent country in the world, with about 90 per cent of all Tajik migrant labourers sending their remittances from Russia. The main motivation for labour migrants is to find work beyond their home country and to send their earned income to their families. According to World Bank data, Tajik workers sent about three billion dollars in remittances from Russia to Tajikistan in 2011 alone. Clearly, Tajik labour migrants' investment in the vitality of their home country is tremendous.

While the earnings of migrants abroad is undoubtedly a lifesaver for their relatives back home in Tajikistan, deterioration of family life has also occurred quite frequently. Children of labour migrants are not united with their parents over years. Fathers do not often get to see their children growing up. Such migrant fathers are estranged from their children, and this often leads to lack of parental feelings of love and responsibility. On their part, teenagers whose parents are migrant workers, consider themselves abandoned and lonely, often feeling vulnerable and anxious. They tend to become depressed, having struggled in their growing up stages without their parents' guidance.

Additionally, boys are forced to shoulder their father's responsibilities in the house. Many children become orphans despite having biological parents. In orphanages and state homes in Tajikistan, the number of abandoned children is growing at a rapid rate.

As a result of many years of shuttle migration, the institution of marriage has also weakened. Young men are reluctant to get married. The number of divorces and the numbers of single mothers with children in Tajikistan is growing. Official government statistics say the divorce rate has gone up 14.3 per cent in 2012 alone. The real number is most likely higher, as many marriages and divorces are not officially registered. Frequently, men leave their wives and children without getting a legal divorce and get remarried abroad. According to data collected by human rights organisations, every seventh Tajik labour migrant will eventually cut off ties with his immediate family in Tajikistan. The image of the close-knit Tajik family that was the strong foundations of Tajik society is tragically crumbling right before our eyes.

During their residence in a strange land, the Tajik migrants' relationship towards one another also changed. They tend to forget about thousand-year-old traditions and their moral standards reach an all-time low, and they tend to move away from their roots. In their home country, they are within the framework of a social environment where they behave according to traditional norms. By opting for bigger cities like Moscow, they tend to be free from the constraints of national, religious and moral living styles. The idea of freedom deviates the Tajik labour migrants from their mountain environment and quite unknowingly they are drawn into the ambit of shrewd employers, apartment landlords, officers in migration services, police, criminals and conmen in Russia.

In such difficult conditions in Russia, there is a gradual decay of the spiritual-cultural qualities in the migrants' lives. It is hard for them to adjust to city life in such a sprawling metropolis, where they often adopt the worst aspects of the host culture and little by little unwittingly lose their traditions. Such a difficult working environment without an inner spiritual solace is extremely difficult to tolerate. In the past, the skills of agricultural workers and artisans, as well as customs and celebrations of the yearly farming cycle were passed on from generation to generation. These customs and holidays related to nature were considered sacred and were highly respected. There was equal acceptance of joy and sorrow as these were natural conditions. The tolerance level today has gone down and ready acceptance of joy and sorrow is fading fast. It is only the oldest generation in Tajikistan that is the last vanguard of morality. Their grandchildren dream of a fast-pace life, thinking of life and employment in Russia like their parents. In fact, the outlook on life of the youth in Tajikistan has fundamentally changed. During a recent survey, when asked, "What do you aspire to be when you grow up?" the majority of children answered: "A labour migrant." We can clearly see here the difference in perceptions among various generations. The Tajik youth ignore the customs of their own land and instead dream of becoming labour migrants, not knowing that in fact those are dreams of a miserable existence in a country that is unwelcome for migrants.

In the novel *The Day Lasts More than a Hundred Years*, Chingiz Aitmatov created the character of the "mankhurt." A *mankhurt* is someone who forgets his past, abandons his national customs, traditions and spiritual value, and loses his moral sense. Seasonal labour migration is perhaps a temporary way of reinvigorating the economy of the homeland, in this case, Tajikistan. However, if this continues for decades, it will have an impact on the future generation in all spheres of life, creating an entire generation filled with *mankhurts*.

We must seek a solution by trying to preserve the shared culture of Northern India and the Pamir region of Tajikistan—this region is the cultural axis that is encountering the maximum difficulties of labour migration. In my opinion, a study of the cultural world of the Pamiri Tajiks and a comparative analysis of this region's customs and traditions with that of the North Indian peoples could be the first step towards spreading awareness about a cultural space and not allowing it to become eroded in a sea of *mankhurts* on both sides of the mountain passes, who are completely unaware of their past, their roots and fellow countrymen. A request from my side is to understand the present difficult situation and here I have expressed my feelings as I belong to that generation that still remembers the shared culture of northern India and Tajikistan but is distressed to see it disappearing with the passage of time.

10. Cultural Dynamics of Afghanistan: Religion and Pashtunwali

Zalmay Wafamal

While the people of Afghanistan are religious, they hold their traditional values and institutions in high esteem. Among many esteemed traditional institutions of different ethnicities and tribes in Afghanistan, the most prominent of these is *Pashtunwali*. *Pashtunwali* is a non-written ethical code of conduct of the Pashtuns in Afghanistan and Pashtun dwelling regions across the Durand Line. This institution has, throughout the history of Afghanistan, governed the everyday life of the people and has even decided on the fate of governments through the decisions made at the *Loya Jirga* (Grand assembly)—the highest decision-making authority in major issues related to the country. *Pashtunwali* is based on several principles, the most important of which are:

Melmastia **(hospitality)**—Showing hospitality and profound respect to all visitors, regardless of distinctions of race, religion, national affiliation as well as economic status and doing so without any hope of remuneration or favour. Pashtuns are widely considered to be the most hospitable people in the world and a Pashtun will go to great extents to show his hospitality.

Nanawatai **(asylum)**—Derived from the verb meaning to go in, this is used for protection given to a person who requests protection against his/her enemies. The people are protected at all costs; in many cases even people running from the law must be given refuge until the situation is clarified. It can also be used when the vanquished party is prepared to go into the house of the victors and ask for their forgiveness. It is a peculiar form of "courteous" surrender, in which an enemy seeks "sanctuary" at his enemy's house. Examples of *nanawatai* were seen even during the Soviet invasion of Afghanistan. The Hollywood film "The Beast" provides a good account of *nanawatai* practised by the Soviet soldiers.

Badal **(justice)**—Seeking justice or taking revenge against the wrongdoer. This applies to injustices committed yesterday or 1,000 years ago if the wrongdoer still exists.

Toorah **(bravery)**—A Pashtun must defend his land/property from incursions wherever he or she might reside.

Subat **(loyalty)**—Loyalty that must be paid to one's family, friends, and tribe members, is upheld.

Imandari **(righteousness)**—A Pashtun must always strive towards thinking good thoughts, speaking good words and doing other good deeds. Pashtuns must behave respectfully towards all creations including people, animals and the environment around them. Pollution of the environment or its destruction is against the Pashtunwali.

Isteqamat **(Trust in God)**—The notion of trusting in the one creator generally comports to the Islamic idea of belief in only one god *(tawheed).*

Ghayrat **(zeal, self-honour or dignity)**—Pashtuns must maintain their human dignity. Honour has great importance in Pashtun society and most other codes of life are aimed towards the preservation of one's honour or pride. They must respect themselves and others in order to be able to do so, especially those they do not know. Respect begins at home, among family members and relatives. The principle of *Kashar* (younger) and *Mashar* (Elder) is another very strong element of Pashtunwali, whereby the elders have a special respectful place in the family, village and country at large. It is this very principle that makes the Jirga a respectful decision making authority where elder representatives of people make decisions at the national level and the nation and the government have to abide by those decisions.

Namus **(Honour of women)**—A Pashtun must defend the honour of Pashtun women at all costs and must protect them from vocal and physical harm.

Pashtunwali dates back to ancient pre-Islamic times and is widely practised among Pashtuns, especially in rural tribal society. In addition to being practised by members of the Pashtun diaspora, it has been adopted by some non-Pashtuns who live in Pashtun regions or close to Pashtuns, and have gradually become Pashtunised over time. Although *Pashtunwali* is believed to date back to the pre-Islamic period, its usage or practice does not breach basic Islamic principles.

Pashtuns all over the world are united by this very institution—*Pashtunwali,* and this unity gets stronger as attempts are made to disunite Pashtuns. The "ONE FOR ALL AND ALL FOR ONE" principle is a very visible and tangible one in *Pashtunwali.* If one is dishonoured, all are dishonoured. If one is harmed, all are harmed. Group interests are higher than individual interests. Through the principle of equality that exists among Pashtuns, the *Jirga* (Assembly) system has evolved among Pashtuns, where all members of the society deserve the right to express their opinion *overtly* and have a say in their future. While everyone fights for their voice to be heard, they all interact with each other in a civilised and respectful manner.

Pashtunwali predates Islam. The Pashtuns accepted Islam as their religion and faith and as part of their socio-economic culture in the eleventh century AD, four centuries after it descended as a religion. In some areas, Islam is sometimes in contradiction with *Pashtunwali*. While these contrasting spheres—Islam and *Pashtunwali*—articulate tension in Pashtun society, they also demonstrate that there are Pashtun tribal democratic ways of coming to terms with these divergences. It also further indicates that Islam is not the only institution among Pashtuns that regulates everyday affairs. Instead, Islam coexists with all Pashtun traditional values.

As a Pashtun scholar, Palwasha Kakar states[1]: "Pashtunwali's relationship with Islam has been a complicated one. Although most Pashtuns are Sunni Muslims, the Pashtun's tribal code is the ultimate authority. Second in allegiance is Islamic law." For the Pashtuns there is no contradiction between being a Pashtun, practising *Pashtunwali*, and being a Muslim and adhering to Islamic law.

According to author Oliver Roy,[2] "Even though the Shari'a and *Pashtunwali* overlap, they are seen as serving different purposes. The Shari'a represents God's Will for humanity on earth and is practised because it is a moral code whereas *Pashtunwali* is seen as a matter of honour." Modern written accounts of Pashtunwali were first seen in the 1950s by authors and members of the *Weesh Zalmian* (the Awakened Youth) political party which later became the *Khalq* and *Parcham* leftist parties and some other liberal movements. They appealed to the history and traditions of the Pashtuns when advocating national awakening and social justice. In their publications, they confidently proffered the rules and values of *Pashtunwali* as educational principles for a modern Afghan nation. This shows that *Pashtunwali* principles and values are very liberal and lean more towards modernisation than extremism.

All through the history of Afghanistan, stability prevailed when these institutions—Islam and *Pashtunwali*—coexisted in a balance, each one addressing matters related to its domain. The Mosque preached religion and the *Dera* (a gathering of the elders of a village) looking after day-to-day affairs at the village level, a *Jirga* solving bigger issues at the district and province level and a *Loya Jirga* (Grand Assembly) deciding on matters related to the nation at the country level. This is how democratic the Pashtun way has always been. This balance and coexistence has helped maintain stability in the country all through, until the balance was disturbed by different colonial powers for their own vicious desires and agendas.

When the strong role of *Pashtunwali* in peaceful coexistence with religion was noticed by colonial powers, who always planned to invade the country but did not succeed, they first of all attacked the institutions that governed affairs in Afghanistan—Islam and *Pashtunwali*—and disturbed the balance that had ensured the peaceful coexistence between the two.

In the early twentieth century, under King Amanullah Khan, Afghanistan was moving fast towards progress and prosperity; the then colonial power provoked fanatic mullahs against the king to overthrow him. That was the first phase of impediment towards progress for Afghanistan. In late 1970s, the then Soviet Union backed socialist regime disengaged both these institutions from the everyday life of the nation by calling mullahs anti-progressive and killing them and labelling the elders of tribes as feudal (big land owners) and either throwing them in their dark prisons or killing them. This was the second phase of impediment towards progress.

In-between these phases, King Zaher Shah recreated balance between religion and Pashtunwali and gave them their lost position and respect again, which led to a four decade era of peace and stability in the country. Pursuing this balance and division of roles, Sardar Mohammad Dawood Khan, the first president of Afghanistan led the country towards a speedy road to progress and prosperity. In his 5-year term, more development projects were completed than ever before or even after.

The Role of Women in Pashtunwali

Women have had their share of practising *Pashtunwali*, not a balanced one though, as per their capacities and capabilities. We have historic examples of different Afghan women who led armies or advised the kings of the time on major political issues. We have examples of Malalai, Nazo Anna, Zarghoona, and many others. On the progressive and democratic front, we have example of Queen Suraya Tarzi, the wife of King Amanullah Khan, who was the first Afghan woman to stand up in front of the *Loya Jirga* and unveil her face stating that it was against the Afghan traditions and also Islam to have women totally veiled, including their face. With that, began a new era of *Roi Luchee* (unveiling of the face) and since the *Loya Jirga* approved of it, this was widely practised in urban areas by women from different walks of life, especially the educated and the working women.

Another example of the role of women in *Pashtunwali* is the high esteem and respect men have for them. For instance, if the men cannot reach a decision to solve a dispute, a woman steps in and requests the two sides to sort out the dispute in a particular manner. Out of respect for the woman, it is compulsory for the men to comply with the demand of the woman to solve the dispute.

Given the over five-thousand-year-old history of Afghanistan, and the success of the Afghan way of governing affairs through a balance and division of role between religion and *Pashtunwali*, it is crystal clear that Afghanistan is old enough to choose its own system and way to peace, progress and prosperity, if it is listened to. The international community must listen to the Afghans and accept the Afghan ways of dealing with problems in Afghanistan and choosing their way of life because the Afghan history has proven time and again that the Afghan traditional ways have superseded every other system to solve the problems of Afghans and help them live in harmony, peace and prosperity.

Notes

1. Palwasha Kakar, *Tribal Law of Pashtunwali and Women's Legislative Authority.*
2. Olivier Roy, *Afghanistan: From Holy War to Civil War* (Princeton: Darwin Press, 1985), p. 52.

11. Transforming the Culture of Conflict: Fostering Peace through Cultural Contribution in Contemporary Afghanistan

Sanaullah Tasal

Introduction

War exerts an undeniably significant influence on the values, norms, behaviour and attitudes which constitute the culture shared within a society. During prolonged armed conflicts the continual exposure to extreme violence in Afghanistan is responsible for the creation of a "culture of violence": the incorporating of violence into the values system of the Afghan, so that it is therefore permitted and overlooked, making violence resilient to peace-building efforts and any conflicts likely to re-escalate into armed conflict.

In order to understand how a "culture of peace" came under the shadow of the "culture of violence," it is necessary to understand how it is transmitted to younger generations and how it is produced and reproduced within Afghan society in the refugees camps in Pakistan. This article aims to explore and understand the phenomenon of the transmission of a "culture of peace into culture of violence and vice versa." Is a "culture of violence" transmitted by those Afghan children and youths who lived away from their country and experienced the war? How should the culture of peace be revived? How to cultivate peace through cultural contribution in contemporary Afghanistan?

Throughout this article I explore these questions focusing on the micro mechanisms that underpin the process of transmission within communities and among individuals. I am also trying to identify the possible factors of Afghan culture which contribute to transmission of culture of violence into culture of peace.

The Culture of Afghans

Afghans have general rules and principles within their culture that help ensure a peaceful living environment between them, and according to which the rights of every individual are secured and which prohibit violence against others. To the extent that the rules and principles of the culture were the dominant structures organising society, not only were everyone's individual rights secured, but there was also a broader peace in the region. Afghans loved and were obliged to the code of *Pakhtunwali*[1] so much, that it has almost gained the status of religion. Afghans are not considering *Pashto*[2] and Islam as two differing things, they are considering *Pashto* and Islam as one. This is the reason why in certain places a Pakhtun finds himself more comfortable with *Pakhtunwali* than his religion. And if you were to call someone "Pashto-less or Pashto-free or cultureless" they would reveal a critical reaction to this as if you had called them they are an infidel or non-Muslim. Some may even show a stronger sensitivity to this.

As a great Pashto poet, Hamza Baba so famously replied to those who claimed Pashto and Pakhtunwali contradicted Islam:

نوتښپ ون وو ناسنا هک مه یادخ /////مياو هز هود هڼګ مالسا وتښپ هت
یو هب[3]

"You keep on considering Pashto and Islam as two differing things, where in my opinion/

If God were to be a human being, he surely would have been a pakhtoon."

In the 1930s, tens of thousands of Pashtuns became an integral part of the movement of nonviolent, civil disobedience against British Colonialism. This movement, called the *Khudai Khidmatgar,* or Servants of God, united formerly hostile tribes to work together towards the goal of ending British colonial rule. Afghans, whatever their ethnic/tribal origin, have over the centuries emulated each other's behaviour—Pashtuns, Tajiks, Hazaras, Uzbaks, Turkmans and other Afghan ethnic and tribal groups have all made their unique contributions to Afghan culture that is more than the total sum of its constituent parts.

For the last four decades, Afghanistan has been ravaged by invasions, civil wars and terrorist activities. As much as all of the other disastrous effects of this intractable violence, the period of acute conflict has disrupted and overturned much of the country's social and cultural traditions and values. All too often, Afghan youth lack the awareness of their cultural heritage and the precedents of peace within Afghanistan. A large portion of the current generation of youth were born and brought up displaced from their homes and heritage in refugees camps in Pakistan and elsewhere. And, many of those youth have been used and abused by nefarious actors, both national and international to perpetuate wars of violence and instability in Afghanistan.

The following compares the pure and peaceful cultural heritage of Afghans with the current understandings of Afghan culture with its influence from many ideologies and the lingering affects modern cultures of violence. The paper will also respond to the questions of how historical Afghan cultural values can be reinvigorated in order to contribute to peace in Afghanistan and Pakistan's FATA region. How do we learn from our shared past in order to transform cultures of violence into a culture of peace?

Afghan Rules and Principles that Help Fostering Peace in Contemporary Afghanistan

In conflict-affected areas, national and international actors can help promote cultural activities in order to give local people ownership of their endeavours and use culture as a vehicle for sustained peace. As I mentioned above that *Pakhtunwali* has played an important role in ensuring stability in Afghanistan and these codes still play a very important role in the tribal structured society of Afghanistan.

Below are three Codes of Pakhtunwali that can play an important role in peace-building in Afghanistan:

The Pakhtun code of conduct is based on equality (Seyal) and applying equality is called (Seyali or competition). Equality, competition, protection of Namus (protection of female members and wealth) and Ezzat (honour) are the centrepieces of Pakhtunwali. Other components of Pakhtunwali are Gundi (rivalry); Qawm (ethnicity or tribe) or Qawmi Taroon (tribal binding); protection of Hamsaya (neighbour or outsiders living with a family or in a village); Jirga (meeting of elders to gather for a specific issue to solve); Pur, Ghach, Enteqam or Badal (revenge) and Nanawati (forgiveness). The application of these rules is called Narkh (informal or traditional law or rules), the implementation of which is being the responsibility of a Jirga, Shura or government. These codes of conduct are an inherited way of life especially for the Pakhtuns in rural areas of both side of the Durand Line.[4]

1. ***Nang, Namus* (Honour):** The main pillars of the Pashtun code: in order to live in Pakhtun family, village or society, you should be able to protect your Honour. (Female, land, property, and religion, Neighbours, Kin and Country are called Namus—honour).[5]

   It is the Pakhtuns' tradition to never compromise on any issue or on a decision they have taken. In case of *nang* and *namus* (honour), they offer any sacrifice that may be sacrifice of life. But he will protect his namus. That is why there is a saying: *Sweeter to me is death than life which is passed day-to-day without honour.*

Pakhtuns are obliged to take care of the (female, land, property and country) of others because if one is unable to care for the honour of another, he is incapable of keeping his own honour. Classical Pashto poet Abdul Hameed Baba has written that يشن ےلتاس سومان و گـنن لب د يچ سومان و گـنن لپخ كـوخ يتاس ئن هب و (Those who cannot protect the honour of others will not be able to keep their own honour.

In the entire world, perhaps it is the unique code of life of Pashtuns, this is the reason why people were saying in the past: when there were Pashtuns there was life.

1. ***Qawmi Taroon*** **(Tribal Binding):** that was an agreement between several tribes for the protection of one another's honour. Afghans used to defend themselves in a union, as long as they knew harm could happen to every member of the community. (*Nan Par ta saba par ma)*
2. ***Meranai, Batoor, Pakhtunpal, Ghazi, Hewadpal*** **(Bravery)**: Historically there have been very clear codes of conduct that authorised the use of violence. And that it was only sanctioned under very strict guidelines—and that not abiding by those rules of violent engagement led to marks against someone's honour and their bravery. Bravery, thus, is not just the ability to use violent force, but the intelligence to know when it is appropriate and abide by the rules of engagement when using it. In Afghan society a person who is brave does not breach the following codes of conduct in the application of violence:

He does not attack women, children, the old or the weak; does not attack an enemy when he or she is in prayer; does not attack an enemy in a *Jirga*; does not attack an enemy during a cultural celebration like a marriage, funeral, or Eid; does not attack places of worship like the mosque or places where a *Jirga* is taking place; does not disrespect the bodies of the deceased and graves of the enemy; and refrains from killing a man who has entered a mosque or shrine in order to forgive the enemy. Whoever fails to follow any of these principles sanctioning and governing the use of violence will be taunted with the words of "Beghairat and benang," or dishonour.

According to the code of conduct of Pakhtunwali children shall enjoy a period of childhood without unnecessary influence. It is a period of life reserved for playing around and having a carefree time. Using a child for war or forcing them to commit suicide attacks goes against the characteristics of bravery in Afghan culture. There is no historical precedent in which Afghan tribesmen have used children in the armed conflicts among themselves or in their hostilities towards the "British" and other occupying forces. Today, the Taliban are using children for jihad and brainwash or used them to be suicide bombers.

Committing suicide is not an act of bravery in Afghan culture. It is considered shameful and un-Islamic in Afghan culture for a person to blow himself up, even in a Jirga or in an enemy's compound. Pashtun are saying, "*Da Nar Ya khrap de ya trap*" (A brave person can hit and cannot be hit.) So, killing or beating the enemy by killing yourself is not bravery.

Whosoever, fails to follow any custom of "Nang" chivalry, Honour (Namus) Qawmi Taroon (tribal binding); Merana (Bravery), is taunted with the words of "Beghairat" (without honour) and be Pakhtun.

How a Culture of Peace Has Been Influenced by Cultures of Conflict and Extremism?

However, as culture is learned and therefore "taught," a culture of violence is also "taught" or rather transmitted, especially to the current Afghan generation, and in this way it persists as part of the system of meanings shared by the community.

The impact of war on Afghan culture is recognised, Afghans are displaced, separated from their families, and are psychologically and physically wounded. They are abducted and trained as fighters and become directly involved in armed struggles, they are abused and killed and they are both victims and perpetrators of the current conflicts. This atmosphere has disrupted and overturned much of the country's social and cultural traditions. The culture of honour, tribal binding and bravery are affected by these unfair conditions and long war.

In the refugee camps, several curriculums with several ideologies that were not relevant to the Afghan culture and values have been developed by Jihadi and non-Jihadi groups and by the international community. These different curriculums were full of violence and war texts and have been taught to the Afghan children in schools and Madrassas.

Culture of Peace after 2001

Since their intervention in Afghanistan, the international community and Afghan government have failed to incorporate the Afghan culture in their peace and reconciliation effort. They failed to understand how to use Afghan culture of patriotism, nationalism, peace, mutual respect, tribal binding in order to achieve peace in the country. They also failed to teach Afghans their own culture that was free of corruption and protecting the rights of others. Instead the international community started accusing Afghan culture (in every Pashtun house there is a terrorist, terrorism is the real culture of Afghans, corruption is the ancient culture of Afghans, etc. ...)

Projection of Afghan culture as a culture of violence only not came from the international community, but this perception of a culture of violence and the celebration of martyrs and those who use violence has become internalised in various parts of Afghanistan.

On the other side, our neighbours and the Taliban used Afghan culture (of honour, chivalry, bravery and taunt) as tools in their war against the Afghan government and coalition forces. Pakistan and the insurgent groups knew that Afghans will fight to the best of their ability if they felt that their culture or religious values have been harmed or mocked. In most of the cases insurgents were showing video clips of foreign troops searching Afghan women, burning holy *Quran*, disgracing Afghan elders and religious scholars (*Mulla*), and thus taunting youth to take revenge on the occupied forces and their Afghan supporters.

Insurgents are making use of widely-available mobile phones with Afghan youths and Afghan national army as a propaganda tool. Insurgents can easily attract them by uploading the suicide attacks ringtones and other Jihad-related songs. The clips sent by the insurgent to subscribers include beheadings, real-life suicide bombings and roadside bomb explosions, coalition forces disgracing the Holy Quran, burning Mosques and killing innocent children and the most appropriate reason for green on blue attacks is these kinds of ringtones and videos.

If we see the Fatwas of the Islamic scholars in Afghanistan and abroad against the suicide attacks it did not work. The reason is that the Taliban are showing to the attackers the movies and photos of the coalition forces searching Afghan women and raiding their houses. So the Taliban are taunting the youth here they are saying:

- يخ هٔن ېد تپ،يمورد ېد لام،يمورد ېد رس
  ده تپ هپ يبوخ لک ېراچ د يړس د[6]

Let the head be gone, wealth be gone but the honour must not go, because the whole of dignity of a man is due to this honour, or Sweeter to me is death than a life which is passed day-to-day without honour.

Green on Blue attacks

In the last few years, Afghan Security forces have turned their guns on their NATO counterparts in increasing numbers; it is usually portrayed as a religious and/or cultural problem in which Afghan troops react to perceived insults by International troops' behaviour. These attackers are not necessarily linked completely to the Taliban; but many security personnel come from conservative and rural areas where such codes (Pakhtunwali) are important and most of the time acted independently, inspired by their need to bring pride back to their tribe or country, and some of them actually done by Taliban members. Those who attacked independently to prevent the loss of pride, or to bring pride back to their tribe or country, people considered them as heroes and were proud of their actions, often building shrines over their graves.

A few years ago, an Afghan border police attacked US troops in Nangarhar province Pacher Agam district while a soldier was taking photos of Afghan women crossing the road. Afghan border police stopped him twice and finally attacked these soldiers and killed seven of them and wounded several others. He was also killed by the foreign troops, and his funeral ceremony was attended by thousands of people across the province and he became a national hero and people built a shrine on his grave.

Compare this kind of attack with suicide attacks on foreign troops; the attackers were not treated like this. Both are attacking foreign troops, the suicide attacker arguing that he is doing so to protect Islam and the other is saying that he has been martyred to protect honour.

Conclusion

The resilience of violence in post-war societies poses a serious challenge for the implementation of peace accords and the construction of a sustainable peace. The experience of war leaves marks both on society and on individuals which last for a long time after the termination of the war.

What has been discussed in this paper shows that *non-violence* was the real culture of Afghans, and deeply rooted in the culture and history of Afghanistan. There are deep historical precedents of Afghans practising peaceful mechanisms for solving their problems either among themselves or with outsiders. Too often, though, these historical examples are overshadowed by well-known periods of acute and widespread violence. The Afghan culture has the potential to bridge tradition with modernity; it has the capacity to express traditional values in a modern setting.

As the withdrawal of international coalition forces in 2014 is approaching, fears among the Afghans are increasing that the complete exit of the coalition forces from Afghanistan will be hard compared to the Soviet exit, because at that time the rules and principles of Pakhtunwali were alive, that ensured a peaceful living environment between different tribes and ethnic groups. This culture of mutual respect between tribes and ethnic groups has been destroyed or undermined by the culture of violence and sectarianism, ethnicity and tribalism which may fuel war and will take the lives of more people.

As a majority of the Afghan nation are chivalrous and tend to display respect to its codes, most of our authors are also keen to impose the culture of violence and firefight in their manuscripts in the interest of the people. These authors and think-tanks should rather indeed begin embedding the long-awaited message of patience, virtue, mutual respect and cooperation and empowering intellectual might in lieu of writings to nurture violence. The culture of peace and non-violence should be revived and must be included in all the peace and reconciliation efforts within and outside of Afghanistan.

Notes

1. The Pakhtun code of conduct is based on Equality, competition; protection of Namus (protection of female members and wealth) and Ezzat (honor) are the centrepieces of Pakhtunwali. Other components of Pakhtunwali are Qawm (ethnicity or tribe) or Qawmi Taroon (tribal binding); protection of Hamsaya (neighbour or outsiders living with a family or in a village); Jirga (meeting of elders to gather for a specific issue to solve); Pur, Ghach, Enteqam or Badal (revenge) and Nanawati (forgiveness). The application of these rules is called Narkh (informal or traditional law or rules), the implementation of which is being the responsibility of a Jirga, Shura or government.
2. Pashto is not only the name of language but the name of the code of conduct as well. Pashto is the foundation of the culture, whenever I am speaking of Pashtu or Pashtun, I obviously mean the culture of Pakhtuns.
3. Haroon Shinwari, *An Introduction to Hamza Baba*, p. 42.
4. Shahmahmood Miakhel (http://pashtoonkhwa.com/files/articles/Miakhel%20-%20Importance%20of%20Tribal%20Structures%20in%20Afghanistan.pdf

5. So Pakhtunwali and its rules can only be understood with reference to the different domains of *Nang* or honour, the basic value of Pakhtunwali and a basic characteristic of a Pakhtun personality. *Sharam* (shame), *Nang* (Honour), *Peghore* (taunt) and *Badal* (revenge) are the central pillars of the Pakhtun Culture. *Sharam* (shame) includes the disrespect of women, family, relation, community, ethnicity, nationality and culture. The strength of *Nang*, the sense of honour attached to each of these domains, varies according to the situation.
6. http://www.asc-centralasia.edu.pk/Issue_65/01_The%20Pashtun_Code_of_Honour.html

12. Gender Studies in Contemporary Afghanistan

Sayed Mohammad Shah

Rebuilding and democratisation of Afghanistan provided tremendous opportunities to womenfolk to gradually claim their basic human rights including health, education, voting in the national elections and accessing work. Currently thirty-eight per cent of the nine million students going to schools are girls while women presence in government services, including the ranks of Police and Afghan National Army is quite visible. Some entered in the politics and made their way to the Afghan Parliament and Senate. Twenty-five per cent of the seats in Parliament and Senate are allocated for women in Afghanistan. Similarly, some women are in leading positions in the Afghan civil society particularly engaged in women's rights activism.

There has also been significant progress on legal framework. Specific achievements are codification of draft laws and regulations such as the Elimination of Violence against Women (EVAW) Law, the Family Status Law, the Guardian Law, Support Centre Regulations, Anti-Discrimination regulations and policies for women prisoners so they can access justice.

Among these, the enactment of EVAW law in August 2009 was a significant legislative step towards ending violence against women in Afghanistan. The article 5 of this law lists 22 acts as violence against women including rape, forced prostitution, setting into flames, causing injury or disability, beating, selling and buying women for the purpose of or under pretext of marriage, retribution of a women to settle a dispute, forced marriage, child marriage, denial of inheritance rights, denying the right to education, work and access to health services, forced drug addiction, harassment and persecution and others.

The High Commission on Elimination of Violence against Women was regularised under the EVAW law in August 2009 to serve as a comprehensive mechanism for the promotion of all aspects of the EVAW law. This Commission is chaired by the Minister of Women's Affairs and has actively engaged in key issues under its mandate. Recently the Commission established its sub-branches in 30 out of 34 provinces of Afghanistan.[1]

Several institutions such as Afghanistan Independent Human Rights Commission (AIHRC), Ministry of Women Affairs (MOWA), United Nations agencies and several other civil society organisations are currently active in Afghanistan to protect the rights of women.

The Afghan Government and its international partners identified in the Tokyo Mutual Accountability Framework benchmarks in five main sectors to support recovery and development for a self-reliant Afghanistan within the larger development assistance framework. The Implementation of the National Action Plan for Women of Afghanistan (NAPWA) and the EVAW law as to two main indicators of the Government's performance in meeting the goals of improving governance, rule of law and human rights has been emphasised.[2]

Despite these significant achievements, the cases of violence against women in Afghanistan have been widespread and 2012 witnessed a drastic boom. The Afghanistan Independent Human Rights Commission (AIHRC) estimates 22 per cent increase in the reported cases of violence against women in 2012. The Commission, Ministry of Women Affairs and United Nations Assistance Mission in Afghanistan (UNAMA) believe the number of cases is much higher than the reported cases.[3] The year 2012 also has in its memories several surprising and heart-breaking events.

The All Afghanistan Ulema Council Declaration of March 2, 2012 while noting that some rights were guaranteed to women under Islam, outlined a code of conduct which was issued for women similar to the position of Islamic fundamentalists. The Council called women "secondary," prohibiting violence against women only for "un-Islamic" reasons and calling for segregating women and girls in education, employment and in public. President Hamid Karzai endorsed the statement, which raised questions about the Government's commitment to protect women.[4]

Subsequently, the Minister of Justice, Habibullah Ghalib's description of battered women shelters as sites of "immorality and prostitution" further deepened that scepticism.[5] Najia Sediqi, the acting head of the Afghan government's Department of Women's Affairs in the eastern province of Laghman, was shot and killed by an unknown gunman as she travelled to work in December. That same month, Anisa, a 22-year-old student and polio vaccination campaign volunteer, was shot to death in Kapisa province.

The late December 2011 arrest and subsequent trial of the in-laws of Sahar Gul—a girl sold into marriage at 13, locked in a basement, and tortured by her in-laws after she refused their demands that she become a prostitute—underlined the threat posed to Afghan girls by unchecked violence against women. The unsolved February murder in Bamiyan of an adolescent girl named Shakila led to street protests in Kabul and Bamiyan, and complaints from Bamiyan officials to President Karzai over what was seen as a cover-up by government officials of a murder. In July, a 22-year-old woman was publicly executed in Parwan province for alleged adultery. Under-age and forced marriage remain common in Afghanistan. Numerous other women in public life were targets of attack in 2012. In the spring and summer, a series of "poisonings" at girls' schools in several provinces, alleged by the Afghan government to have been perpetrated by opponents of girls' education, escalated fear for schoolgirls and their families.

The Ministry of Women Affairs (MOWA) believes that violence against women has always been widespread in Afghanistan and the reasons for 22 per cent increase during 2012 are proactive reporting by media, more awareness of women about their rights and existence of relevant institutions to support and protect women's rights.

> "Violence against women is not a new phenomenon; it has always been in Afghanistan. In the past, there was no formal institution to pursue cases and the media didn't actively report cases on large scale. Now we have active media, women are more aware about their rights, institutions have been established that register cases of violence against women and pursue them. However, I would claim that there are still many cases of violence which do not reach us." (The Deputy Minister for Women Affairs, Sayda Mojgan Mostafavi)

The root of violence against women in Afghan society is embedded in harmful traditional and cultural practices which are sometimes attributed to religion as well. These harmful practices lead to pain, suffering, humiliation and the marginalisation of millions of Afghan women and girls, violating the most basic human rights of half the population.

The UN's Committee on the Elimination of Discrimination against Women (CEDAW Committee) describes harmful traditional practices as:

> Traditional attitudes by which women are regarded as subordinate to men or as having stereotyped roles" and perpetuate "widespread practices involving

> violence or coercion, such as family violence and abuse, forced marriage .... Such prejudices and practices may justify gender-based violence as a form of protection or control of women. The effect of such violence on the physical and mental integrity of women is to deprive them of the equal enjoyment, exercise and knowledge of human rights and fundamental freedoms.

Trends, Patterns and Types of Violence against Women

Prevalent forms of violence against women included battery and laceration, sexual violence and harmful practices[6] such as early and forced marriages, often leading to self-immolation, baad, which is use of girls in marriage to settle disputes and the so-called Honour Killing.

Forced Marriages

A marriage, in which the free and full consent of one or both of the intending spouses is not taken, is a forced marriage. According to a 2008 report by UNIFEM, 70 to 80 per cent of Afghan marriages are forced.

Baad

Baad is a practice of giving away of girls to settle disputes. This is one of the most egregious types of violence against women in Afghanistan. *Baad* allows communities or families to settle crimes such as murder, in theory to restore peace and order between the conflicting parties, by transferring punishment for the crime to a woman or girl. The "honour" of the aggrieved family is "restored" through punishing the woman for a crime she did not commit. The merit of this practice in resolving disputes is highly dubious; often conflict and enmity between families or groups continue. Girls given in *baad* are often treated like slaves—they endure mistreatment, physical violence and humiliation as retaliation for the crime committed by a male family member.

Baadal—Exchange Marriages

Exchange marriages are mutual arrangements between families to exchange daughters. The families avoid monetary negotiations and the cost and risks of incurring debt. The practice denies women the right to freely enter into a marriage based on consent—as required under international, national and Sharia law. The practice also contradicts Sharia law requirements that forbid one man to give his daughter in marriage to another to avoid *mahr* (dowry payments).

One widely reported consequence of these marriages is that in-laws punish brides reciprocally in exchange for any reported mistreatment or punishment of their own daughter.

Child Marriage

"If you hit a girl with your hat and she doesn't fall over, it's time to marry her."

Child marriage constitutes one of the most severe forms of child abuse with a disproportionately negative impact on the girl child. It is both a cause and consequence of the most severe form of gender discrimination. The practice harms girls by denying them their childhood and forcing them into marriage (as children they are unable to make a free and informed choice about a future spouse). The practice also denies girls the right to education and health, as early marriage leads to early childbirth for which girls are mentally and physically unprepared. Due to widespread poverty, child marriage also leads to "selling" of girls, particularly to much older men, who can pay impoverished families for a young girl's marriage. As older men often take young girls as additional wives, the practice of polygamy emerges. Under-age marriage is common across Afghanistan, in all regions and among all ethnic groups. According to UNIFEM and the Afghan Independent Human Rights Commission, fifty-seven per cent of Afghan marriages are child marriages—where one partner is under the age of sixteen.

Forced Marriage of Widows and Inheritance Rights

Harmful traditional practices not only curtail Afghan women's rights before and during marriage but also after their husband dies. Forced marriage of widows stems in part from widows being considered the property of their in-laws, but is also often due to the desire to deny a widow her right to inheritance by marrying her to a relative and keeping any inheritance within the family. The woman concerned is thus forced into a marriage against her will, contrary to all national and international law, as well as Sharia law—where consent is a prerequisite for any marriage.

Restrictions on Women's Freedom of Movement

"It is better to confine women and girls at home and safeguard their chastity and modesty."

Women's participation in public life is constrained due to restrictions on freedom of movement.

This restriction is the result of both arbitrary and misinterpreted references to religion as well as to widespread insecurity in areas throughout Afghanistan. It represents a major barrier to realising the full range of women's rights; denial of women's freedom of movement prevents women from engaging in work, and accessing many other rights, such as education and adequate health care.

"Honour" Killings

Where women are perceived as receptacles of family honour, their opposition to family dictates about marriage often puts them at risk of brutal physical punishment. So called "honour" killings recognise a man's right to kill a woman with impunity because of the damage that her immoral actions have caused to family honour. It is a killing of a family member by one or several relatives who believe the victim has brought shame upon the family. The perceived dishonour is often the woman's flight from a forced marriage, choosing her own marriage partner, or engaging in questionable conduct with the opposite sex. An "honour" killing is, given the nature of the crime and its link to cultural notions of honour, a harmful traditional practice.

Self-immolation

Self-immolation is one of the most tragic consequences of harmful traditional practices and violence against women in Afghanistan. The authorities investigate very few cases where family members of women who set themselves alight are alleged to have caused the act. This is due to lack of evidence, but also due to reluctance on the part of state authorities to investigate or prosecute such cases.

Running Away

When social and cultural circumstances do not allow women and girls to oppose harmful traditional practices, or to escape violence, they sometimes resort to running away. While "running away" is not a crime under Afghan law, law enforcement authorities often arrest, jail and even prosecute girls for running away, usually qualifying the charge as "intention" to commit *zina* (sexual intercourse outside of marriage). Under Article 425 of the Penal Code a man who elopes with a woman who is eighteen years or older is not deemed to have committed an act of kidnapping. This implies that a woman, aged eighteen or above, who "runs away" to marry is not guilty of a crime. Running away can lead to conflicts among families or communities. Sometimes, as in the case mentioned above, families are compelled to give away another girl through *baad*. Runaways also sometimes face the risk of being murdered in "honour" killings by their relatives.

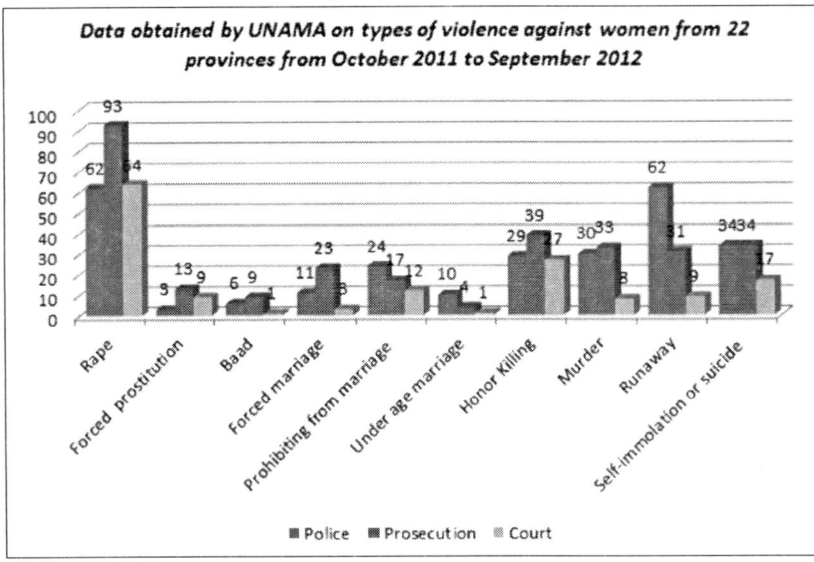

Weaknesses of Justice System

The weakness of justice system has also been a potent threat to the women in Afghanistan. A recent Human Rights Watch report, "I had to Runaway" estimated that of the about seven hundred women and girls currently detained in prisons across Afghanistan, four hundred and seventy have been found guilty and imprisoned on the charge of fleeing from home with the intent to commit adultery.

It is despite that on September 16, 2012, the Minister for Justice, Habibullah Ghalib, the Minister for Women's Affairs, Hussn Banoo Ghazanfar and Deputy Interior Minister, Baz Mohammad Yarmand strongly condemned the imprisonment of women and girls who were charged with running away. They said running away was not a crime. However, these women and girls were arrested under the Sharia law, which terms running away a crime under some circumstances.

According to the Senior Researcher at Human Rights Watch, Heather Barr, the Supreme Court had sent a memo to judges instructing them that if a woman run away and goes straight to the police or to her family members, then that is not a crime but if she goes elsewhere with a non-family member, then it is intent to commit adultery "Zina," a crime under Sharia Law. In many cases, the women and girls who ran away from homes to escape violence against them get further victimised by ending in the prison.

> "When people victimise women they are not arrested and not punished and the women who are victims of these crimes, they are often treated like criminals." Heather Barr, senior Researcher at Human Rights Watch[7]

Some experts indicate the risk that after running away from homes, young girls could fall into the hands of human traffickers and end up in sex industries in other countries.

Women Victim's Access to Justice

The women victims of violence face different challenges in accessing justice due to several factors. Majority of women do not report their situation to law enforcement and judicial institutions due to cultural restraints, social norms and taboos, customary and religious beliefs relegating women to subordinate position, fear of social stigma, exclusion and at times even threat to life. Eventually, many cases of violence against women remain unreported to the formal law enforcement and justice institutions.

Dominance of Traditional Justice Mechanisms

In major parts of Afghanistan, particularly the south-east, south and eastern parts, traditional justice mechanisms are excessively entrenched. In most rural communities, issues are resolved through customary law carried out by elites and elders. Complaining to formal government institutions is considered shameful and taints a family's dignity.

Even local authorities, including professional prosecutors and judges, refer a majority of women's violence cases to local committees. The elders decide not only the cases but also influence what reaches higher levels of the legal system, meaning that some cases are never officially registered.

In Daikundi province, a man stabbed his sister-in-law multiple times. The victim survived and police arrested the alleged perpetrator. The case was resolved by community elders who advised the man not to bother the woman further. There was no jail time.[8]

Law Enforcers' Discriminatory Attitudes and Low Priority

The law enforcing authorities sometimes do not take violence against women cases seriously and act on them very slowly. Many officials consider cases of violence against women a family matter and prefer that they be dealt with at the family and community level.

> "During the holy month of Ramadan, a woman reported to a police station claiming that her husband had beaten her and broken her tooth because she had mistakenly put some extra salt in the food. Instead of taking legal action, the policeman mocked: 'now this is also violence against women … some NGO people will show up soon to help her.'" (A female defence lawyer in Kabul, Binafsha Ameeri.)[9]
>
> "Police behaviour could be the manifestation of social perception and attitudes towards women, because they come from the same society; there is need to change perceptions, which takes ages." (The Head of Human Rights and Gender Department of Kabul Police, Samanwal Saifuddin Wafa.)[10]

Similarly, United Nations Assistance Mission in Afghanistan (UNAMA) in its report[11] refers to an interview with a prosecutor in Maimana that he believed empowering women led to more divorces. The report quoting him says, "Women also tended to misuse the law to their advantage, and that the law does not provide protection for men who were mistreated by women."

Consequently, the issue of violence against women in Afghanistan requires further political commitment, increased mobilisation and constant awareness raising among the communities against the harmful traditional practices, effective implementation of the state laws and ensuring women's access to justice in every nook and corner of Afghanistan.

Notes

1. Sayeda Mojgan Mostafavi, Interview with Deputy Minister for Women Affairs, January 2013.
2. UNAMA Report: "Still a Long Way to Go: Implementation of the Law on Elimination of Violence against Women in Afghanistan," p. 17.
3. This information is based on discussions with the representatives of these organisations in separate meetings.
4. Afghanistan: Rights at Risk as Military Drawdown Advances. http://www.hrw.org/news/2013/02/01/afghanistan-rights-risk-military-drawdown-advances

5. Afghanistan: Rights at Risk as Military Drawdown Advances. http://www.hrw.org/news/2013/02/01/afghanistan-rights-risk-military-drawdown-advances
6. The definition of patterns, types and trend of harmful traditional practices has been derived from United Nations Assistance Mission Report "Harmful Traditional Practices and Implementation of Law on Elimination of Violence against Women in Afghanistan," December 9, 2010.
7. Interviewed by author.
8. This has been quoted from author's article for UN Newspaper in Afghanistan "Caught Between Modern Law and Tradition," issue 1 (2012).
9. Interviewed by the author.
10. Interviewed by the author.
11. Still a Long Way to Go: Implementation of the Law on Elimination of Violence against Women in Afghanistan, December 2012.

13. Media's Image Management as a Mechanism of Expansion of Cross-cultural Interaction of India and China with Tajikistan

Dmitry E. Nikolaev

Introduction

In the contemporary period, in every society there is a problem of finding a balance between two mutually exclusive directions of development. The first direction is caused by the participation of the majority of states in the global integration process and involves the influence of interacting cultures. The second direction aims at the preservation of one's own cultural and civilisational identity, customs and traditions.

An additional factor that complicates the search for the optimal balance between the openness of the country and its insularity is the tendency of people to engage more and more in cross-cultural interaction. In cultural interaction, not only are government officials involved but also society as a whole. The extent of such participation is clearly growing.

In these circumstances, the state and the active social groups (in business, media, culture) can either keep themselves aloof, allowing cultural integration to take place spontaneously and uncontrollably, or conversely can try to control such processes. Spontaneous integration shows lack of balance between openness and insularity of a society. At the same time, there are unimagined consequences for "small" cultures that have a risk of being assimilated by the more powerful ones. The unmanaged intercultural interaction carries a risk of inter-ethnic, inter-religious and inter-cultural conflicts.

From our perspective, the integration processes can be really effective if they are predictable and manageable to some extent. And the efficiency of prediction and control depends on the adequacy of the monitoring of the dynamics of cultural and information space (in other words, in order to effectively make changes in any system, it would be useful to have some ideas about its current state).

In this paper we briefly describe the main ideas which reflect a possible approach to dealing with media images based on the images of the two leading Asian powers—China and India, as they are presented in the mainstream media of a small Asian country, i.e., the Republic of Tajikistan, which has just made a mark in global processes.

In order to avoid different interpretations of key terms, we will specify how they have been used in this paper.

The image which is assessed is a fictitious set of characteristics about a particular object that is formed in the mind. This set of characteristics with respect to a country can be formed under the influence of impressions after visiting the country and also after communicating with its citizens, under the influence of fiction and non-fiction literature and under the influence of the views of other persons. Media also has serious impact on the image of the country due to the fact that they largely shape the information space around us. The information space is part of the reality within which information circulates. The difference between the information space and other forms of social space is that the rise and development of the information space are entirely related to information exchange between the social actors.

Media reports often contain evaluation features of a described object. For example, the article may contain some words of admiration for the values of the country or may have some derogatory epithets. The total evaluative background of the article is generated under the influence of these characteristics. The evaluative background of the article determines the positive or negative portrayal of the object in the text.

For a detailed analysis of the text it seems important to take into consideration the so-called secondary meanings of words used by the authors of the articles. The secondary meaning of the word is: (1) an additional, not relevant in the current context, and often refers to an ambiguous word; (2) a meaning of a homonym to a given word.

Methodology

The primary method of research we have chosen here is the content analysis. At the same time we have used a quantitative version of the content analysis (focused on the frequency of appearance in the text of certain characteristics (variables of content) and qualitative version (which allows us to make the conclusions based on only the presence or absence of certain characteristics).

Thus, we have identified the main topics, in connection with the case studies mentioned here, i.e., India and China. We have allocated 17 such topics. In our opinion, there is a good description of the themes in relation to India and China in the Tajik media.

For a more in-depth study of context, which refers to India and China, we picked out the secondary meanings of linguistic units used by journalists to describe these two countries. Analysis of the frequencies of the selected secondary meaning gave us the possibility to identify the main topics not directly related to the factual content of the article, but which can be perceived by readers. We relied on the research of psychologists who have demonstrated the significant effect of secondary meanings on the images that have been formed during the perception of the text by the reader.

In our research we analysed the publication in nine leading media of Tajikistan (in Russian language) for the period January 1-December 31, 2012, in which India and/or China has been mentioned.

Media List

1. "Asia-Plus"—an independent news agency and a newspaper.
2. *Khovar*—the state national news agency.
3. *Nezavisimoyemnenie*—an independent news aggregator.
4. *Avesta*—an independent news agency.
5. *Pressa.tj*—an independent website that publishes the content of *Tojikiston*, "Crime-Info," *Oila* newspapers.
6. "Business and Politics"—an independent information resource and a newspaper.
7. *Vecherka*—an independent newspaper.
8. *Vecherniy Dushanbe*—an independent newspaper.
9. "News Digest"—an independent newspaper.

Results

General Data

We analysed 1,194 articles in which India and/or China were mentioned. China was mentioned in 1,022 articles, India was mentioned in 274 articles. In 102 articles there was reference to both countries.

Diagram 1. The ratio of the number of articles that mention China and India

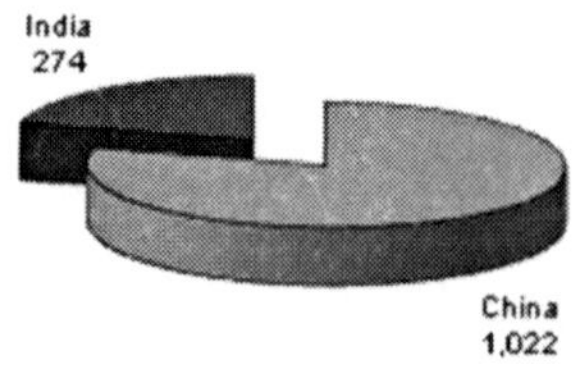

However, there were only 163 articles in which the main theme was China, and 27 articles where the main theme was India (15.95% and 9.85% respectively).

Diagram 2. The articles in which with China is connected the main or a secondary theme, %

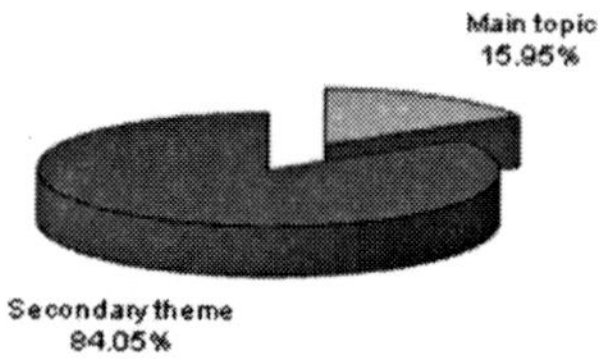

Diagram 3. The articles in which with India is connected the main or a secondary theme, %

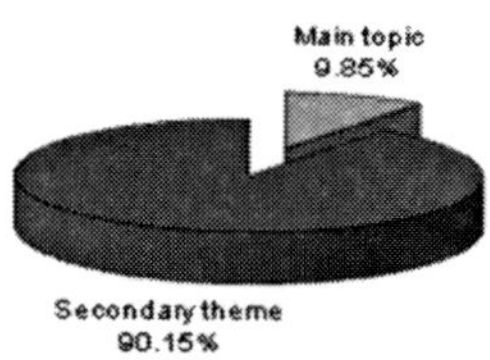

The total number of mentions is 2,884 for China and 593 for India.

Diagram 4. The ratio of mentions of China and India

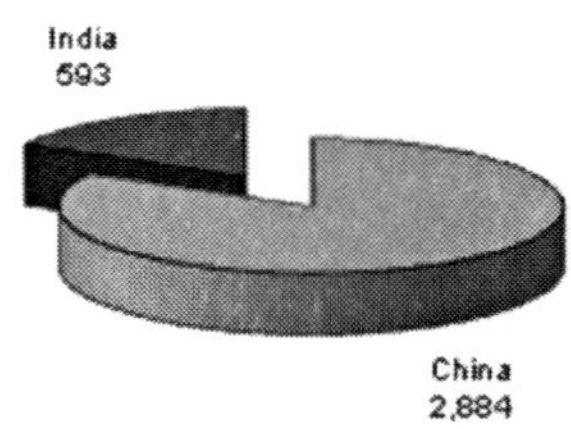

Around 85.80% of references to China and India do not carry the obvious emotional colouring, and 5.04% of mentions are accompanied by pronounced positive assessment, 9.15% by negative.

Diagram 5. The evaluative background of mentions of India and China

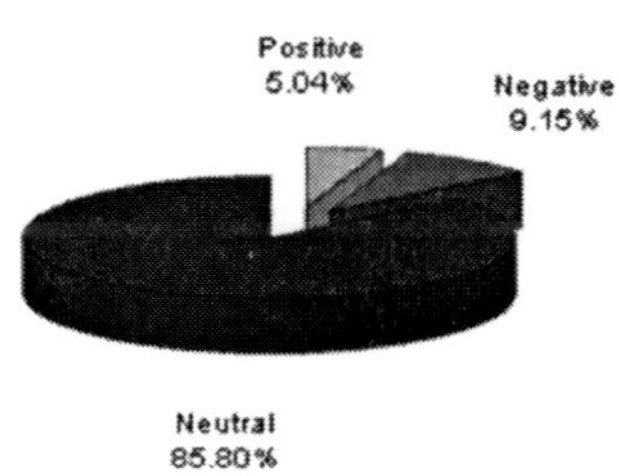

There are statistical differences between the evaluative background of China and India as mentioned categories. In the case of China, the positive references are 5.97%, negative references almost twice as much, i.e., 10.57%.

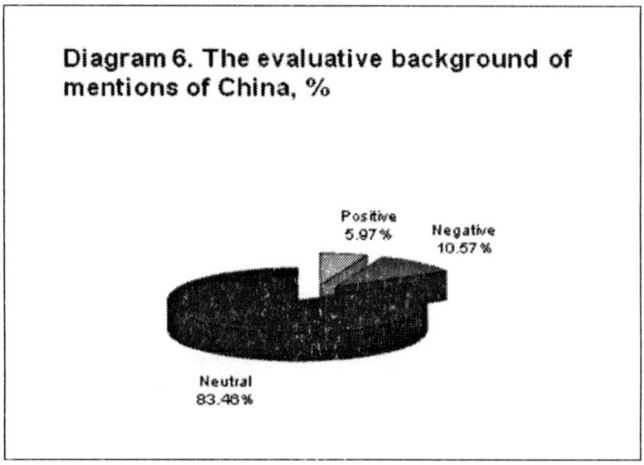

For India, the corresponding figures were 1.50% and 3.75% respectively.

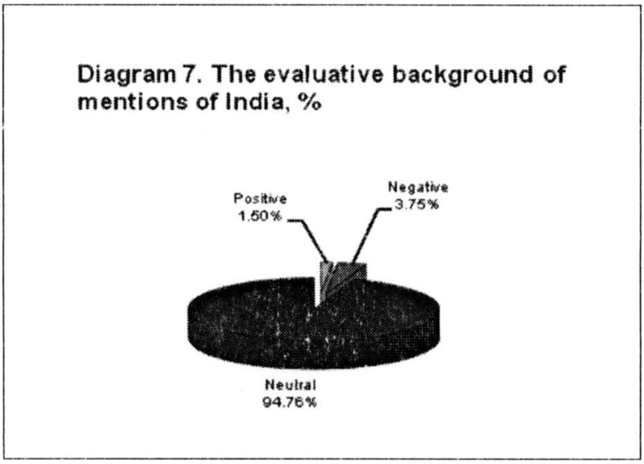

China

The main theme of the publications that mention China in the Tajik media is that of bilateral economic cooperation (35.4% of total mentions). China's soft loans and China's investment in major projects, especially in infrastructure (roads, tunnels, power plants, etc.) are main subjects of discussion.

Rarely is China mentioned in the statistics (e.g., background information and the ratings, number of Internet users or world ranking in terms of press freedom) and in relation to sports (14.74% and 12.30% respectively).

Diagram 8. The themes of mentions of China

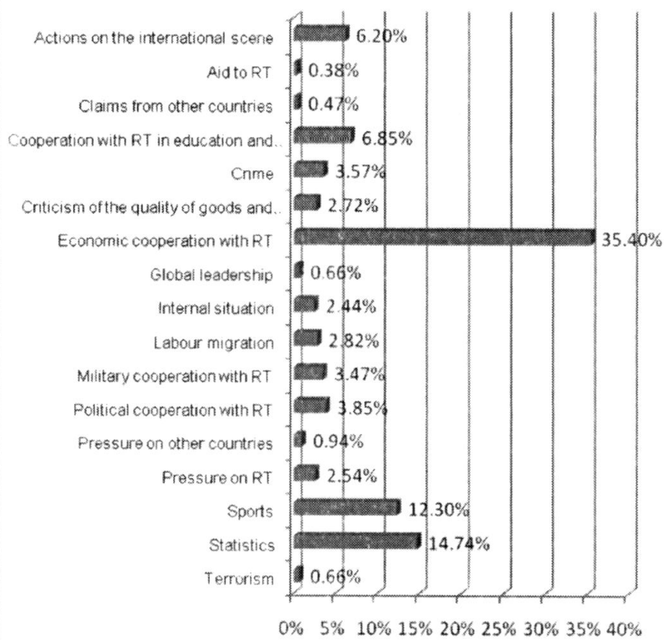

The theme of bilateral cooperation in the fields of education and culture is placed in the fourth position (6.85%). Most articles on this topic describe Tajik students being educated in Chinese universities. Also joint cultural projects are mentioned.

Discussion of China's actions on the international stage, not directly related to Tajikistan (6.2%) comes in the fifth place. Most of the articles are devoted to the analysis of contradictions between China and the United States on the main themes with global attention, i.e., the Iranian and North Korean nuclear programmes, the situatio n in Syria, etc. Significant is the discussion about underlying tension between China and Russia in the Central Asian region.

Not much attention is given to the political cooperation between Tajikistan and China (only 3.85%). In this case, the theme is reduced mainly to statements of high-level talks, rhetorical statements about mutual trust and strategic partnership.

The theme of crime acquires the seventh position (i.e., 3.57%). Here two themes are mostly discussed—the fact of abduction of Chinese businessmen in Tajikistan, as well as fraudulent measures by the Chinese, from which employees of joint factories suffered. Despite the fact that the Central Asia is a leader in the Eurasian region in the production of drugs, the drug topic is mentioned only in reports of the round tables with the participation of anti-drug agencies from different countries.

The mentioned percentage (3.47%) is followed by a discussion of military cooperation with Tajikistan within the framework of the SCO. One of the most pressing issues for the media in Tajikistan is the topic of labour migration. However, in most cases the discussion of this topic involves only Russia and Kazakhstan. Therefore in our study only a 2.82% percentage that mentions of China is related to this topic.

The issue of quality of Chinese goods and services is in the tenth place in terms of the frequency of discussion (i.e., 2.72%). A wide range of items—from pens to transplantation surgery is criticised. In 2.54% of cases, the Chinese publications hardly mention the political and economic pressure from China on Tajikistan. They discuss the factual details amounting to this pressure (e.g., transfer to China of the large part of Tajikistan's territory) and hypothetical threats which are growing proportionally to the financial debt.

Only 2.44% of the discussions are related to various aspects of the domestic situation in China (politics, social condition, etc). Less than 1% is on themes like the pressure of China on other countries (especially on Tajikistan's neighbours in the region—which is 0.94%), the issue of terrorism, the dominance of China in the world's economy and politics (each at the rate of 0.66%), claims by other countries on China (of about 0.47%), as well as the provision of grant aid to Tajikistan (0.38%).

India

In the case of India, the distribution by the number of mentions is of a fundamentally different nature. Here there is clearly no single dominant context.

Of the mentions 20.81% are connected with statistics and ratings. The authors have noted India's position in the rankings of the population, the level of welfare of the inhabitants, the level of Internet censorship. It can be seen that the journalists' attention to sports was almost the same (i.e., 20.19%).

Slightly behind the above category come the topics of bilateral cooperation in the field of education and culture (i.e., 18.32%) and economics (i.e., 16.77%). In journalists' perceptions, bilateral cultural interaction basically consists of international celebrations of Nowruz and of the participation of Tajik actors and directors in film festivals held in India. Interaction in the economic sphere is often discussed in the context of India's plans to participate in the projects of modernisation and construction of hydropower plants in Tajikistan.

Diagram 9. The themes of mentions of India

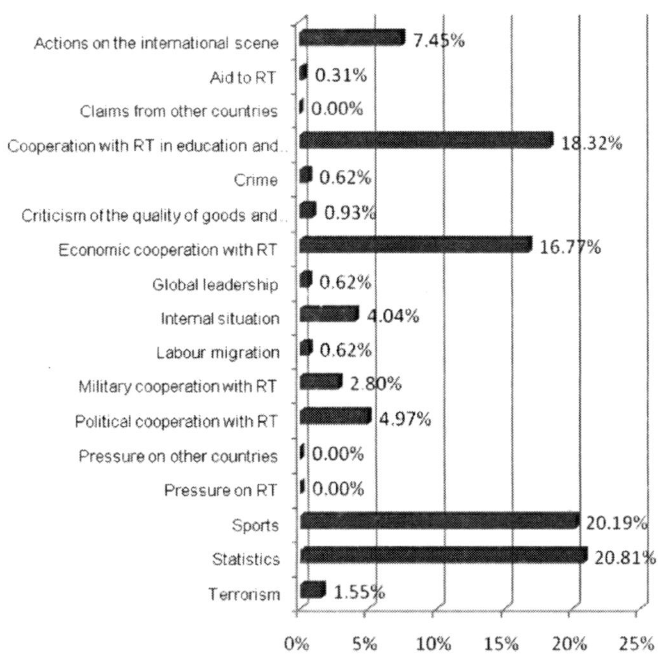

Much less attention (7.45% of total mentions) is paid to the descriptions of India's actions in the international arena, not directly related to Tajikistan. For example, a lot was said about the consistency of India's foreign policy towards the United States.

Of the references 4.97% are related to the description of the political cooperation between the two countries, India and Tajikistan. First of all, we mean here the publications of the official press releases, communiqués and statements after the talks and summits. Fewer mentions (4.04%) refer to discussions of the internal situation in India. And the greatest attention here is paid to road and rail disasters, crimes against sexual integrity, and so on.

The theme of military cooperation with Tajikistan accompanies 2.80% of mentions of India in the studied media. The Indian interest in the reconstruction of the Aini military airfield and the potential possibility for a similar reconstruction of the airfield in Farkhor are often discussed. The problem of terrorism (1.55%) is discussed from the standpoint of regional threats posed by religious terrorist organisations, which is a common worry for both India and Tajikistan.

A number of topics in the research study are related to isolated cases. These topics include, for example, the critical approach to Indian goods and services (0.93%). Criticism here is of non-specific nature. Cheap Indian goods as well as the Chinese and Turkish goods are opposed in comparison to high-quality European and American ones. The theme of crime (0.62%) in Tajik press is in no way linked to the bilateral relations—it is a more global issue. Also the topics of labour migration (0.62%), India's leading position in the world (0.62%), India's assistance to Tajikistan (0.31%) in various international programmes find rare mention.

Such topics as the India pressure on Tajikistan and on other countries as well as claims to India from other countries are not present in the material under study. It is also necessary to note the complete absence of articles on the history of China and India, on the mentality of their citizens, as well as the almost non-existent material on the cultural features in India and China (maybe there is only one study on either country).

Analysis of Secondary Meanings

Analysing secondary meanings of linguistic units used in the descriptions of India and China, which are not directly related to the factual content of the article can have an additional impact on the reader. The following results were obtained:

1. In describing the interaction between Tajikistan and India, journalists show the past matters more. Similar is the frequency in describing the interaction between Tajikistan and China. Also they predict that the future lies with China. Thus, in the case of China, we can speak about some kind of a balance—they associate with China not only the past but also the future. But with regard to India the future orientation looks rather thin.
2. The descriptions of the interaction between Tajikistan and China in the Tajik press are usually accompanied by a discussion of very specific fields and objects of interaction. The descriptions of the relationship with India are often vague and are described in rather general terms.

3. The mentions of India usually relate to competition. In the case of China the competitive profile is significantly less.
4. The descriptions of the relationship with China are usually accompanied by doubt, sometimes by risk. This is not a typical description in the case of India.
5. One of the most significant topics that accompany the mention of China in the sources is the ever-increasing theme of growth. This topic is not so relevant for India.
6. The mentions of India are often accompanied by characteristics of originality, individuality, uniqueness. In the case of China this trend is not seen.
7. In the case of China there is focus on the creation of tangible and intangible objects from zero level. For India the typical focus is on the development and modernisation of what already exists.

Discussion

The results of the study show that the images of India and China in the media of the Republic of Tajikistan firstly, are spontaneously formed, and secondly, are lopsided and often erroneous. Thus, the image of China as a country that pursues in Tajikistan only its own economic interests, the presence of topics connected with the criminal record in Chinese business naturally raise many doubts and fears about the success of bilateral cooperation. The Chinese are desirous of economic success, concrete and businesslike mentality, intent to build infrastructure in Tajikistan by themselves, using their own equipment and at their own expense. In the eyes of Tajiks, their actions tend to validate such fears in the society.

Generally speaking the image of India is quite blurred and unstable. Against the background of the presence of India in the information space, the prospects of bilateral cooperation are limited to several projects in the field of hydropower, the potential presence in Tajikistan of the Indian Air Force group and joint participation in the celebration of religious holidays and festivals.

Unfortunately we can state that only a very small portion of the examined 1,194 articles may give the readers some information about the culture, traditions, way of life and mentality of the peoples of India and China. A considerable amount of material is devoted to the tragic accidents and incidents that have occurred in these countries.

Undoubtedly, the overwhelming dominance of the official information in the materials on India and China cannot be justified by the features of the examined media. The reason rather lies in the absence of other newsmakers and events connected with these two countries. In the media that is examined here, which is formally political and social, considerable space is allocated for regular interviews with scientific and cultural personalities, for discussing actual social, domestic, and religious issues. Even fragments from prose and poetry are published there. However, India and China are too often referred in the texts of official communiqués and press releases, which are hardly read until the end by the majority of readers.

Can this situation suit India and China? Yes, it can. It is possible that self-removal from the targeted formation of image of the country is voluntary and has good reasons.

However, in our view, this strategy is not effective. Mutual incomprehension and hostility can be a major obstacle to the integration of different levels—from the individual level to the level of the state. As a result, various spheres of cooperation can suffer—from the economic sphere to cultural exchange and environmental protection measures. For China, it will also affect the quality of life of tens of thousands of migrants working in Tajikistan.

The filling of the information area of Tajikistan can be offered as the primary method of adjusting and supplementing the media images of the two countries. This on the one hand, must demonstrate openness and attractiveness of the Indian and Chinese cultures, and on the other it must use very available and easily understood forms of presentation.

For this purpose it is advisable to establish the extensive information involving different sectors of society. The most actively used areas are those in which India and China are the leaders in Asia, and perhaps in the world. For example, modern and traditional medicine, health practices, education, science, modern technology, tea culture, traditional cuisine, etc. Research carried out by us in Russia, shows that among the materials published in the media, those of them are in demand for most readers that contain information to enable the reader to solve an actual problem for him. In our view, this strategy will be successful in Tajikistan too. Materials that prove to be options in India and China are solutions to the urgent problems of Tajikistan (eradication of poverty, improvement of public education, access to quality healthcare, development of agriculture in challenging conditions, methods of prevention and settlement of inter-religious and inter-clan conflicts, the fight against extremist religious movements and so on) will undoubtedly attract the attention of readers. From our point of view, the solutions to these problems are in demand at the state level and also at the levels of the region, municipality and family.

Finally we want to emphasise once again that media images' management with a relatively small financial and organisational cost can significantly improve the effectiveness of intercultural communication, which in its turn will give impetus to the further development of bilateral relations in the humanitarian, economic and political spheres.

Notes

1. A. Iu Agafonov, "Priming effect as a result of the nonconscious activity of consciousness," *Journal of Russian and East European Psychology*, vol. 48, no. 3, 2010, pp. 17-32.
2. J. McGarry and B. O'Leary (eds.), *The politics of ethnic conflict regulation* (London: Routledge, 1993).
3. A. V. Mozolin, *Image analysis methodology and the position of image in the information space* (in Russian), 2004. Retrieved from http://www.rc-analitik.ru/file/%7Bca1dd929-1ac5-46af-bf15-6db844ee7a14%7D

14. The Civilisational Identification and Consolidation of Central Asia in the Cultural Space of the Internet

Aleksey Arapov

The New "Geographical" Space

A rapid development of the Internet as a worldwide network of digital multimedia resources has been a general global trend of the first decade of the twenty-first century. Based on this "web" of computer and mobile communications a virtual world originated through modern digital formats accelerating educational, media, games, culture and business processes. At its core, the Internet is a new "geographical" area of human development. Throughout the world development of Internet technology appears as a factor increasing the efficiency and competitiveness of individual countries, communities, individuals in business, education, science and culture. The number of Internet users worldwide has exceeded 2.5 billion (more than 36% of the world population) and continues to grow steadily. It is important that at the same time "life" spent by people in this virtual world has been constantly increasing.[1] Internet reloads the very principles of working with information. In the place of the passive, the viewing formats of media and marketing, new active network formats come into being with reverse Internet communications, crowd sourcing and decentralisation of information flows. This, in turn, dramatically changes the model of such basic information resources as a book, library, museum, television, social and business advertising.

From the time the printed book emerged in China, at the beginning of the eleventh century, and laborious handwritten books were replaced, the availability of text information and the number of readers have increased enormously. Beginning from the 1990s e-books became the standard, where text and illustrations lost their physical form and were embodied in a digital file. A great volume of book publications, accumulated for centuries, has been digitised for three decades, and thanks to the Internet, finds universal access. Such notions as a rare book and number of published copies, etc., lose their habitual meanings. New books, newspapers, magazines[2] and textbooks are already being created in digital format, and a tablet has come to replace books in students' schoolbags. High speed and efficiency of communication on the Internet has launched a process of global transfer of public services, business, education, media, entertainment, and others into the virtual world. It is now accepted that whatever is not represented on the Internet does not exist. Possessing strategic opportunities and prospects the Internet becomes an arena for business and cultural rivalries, and even information wars in the new digital format.

Internet as a Cultural Space

Nowadays every culture, every ethnic community is facing the challenge of presenting itself online. For cultural self-sufficiency, it is no longer enough to have geographic, political, linguistic isolation. The main thing now is a willingness to withstand open civilisational competition of ideas, values, and images. Thus, despite the dominance in the Internet of the most widely spoken languages, such as English and Chinese, Spanish and Portuguese, Arabic, German, Russian and French, the growth of opportunities for robot translators such as Bing and Google Translator has increased thereby removing language restrictions in the perception of information. So Eastern language speakers have access to messages in the Western languages, and vice versa.

The global nature of the Internet is forming a new cultural type of a human—*Homo Interneticus*. This is a pro-Western type, whose norm is a multicultural environment, an unlimited number of communications, anonymity of contacts, the use of "masks," access to taboo topics of the real society. The Orient has not yet given adequate answers to the technological challenges of the Internet as a product of Western culture. If a symbol of cultural threats to the East in the middle of the twentieth century was "House of Gandhi,"[3] where "the winds of other cultures broke into its windows and doors," now in connection with the Internet, this symbol is "House of Nasreddin,"[4] which generally "has no walls and roof, and there is only the door."

While Asian cultures are still slowly deploying themselves in the Internet and are inferior in scale to that in North America and Europe, the West manages to culturally intercept online a significant part of Asian youth.

But the East, having a large-scale human resource and deep humanitarian civilised worlds such as China, India, Iran, Central Asia, the Arab East, is able to take the initiative in cultural influence on the Internet. It is thanks to the openness and ubiquity of the Internet that for the first time, there appears a possibility of civilisational expansion in the world of ideas, holistic doctrines, art, music codes of the East, which until now have been closed within the borders of their cultures. In this article the subject of our interest is Central Asia, the ancient historical and cultural region in the centre of Eurasia, the modern "kernel" of which is formed by a group of post-Soviet countries and Afghanistan.

The Historical and Cultural Importance of Central Asia

The very characteristics of the "central" reflects the location of the region between the most important historical and cultural territories of Asia, in the north-west—Russia (Russia) and Eastern Europe, to the west—Iran (Persia), Mesopotamia, Iraq, the Caucasus, in the south, south-east—Hindustan and Tibet, in the east—Mongolia and China. Hence the status of Central Asia as a major economic crossroads of Asia, a key node of the continental trade routes including the strategic Silk Road. Throughout ancient and medieval history, from the first century BC, the lands of Central Asia were consolidated under large powers: the ancient Bactria, Khorezm and the Greco-Bactrian kingdoms, and the Parthian, Kushan Empire, Turkic khanate, powers of the Samanids and Ghaznavids, Karakhanids, Seljuks and Khorezm, Kara-Khitays and Chengizids and Temurids, Sheibanids and Astarkhanids. That is where the common cultural roots and civilisational unity of the peoples of the region, who today number more than 100 million people, is situated.

The crossing of paths and high intensity of trade through Central Asia in ancient times and in the Middle Ages, as well as the association with a diversity of political and cultural contacts have created the conditions for interaction and mutual influence of neighbouring civilisations, and provided conditions to form their own civilisational traditions in Central Asia. Because of the geographical features, the region's major vectors of external influences during the ancient and medieval history was "Western" (from Persia), embodied in the early Persian Achaemenid culture, Hellenism, Middle Ages Persian Sassanid Zoroastrian culture, the Arab-Muslim culture, and "Eastern"—(through Altai and north-western China)—early Chinese of the Han Empire, Huns of the Tang Empire, Kara-Khitays and Mongols. The

"Southern" (Indian) vector of influence was particularly strong in the periods of the Greco-Indian kingdoms of Kushan Empire, the Delhi Sultanate and the Mughal power (Baburids). The main feature of the civilisation of Central Asia was its historical mission of a mediator between the neighbouring civilisations of Asia and Eastern Europe. We have to remember that through Central Asia Chinese silk and Indian figures came to Europe.

Geo-cultural Location of Central Asia in the beginning of the Twentieth and Twenty-first Centuries

Cultural processes in this eastern area in the eighteenth to twentieth centuries were severely influenced by external factors related to the "Great Game." At the end of the first half of the nineteenth and twentieth centuries as a result of geopolitical confrontation between Russia (and its successor in 1920-1980—the Soviet Union), the United Kingdom and China, Central Asia, with the exception of Afghanistan, almost lost its state form. On the territory of Central Asia and Kazakhstan there were established national republics of the Soviet Union, in East Turkestan—there was formed Xinjiang Uygur Autonomous Region of China. In the second half of the twentieth century, the place of Great Britain in the geopolitical rivalry was taken by the United States of America. One of the consequences of confrontation with the Soviet Union from the late 1970s was transformation of Afghanistan in the arena of continuous hostilities that led to the death of a civil state.

The fall of the "Iron Curtain" after the collapse of the Soviet Union in 1991 led to the formation of independent post-Soviet states: Kazakhstan, Kyrgyzstan, Tajikistan, Turkmenistan and Uzbekistan. For the past years these countries have been experiencing an intense process of historical and cultural identity of the Kazakhs, Kyrgyz, Tajiks, Turkmens and Uzbeks, who became titular nations of their states. This aggravates further cultural separation of the peoples of this part of Central Asia, started in the years 1924-1929 by Soviet national cultural disengagement in Central Asia and Kazakhstan. At the beginning of the twenty-first century the troops of the coalition of religious orthodoxy of the Taliban were defeated and Afghanistan restored to its state status, thus acquiring new potential for national-cultural development. The main point there is to develop ideas and formats for cultural unity of the Afghan people: Pashtuns, Tajiks, Uzbeks, Hazaras, etc.

The revival of independent national states in the region, despite its multi-statehood gives Central Asia a chance to not only manifest itself once again as a subject of international relations, but also update its general civilisational self. The factors working for cultural unity are the millennium long coexistence of Farsi and Turkic language traditions, common field of musical rhythms, craft ornaments, traditional architectural forms, and ritual formats of urban and rural communities. We have to note here that, due to the historical realities of the post-Soviet states, and despite the presence of their national languages : Uzbek, Tajik, Turkmen, Kazakh, Kyrgyz, Karakalpakstan and other languages, in the area of inter-regional (inter-ethnic) communication, Russian is still broadly used. This is why these countries appear in within the sphere of influence of the Russian-speaking Internet. The Internet in Afghanistan is largely in the English-speaking space. Labour migrants in Russia from Uzbekistan, Tajikistan and Kyrgyzstan, as well as migrants and refugees from Afghanistan to the United States and Europe become mediators of new features, and in particular, the conductors of Internet communications in their countries.

The Balance of Secular and Islamic Cultures in Central Asia at the Beginning of the Twenty-first Century

An important factor in the historical and cultural integrity of the region in medieval, modern and contemporary history is its Islamic confessional unity with the dominant Sunni Hanafi tradition and the rule of law.[5] In this aspect, Central Asia manifests itself as the eastern "island" of Sunni Islamic tradition, separated from the western territories by Shi'ite Iran, which borders to the east the Buddhist cultural tradition, the north—Christianity, the south—Hindu cults.[6] With its different ethnic and cultural traditions and its contribution to cultural development, the region can be compared with the Arab world. It is important to mention the contribution of Central Asian spiritual persons in Hadith study (Imam al-Bukhari, Muhammad al-Termezi, Abu Dawud al-Sistani), Sufism ('Abd al-Khaliq Gijduvani, Najm al-Din Kubra Ahmad Yassavi, Bahuddin Naqshband, Hodge Ahrar), Islamic science (al-Khwarizmi, al-Ferghani, al-Farabi, Biruni, Ibn Sina, Gias al-Din al-Kashi, Ulugbek, Ali Kushchi), Islamic poetry (Ferdowsi, Jami, Navoi).

From the time of Takhirids and Samanids Central Asia had common Islamic centres of higher education, where in the Middle Ages the most outstanding position was occupied by Bukhara (its value was retained until the twentieth century). What matters is the fact that the region, starting with the tenth to the thirteenth centuries was the historic centre for the spread of Sufism and Sufi tarikats and part of those communities ("Nakshbandiya," "Nakshbandiya-Mudzhaddiya," "Suhrawardiyya") retained some influence on the traditional Muslim communities (especially in Afghanistan). The generality of these spiritual principles found expression in the unity of forms and traditions of Islamic architecture, to the mosques, caravanserais and mausoleums of Samarkand, Bukhara, Merv, Balkh, Herat, Termez, Tashkent, Kokand, Kabul, Khiva and other cities in the region built on common canons. With all the depth of the Islamic origin in Central Asia region there has been a historically stable secular form of the government, as well as secular forms of Islamic culture.[7] This is also a favourable factor for spreading the Internet as a medium of open, secular communications with no denominational restrictions.

Central Asia Online

The reality of the historical fate, technical and cultural processes in specific countries reflects their involvement in the space of the Internet. According to public data the Internet coverage in modern Central Asia is already relatively high, more than 30 million people (more than 30%), with the dominance of the output to Internet resources via mobile phones. The coverage figures are quite different for specific countries of the region: the maximum numbers are in Kazakhstan and Kyrgyzstan—more than 60%, average—30-50% in Uzbekistan and Tajikistan, the lowest—5-10% for Afghanistan and Turkmenistan.[8] The scenario for the online process here with some delay should follow the global trends, including crucial in the recent years building of a global social networking (Web 2.0), such as Facebook, Google+, YouTube, Twitter, and Wikipedia.

The leading network of Facebook (FB) already covers more than 1.1 billion people or approx. 16% of the world population. There are about 1.7 million people (1.5%) in Central Asia in FB, i.e., it lags behind world standards from countries such as the US (58%) and Turkey (52%)—in the three dozen times. The number of Facebook users at the beginning of August 2013 in the countries of Central Asia is presented in the table below:

	Country	Number of Facebook users, thousand people	% of the population
1.	Afghanistan	600	1.69%
2.	Kazakhstan	660	4.00%
3.	Kyrgyzstan	152	2.76%
4.	Tajikistan	60	0.86%
5.	Turkmenistan	11	0.22%
6.	Uzbekistan	240	0.80%
	Total:	1,723	1.69%

Source: Open analytical data of Facebook, currently being researched by the author.

This data certifies that the processes of online socialisation here is just beginning and FB involvement noticeably inferior to neighbour countries such as Iran (20%) and Pakistan (4.6%).[9]

Cultural Self-identification of Central Asia Online

A user's activity in the network starts with self-identification on a "friend or foe" principle, leading to the inclusion in one and disconnection from the other through links and information flows. Thus commences the cultural and ethno-cultural filtering, selection and protection of the environment with familiar ideals and values of the historical and cultural heritage. In FB format this occurs by subscription to themed pages or entry into communities of particular interests. Undoubtedly so far a dominating idea for most people is identification with the culture of their own country. In Iran, in this regard, we note the activity of the pages in FB as "Explore the beauty of Iran" (21 thousand, 10.12[10]), "Iran Art & Architecture" (33.8 thousand, 09.11), "Iran Archaeology" (8.8 thousand, 07.10), Pakistan—"Explore the beauty of Pakistan" (160 thousand in 2012), "Pakistan Art & Architecture" (15.9 thousand, 01.12). In Afghanistan, a similar activity was recorded with the establishment of such pages as "Afghanistan In Photos" (44.7 thousand, 02.12), "My Afghanistan Best At All" (54.6 thousand, 02.11), "Afghan Culture" (114 thousand, 02.10). In the post-Soviet countries in the region that process does not have the sufficiently large scale, but it is possible to note the emergence of such FB groups as "Welcome to Uzbekistan" (20 thousand), "I love Uzbekistan" (10 thousand) and "UzNetwork" (9 thousand).

The First Experience of Consolidation of Central Asia in the Social Networks of the Internet

Internet users in the Central Asian countries perceive with interest each other's information and cultural flows of regional importance. Such resources as the FB page "Central Asia" (6.3 thousand, 09.10) and the group "Central Asia Today" (4.7 thousand, 02.13) may be presented as a proof of this. The factors for regional cultural consolidation are the commonness of the architectural landscape of Islamic architecture, the Sunni tradition of Islam, which explains popularity of such FB sites as "Islamic Heritage" (10.5 thousand, 03.11) and "Islam Art & Architecture" (26.9 thousand, 12.09). A network of online community is like a virtual "city," i.e., here for cultural consolidation there will be needed experience, image, the semantics of an ideal type of a city, which this community presents. The West states its standards, the East—has the right for its own. The historical experience of Central Asia may claim for such a "virtual building" mental traditions and common forms of a City, expressed at the time by Al- Farabi, the Sufi brotherhoods, Alisher Navoi, etc.

The Project "Marakanda"

Indicative are the results of the construction of such a "city" in the FB in the frames of the project "Marakanda," virtually realising general interest in the history and culture of Central Asia.[11] For a year since August 2012 two parallel FB pages in Russian and English languages have been operating (www.facebook.com/Marakanda.ru and www.facebook.com/Marakanda.net), with total coverage of about 7.3 million people. The basis of the audience of "Marakanda" is made of young and middle age people: 18-24 years—17%, 25-34 years—32%, 35-44 years—23 %. At the second step, i.e., through friends of fans, "Marakanda" messages in FB reach 1.8 million people.

Foremost among the two-and-a-half thousand publications in "Marakanda" have been visual material presenting Afghanistan, Kazakhstan, Kyrgyzstan, Tajikistan, Turkmenistan and Uzbekistan, complemented by publications from the neighbouring countries: Iran, Pakistan, India and China. Positive ratings ("like"), comments and republishing show that subscribers of "Marakanda" have a sense of cultural commonality, proximity or even identity in pictorial semantics, traditions, architectural forms, craft aesthetic, musical rhythms. Indicative is a high interest to the pre-Islamic culture, Zoroastrianism, and Iranian Türkic epic, tolerant attitude to the lost Buddhist tradition. The publications and readers' comments in "Marakanda" naturally exhibit a representation of a single body of civilisation in the region, the unity of the historical destiny of the peoples of Central Asia.

"Marakanda" as a virtual "city" becomes a venue for cultural communication, absorbs and ranks visual images, art codes of traditional culture, applied arts, architecture, sacred spaces, houses, creates a new form of society, encourages interest in the new knowledge. Young audience within this Internet project discovers significant, but till date known artistic codes of Central Asia, gives them a high aesthetic and ethical evaluation. An unexpected effect of this cultural project was the fact that, actually, the Central Asians constitute only one-third of the "Marakand people," while the rest of the visitors of the virtual "city" represent external cultural worlds. One-fifth of the audience of "Marakanda" emerged from Russia and the European CIS countries, the same number from the eastern and south-eastern regions of the Islamic world (we note the high level of participation from Turkey and Egypt, Iran and Pakistan), as also from North America and Europe.

This wide range of audiences shows a considerable influence of the "soft power" of Central Asian culture, presents a positive interest and sympathy to it from the external cultures of both East and West and the willingness to "feed on" her images and sympathise with her subjects. General Central Asian angle of perspective, supported by "Marakanda" creates a feeling of civilisational fullness, which, in particular, is very important for the restoring of self-consciousness of Afghanistan destroyed by the war.

Conclusions

It seems that open digital space of the Internet, its social Web 2.0 formats are now becoming one of the resources and tools for the consolidation of a new civilisation in Central Asia, its effective interaction with both post-Soviet cultural space, a modern Euro-American cultural world and the traditional worlds of Asia. The synthesis of Eastern tradition and Western technology can create new and unexpected effects of cultural transformation, similar to those in the twentieth century which gave rise to such phenomena as Indian cinema, Chinese opera, Japanese animation, Uzbek theatre. If the essence of the Western way of progress have been technology parks, a model specified by the California Silicon Valley Technology Park (USA), the asymmetric response of the East may be seen not in the technical but in humanitarian sphere, perhaps—in the form of humanitarian parks of Eastern cultures, including the use of virtual formats offered by the Internet.

Notes

1. In Europe, the average time, which online users spend in this virtual world is more than 1 hour per day.
2. For example, the agency «Tengrinews» in Kazakhstan and the edition «gazeta.uz» in Uzbekistan.
3. The famous saying of Mahatma Gandhi: "I do not want my house to be walled in on all sides and my windows to be stuffed. I want the cultures of all the lands to be blown about my house as freely as possible. But I refuse to be blown off my feet by any."
4. Nasreddin, well-known in different nations of the Middle East as "Hodja Effendi," "Nasreddin Hodja," "Mullah Nasruddin," is the legendary hero of popular instructive parables and funny stories.
5. The local Shi'ite and Ismaili communities in Afghanistan and Tajikistan recognise prevailing significance of Sunnism in Central Asia.
6. In this view, Mongolia with its Buddhist religious tradition is beyond Central Asia and this country should be considered as a frontier region.
7. A. H. Saidov, Y. S. Umansky and A. V. Arapov, The Secular way in the spirit of Islamic Culture: Reflections, Tashkent, 1995 (monograph in Russian).
8. For comparison, Iran and Pakistan coverage of the Internet is 15-20%, Turkey—40%, USA—80%.
9. A small number of users of the FB network in Central Asia is also related to the fact that in this region has enormous influence the Russian social networks such as "Odnoklassniki (Classmates)," "VKontakte" and "Moi Mir (My World)." Thus, in particular, the number of users of the "Odnoklassniki" network in Uzbekistan has exceeded two. In addition the MAIL.RU Group launched version of "Odnoklassniki" in the Uzbek language, which already has 660 thousand users. It is significant that 90% of them are connecting with the "Odnoklassniki" network by mobile phones.
10. Month and year of the opening of the page or community to Facebook.
11. The author of the article is one of the initiators and content editors of this project.

15. The Notion of Siege in Israeli Cinema: "Beaufort" a film by Joseph Cedar

Chana Anzi

Before addressing the theme of my paper which deals with Israeli cinema and the film *Beaufort* as a case study, let me start with an observation. Film, as a composition of various elements (sound, visual, props, lighting, rhythm, etc.) might entail an internal premise which does not give itself easily through literary analysis of characters and plot. The cinematic language, which manipulatively places itself in the background, should be decoded in order to reveal what is subconsciously presented on screen.

The acclaimed film "*Beaufort*" from 2007, directed by Joseph Cedar, portrays the last days of the IDF's (Israel Defense Force) occupation in South Lebanon, which was aborted after eighteen years of holding due to the protest of "Four Mothers" movement to "Leave Lebanon in Peace." The movie which was nominated for the Oscar in 2008 and won several Israeli and international awards follows the story of a young commander Liraz Librati, and his unit posted in the twelfth century Crusader fort *Beaufort* on the verge of the Israeli withdrawal from Lebanon. It chronicles the daily routine of the soldiers, their feelings and fears along with tragic episodes which continuously hit them: the death of Ziv, an engineering corps soldier, while opening access to the post, the deadly mortar shell attack on the Beaufort and the missile that killed Biton in the green post.

The conflict of the film is embodied through representatives of opposite political views; the protagonist and the bereaved father of Ziv, the sacrificed engineering soldier, who is never actually a real figure in the film, but rather an image that the commander Liraz sees on the screen or in a vision. Liraz is a highly motivated commander, who blindly believes in the army and the state. Ziv's father, on the other hand, belongs to the pacifistic "Four Mothers" movement, and did not even know that his son was in Lebanon, he blames himself for not being able to evoke the ideal of the sanctity of life in his son.

Liraz's personal journey is depicted parallel to the developments of the plot, starting out as an ultra-patriotic soldier, who believes in the army and disagrees with the withdrawal from Lebanon (which he blames the four "grandmothers" movement for—this is a derogative terminology), but through the multiple deaths of his subordinates, and several occasions in which he finds himself dysfunctional and even at fault—he goes through a transformation which is hinted gently in the film.

The film leads the viewer from the patriotic and nationalist ideals of warfare, sacrifice and bonding to the land (Liraz claims that he cannot leave the Beaufort Mountain) to the moderate and pacifistic values of sanctity of life. Nevertheless beneath the conflict that the film addresses, lies the Israeli notion of Jewish existence which can be revealed through an analysis of the cinematic ways of expression.

Nitzan Ben-Shaul in his essay "Israeli Persecution Films" (2006) analyses the notion of "Siege" in Israeli Cinema, which he ascribes to the tragic history of the Jews and the Jewish insecurity complex. He reviews three Israeli films from the 1960s to the early 1990s and proposes nine cinematic elements which evoke notions of "Siege": claustrophobia, agoraphobia, violence, threatening encirclement and suspicion.

The nine elements are:

(1) Shadowy patterns of lighting;
(2) Visual and aural configurations composing closed and labyrinthine spatial formations;
(3) Open threatened spaces where there is no refuge;
(4) Unexpected, abrupt editing patterns and camera movements creating violent surprises;
(5) Temporal circular structures whose synchronic framework disjoints their diachrony;
(6) Fatalistic or bounded story structures;
(7) Recurrence of suspicious and violent interactions among characters;
(8) Conspiratorial modes of action;
(9) Thematic and formal isolation of threatened individuals or groups.

In addition, I suggest a few more "Siege" elements that can be seen in *Beaufort*:

(1) The enemy is never seen on screen (just as in a Siege)
(2) Throughout the film it is difficult to differentiate the faces of the soldiers
(3) The film is Monochromatic (sticking to colours of green, gray and black)

Similar cinematic patterns exist in *Beaufort* alongside other elements which contribute to the sensation of Siege in the film. My argument is that although the film is able to shake the Israeli military ideals in the name of human values, it is unable to overcome the "traditional" Israeli notion of "Siege" while dealing with the South Lebanon conflict.

In this paper I tried to show that the cinematic language of *Beaufort* reveals one of the Israeli internal cultural notions which is not apparent in the symbolic reading. It brings to the surface the embedded and probably impossible-to-get-rid-of "Siege" perception which is common among Israeli-Jews.

References

Bar-Tal, D. "The Massada Syndrome: A Case of Central Belief." The International Center for Peace in the Middle East, Discussion Paper 3, May 1984.

Ben-Shaul, N. Israeli Persecution Films. *Traditions in World Cinema.* Edinburgh:Edinburgh University Press, 2006, pp. 160-176.

Globalising Geographies Perspectives from Eurasia

Edited by

Anita Sengupta
Suchandana Chatterjee

Maulana Abul Kalam Azad Institute of Asian Studies
Kolkata

in association with

KNOWLEDGE WORLD

KW Publishers Pvt Ltd
New Delhi

The **Maulana Abul Kalam Azad Institute of Asian Studies** (MAKAIAS) is an autonomous body under the Ministry of Culture, Government of India. It was set up at the joint initiative of the Government of India, Department of Culture, Ministry of Human Resource Development and the Government of West Bengal. Based in Kolkata, it was registered as a Society under the West Bengal Registration of Societies' Act of 1961 on the 4th of January 1993, with Prof. Nurul Hasan, the then Governor of West Bengal, as the President of the Society. It is funded by the Department of Culture, Government of India. Presently, His Excellency, Governor of West Bengal, is the President of the Society.

MAKAIAS is a centre for research and learning with a focus on social cultural, economic and political / administrative developments in Asia from the middle of the 19th Century onwards, with special emphasis on their links with India, and also on the life and works of Maulana Abul Kalam Azad. It operates out of Azad Bhavan in Salt Lake as well as the Maulana Azad Museum located at 5 Ashraf Mistry Lane, Kolkata.

ISBN 978-93-83649-29-7

KNOWLEDGE WORLD

Published in India by

Kalpana Shukla
KW Publishers Pvt Ltd
4676/21, First Floor, Ansari Road, Daryaganj, New Delhi 110002
Phone: +91.11.23263498/43528107
Email: knowledgeworld@vsnl.net • www.kwpub.com

Printed and Bound in India

2011 FPBA BEST PUBLISHERS AWARD (ENGLISH)

CONTENTS

For

Professor Barun De

(1932-2013)

Contributors

Anita Sengupta, Fellow, Maulana Abul Kalam Azad Institute of Asian Studies, Kolkata, India, e-mail: anitasengupta@hotmail.com

Farkhod Tolipov, Director, "Knowledge Caravan," Tashkent, Uzbekistan, e-mail: farkhod_tolipov@yahoo.com

Suchandana Chatterjee, Fellow, Maulana Abul Kalam Azad Institute of Asian Studies, Kolkata, India, e-mail: suchandanachatterjee@hotmail.com

Vladimir A. Lamin, Director, Institute of History Siberian Branch of Russian Academy of Sciences, Novosibirsk, Russia, e-mail: lamin@history.nsc.ru

Yanina A. Kuznetsova, Candidate Science (Hist), Institute of History Siberian Branch of Russian Academy of Sciences, Novosibirsk, Russia, e-mail: scriptor@history.nsc.ru

Dmitry Vladimir Shlapentokh, Associate Professor of History, Indiana University, Indiana, USA, e-mail: dshlapen@iusb.edu

Anar Somuncuoğlu, Lecturer, Hacettepe University, Faculty of Economics and Administrative Sciences, Department of International Relations, Ankara, Turkey, e-mail: anarsomuncuoglu@yahoo.com

Denis Ananyev, Senior Researcher, Institute of History, Siberian Branch of Russian Academy of Sciences, Novosibirsk, Russia,
e-mail: denis.ananyev@gmail.com

Emilian Kavalski, Associate Professor of Global Studies, Australian Catholic University (Sydney), Australia and Book Series Editor of "Rethinking Asia and International Relations,"
e-mail: Emilian.Kavalski@acu.edu.au

Michael Fredholm, Stockholm International Program for Central Asian Studies (SIPCAS),
e-mail: Michael.Fredholm@hotmail.com

Arpita Basu Roy, Fellow, Maulana Abul Kalam Azad Institute of Asian Studies, Kolkata, India, e-mail: basuroyarpita@gmail.com

Alexey Zelenskiy, Docent of Philosophy, Sociology and Political Science, Department of Social and Political Sciences, Kazakh-German University, Almaty, Kazakhstan, e-mail: alzelenskiy@yandex.ru

Diloram Karomat, Fellow, Maulana Abul Kalam Azad Institute of Asian Studies, Kolkata, India, e-mail: dilkaramat@yahoo.com

Sanjay Chaturvedi, Professor of Political Science and Honorary Director, Centre for the Study of Mid-West and Central Asia, Panjab University, Chandigarh, India, e-mail: csgiorg@gmail.com

Introduction: Perspectives on Transformed Geographies in Eurasia

Anita Sengupta

An abiding feature of the modern world is its complex connectivity. This is perhaps best exemplified by the networks of interconnections and interdependences that characterise every aspect of modern social life. It is this connectivity that pervades all accounts of globalisation. Connectivity can be simply taken to imply global-spatial proximity in the sense of the shrinking of distances through the dramatic reduction of time taken to cross them. At another level of analysis connectivity shades into the idea of spatial proximity via the idea of "stretching" of social relations across distance. The discourse on globalisation is replete with metaphors of global proximity of a "shrinking world." The creation of globalised spaces also inevitably implies the creation of a degree of cultural "compression." The resulting de-territorialisation is then taken to fundamentally transform the relationship between the places that one inhabits and cultural practices, experiences and identities.

Yet, paradoxically, this world of expanding de-territorialised boundaries is also a world of many more and, in numerous cases, stronger states. And the politics of identity is, even today, largely determined within the old structure of the state. The extent to which groups have boundaries and conversely the extent to which cultures have borders, in other words, the relationship of culture to territory, remains a significant part of the discourse on identity given the complex ways in which frontiers, even those determined by imperial partitions, continue to influence the determination of cultural identities in regions such as Eurasia. Yet, the question as to whether there is an essential correspondence between territory, nation, state and identity remains unanswered. The cultural permeability of borders, the experience of people who are more comfortable with the notion that they are culturally tied to many other people in neighbouring states and the rigidity of states in their efforts to control cultural fields that transcend their borders demands that a variety of political and cultural boundaries be constructed. In fact the durability of cultural frontiers long after the political borders of the state have shifted implies the widening of perspectives to take note of the formal and the informal ties between local communities and the larger polities of which they are a part.

The Eurasian engagement with geographies of globalisation includes issues such as energy and transportation, management of resources, environment as well as demographic patterns and flows. It would also need to take note of challenges encountered by social groups and communities in the face of globalising tendencies and intricate patterns of roads and routes. The role of emerging alternatives within the region and community partnerships in Eurasia also needs to be addressed. As the world re-crystallises along new political, economic, social and cultural lines, this volume seeks to examine these issues in the Eurasian context through an understanding of the intersection of space and place in Eurasia; Eurasian engagement with globalisation in terms of shifting spheres in politics, economics and culture and levels of integration; connectivity and routes in a globalised Eurasia; challenges, strategies and architectures in the region and its neighbourhood and alternative globalisations. Most of the articles in the volume were presented at a seminar on *Geographies of Globalisation in Eurasia* organised by the Maulana Abul Kalam Azad Institute of Asian Studies in October 2013. A few have been commissioned from experts.

Spaces into Places

A significant transformation in the Eurasian space has been in terms of changes in political geographies with the construction of clearly demarcated political spaces within securitised borders of states. The changes in political geographies also becomes significant for a broader understanding of the geopolitics of identity within the region. Once borders are drawn a process of coming to terms with it follows as states attempt to legitimise the lines that are more often than not drawn as a result of imperial partitions. In the course of this legitimation, states are transformed into nations and culturally identified with the dominant group within its borders. Identity within the limits of the border is transformed into *national identity*. The making of political identity has inevitably been accompanied by a search for territorial spaces as the legitimate homeland of communities. This sense of spatial identity gained momentum in the wake of post-imperial attempts at assigning clearly demarcated spaces to groups defined as "nationalities" and the subsequent acceptance of identities as place bound. The assertion behind this emphasis is the claim that every community essentially belongs to its "homeland." The sense of exclusiveness was enhanced by the naming of the entities after the majority national communities, Kazakhstan, Uzbekistan and so forth literally meaning "land of the Kazakhs, land of the Uzbeks." The "national" problem today, therefore, has a distinct territorial dimension. That is, indigenous nations resident in the state lay claim to particular geographic regions as their respective *national homelands*. The boundaries of these national homelands are perceptual and their legitimation claimed by nationalists who are both looking back to a mythical golden age when the "nation" dominated vast lands, and also looking forward to a time when it will once again regain sovereignty over the territorial spaces it considers home. In multinational homelands this exclusivity often becomes problematic as, very often, the claims of nations overlap.

It has been argued that how political space is constructed and where the boundaries are located also becomes significant in terms of a broader understanding of developments within the region since a boundary does not exist just at the border but manifests itself in numerous institutions like education, media, novels, memorials and ceremonies and spectacles.[1] It becomes crucial in determining not just cultural contacts across boundaries but also the flow of goods and people and therefore also economic contacts. This is particularly relevant in post-colonial situations where state borders in any case make little sense in economic and social terms. However this posturing remains significant in terms of the projection of the state as a sovereign entity. What is also interesting is how changes in the geographical space that is identified as a "threat" could well mean that at certain junctures the posturing becomes more important at a particular front than at others. This posturing is therefore important in terms of a performative role that borders play not just in identifying a collective "inside" but also in defining an alien "outside." Where not just the material but conceptual boundary is located becomes crucial, not just by those circumscribed by it but also for many others outside its limits whose everyday life is dependent on its fluidity. In fact the assertion of territoriality is often reflected in terms of "perceptions of threat" thereby bringing to the forefront the significance of an understanding of the performative role that borders play for the modern state. It also becomes important in analysing the way in which regional geopolitics is perceived and constructed by the states themselves through an assertion of control at the borders but also through a depiction of threat from beyond.[2] Farkhod Tolipov in his article, *Central Asians: Peoples of the Region or Citizens of the States*, examines how the geopoliticisation of relations within the Central Asian states and the geopoliticisation by state leaders and elites of their own territories has resulted in national-regional dualism and skewed perceptions of regional geopolitics in the region.

Conceptions of homelands and how these affect the sense of nation and community is also significant for an understanding of the relationship between territoriality and nationalism. An understanding of the concept of homelands has become particularly significant for the Eurasian region in the wake of the emergence of the sovereign states as they offer new insights into changing notions of sovereignty and territoriality. The legalisation of political boundaries, however, has complicated this search as most demands for homelands do not correspond to present demarcations. And in any case, most concepts of homeland overlap with that of others leading to potential conflict situations. Narratives of displacement become significant here and in most cases the reassertion of identity is based on ideas of a mythical space to which the community claims special rights. The determination of previously determined space brings to the forefront the significance of identification of homelands and the claim that the current boundaries of the state correspond to these ancient homelands. Along with this, the construction of a "post-Soviet" identity becomes imperative for the legitimation of the new states. Transformations in political geographies influenced the construction of "geostrategic discourse" in the post-Soviet states and these discourses in their turn have affected the geopolitics of identity. On the one hand, the assertion of a securitised border is justified through perceptions of "threat" and, on the other, a legacy of shared cultural practices mediates the gap between borders and the more fluid conception of frontiers.

Territorial boundedness, however, remains central to the assertion and representation of the state as sovereign. It is difficult to imagine the concept of the state without a corresponding finite stretch of territory. However, excursions into the state's geographical margins show that even the borders of the most securitised states are more porous than any map would convey. For those living in the borderlands of states and especially in areas where the location of the international boundary is, or has been historically contested, the divergence between the cartographic division of national space and the everyday experience of the "border" is not merely of academic interest. Quite how state assertions of "territorial integrity" should translate into the movement of goods and people across the state's edge is a question on which daily life invites reflection. How to have "secure" borders that can nonetheless allow free trade across them? How to prevent resources from being siphoned out illegally, without this entailing draconian document checks every few kilometres? How to sustain relations with friends and relatives across a border when transport is increasingly fragmented along national lines? What to do with uncultivated territory, the jurisdiction of which is contested, in a situation of acute land shortage? How to balance limit and flow, connection and separation, inclusion and exclusion? All of these are issues that one is constantly confronted with in Eurasia. Suchandana Chatterjee in her article *The Russian Regional Gaze: From the Far East to the Far North* looks into some of these issues and argues that Russia's geopolitical reorientation at its Far Eastern margins entails Russia's eastern reach through railway corridors across Russia and bridge-building projects in the Pacific. Such projects herald the extension of its frontiers and have been showcased in a major way in the context of Europe-Asia connectivity. However, it has a significant impact on those living at its borderlands.

A significant way in which frontiers were expanded was through the development of maritime and land routes. In their article, *The Northern Periphery of the Great Silk Road,* Vladimir Lamin and Yanina Kuznetsova discuss the establishment of trade relations from Siberian cities to India where the expeditions explored land, rail and sea routes emphasising the fact that examinations of exchanges across Eurasia should not be limited to land routes given the history of maritime interactions. On the other hand, the Silk Road is now used as a metaphor for oil pipelines. Given the importance of oil and gas, pipelines have now acquired rhetorical significance. This is reflected in geopolitical narratives that have been reoriented and rhetorical boundaries that have been redesigned to create new conceptual boundaries based on energy. Such shifts in geopolitical thinking, influencing where a region is geopolitically situated based on availability of resources, has resulted in interesting shifts in strategic geography and reorientation in Eurasia.

Space, Memory and Identity

While the transformation of frontiers into borders has led to changes in political geographies, the idea of Eurasia as a geo-cultural space has opened up new possibilities of imagining this space. Aleksandr Dugin for instance points to a particular way of imagining Eurasia when he notes, "Eurasia does not have fixed boundaries. Eurasia is a civilisational structure, it is a geopolitical pole."[3] The term Eurasia or *Evraziia* was used by the Eurasianists to indicate a different "geographical world," different from both Europe and Asia. It has been argued that the Eurasianists' "geographical world" of Eurasia can be called a mega-region.[4] Eurasianists sometimes used the word "continent" to refer to this mega-region but that usage was for them metaphorical rather than scientific. In the new world of Russia-Eurasia the Eurasianists declared cultural independence from both Europe and Asia. Eurasianists strongly identified ethnic Russians with other Eastern Slavs and peoples of the

Eurasian mega-region, Finno-Ugric, Turkic and Mongolian. Eurasianists did not however define the boundaries of Eurasia with precision and in fact their various versions of Eurasia overlapped. Still the expanse of their "Eurasias" roughly coincided with the boundaries of the pre-1914 Russian Empire. For traditional Eurasianists, Eurasia was separated from Asia to its South by high mountains and impenetrable deserts, to its West Eurasia was separated from Europe by what Savitskii called the "region between the Black and the Baltic Seas." Eurasianists devised a series of detailed arguments to justify this as the legitimate geographical divide. A strict interpretation of this geographical scheme excluded all of Russia's territory east of the Lena River. On the other hand some regions that fall outside Russia's political borders—a large part of western China for instance—was seen as an integral part of Eurasia. Eurasianists argued that there was no discernible break across the Urals, linguistically, culturally and economically there were only continuities from the west to the east.

It has been argued that in its most extreme version, the Eurasian heartland is presented by the Russian geopolitical school as the "geographic emanation field" for the realisation of an objective that longs for the expulsion of the Atlantic influence from Eurasia. In contradistinction from the principles of the Slavophiles, which call for the unification of all Slavs, Eurasianism is oriented southwards and eastwards and envisages the merger of the Orthodox and Muslim populations. As a geopolitical vision, Eurasianism is a curious medley in which communist ideology, nationalism and orthodox fundamentalism coexist. Although their principles are often contradictory these three ideologies incorporated into the field of the geopolitical Eurasian vision constitute for many Russia's "third way."[5] There is a vital geographical component to Eurasianism, dictating that Russia should control the Eurasian heartland including Central Asia and the Caucasus. Central Asia occupies a complex place in Eurasianist thinking. It is included in all the movement's geographical definitions of Eurasia but not in its historiographical or ethnological discourses.[6]

From 1991 to 1996 the Eurasianist idea became increasingly attractive since it fitted with the reality of the eastward movement of Russia's borders and justified a focus on the renewal of ties with the CIS states as well as Russia's eastern neighbours. Tsygankov argues that Eurasianism contributed to changes in Russian foreign policy and has been gaining influence among both politicians and intellectuals since the December 1993 parliamentary elections.[7] Eurasianist ideas also flourished at this time because economic disparity between Russia and the West was increasing and security concerns and cultural differences between Russia and Europe were reinforcing the historic feeling of Russian "otherness" from Europe. Eurasianism was a useful alternative concept with which to guide Russia's foreign policies and to provide support and credence to a range of political orientations. In this volume, Dmitry Shlapentokh examines one such Eurasianist orientation in his article, *Dugin's Early Eurasianism and the Problem of Recycling Ideology.*

Eurasianism has also been emphasised in the political and ideological discourse of contemporary Turkey, which is today ideally situated, not just geographically but politically, economically and culturally, to be identified as "Eurasian." In the political and ideological discourse of contemporary Turkey, a variety of definitions of Eurasia has had their adherents and remains significant as discursive re-conceptualisations, at the juncture of geographical and sociological imaginations. Similarly, alternatives that critique traditional definitions as also the interests that they represent are equally significant. During the 1990s representatives of a large number of pro-Islamic and pro-Turkic political forces elaborated a model of Turkey's Eurasian policy as an alternative to traditional pro-Western policies. This was based on the idea of cooperation among the most important powers of Eurasia, Turkey, Iran and Russia. Part of this turn towards Eurasianism was based on the advantages of the representation of Turkey as "the" model for a vast region where there was apprehension of a turn towards Islam. Over the years views concerning Eurasia and Turkey's place in it have been transformed, not just among the academia but also within circles that had traditionally been Kemalist, like the army. Official military documents now represent Turkey as a "country of Eurasia" committed to enhance ties both with the West and the East. Since the end of the 1990s the political establishment itself and the leaders of both the Democratic Left Party (*Demokratik Sol Parti,* DLP) as well as the JDP (*Adalet ve Kalkinma Partisi,* AKP) that followed have insisted on a region oriented foreign policy based on Turkey's position at the crossroads of Europe and Asia. The Eurasian direction of Turkish foreign policy is also reflected in the political programmes of other parties like the Social Democratic People's Party (*Sosyaldemokrat Halk Partisi*, SHP) and the Party of New Turkey (*Yeni Turkiye Partisi*, YTP).

While Eurasianism lacks credibility in strategic terms, its lure itself is said to be indicative of an eastward shift. Eurasianism in Turkey remains a foreign policy option advocated by groups with different ideologies, approaches and attitudes regarding Turkey's position in the post-Soviet international arena. There are, however, serious obstacles for this option to be put into effect. Turkey continues to have a primarily pro-Western policy, now increasingly tempered by its interest in the Middle East, and the Eurasian region seems to be of secondary importance. It is also emphasised that Turkey is just one of the players in the region and definitely not one of the most significant. The general impression is that the three biggest players in the region, Russia, China and the United States are becoming more and more involved with the region in addition to actors with less influence such as India, Iran, Japan, and the European Union. Any shift that Turkey showed in its foreign policy would make all these actors uncomfortable.

Therefore, by the turn of the century the trend of seeking to institutionalise relations with the Central Asian states had taken a back seat. The discourse of Turkish foreign policy shifted from rhetoric about the "Turkic century" in the early 1990s to "Eurasianism" in the 2000s.[8] A number of factors including a change in the ruling party in Turkey, Turkish-Russian rapprochement, the fact that Moscow was looking askance at the Pan Turkic organisations and most importantly transformations within the Central Asian Republics were responsible for this. Tunc Aybak argues that Turkey's foreign policy drive towards Central Eurasia aimed at establishing ethnic and cultural links with Turkic states suffered from several weaknesses.[9] First, and most important, was the lack of historical continuity. Historically Central Asia was never a part of the Ottoman Empire and the Muslims of Central Asia were regarded as foreigners. Pan Turkism only became an influential ideology during the last days of the Tsarist rule. And even then, it had failed to elicit wider popular support. During the period of the Soviet Union, Turkey had maintained bilateral relations with the federal centre rather than the titular Turkic Republics. Jacob Landau notes that Pan Turkism as an ideology still existed in certain political circles and was adopted by various minor nationalist parties throughout the Cold War, but it held little appeal for the Republican state elites of Turkey.[10] Even when these parties shared power with other major parties in coalition governments, Pan Turkism hardly informed key foreign policy decisions. A second reason was geographical contiguity. Central Asia is geographically detached from Anatolian Turkey. There is today also significant cultural diversity. Even though the Turkic languages share a common linguistic branch, the vernaculars are today highly diverse. In the Central Asian region the vernaculars were also historically influenced by Persian and Russian. Anar Somuncuoğlu looks into some of these issues in her article, *Turkey in Eurasia: Identity and Foreign Policy.*

There is, therefore, the need to take note of the fact that the Eurasian debate itself is not a monolithic whole and in its various forms serves distinct purposes. Caroline Humphrey has noted that the concept of "Eurasia" has enabled the governing circles of many Asian regions of Russia to create distinctive ideas about the nature of their existence within the Federation. The idea of "Eurasia" is also providing an arena for new political relations to be formed between the provinces. She has argued that Eurasia is likely to be highly influential both in conceptualising federal relations and in shaping the political-cultural character of the constituent regions.[11] However, not all reactions to Eurasianism have been positive. There have been critiques like Urkhanova from Buryatia who have argued that Eurasianism is built on Russian great power statehood. As a result the "imprecise inclusiveness" of Eurasianism is a cloak for renewed Russian imperialism. Yet, she argues that the Buryats cannot refuse Eurasia as they have been part of it during the Soviet period.[12] In fact the Siberian region covers nearly a quarter of what is identified as Eurasia today. Humphrey notes that the idea of Eurasia has resurfaced among the new generation of leaders in the Inner Asian regions and Central Asia as an escape from their peripherality. She argues that it provides an arena of political imagination where the Inner Asian people can claim a dignified place.

One aspect of this is evident in the new historiography from Siberia that looks at Siberia's role in the future globalised world in terms of a bridge between Europe and Asia. Denis Ananyev in his article, *Siberian Regionalism in the Second Half of the Nineteenth to the Early Twentieth Centuries: Views in Historiography*, looks into the antecedents of the regionalist movement (*oblastnichestvo*) which advocated far-reaching autonomy, liberation from colonial dependence and free economic development of Siberia. More than a century has passed since the death of Nikolai M. Iadrintsev, author of the well-known classic, *Siberia as a Colony.* Although these years have brought significant changes in the global arena, it has not significantly transformed the position of Siberia vis-à-vis European Russia. The persistence of the relationship is rooted in the nature of economic development in Siberia, which has reinforced efforts to transform the economy as well as the political relationship. The re-emergence of Siberian separatism has led to debates about the viability of economic reforms without the expansion of regional sovereignty. The subsequent efforts for uniting Siberian territories through the Siberian Agreement are projected as an attempt to coordinate economic reforms at the regional level.

Globalising Political Geographies

It has long been recognised that security is essentially a contested concept and there is no term that is as uncertain and unstable as "security." The end of the Cold War rendered the settled, hegemonic understanding of security unstable and vulnerable to contestation. This traditional understanding was defined by Stephen Walt as the "threat to use and control of military force" and it translated into security for states against threats posed to them largely by other states. Much of the early critical work in security studies demonstrated the politics of this concept of security; who it worked for and who it worked against. There were subsequently two ways of understanding security; the first explored the way in which security came to be understood and practised and with what effects, and the second in terms of the forms of security that were masked or actively opposed by the dominant understanding. Prior to 2001, the discussion on security was dominated by the understanding of security as state centric, military security. While a range of alternative understandings was being developed they were articulated exclusively in relation to the conventional conception. The events of 9/11 and, more importantly, the decisions taken in response to these events, fundamentally altered the terrain of contest over security.

The global war on terror dramatically reinforced the significance of security, which had been seemingly on the wane since 1989, but the notion of security that came with it was different from that which had come before.[13] In the post 9/11 world, security became a much more expansive, fluid and uncertain concept. While the state employed traditional military means to achieve security, the state no longer seemed to be the container of security. Terrorism, as the primary security threat, seemed to render the stark division between external and internal threats meaningless. This uncertainty of security has multiplied the sites at which "security" may be found. Traditional sites, such as militaries and conflict, have been re-articulated but they have been joined by border fences, detention centres, airport security counters, places of worship and even universities. However, even as insecurity processes become increasingly transnational and even global in their dynamics and scope, many states continue to be profound sources of insecurity both to other states and people. A plethora of issues constitute pressing security concerns today. These include environmental threats and climate change, the situation of forced migrants and refugees, nuclear instability, security and proliferation, interstate security dilemmas, trade in small arms, concerns about the militarisation of space and proliferation of robotic military technology. This is compounded by endemic human insecurity represented by the experience of women in conflict zones, deep and widespread poverty, human rights abuses and the targeting of minorities. Globally this amounts to a complex and interconnected array of concerns that no state or security organisation can afford to neglect. It has been argued that this globalisation of insecurity, in such complex interconnected forms requires a change in state approaches and commitments and efforts to improve global security governance.[14]

In the last decade there has, therefore, been a broadening of the notion of security from states to societies and an increasing differentiation of security arrangements. It has been proposed that this transformation be conceptualised as *security governance*, characterised by a fragmentation of initiatives among a diverse group of actors. Security cannot just be defined in terms of security at the borders. It needs to be defined in "cosmopolitan" terms through an array of issues like movements across borders, radicalism within states, the sharing of water, and various multilateral attempts at combating insecurity. Emilian Kavalski in his article, *China's Security Governance of Central Asia*, identifies the main elements of China's involvement in the region both in terms of a normative power but also in terms of its socialising propensities. He argues that the Chinese understanding of security governance is prompted by a sense of insecurity that is driven by its own domestic and social experiences. The management of diverse security predicaments at home underwrites its involvement in security governance practices internationally.

Since 9/11 security narratives in Eurasia have been intertwined with the impact of Islam. The relationship between Islam and security in Eurasia has significant historic depth, on account of the Russian encounter with Islam. Russia's discursive imagery has fluctuated from fear of encirclement to aspirations for domination, from resistance to accommodation between cultural alienation and Eurasian affinity. These fluctuations speak of a long history of both soft and hard securitisations of Islam in Eurasia.[15] The collapse of the Soviet Union opened the region and its competing narratives to outside influences and penetrations. The global narrative, defining Islam as the primary post-Cold War threat and civilisational challenge found its way into the region where it was adopted by post-Soviet elites. Regional actors and great powers all tapped into the prevailing discourse to deal with their own specific political or ethno-territorial challenges. Eurasian Islam that has had its own distinctive history and local/regional socio-political complexities, was catapulted into a larger Muslim world not through cultural, economic or political integration but via a narrative process of securitisation on a global scale. The process of securitisation embraces a broad spectrum of narratives and views that encompass individuals, social groups and movements.

Michael Fredholm in his article, *Daydreams and Nightmares: Dreaming of the Al-Qaeda and the Once and Future Caliphate,* looks at the other side of this globalised narrative when he examines *jihadist* narratives on globalised Islam. He looks into the Russian speaking *jihadist* networks of North Caucasus, Urals, Azerbaijan and Central Asia to argue how these narratives are about the dreams and nightmares of the proponents rather than any ideological development. He also looks into the counter-narrative that has resulted as a reaction against the jihadist "dream" which has itself generated global sympathisers.

While security concerns have assumed salience across the globe, Afghanistan's proximity to Central Asia has meant that security, or perceptions of insecurity, dominates the strategic discourse in the region. Issues that stand out include the challenges that the Central Asian states will face in terms of stability, ethnic tensions, radicalisation of youth, destabilisation of commodity flows and energy security and the impact that these could have on Central Asian society. However, security cannot just be defined in terms of security at the borders. It needs to be defined in "cosmopolitan" terms through an array of issues like movements across borders, radicalism within states, the sharing of water, and various multilateral attempts at combating insecurity. As International Security Assistance Force troops prepare to leave Afghanistan, the future of Central Asian security has become a major subject of policy discussions not only within the region but also in the capitals of neighbouring states. While the Collective Security Treaty Organisation and the Shanghai Cooperation Organisation work out detailed plans to cope with shared security concerns, the idea of a "spillover" is increasingly being debated by security experts. In fact analysts have argued that the Central Asian states have once again raised the question of growing terrorist and extremist risks to attract greater military assistance packages from Russia, China and the US. Washington's postwithdrawal stabilisation strategy for Afghanistan appears to rely heavily on regional economic development schemes through an initiative known as the New Silk Road Strategy. Two US-sponsored initiatives have been on the cards—the establishment of a regional energy market via the construction of transmission lines connecting South and Central Asia and a long planned pipeline connecting Turkmenistan to South Asia, TAPI. The success of the strategies to link the two regions would be dependent on economic viability as well as prevailing political and security conditions. Moreover, it remains to be seen whether all the states would agree on a single strategy of development. In fact, there are already existing alternatives to the New Silk Road Strategy with the Chinese vision of a Eurasian Land Bridge linking China and Russia to Europe via Kazakhstan and the International North South Transport Corridor project supported by India, Russia and Iran which are at different stages of implementation. One of the effects of the scheduled pull-out of the international troops from Afghanistan has been a reported upswing in the activity of Central Asian militants in northern Afghanistan and the attendant anxiety that these groups might be engaged in destabilising activity in Central Asia.[16] Arpita Basu Roy in her article, *Afghanistan and Central Asian Security*, looks into some of these issues in detail.

Globalising Cultural Geographies

Historically, Central Asia's cultural geography has been home to a diversity of faiths. Yet, the general impression that one gets, from any discussion on Islam in the Central Asian region, is of a religion of an all-pervasive character and one that completely overwhelmed the earlier traditions prevalent in the region. That this is less than the whole truth became evident when in the course of the current rediscovery of "roots" the search was more towards a pre-Islamic tradition than one simply in search of Islam. The multiple religious experiences of the region, in particular in the nomadic case, assumed numerous forms ranging from animism, totemism, shamanism, and polytheistic cults as well as Islam, Buddhism, Zoroastrianism, Manichaeism and Nestorian Christianity. A revival of all these forms in contemporary Central Asian literature in recent times is a pointer to their continuing relevance in society. Moreover, in the Central Asian situation, one would have to begin with the recognition of the fact that "an Islam" was never a reality in the region. Islam, in Central Asia does not have a monolithic structure, and various other trends like Sufism or even pre-Islamic faiths exerted influence and wielded power. In fact states like Uzbekistan recognise

Navroz, the festival symbolising the arrival of spring and a remnant of Zoroastrian tradition, as an "Uzbek" national tradition with a national holiday on the day. It is also important to remember that Islam itself is not monolithic. Apart from the major split between the Sunnis and the Shias, there were also different doctrinal tendencies—traditionalist, fundamentalist and, in the nineteenth and twentieth centuries, modernist. There is also the interplay in the region between dogmatic religion, Sufism and popular piety, "official" Islam and "popular" Islam. All these streams share one faith, but the social structures in which their common Islamic sentiment developed, differed, as did their political experiences. In fact there are also regional differences in the practice of Islam even among the so-called "settled" peoples.

This leads to the realisation that in most scholarship on religion in the Central Asian region, the emphasis on the crucial role of "an Islam" probably resulted primarily from the supposed Soviet-era emphasis on the identification of a structure that was to become the principal focus of anti-religious propaganda. As a result, it was pointed out that the current structure of Islam in the region is said to owe much of its organisational and academic existence to Soviet efforts. This, however, ignored the fact that there was recognition of this diversity in Soviet ethnographic literature, which mapped the contours of these beliefs in detail. Examinations of Soviet research on the religious and cultural traditions of the region points to the fact that there was detailed examination of other religious traditions, albeit as *perezhitki* or survivals of older traditions that the socialist system would replace. This assumes importance in the light of the fact that official Soviet Islam was recognised as having remained a link in the chain of the modernist *Jadidist* version of Islam. Among the early forms of religion, totemism had attracted the attention of Soviet scholarship; attention had also been focused on magic, mythology and folklore. Soviet ethnography had also focused attention on syncretism, for example, on the syncretic character of "everyday Islam" with the survivals of pre-Islamic "cults," which having been absorbed by Islam, created distinctive everyday religious phenomena among different Muslim peoples. V. N. Basilov cites the works of O. A. Sukhareva, G. Snesarev, T. Bayalieva and L. Lavrov to show extensive studies of pre-Islamic relics among the Uzbeks. He also pointed to literature that shows that besides the mainstream Islamic thoughts and beliefs, Sufism in its popular forms had absorbed certain pre-Islamic traditions of the region. Current studies on everyday life in the region point to a similar syncretism with the coexistence of "*namaz* and wishing trees" signifying the diversity of everyday religious life.[17]

While the reality was that of a society with multiple religious traditions, the imperatives of the post-Soviet era demanded the projection of a singular faith that would form the basis of the foundation of the new state. However, faced with global "radical" challenges in the post-independence period, the emphasis soon shifted to the many pre-Islamic traditions of the region. As such the political rhetoric of revival emphasised the multifarious traditions of faith rather than the structures of an "Islam." A. K. Sultangalieva, in her examination of Islam in Kazakhstan, argues that in the Central Asian region Islam was more of a historical peculiarity than a historical force but also an intra-ethnic phenomenon rather than a defining societal characteristic. Islam was introduced to Kazakhstan over a period of eight hundred years, from the eighth to the sixteenth centuries. It appeared not in one continuous wave but in a gradual current. Islam therefore never replaced other pre-existing faiths in the Kazakh steppes, such as Turkic animistic beliefs and Zoroastrianism. Instead it became synthesised with them. Moreover the influence of Sufism, an unorthodox, mystical branch of Islam brought to the region by the missionaries from Bukhara, became an important element of local faith. Sultangalieva points out that in contrast to a number of other Muslim regions, the inhabitants of the Kazakh steppes did not consider the Sufi brotherhoods as heretical.[18] Islam in Kazakhstan was further diluted by the practice of "Chenghism," a system of beliefs introduced after the Mongol invasions that placed a particular emphasis on a genealogical connection with Chenghis Khan. More significantly this existed alongside Islam while blatantly refuting Islam's central tenet, there is no God except Allah.

Over the years the Kazakh government has also taken steps to reduce the impact of Islam. In fact the officially declared policy is one where there is convergence of faiths represented by the Palace of Faiths. "The

Heart of Eurasia" is an officially promoted identification of the capital Astana and metonymically of Kazakhstan itself.[19] This title corresponds to an often heard ideological claim that Kazakhstan is situated at the centre of civilisational connections between the East and the West, and between the North and the South of the continent. The country is populated by the representatives of 130 national minorities and has representatives from a great variety of religions. For the first two decades of independence President Nazarbayev has focused on the fact that Kazakhstan is either one of few countries, or may be the only multinational and multi-confessional country where inter-ethnic or religious conflicts are absent due to its tolerant and peaceful traditions.

Alexey Zelenskiy in his article, *The Point of Convergence: Reasons for New Age Spirituality in Kazakhstan*, argues that this absence of conflict can only be justified in terms of the emergence of a New Age spirituality which is a global spiritual trend. A common interpretation for the emergence of New Age spirituality is in terms of a compensatory response to global challenges and threats of the late twentieth century, such as the ecological crisis, the discrediting of Christian values, social disintegration, existential uncertainty and others. An impact of New Age values on secular spirituality as well as on social institutions and state decision-making is unambiguously detectable in Kazakhstan in particular. Just after its "official inauguration," New Age culture reached Kazakhstan in late Soviet times in the 1970s-1980s. According to Zelenskiy, a decade later it was already widely represented by "astrologers, theosophists, UFO enthusiasts, cryptologists, messiahs, occultists and so on." However, there is a certain hostility of the official authorities to both domestic and foreign messianic sects, like Ata Zholy, Allya Ayat or Scientology. Neither received official registration. Zelenskiy argues that the state recognises Islam as the traditional religion of Kazakhs instead of shamanism or the religion of Tengri. However, he emphasises that one should not forget the place of shamanism and Tengri at the level of traditions and customs, and the fact that these traditions and customs had an existence prior to Islam.

Like religion, music readily spreads beyond the land of its origin as people carry their music with them when they travel, as they bring with them their own faiths and rituals. Familiar chants, songs and instruments sustained pilgrims and traders who at the same time absorbed musical influences they encountered in their travels. Musical traditions are portable, but they are also durable, and stubbornly take root in the lands where they were born. One of the most powerful surviving features of the old Silk Road today is the variety of music performed, on instruments old and new, indigenous and imported everywhere from the shores of the Mediterranean to the shores of the Pacific. This is a living musical heritage that links thousands of years of trade and exchange among the people of the Silk Road. Religion, of course, had been one of the most important cultural forces to promote the dissemination of music along the Silk Road. Islamic Sufi orders, who traditionally welcomed the use of music, chant and sacred dance as elements of prayer, were instrumental in spreading spiritual songs among their adherents. Wandering dervishes, holy men, and religious storytellers used song and chant as a means of proselytising the moral values of Islam to audiences that gathered to hear them in bazaars, caravanserais and tea houses. Similarly, Buddhist monks also brought forms of scared chant from one part of Asia to another. Music along the Silk Road illustrates overarching regularities not only in the way that it is physically produced, but also in the role that it plays in society and culture.

As Theodore Levine points out, in music as in other aspects of culture, the history of the Silk Road has largely been the history of interaction between two large cultural domains; the sedentary world and the nomadic world.[20] Nomadic and sedentary people have coexisted in Eurasia for centuries and their relationship has often been problematic. Yet despite periods of hostility, pastoralists and sedentary dwellers have both relied on an intricate cultural and commercial symbiosis that is one of the hallmarks of Inner Asian civilisation. This is evident in the way that music and musical instruments have travelled from one cultural realm to another. In her article, *The Silk Route in Mustafo Bafoev's Imagination*, Diloram Karomat examines Uzbek composer Mustafo Bafoev's composition *Buyuk Ipak Yo'li* to highlight the connections of the cultures along the Silk Road.

While cultural geography traditionally included the study of religion, language, music, art and other cultural aspects (how they related to spaces and places where they originated and then travelled as people continually moved across various areas) it is now increasingly being expanded to include cultural landscapes as they link culture to the physical environments where people live. The adaptation of humans to their environment, which also includes how beliefs and institutions in a culture regulate its interchanges with the natural ecology that surrounds it, therefore assumes importance. The present geological age, the "anthropocene" period, is viewed as one during which human activity has been the dominant influence on climate and environment and there has therefore been concern about the way in which human groups make decisions about how to use their natural environment. Climate change in the Circumpolar Arctic and the subsequent opening of Arctic shipping lanes, illustrates one such case of intervention which invokes both hopes and fears among the "Arctic" and "non-Arctic" states. The diminishing Arctic sea ice cover is a fact, and with the Arctic Ocean becoming more accessible, shipping is bound to increase. There is already more regional traffic, mostly related to development and export of petroleum resources. As the "summer window of opportunity widens" occasional transit may also occur. While an immediate shift of the Atlantic-Pacific route is not on the cards, processes to address protection of the Arctic environment and the livelihoods of inhabitants needs to be initiated. In recent times, cultural ecology has come under criticism from political ecology for ignoring the connections between local systems and the larger political economy. In his article, *Northern Eurasia in the Era of Climate Change: Rhetoric and Reality of the Northern Sea Route*, Sanjay Chaturvedi moves beyond this duality and examines the Circumpolar Arctic as a lived space but also in terms of linkages, resource potentials and routes of access that has legitimised its place in the global economic system.

Globalisation and Regional Initiatives

Despite the argument that globalisation is ushering in the so-called "global" village, the process of construction, deconstruction and reconstruction of regional identities and organisations continues. It can be argued that globalisation reinforces the need to identify more and more with one's regional identity lest one is lost in the seemingly endless boundaries of the global village. There then remains the possibility that "region" becomes even more relevant in the context of globalisation as the individual is likely to use region as an instrumental category to resist marginalisation in a globalised world. In this search for alternative boundaries linkages that move beyond the bounded ones of the state or the endless ones of the "global" village often assume significance. Exploring regional linkages also assume geopolitical significance in terms of projecting a unified perspective on certain issues that then carry more political weight on the international arena. The seminar on *Geographies of Globalisation* was followed by a round table on *Are regional initiatives meaningful in the Eurasian context?* which examined regional organisations in Central, West, South and South East Asia from a comparative perspective. This section is an attempt to bring together some of the ideas that were generated in the round table on Central Asia and Eurasia.

The term "multilateral" can refer to an organising principle, an organisation or simply an activity. Any of the above can be considered multilateral when it involves cooperative activity among many countries. "Multilateralism" as opposed to "multilateral" is a belief that the activities ought to be organised on a universal, or at least many-sided, basis for a "relevant" group. It may be a belief both in the existential sense of a claim about how the world works and in the normative sense that things should be done in a particular way. As such multilateralism is "designed" to promote multilateral activity. It combines normative principles with advocacy and existential beliefs. While a debate on the reform of the United Nations, as the principal global multilateral forum, had been an ongoing process, a multilateral approach towards regional issues, particularly security issues, with emphasis on confidence building, preventive diplomacy and conflict resolution, are being increasingly accepted as significant to the maintenance of regional security and promotion of regional development.

Multilateral confidence-building measures reflect the belief that through regularised dialogue and consultation, existing and potential conflicts can be effectively managed without the necessity of recourse to coercion. It is pointed out that multilateralism is distinctive, not merely because it coordinates national policies in groups of three or more states, which is something that other organisational forms also do, but additionally because it does so on the basis of certain principles of ordering relations among states.[21] However, an understanding of multilateral initiatives remains incomplete without a close reading of how regions perceive their "national" and "regional" security. Underlying these national priorities are a set of assumptions about the security of the state and how shifting alliances with other states can best preserve this. This rather realistic understanding of the situation, of course, is not without its problems. Not the least of which is that states often do not act as unitary and rational actors. In actual situations state decisions are often determined by the interplay of domestic and international factors and influenced by partisan interests. It is in this background that one would need to look into the emergence of a regional dialogue in Central Asia and Eurasia.

Writing in 1994 and echoing many others, Martha Brill Olcott had pointed out that the disincentives for regional integration in the Central Asian region was such as to ascribe to the eventuality of such integration the possibility of a myth.[22] The argument for this ran as follows: Rivalries within the region coupled with the fact that independence had been embraced with enthusiasm by each of the states, who also immediately began exploring independent developmental and economic relations with other international bodies, would effectively ensure that attempts to create any organisation designed to treat Central Asia as a single unit would remain a "spectre conjured to ward off specific threats or problems."[23] The "weak state" structure argument was also put forward to point out that the Central Asian states, confronted as they were with the necessity of national consolidation, would be unable to take any action towards regional integration.[24] Otherwise, according to Olcott, regional integration and cooperation would only prove to be workable in such minor incentives as educational and scientific policy, a regional commission on the media and in commissions to address ecological conditions in the Aral Sea or the disappearing caviar yields of the Caspian. While the author also noted that the less than three years that had passed were insufficient to correctly indicate the complete failure of efforts at integration, yet she was of the opinion that the five states were being increasingly drawn apart rather than being brought together.

It is generally accepted that the purpose for any regional organisation is twofold: the acceleration of economic development and the reinforcement of regional stability and security. The role of multilateral regional initiatives on a Central Asian level as primary providers of security has not been rated very high. It has been observed that such initiatives have been unable to convey hard defence guarantees, create joint military units, negotiate arms reductions or enforce the end of overt conflicts. However, a correct assessment of these initiatives would have to begin with noting their existential significance as groups of states that recognise themselves as sharing some elements of community and can define their national identity as complementary rather than adversarial to their neighbours. Regular meetings and the creation of personal ties encourage *esprit de corps* and may help to defuse crises. In fact non-traditional security issues like environment, defence against pollution, water management, drug smuggling, organised crime, migration and refugees have provided more useful areas for regional discourse. In addition there have been attempts at economic cooperation with an understanding that economic development is conducive to the security of the region.[25]

Within Central Asia, Kazakh commitment to multilateral initiatives has been strongest. This commitment has extended not just within the Central Asian region but also on a broader Eurasian level. On a practical level Kazakh effort at integration on a Eurasian level has involved numerous initiatives. Kazakhstan has emerged as a leader in efforts at promotion of regional economic and political integration in Eurasia. Under President Nursultan Nazarbayev, Kazakhstan has followed a foreign policy that has sought to maintain good relations with the most important external powers. In addition there has been an attempt to strengthen ties with countries of Central Asia and the Caspian Sea basin. Kazakhstan also plays a prominent role in most of Eurasia's international institutions and organisations like the Commonwealth of Independent States, the Collective Security Treaty Organisation, the Eurasian

Economic Community, the Shanghai Cooperation Organisation, the North Atlantic Treaty Organisation and the Organisation for Security and Cooperation in Europe. In line with this the President has stated the objective of making Kazakhstan a "transcontinental economic bridge."[26]

In keeping with this there have been efforts at improving regional transportation, pipelines and communication networks, reducing custom and other man-made barriers to trade, encouraging tourism and other non-governmental exchanges while strengthening labour mobility in Eurasia and promoting Kazakh private investment in other Eurasian economies. The strong Kazakh support for regional integration results in part from a recognition that Kazakhstan will benefit from enhanced ties among Eurasian countries. There is also a conviction that through this integration at the Eurasian level Kazakhstan and its neighbours will achieve greater room to manoeuvre among the great powers active in the region and reduce the risk of their becoming dependent on any one supplier, customer or market. The increase in regional prosperity that economists predict will ensue from this integration would help Kazakhstan expand its economic activities and realise its potential as a natural crossroads for east-west and north-south commercial links based on the reduction of man-made political and economic obstacles to the free flow of goods and people among Eurasian nations. It has been argued that Kazakhstan's geography allowed it to exercise a decisive influence in two of Eurasia's most important subregions—Central Asia and the Caspian Sea.[27]

In addition Kazakhstan has presented repeated proposals for a Eurasian Union covering a range of cooperative endeavours in the areas of politics, economics and security. The idea of a Eurasian Union was conceived in the mid 1990s and was intended to promote economic, social and, to a limited degree, political integration across the post-Soviet space. The Eurasian Union was conceived with the idea of first establishing a customs union and a common economic space and to enable the citizens of the post-Soviet successor states to travel visa free across newly erected borders. President Nazarbayev argued that the Commonwealth of Independent States had been impotent. In contrast the Eurasian Union would be empowered and legitimised by an executive committee and a parliament. The effort would be to erect an effective institutional framework for economic integration and mutual security in order to avoid unnecessary expenses of border control. President Nazarbayev argued that much of the world was integrating and in the post-Soviet space this integration should work better since till recently it was an integrated economic space. While this initiative failed, President Nazarbayev reaffirmed his commitment to a union launching a new initiative in April 2007 that focused on borders and water management issues that had long complicated relations among the Central Asian states but also matters that could only be resolved collectively. The November 2007 decision to award Kazakhstan chairmanship of the Organisation for Security and Cooperation in Europe (OSCE) in 2010 recognises the country's growing importance in Eurasia. Kazakh officials have characterised this as an endorsement of their country's successful economic and political reforms, their leading role in Europe and Central Asia and their contribution as a bridge between the former Soviet republics and other OSCE members.

On the broader international front the rhetorical significance of the Eurasian union is stated as a self-evident move. The President argues

> ... it is absolutely clear to us that the main tendency in world development today is global integration, and the inspiring example of the member countries of the European Union is finding support in the most varied regions of the world. Moves towards unification are evident in the countries of Latin America, South East Asia and the near East. Along the same lines is the idea, advanced by Kazakhstan and having many adherents beyond its frontiers, for the creation of a Eurasian Union on the territory of the former Soviet Union. This not only pursues obvious economic objectives but also assumes the integration of the former Soviet Republics in the fields of science, culture, education and information. I feel sure that in the next century and beyond, the united subcontinent of Europe and Asia must develop as a single unit for the future of our children and our descendants and that there will come a day when Europe and Asia will develop together, drawing upon their huge natural and human resources.[28]

The Eurasian idea is therefore presented as the ideal for the future not just on a political and economic level but also at a cultural level. President Nazarbayev has called for the establishment of a Eurasian research centre that will focus on the unique spiritual heritage of the Eurasian people.

A very significant multilateral effort on a pan-Asian level initiated by the Kazakh President Nursultan Nazarbayev is the Conference on Interaction and Confidence-Building Measures in Asia (CICA). The CICA vision for security in Asia elaborates on multilateral approaches towards promoting peace and security and visualises itself as the forum for dialogue, consultation and adoption of decisions and measures on the basis of consensus on security issues in Asia. CICA originated with the idea that there was necessity for a pan-Asiatic system of security which, while addressing problems of security and confidence building, would also keep in mind cultural origins, national peculiarities and also the complicated history of relationships among them. The purpose behind the initiative was the creation of a system of security in Asia where safety would be guaranteed by the whole complex of measures. CICA has been involved in dialogue over three groups of issues—military-political affairs, socio-economic development and humanitarian concerns. CICA identifies certain elements as challenges to security and seeks to find ways to eliminate them. In this context it resolves to support efforts for the elimination of weapons of mass destruction, to ensure the establishment of nuclear free zones, to curb excessive accumulation of conventional armaments, condemn terrorism, not to render any assistance to separatist movements in other states, reject the use of religion as a pretext for terrorists and separatists, emphasise the significance of curbing the movement of illicit drugs and corruption. In the context of achieving these objectives the CICA will take necessary steps for the elaboration and implementation of measures aimed at enhancing cooperation and creating an atmosphere of peace, confidence and friendship. All states are encouraged to resolve their disputes peacefully through negotiations in accordance with the principles enshrined in the UN Charter and International law.[29]

The Central Asian experience, however, has not been uniform. There are interesting examples of the Central Asian states participating in different interstate organisations and in plans involving states outside the region simultaneously. For example, with the exception of Turkmenistan, the Central Asian states are participants of both the SCO and various NATO programmes. Kyrgyzstan joined the World Trade Organisation in 1998, although this contradicted with the principles and interests of the customs union of various post-Soviet states and of the Eurasian Economic Community, headed by Russia, which was set up on the basis of the customs union in October 2000, and of which Kyrgyzstan was also a member. Kazakhstan has been involved both with the Tengiz-Novorossiisk and the Baku-Ceyhan oil pipeline projects, the main lobbyists for which are, respectively, the Russian Federation and the USA. Of course this policy has had its share of critics within the region. Talgat Ismagambetov, notes that while this allows the Central Asian states to manoeuvre between the interests of the three world powers and where possible to extract for themselves certain short-term advantages, it does so without solving any problems related to the entire area of their national security.[30]

It is not surprising therefore that alternatives to the multi-vector policy have emerged. It has been argued, for instance, that Central Asia should be considered as an independent "security system."[31] As such participation of the Central Asian states in a single anti-terrorist coalition should be supplemented by their independent cooperation in this sphere. It has been argued that a "market" for security and anti-terrorist activities has taken shape in Central Asia where a number of international organisations offer their "professional assistance" in the field of regional security including UN agencies, EU, OSCE, CSTO, NATO and SCO. In addition there are a number of bilateral security agreements like the Uzbek-Russia strategic partnership, the CSTO joint military exercises and the Kazakhstan-China strategic cooperation established in July 2005. As such, it has been argued that Central Asian states find themselves deeply entangled in this "market."[32] In order to avoid entanglement, arguments have been put forward for the states in the region to manage their security on their own in order to escape the effects of "geopolitics and reliance on extra-regional powers."[33] In any case, it has been emphasised that the Central Asian states need to reject the "zero-sum game" and adopt a "win-win" strategy. Criticising "inadequate old-fashioned zero-sum game geopolitics," it has been argued that instead of regarding the states of the geopolitical triangle—US, Russia, China—as permanent rivals and worse still regarding themselves as victims of geopolitical rivalry, the states should take measures towards inviting all sides of the triangle to constructive cooperation in Central Asia. As for the powers involved, geopolitical pluralism rather than geopolitical antagonism will be based on the economic incentive of energy security. While inconsistencies between the regional and the global are accepted, the need is to focus on areas where regional initiatives are required and also identify overlaps between various regional initiatives.

However, it is also true that the direction that multilateral initiatives assume within the region is yet to be seen. In the light of such varied developments the observation of the Viennese philosopher, Ludwig Wittgenstein, in 1929, seems particularly relevant. He noted:

> When we think of the world's future, we always mean the destination it will reach if it keeps going in the direction we can see it going now; it does not occur to us that its path is not a straight line, but a curve, constantly changing direction.[34]

Notes

1. Nick Megoran, Gael Raballand and Jerome Bouyjou, "Performances, Representation and the Economics of Border Control in Uzbekistan," *Geopolitics*, vol. 10, no. 4, 2005.
2. Megoran, Raballand and Bouyjou, "Performances, Representation and the Economics of Border Control in Uzbekistan."
3. Aleksandr Dugin, *Geopolitika Postmoderna: Vremena Novykh Imperii Ocherki Geopolitiki XXI Veka* (St. Petersburg: Amfora, 2007).
4. Ilya Vinkovetsky, "Eurasia and its Uses: the History of An Idea and the Mental Geography of Post-Soviet Space," unpublished paper presented at the 2007 Annual Soyuz Symposium on *Locating Eurasia in Post-socialist Studies: The Geopolitics of Naming,* April 27-29, 2007, Princeton University.
5. Olga Koulieri, "Russian Eurasianism and the Geopolitics of the Black Sea," www.da.mod.uk/CSRC/documents/Special/S43/S43.pt4

6. See Marlene Laruelle, *Russia's Central Asian Policy and the Role of Russian Nationalism,* Silk Road Paper April 2008, http://www.isdp.eu/files/publications/srp/08/m108russiacentral.pdf
7. Andrei P. Tsygankov, "Hardline Eurasianism and Russia's Contending Geopolitical Perspectives," *East European Quarterly,* no. 32, 1998.
8. Tunc Aybak, "From Turkic Century to the Rise of Eurasianism," in Gerald MacLean (ed.), *Writing Turkey, Explorations in Turkish History, politics and cultural identity* (London: Middlesex University Press, 2006).
9. Aybak, "From Turkic Century to the Rise of Eurasianism."
10. Jacob Landau, *Pan Turkism in Turkey: A Study of Irredentism* (London: Hurst, 1981).
11. Caroline Humphrey, "Eurasia, ideology and the political imagination in provincial Russia," in C. M. Hann (ed.), *Post socialism Ideas, ideologies and practices in Eurasia* (London and New York: Routledge, 1993).
12. See Humphrey, "Eurasia, ideology and the political imagination in provincial Russia."
13. David Mutimer, Kyle Grayson and J. Marshall Bejer, "Critical Studies on Security: An introduction," *Critical Studies on Security*, vol. 1, no. 1, 2013.
14. Antony Burke, "Security Cosmopolitanism," *Critical Studies on Security*, vol. 1, no. 1, 2013.
15. Mohiaddin Mesbahi, "Islam and Security Narratives in Eurasia," *Caucasus Survey,* vol. 1, no. 1, October 2013.
16. Saule Mukhametrakhimova, "Afghan pullout risks Central Asian Security," *JK Alternative Viewpoint,* August 23, 2013.
17. See David W. Montgomery, "Namaz, Wishing Trees and Vodka: The Diversity of Everyday Religious Life in Central Asia," in Jeff Sahadeo and Russell Zanca (eds.), *Everyday Life in Central Asia, Past and Present* (Bloomington and Indianapolis: Indiana University Press, 2007).
18. A. K. Sultangalieva, *Islam v Kazakhstane: Istoriia, etnichnost obshchestvo* (Almaty: Kazakhstan Institute of Strategic Studies, 1998).
19. Nursultan Nazarbayev, *V serdtse Yevrazii* (In the Heart of Eurasia) (Almaty, Astana: Zhybek Zholy, 2010).
20. Theodore Levine, "Music and Musicians Along the Silk Road," Smithsonian Folklife Festival, The Silk Road Connecting Cultures Creating Trust, www.festival.si.edu/past.../silk_road/programme_theodor_levine.aspx
21. John Gerard Ruggie (ed.), *Multilateralism Matters, The Theory and Praxis of an Institutional Form*, (New York: Columbia University Press, 1993).
22. Martha Brill Olcott, "The Myth of 'Tsentralnaia Aziia,'" *Orbis*, Fall 1994. Similar ideas were expressed by others who pointed to economic, political and social reasons of discord. See for instance, Anatoly Khazanov, *After the USSR: Ethnicity,*

Nationalism and Politics in the Commonwealth of Independent States (London: The University of Wisconsin Press, 1995).

23. Olcott, "The Myth of 'Tsentralnaia Aziia.'"
24. See for instance Paul Kubicek, "Regionalism, Nationalism and Realpolitik in Central Asia," *Europe-Asia Studies,* vol. 49, no. 4, 1997.
25. Mashan Meiirzhan elaborates on the role of the Central Asian Economic Union in this regard in his article, "Regional Security as a System Factor in Central Asian Integration," in Jasjit Singh (ed.), *Peace and Security in Central Asia* (New Delhi: IDSA, 2000).
26. From the *Address by H. E. Mr. Nursultan Nazarbayev, President of the Republic of Kazakhstan to the twenty-eighth session of the General Conference of the United Nations Educational, Scientific and Cultural Organization,* Paris, November 15, 1995.
27. Richard Weitz, "Kazakhstan and the New International Politics of Eurasia," Silk Road Paper, July 2008, Central Asia-Caucasus Institute and Silk Road Studies Programme, www.silkroadstudies.org
28. From the *Address by H. E. Mr. Nursultan Nazarbayev, President of the Republic of Kazakhstan to the twenty-eighth session of the General Conference of the United Nations Educational, Scientific and Cultural Organization.*
29. For a detailed analysis of CICA see Murat Laumulin, *The Security, Foreign Policy, and International Relationship of Kazakhstan after Independence, 1991-2001* (Almaty: Kazakhstan Institute of Strategic Studies and Freidrich Ebert Shiftung, 2002) and M. Ashimbaev et al. (eds.), *New Challenges and New Geopolitics in Central Asia after September 11* (Almaty: Kazakhstan Institute for Strategic Studies, 2003).
30. Talgat Ismagambetov, "Some Geopolitical Peculiarities of Central Asia, Past and Present," in Sally N. Cummings (ed.), *Oil, Transition and Security in Central Asia* (London and New York: Routledge-Curzon, 2003).
31. A security system, as defined by Barry Buzan, is a group of states whose security interests bind them sufficiently closely so that their national security cannot be realistically considered separate from each other.
32. Farkhod Tolipov, "East vs West? Some Geopolitical Questions and Observations for the SCO," *China and Eurasia Forum Quarterly,* July 2005.
33. Farkhod Tolipov, "Multilateralism, Bilateralism and Unilateralism in Fighting Terrorism in the SCO Area," *China and Eurasia Forum Quarterly*, vol. 4, no. 2, 2006.
34. Ludwig Wittgenstein, *Culture and Value* (Chicago: University of Chicago Press, 1980).

Spaces into Places

1. Central Asians: Peoples of the Region or Citizens of the States?

Farkhod Tolipov

Two Introductory Remarks

The author of this paper was recently a Fellow at the NATO Defence College in Rome and had a unique opportunity to attend lectures of different guest-officers from NATO HQ and experts from think tanks; to carry out research on NATO's role in Central Asia after 2014; to discuss with colleagues the security challenges the region faces nowadays, etc. From this experience I returned home quite confused by controversial and paradoxical revelations. Though I was of the opinion that NATO should keep its high profile in our region, my position was rejected by all whom I talked to in the NATO institution. My colleagues referred to fatigue among European countries and the US after the Afghan campaign and reluctance to remain in Central Asia. At the same, it is the widespread opinion and concern among primarily Russian and Chinese expert community, as also among Uzbek, Kazakh and other Central Asian official and academic circles, that the US/NATO intends to establish its permanent military presence in Central Asia, concerns which are not verified. My analytical confusion caused some suspicions that something is wrong with Central Asian geopolitical scholarship.

Very recently, I participated in a forum "Dialogues on the Great Silk Road" organised in the Issyk-Kul by the Mukhtar Auezov Foundation. That forum, without exaggeration, was saturated and pervaded with passionate expressions of cultural, historical and national unity of all Central Asian peoples and rejection of artificial division of the region into five sovereign states. The forum loudly called for restoration of the regional commonality. At the same time, it is a prevalent opinion and stereotype that the peoples of the region are deeply divided along different lines and do not and cannot constitute a single polity. In this instance also my analytical confusion caused serious suspicion about Central Asian regionalism scholarship.

Theoretical Assumptions

This research proposes new contemplation on the phenomenon of regionalism in Central Asia, based on consideration of juxtaposition of new phenomenon of what is called "micro-geopolitics" and the old phenomenon of national-regional dualism—two realities that characterise the "ecumenic" evolution of peoples and states of Central Asia since gaining independence in 1991.

The micro-geopolitics refers to the geopolitisation of regional relations between Central Asian states and by state leaders and elites of their own territories. This phenomenon differs from classical geopolitics of great powers and became, in fact, a by-product of the latter. The situation can be described in the notion of "regime of micro-geopolitics." The national-regional dualism means a specific spatial phenomenon reflected in contradiction between "unidimensional" static borders of the states of Central Asia and "multidimensional," dynamic frontiers of self-determination of peoples of these states. In many observations of Central Asia socio-spatial realities of this region are taken from dualist perspective, namely, such constructs as sedentary-nomadic, Turkic-Persian, upstream-downstream, small-big, strong-weak divisions between the Central Asian countries. Moreover, the very definition of the frontiers of Central Asia and its composition remains an actual subject of an academic search and is not yet complete.

Both micro-geopolitics and national-regional dualism have evidently an existential territorial dimension; and juxtaposition of these two spatial realities has caused quite sophisticated and biased political process related to the defining of the region of Central Asia and led to an articulation of "territorialisation" of social being which manifests itself in subregional clan and kinship relationships on the one hand, and mega-regional cross-border way of life of local population on the other. Such a controversial, dual link between space, peoples and polity needs to be deeply elaborated, given an artificial division of this region in early twentieth century, dramatic geopolitical implications of the collapse of the Soviet Union in 1991 and new articulation of a spatial dimension of the Euro-Asian integration project in early twenty-first century.

This research is designed within the framework of constructivist methodology and the school of critical geopolitics. However, despite this relatively novel approach to the understanding of relationships between space, peoples and polity, it still remains quite narrow for explaining those relationships without an interdisciplinary approach to the problem which would incorporate historical views, study of demographical and migration processes as well as ideological aspects of the nation- and state-building in Central Asia as related to the habitat. Finally, comparative analysis of the very phenomenon of regional integration in Europe and in Central Asia yields quite telling lessons. These last directions of research do not fit in the frames of this analysis but were mentioned just to point out to the complexity and sophisticated character of driving forces of overall regional relationships in this part of the world.

Global Challenge and National Interest

So-called newly independent states of Central Asia which came into existence due to the dissolution of the Soviet Union have faced since 1991 a twofold existential reality: the challenge of a new era of globalisation and the legacy of old era of sovereignty. Throughout the period of independence—for more than 22 years—these states have dealt with the seemingly paradoxical task of meeting the challenge of globalisation on one hand, and asserting newly acquired sovereignty on the other. This paradoxical task stipulated their contradictory behaviour as actors of international relations.

The challenge of globalisation consists not simply of rising interdependence per se of countries and peoples of the world to which newly independent states have to adapt themselves but of expanding institutional and political engagements and arrangements which require special institutional and normative adaptation and correspondence of these states. At the same time, "fundamentalism of sovereignty" obviously makes them prioritise what is called national interests. Unleashed in 1991, "freedom of national interests" caused metamorphoses of identities and policies. Combined with the challenge of globalisation the challenge of sovereignty created a perplexing situation for states and political regimes of Central Asia.

This situation further confused the political process. The most illustrative manifestation of this confusion is the revelation that the countries of the region still see the world through the old and obsolete lenses of classical geopolitics and power struggle. Interesting and symptomatic in this respect are the activities of international organisations in the region and attitude of Central Asian states towards them which testify non-compliance of Central Asians with international norms. As a result, the actuality of and appeal to multilateral formats in addressing contemporary challenges the world is facing coincided with actuality of and appeal to nationalism in newly independent states of Central Asia. So, international organisations with their international agendas encountered the motion of Central Asian nations in the opposite direction. Central Asian countries' national agendas have not yet been satisfied, but they are forced by contemporary international reality to satisfy international (and regional) agendas.

The complexity confused researches as well. The overall researches of current Central Asian regional developments, to my mind, lack accurate elaboration on three problems in dialectical conjunction, namely, context, contest and consent ("C3"). In other words, one has to comprehend the nuanced context of analysis; evaluate as precisely as possible the real and mythic roots of contests over certain things, such as values, resources and power; propose fundamental solutions of problems and ways towards reaching consent. From this perspective, I would like to point out to the contradictory context of globalisation and sovereignty which are the main factors of ongoing contests among Central Asians over territory, water, resources, power and so on. I would like also to point out that more often than not the consent among Central Asian countries is being constructed, at least within discursive framework, on the wrong basis because crisis management and conflict prevention efforts in the region take mostly the form of mitigation, mediation, confidence-building and the like. However, these measures do not yield fundamental solutions.

Micro-Geopolitics

Let us ask ourselves: what would happen or what would be the course of events should the Soviet Union still exist? Geopolitical environment and peoples' identities of Central Asians would be, so to speak, Soviet-made. We know that none of the former Soviet Central Asian republics was ready for independence and each was ready to sign a new Union Treaty in 1991. After independence they all rediscovered the world, their own history and the land in which they live. After all, they became micro-geopolitical actors. We know that classical geopolitics is all about the great power rivalry over particular territory; it is all about the great power's aspiration on establishing its control or domination on a particular territory. Micro-geopolitics is all about small countries' aspiration on utilisation of the geographical assets they possess and "selling" these assets to great powers. Former targets and objects of great power geopolitics, or Great Game, these small countries of Central Asia try to play off the "Small Game" card with each other and with great powers.[1]

It is not by accident that the concept of "bridge" is widely used by all political regimes of Central Asia when they try to demonstrate their geostrategic significance. Portraying itself and its territory as a bridge connecting one geostrategic region or great power of the continent with another became an obsession of political regimes of all five countries concerned. It has to be noted here that, on the one hand, central and bridge-like geographical location of Central Asia as heartland of Eurasia is a reality. Its significance was well described, for example, by Ross Munro: "A new Silk Road of modern railroads and highways that would effectively give China a land route far to the west, ultimately to Europe and to an Iranian opening on the Persian Gulf, would have enormous strategic consequences, possibly comparable to the impact that the advent of Suez and Panama Canals once had."[2] But, on the other hand, "bridge-ism" or, more appropriately, "sovereign bridge-ism" led to very rewarding view on the geographical being ("geo-being"). Combined with historical myths about lands and territories, borders and frontiers of any individual country of the region, it has a negative impact on identities and regional relationships of Central Asians because intentionally or unintentionally, it leads to distortion of history and also nationalisation of this history.

I did not ask what would be the course of events should the Soviet Union still exist today only out of curiosity. It was just to remind that the immediate reaction of Central Asian republics to the dissolution of the former superpower was the establishment of their own regional unity. This very fact revealed the unique historical heritage preserved over centuries despite the construction of the Soviet "melting pot." Central Asian regional structure had passed through a number of important stages since 1991 and possessed a profound potential of nurturing regional identity out of five nations, but this evolution was artificially interrupted in 2005.[3] Since then the potential for regional discord between and among Central Asian countries has shifted from latent level to dominant factor of the regional affairs. Central Asians could not cope with such challenges as territorial claims, disputes over water distribution, inter-ethnic conflicts on their own and the idea of international agents' mediation appeared as a recipe for conflict prevention, simulation of regional cooperation and development in this region. However, various multilateral initiatives have not yet resulted in considerable regional cooperation based on mutual trust and corresponding political will.

Anita Sengupta rightly noticed that a variety of regional organisations that emerged in Central Asia, although perceived as agents of economic development and security providers, in fact, have been unable to convey hard defence guarantees, create joint military units, negotiate arms reductions or enforce the end of overt conflicts. She points out that "a correct assessment of these initiatives would have to begin with noting their existential significance as groups of states that recognise themselves as sharing some elements of community and can define their national identity as complementary rather than adversarial to their neighbours."[4]

Currently, the overall relationships between Central Asian countries, unfortunately, are far from fraternal, at least because the national interest approach to whatever problem arises in their relations just exacerbates the problem instead of removing it. Interestingly, almost any conflict-prone situation in the region directly or indirectly has a territorial dimension which stipulates micro-geopolitics. Suffice it to enumerate basic conflictual issues which are "territorialised":

- construction of the Rogun Hydro-Power Station (HPS) in Tajikistan;
- construction of the Kambarata HPS in Kyrgyzstan;
- Tajiks claims of Bukhara and Samarkand;
- Inter-ethnic tension between Uzbeks and Kyrgyz in the South of Kyrgyzstan;
- Mining by Uzbekistan of some sections of the Uzbek-Kyrgyz and Uzbek-Tajik border;
- Sporadic clashes of border guards on the border area between Kyrgyzstan and Uzbekistan, Tajikistan and Uzbekistan, Kazakhstan and Uzbekistan, Turkmenistan and Uzbekistan;
- Maintaining the visa regime between Central Asian states;
- Mutual territorial claims and incompleteness of delineation and demarcation process between these states;
- The problems of enclaves between Kyrgyzstan, Tajikistan and Uzbekistan;
- The problem of transport communications and pipelines across the region;
- Uzbekistan's accusation of the Tajik side for its dirty aluminium production in Tursunzoda city which has negative environmental impact on the adjacent territory of Uzbekistan;
- Unresolved status of the Caspian Sea.

National-Regional Dualism

Carlo Tullio-Altan, one of the modern researchers of the concept of a "nation," distinguishes the following symbolic landmarks of national identity: epos (historical memory), ethos (rules for living together), logos (common language), genos (family relations and lineage) and topos (territory).[5] However, such thinkers as Max Weber or even Josef Stalin might disagree with such description of a nation. In particular, Max Weber pointed out to the difference between the very *idea* of the nation and *empirical scope* of given political association. He defined the concept of nation in the following way: "a nation is a community of sentiment which would adequately manifest itself in a state of its own; hence, a nation is a community which normally tends to produce a state of its own."[6] In most definitions of the phenomenon of the nation it is primarily associated with a certain political affiliation. All the symbolic pointers of national identity—epos, ethos, logos, genos and topos—are at the same time the objective facts of history and subjective perception (interpretation) of that history. I would argue that if political affiliation and allegiance are central for understanding the phenomenon of the modern nation, then the dialectical interaction, mutual exchanges and constituting relationships between the nation and the state are crucial for their coexistence. This is especially true, in my opinion, of nations and states of Central Asia which were shaped respectively as a modern political community and a modern political institution to a great extent due to the Soviet institutionalisation. Moreover, this Soviet political initiative and innovation was picked up after its dissolution by the so-called newly independent states of Central Asia. In our case, it is not so much a nation constitutes and manifests itself in a state of its own as its opposite—a state shapes and manifests itself in a nation.

That is why national ideology was very important for shaping a nation and justifying the being of the state. The process of producing nationhood out of the statehood required not only profound mobilisation of historical memory but also creation of mythology which would push that memory in a "right direction." Nation-building process in Central Asia goes hand-in-hand with mythology-making. This process is leading to alienation of Central Asians from each other, the tendency that was well described by the Uzbek sociologist Alisher Ilkhamov. He pointed out to the principles of "us" versus "others" which became a driving force of the policies of states of the region vis-à-vis each other. "The national ideologies are made by distortion of native history and national identity. The practice of administrative subjection of academia and the rejection of academic freedom continues beyond Soviet Union's dissolution, with even more arbitrary rewriting of national history. As a consequence, a number of officially adopted historical doctrines produced by court and tame scholars have emerged. These doctrines tend to distance the Central Asian peoples, their histories and national symbols from each other."[7]

Today, in its attempt to explain the regional relationships and overall developments, Central Asian scholarship more often than not is utilising such dualist constructs as sedentary-nomadic, Turkic-Persian, upstream-downstream, small-big, strong-weak divisions between the Central Asian countries. However, such a linear approach to regional affairs overlooks profound interdependence of peoples of the region. Nomadic peoples are no longer nomadic at least since the establishment of Soviet rule and urbanisation; Turkic-Persian peoples are not completely separated from each other and their lives and history deeply overlap; upstream and downstream countries actually belong to the same ecosystem; the stronger state cannot and has not, so far, imposed its will upon the weaker one, so such a division is also artificial; "small" and "big" characteristics cannot be criteria for consideration of prospects of integration and disintegration because there are small and big countries everywhere (especially in Europe) where integration has taken place.

Finally, there was another reason for my mentioning the Soviet Union as a political association to which former Soviet Central Asian republics were ready to hand over their allegiances in 1991. It was a "melting pot" for peoples of the region. I would argue that the region has for centuries evolved as a "melting pot" for tribes and ethnic groups. Anita Sengupta rightly noted the "complexity of a situation where the people of the now sovereign republics of Central Asia had been linked for centuries by community of language, extended contact, ethnic and cultural interaction and similar historical development" which resulted in emergence of different short- and long-lived political unions.[8] The only phenomenon of the Uzbek nation which "federalistically" originated out of 92 ancient tribes, whose names are often repeated in the tribal composition of neighbouring nations, is a clear-cut example of the "melting pot" geography of Central Asia.

Interestingly, even the Soviet Union, despite its authorship of the creation of modern Central Asian republics and nations, served as a "melting pot" because such a division was conditional as long as there existed supranational polity. When the Soviet "melting pot" itself melted the notion of "national identity" became the "weapon of mass construction" which was a serious new cultural, ethnic, psychological and historical challenge for self-consciousness, self-perception, self-determination and self-assertion of peoples of the region. "Indeed, identities in general and 'national' identity in particular is faced with a constant process of transition as political boundaries are reorganised and some states cease to exist while others come into being, defining identities on newer basis."[9] From such contemplation we can presume that perhaps a new "melting pot" will and should evolve in Central Asia out of experimentation on nation- and state-building without due acknowledgement of region-being. All in all, it is impossible to distinguish in the Central Asian context where the national life ends and the regional life begins, and vice versa. National-regional dualism in Central Asia is a matter of fact and this fact requires revision of some academic approaches to the study of Central Asia based on the new principle of indivisibility of the region.

Dualism by Kazakhstan and Uzbekistan

There is another, so to speak, non-conventional dualism in the region which has an impact on Central Asian geopolitical status quo and thereby on integration versus disintegration moods. This dualism emerged out of mythic perception of competition between Kazakhstan and Uzbekistan—two strongest states of Central Asia—for the leadership in the region. It is really astonishing that both countries "forgot" their region by taking two different stances in their foreign behaviour: Kazakhstan overextends itself by obsession with global project-mongering; Uzbekistan, to the contrary, decided to reduce its "regional presence," albeit not totally, and proclaimed bilateralism as a driving principle of its foreign policy. So intersection of space and place in Central Asia is undergoing nowadays a dramatic metamorphosis. Kazakhstan by overextension and Uzbekistan by self-restraint both have isolated themselves from the region and failed to give a lead in regional affairs;[10] the region as a space and as a place is being de-territorialised not so much due to the global trends of de-territorialisation as due to, so to speak, Kazakh-made and Uzbek-made instruments of "Geopolitical Positioning System" (ironically, "GPS").

Indeed, Astana constantly invents new instruments for their geo-positioning in space and place such as Path to Europe, Eurasian Union, Conference on Interaction and Confidence Measures in Asia, Central Asian Union, Union of Kazakhstan and Kyrgyzstan, etc. In February 2014, President of Kazakhstan Nursultan Nazarbayev once again invented one more "GPS," namely, renaming the country from Kazakhstan into Kazakh Yeli which means the Kazakh people but loses the geographical and political connotation that the suffix "stan" clearly reflected. Most of the observers discerned in this trick a deliberate attempt to distance the country from other Central Asian "stans"—Kyrgyzstan, Tajikistan, Turkmenistan and Uzbekistan. Such a national exceptionality outlook can further distort the geographical and historical outlines of the single "regional village" of five "stans."

Uzbekistan, in turn, has taken an insular stance in the region and its "GPS" instrument is typically used when Tashkent capitalises on Uzbekistan's central position in the region and exerts pressure on Tajikistan by blocking roads or resisting the construction of the Rogun HPS; or does not interfere when Uzbeks are massacred in Osh city of Kyrgyzstan; or one-sidedly mines segments of the border with Kyrgyzstan and Tajikistan; or abandons the CSTO while other Central Asian states remain the members of the Organisation, and so on. Actually, similar views can be noted with regard to other "stans" concerned, though Kazakhstan and Uzbekistan obviously bear the main responsibility for regional affairs in Central Asia. Therefore, while Central Asians are entering the global village, they at the same time are significantly destroying their own regional village of Central Asia. They increasingly demonstrate that there are 5 places as residences of their peoples and there is not a single space as their historically common habitat.

Is Eurasia a Response to the Global Challenge?

After the dissolution of the former Soviet Union the geographical territory that this superpower occupied ceased being a single space of habitat for the peoples who lived together within it for more than 70 years. This space was turned into a number of places which were called "independent states." The political and arbitrary disruption in 1991 of the once territorial connectivity of Eurasian lands had brought about re-structuring of the geographical space and political places where more than 100 nationalities and ethnic communities were erstwhile well accommodated.

Central Asia became such an area which geopolitically and in terms of self-determination of peoples is fluctuating between the Euro-Asian and Euro-Atlantic spaces. And this is one of the strongest manifestations of globalisation in this part of the world. It is not accidental, therefore, that the political project and ideology of Eurasianism was recalled soon after the collapse of the USSR. The Russian President Vladimir Putin and Kazakhstan's President Nursultan Nazarbayev are perhaps the most prominent proponents of this project nowadays. However, the Eurasian doctrine, attractive and strong as it is, implies not just a somewhat co-habitation of peoples and countries within one polity but Russia as a pillar or centre of gravity for them. So the success or, rather, acceptance of this doctrine by the peoples to whom it is addressed, will depend primarily on Russia. The collapse of the USSR, which in fact was a Eurasian Union, during the presidency of Boris Yeltsin, was at the same time a blow on Eurasianism. The main proponents of Eurasianism themselves today are globally oriented in all spheres ranging from economy to security.

In particular, neo-Eurasianism can no longer take the ideological meaning of the "protection of smaller (weaker) peoples" by Russia as this doctrine had in the past. I think it will have a chance to be embodied as a model only if it recognised that smaller nations, actually independent states, are able to either protect themselves or seek protection outside the Eurasian space. So the question of Eurasianism is not so much a matter of protection or security of countries situated on this region as it is a matter of proper modern accommodation of this vast space as such. It is a question of transport, communication, trade, cultural exchanges, and so on. This is indeed the vast continental zone that needs a new geopolitical accommodation. The presence of China in Eurasia on the one hand, and the openness of Eurasia itself to the West on the other, essentially modifies the content and function of the Eurasian doctrine.

Meanwhile, if Eurasianism is envisioned as a principle of creation of the "common home" and joint identity, that is, the principle of interstate integration, then it should evolve not so much on the security substance as on the normative one. For Central Asia it means, if accepted, the political shift from the regional spatial being to the macro-regional one. However, the *paradox of macro-regionalism* as a stage where the solutions of problems of regionalism can be found is hidden in the nature of those problems themselves: macro-regionalism implies indispensable mediation role of great power in resolving regional problems; however, while the decision can be made on the macro-regional level its implementation will be on the regional one, that is, the problem will be returned back to those in the region who delivered it "up" by invoking great-power mediation. The joining of Uzbekistan to the EvrAzES organisation in 2006 and abandoning it right in 2007, is an illustrative example of the so far vagueness of the continental Eurasian doctrine.

It will be pertinent to mention, in this regard, former Armenian Foreign Minister V. Oskanyan's observation of the Armenian hesitation between the European Union and Eurasian Union, "... the situation is uncertain, the foreign policy lacks an ideological basis. We don't know where we are going and what our purpose is. The country is drifting ... If we are unable to perceive clearly the ideological basis of our foreign policy external actors will be likely to interpret everything in their own way and act in accordance with their own interests. But our interests do not always coincide, even collide with theirs. First of all, we should define which path we going along ..."[11] I am confident that such a discourse is very relevant for Central Asians, as well.

Conclusion

So who are the Central Asians: peoples of the single region or citizens of five states? One can assume that two schools of thought compete with each other regarding this fundamental question. One school sees the region as fragmented, another as united. This dichotomy concerns not only academia but elites and political regimes as well. Elites' specific comprehension of globalisation and preoccupation with national interests, in fact, distorted the methods of construing and constructing the nation-state and securing it in each Central Asian country. However, the elitist approach to this issue obviously lacks the voice and, so to speak, contribution of the demos.

The way out from this intellectual and political deadlock obviously lies along the way of *democratic* recognition of national-regional dualism and overcoming destructive geopolitics. It would also mean shifting analysis and policymaking beyond the elitist national sovereignty and national interests' frameworks and acknowledgement that sovereignty and interests can be regional. I believe that these seemingly fossilised terms should be revised and made globally adjustable. After all, "[t]he ontological problem is that interests may not be assumed a priori, but are a malleable product of a complex web of social interaction."[12]

As anywhere that integration takes place, there are Central Asian pessimists and Central Asian optimists regarding the future unification of the region. In any case, during the whole period of independence a phenomenon of "national-regional" dualism revealed itself. Centripetal tendencies juxtapose with centrifugal ones. Nation- and state-building processes intermingle with the regional evolution. That is why the main characteristics of the status quo in the region can be formulated as follows: *united in culture, divided in politics; united in traditions and heritage, divided by circumstances; united by geography, divided by geopolitics.* The Great and Small games by which Central Asians seem to be entangled could not but undermine their comprehension of the common responsibility for the regional affairs. From this viewpoint, the new strategy of region-building becomes expedient at the new stage of the Central Asian development after gaining independence. After all, the Eurasian affiliation, if any, of Central Asians should be preceded by the full accomplishment of the Central Asian regional integration project. Otherwise, the premature Eurasian format of integration will symbolise forever inability of Central Asians to unite on their own.

Notes

1. F. Tolipov, "Micro-Geopolitics of Central Asia: A Uzbekistan Perspective," *Strategic Analysis*, vol. 35, no. 4, July 2011.

2. R. H. Munro, "China, India, and Central Asia," in *After Empire. The Emerging Geopolitics of Central Asia*, J. Snyder (ed.) (Washington: National Defense University Press, 1995), 130.
3. F. Tolipov, "Geopolitical Stipulation of Central Asian Integration," *Strategic Analysis*, vol. 34, no. 1, 2010.
4. Anita Sengupta, *Restructuring Regional Alignments in Eurasia: the Emergence of a New Dialogue* (Kolkata: MAKAIAS, 2008), 26.
5. C. Tullio-Altan, *Gli italiani in Europa. Profilio storico comparato delle identita nazionali europee* [Italians in Europe. A comparative historical profile of European national identies], Bologna: Il Mulino, 1999: 12-13. Quoted in A. Ilkhamov, "Post-Soviet Central Asia: from nationhood mythologies to regional cold wars?" in *Towards Social Stability and Democratic Governance in Central Eurasia. Challenges to Regional Security*, Irina Morozova (ed.) (NATO Science Series, Amsterdam: IOS Press, 2005), 87.
6. Quoted in John Hutchinson and Antony D. Smith (eds.), Nationalism, Oxford University Press, 1994: 25.
7. Ilkhamov, "Post-Soviet Central Asia," in Morozova (ed.), *Towards Social Stability*, 85.
8. Anita Sengupta, *Frontiers into Borders. The Transformation of Identities in Central Asia* (Kolkata: MAKAIAS, 2002), 144.
9. Sengupta, *Frontiers into Borders*, 176.
10. F. Tolipov, "Uzbekistan and Kazakhstan: Two Failed Leaders of Central Asia," *Himalayan and Central Asian Studies*, vol. 16, nos. 3-4, July-December 2012: 172-82.
11. Quoted in Roman Melikyan, "Eurasian Union, European Union and the Armenian Complementarism," *Central Asia and Caucasus*, vol. 14, no. 2, 2013.
12. Jan Angstrom and Jan Willem Honig, "Regaining Strategy: Small Powers, Strategic Culture, and Escalation in Afghanistan," *Journal of Strategic Studies*, vol. 35, no. 5, October 2012: 670.

2. The Russian Regional Gaze: From the Far East to the Far North

Suchandana Chatterjee

Discussions about Russia's changing energy pivots indicate a shifting Russian gaze from the Far East to the Far North. Myriads of factors have affected the change. In the aftermath of the Cold War, the importance of resource-rich regions like Siberia and the Far East[1] in connection with Northeast Asian energy grid was seriously considered. Russian options were related to trade and economic cooperation, energy and infrastructure—which regions like the Russian Far East and Eastern Siberia were able to offer. An alternative viewpoint rated Siberia and Far East as underperformers[2] that resulted in Russia's weak economic engagement with APEC. Some Russian sympathisers are of the opinion that in Russia's APEC policy, there was a will to return to the Primakovian policy of balancing strategies.[3] Some observers have marked a China turn in President Putin's official pronouncements in St. Petersburg International Economic Forum in June 2013.[4] Russia's search for diversified energy routes in the East is evident. She is trying to balance relations with her Pacific neighbours, mainly through re-engagement with APEC community.[5]

The Russian gaze had also drifted to icy regions of the Arctic region that has led to fresh parleys with Scandinavian countries and Canada about maritime control over regions classified as Exclusive Economic Zones (EEZ) that seems to be out of bounds of the UN Charters on the high seas. "Arcticism" is a somewhat romantic image that dates back to the eighteenth and nineteenth centuries when Russia launched her exploratory missions. An idealistic scenario would have been the acceptance of Russia's claim over the Arctic seabed as part of the historic Russian past and also as part and parcel of an economic zone that includes the Siberian shelf. But, that is not the case. The "idea of the common good" is not being considered here—much graver issues of military and naval containment in the endangered environment of the Arctic have raised questions about resource-based development ethics of the Great Powers, in this case, Russia. This paper seeks to deal with the Russian regional gaze in (a) Siberia and the Far East and (b) the Arctic.

In the Community of Asia

Immediately after the end of the Cold War, Russia's policy towards her neighbours was based on the notion of "leaning towards the West, stabilising the South and going East."[6] The desire for a new business atmosphere made Russia look in the direction of the East. The most attractive regional bloc was the Asia-Pacific and its economic component APEC. ASEAN, a 27-nation forum and the East Asia Summit that has evolved out of ASEAN, were also given attention. The main agenda was connectivity and development of the Far East, and consolidation of partnership relations with East Asian countries was discussed within that framework.[7] Russia's most recent initiative has been to strengthen its programme of action in APEC 2012 in Vladivostok by supporting APEC model of horizontal integration. Keeping in mind energy as its calling card, Russia has been projecting Siberia and Russian Far East as the scene of action for APEC involvement.

The question of *entering* the Asia-Pacific region cropped up since the time of *glasnost* and *perestroika* with the hope of economic integration across borders. In the 1990s, regional integration through routes of access was seriously thought of through surface connectors as the Trans-Siberian railway and through bridge and road formula. Russian border cities like Blagoveshchensk were rebuilt as bridges for regional integration. Siberia mattered most in Russia's Asia policy that was oriented towards resolving the Sino-Russian border dispute in the Amur basin—a region that was subjected to Russian penetration in the 1560s, built as a fort and a trading port for furs. Gorbachev-Deng Xiaoping's joint pledge "to close the past and open the future" was a step forward to initiating negotiations about normalising relations, though there was enough speculation about acknowledging Chinese rights of navigation beyond Khabarovsk.[8] Events like the Year of Russia in China (2006) and the Year of China in Russia (2007) sought to strengthen scientific and technical cooperation between the two countries. So, theoretically speaking, the external engagement of multiple actors within the format of "a community of Asia" and the convergence of interests in the Asia-Pacific region was greeted with enthusiasm.

Scene I

Siberia and the Russian Far East

In its search for markets of energy, Siberia has earned a new name, i.e., a Pacific gateway,[9] with obscure places on the Sino-Russian and Russo-Japanese Pacific borderlands (also including river islands) being posed as the hub of Russia's energy routes.The Asia-Pacific region has evolved as an attractive option because of the prospects of access to markets and sources blessed by cheap local energy resources that can travel through lesser distances. In this, Russia feels the pressure of China because it has sought to diversify the huge need of energy with alternative energy sources like nuclear power, domestic shale gas and renewable energy.

The questions that are raised are whether Siberian and the Far Eastern oilfields will continue to be considered useful from the new perspectives of infrastructure connectivity, market connectivity and technology connectivity. China's forays into the regional market through routes of infrastructure and technology have generated multi-level regional competition. The Japanese model of balancing Chinese competition in the Asia-Pacific region introduced new levels of debate in the energy arena. Chinese joint ventures became active and provincial authorities set up economic cooperation zones in Khabarovsk territory in Heihe, Suifenhe and Hunchun.[10] Provincial authorities gradually became more proactive by encouraging the activities of mediators in the Amur region. The possibilities of creating free economic zones and Special Economic Zones (SEZs) in which these mediators would operate created a new environment for interaction.

Since 2003-4, as Russia pushed forward its new energy strategy in the region, a web of energy deals surfaced. China started projecting its own energy interests, by advocating shortened routes (Angara-Harbin route) and combining oil and gas routes via Daqing and also ruled out Mongolia as a transit route. The main interest was in oil exports to the West. Gas arrangements became a tenuous issue. Japan at this stage became more proactive and the Nakhodka route was projected as bringing second life along the BAM territories (Baikal-Amurskaya) region. China pressed forth with a combined route, i.e., the Daqing-Nakhodka route. Japan also had its own agenda. Nakhodka was better suited compared to Daqing as it was closer to East Siberian oilfields. The Irkutsk Regional administration toyed with the idea of having a Baikal pipeline that would be integrated with Nakhodka and Daqing routes and perhaps this would help to keep the negative aspects at bay. Similar competition started with the Vangkor project, a northern oilfield of Russia in which Rosneft eliminated its competitors smoothly, with an eye on the Northern European destinations. In 2009, the Vangkor oilfield was launched with a lot of enthusiasm and this was the first step in Rosneft's plans for the development of the East-Siberian oil and gas province, with aims to supply Asia, mainly China and Japan with oil through the East Siberia-Pacific Ocean transport pipeline (ESPO). Both the Chinese and Russian governments promised guaranteed oil supplies to each other after the ESPO deal. The investment potential of Vangkor was huge. There was much discussion about the multi-tiered collaboration of Rosneft. The Vangkor and Anglo-Siberian deal gave the Vangkor project an international image.

ESPO

China relied on Russia to divert its oil imports away from the Persian Gulf. Milestone projects were unleashed centred in Siberia. Besides the drilling projects of Rosneft and Sinopec in Sakhalin oilfields and oil exploration in Siberian oilfields, significant strides have been made since the East Siberia-Pacific Ocean Pipeline project (ESPO) that is supposed to replace the costly transportation of oil through railways. The two sides in 2003 first endorsed a pipeline proposal linking East Siberia and Daqing. This Chinese proposal was supplemented by the YUKOS proposal of Chita-Daqing pipeline that was replaced in 2006 by the ESPO project (*Vostochnaya Sibir Tikhii Okean* or East Siberia-Pacific Ocean Pipeline) that would originate in Taishet and end at Skovorodino with a spur connection in Daqing. From Skovorodino, the pipeline would be extended to Nakhodka port on the Pacific coast. This is a 4,800-kilometre pipeline exporting Russian crude oil from Taishet to Asia-Pacific markets (Kozmino via Skovordino).[11]

The ESPO project is a controversial subject. Energy experts doubt that Russia's oil reserves in East Siberia will be sufficient to meet the growing needs for oil. To re-route the oil from west to east Siberia would mean more costs. This would create a further delay in the milestone projects and would also increase capital expenditure. This means financiers of the project would face tough competition from each other. Also, there seems to be several ecological objections. The route of the oil pipeline is quite complicated crossing about 50 big and small rivers, tens of highways and railroads and mountain ranges. This geographical overlay of rivers and mountains and the high level of seismic activity will inevitably create a danger during construction work and would be risky for the pipelines. According to Greenpeace activists, the pipeline crosses the largest river in Lake Baikal—the River Angara—and a slight oil leakage will pollute the river, Lake Baikal and its marine resources.

Despite these legitimate concerns, the ESPO pipeline is the biggest prestige issue in Sino-Russian energy relations. The ESPO was Russia's trump card to dilute the EU and American engagements through Nabucco. From the Chinese side, one does see its interest in diversifying the energy supply route. The Russian interest is the East Siberian oilfields which would serve as the access route to the Asia-Pacific region. Russia's interest in retaining the Pacific route prior to the Daqing spur may be related to its interest to warm up its relations with Japan in order to use it as a mechanism for connecting with the markets of Europe as well. So, analysts view the ESPO project as a Russian diplomatic and geopolitical tool rather than an economic one. Threat or no threat from China, the issue of energy in Eastern Siberia and the Russian Far East has been given a lot of attention.

Connectivity Issue: The Baikal-Amur Railway

Added to the Putin wish list is the revival of the Baikal-Amur Railway. Russia has also been considering plans to develop the legendary Trans-Siberian Railway as an international transport corridor linking Europe and the countries of the Asia-Pacific region. The classic mainline is expected to be refurbished under a multibillion-dollar government plan that aims to improve infrastructure. The plan was announced by President Vladimir Putin at the St. Petersburg Economic Forum at the end of June 2013. The modernisation of the Trans Sib and its main artery the Baikal-Amur Railway Line has been sanctioned. The BAM was the product of a Soviet railway project in the 1970s that took a decade to construct. The project ended in 1984 that linked the Trans-Siberian line between Krasnoyarsk and Irkutsk at a small junction called Taishet and ran north of Lake Baikal parallel to the main line before arriving at the Pacific Ocean port of Sovetskaya Gavan. The BAM fell into disuse within eight years due to the lack of freight passage through such harsh climatic regions. A portion of it in north-western Buryatia was revived in 2003, but the track was largely underutilised. Subsequently, the plan for revival of the BAM as a mode of heavy freight traffic for the transport of timber, coal, minerals and oil extracted from the nearby regions has been worked out.

Several new boomtowns came up around the BAM tracks in the late 1970s. Tynda is one such town that emerged from nowhere and offered its services along the railway line. It has all the features of a Soviet town and is called the unofficial capital of the BAM. Tynda is a major railway junction for access to both China to the southeast and Yakutia, which is connected to the region with the Amur-Yakutsk mainline, also known as the "Little BAM." Another boomtown is Blagoveshchensk, which is 568 kilometres away from Tynda, and shares a river border with Heihe in China, a Manchurian boomtown that is located across the Amur. Natalia Ryzhova has described how since 1993, with the opening of the Chinese-Russian border in RFE, informal border trade has been triggered off which has led to easy movement of hidden goods and services passing along established customs points. Her case study of the Heilongjang province indicates the spontaneity of privatisation and the institutional vacuum that have accounted for unprecedented business practices through various "channels" in the "grey zones."[12] Another riverside town is Komsomolsk-na-Amure which is an industrial powerhouse and stands out for its European architecture. Tynda is also very close to the Sakha republic which is a storehouse of diamonds. The terminal station of the BAM is Sovetskaya Gavan (Sovgavan), a port on the Tatar Strait. The raison d'être of Sovgavan is its timber industry, which now supplies nearby China. As Russia tends to have a firm grip over the Asia-Pacific, such small towns on the Pacific Coast seem to have brighter prospects.

The prospects became evident in the statements of the Minister of Development of Siberia and the Far East, Viktor Ishayev, who reported in the St. Petersburg Forum in June 2013 about plans to build a second spur of the Baikal-Amur Mainline that will connect Sakhalin Island and the mainland by means of a bridge. This railway line will also be extended to Korea and China. The Transsib-BAM project seems to have a huge job prospect by the year 2020. There is a growing hope in Russia about the Far East being transformed into a transcontinental transit hub which will reverse previous negative tendencies of outmigration from that region. Russia is aware of similar projects in Kazakhstan and China about connecting border territories with Europe through the Pacific. The nearby port of Vanino also acquired prominence after oil and gas companies became entrenched in Sakhalin.

"The Other Far East"[13]

Armed with the three bridges and one road formula, the APEC summit of 2012 in Vladivostok was showcased in a major way. The main desire is access through Russian "multilane bridges and one road" to the Asia-Pacific region and Europe. The Federal Ministry for the Development of the Far East based in Khabarovsk, on the banks of the Amur River, was set to become the hub of Russia's new Eastern policy. A number of major projects were planned in the Far East, including a road network. The projects include the modernisation and reconstruction of the Trans-Siberian Railway, which has the potential to generate an annual income of $18-20 billion; the construction of the Trans-Korean Railway to the port of Busan; a number of major motor roads and the development of the Northern Sea Route, which will facilitate the development of new deposits and reduce the transportation costs by 40%. The new Ministry proposed building massive bridges from the mainland (Khabarovsk region's Selikhin) to the island of Sakhalin in order to turn the island into a third door to the Pacific. Similarly rail tunnel links would connect Sakhalin with the Japanese island of Hokkaido.[14] However, the bridge building projects had several lapses.[15]

Plans were underway to build a petrochemical plant, an LNG plant and an oil refinery in Sakhalin. In addition, work on a major shipbuilding cluster seems to be in progress. The purpose was to boost the development profile of the Primorye Territory and other regions in the Russian Far East. An ambitious scheme is a section of the ESPO pipeline that will be entrenched in Primorskiy territory.

There were plenty of reports on the newness of the "other Far East":

> Arriving in Vladivostok by sea last month, there is still snow on the shore, tucked into folds of the ground so that the dark hills and bright white shadows give the landscape the look of a photographic negative. The sea lanes are clear, however, allowing the nuclear icebreakers to rest in dock, and the port of Russia's easternmost major city is already busy, looking at once godforsaken (the lack of vegetation creates a lot of dust) and pleasantly busy (there are cranes, of every sort, everywhere).
>
> The bay that the city commands has been called the Golden Horn since the 1860s, but a faint geographical resemblance aside, it is hard to defend the comparison. While Istanbul was a fulcrum between east and west, this city's name betrays which way it leans: Vostok is Russian for "east." From here it's cheaper to fly to Japan than to major cities in Siberia. Residents have just one hour of their workday to do business with Moscow, due to the seven-hour time difference. Korean-branded buses ply the streets, and the best hotel in town is called the Hyundai.

Popular attitudes, especially among the young, also seem to be changing:

Marina Rashchepkina, a second-year translation student at the Far Eastern Federal University, said many people in her hometown of Amursk, around 500 miles north of Vladivostok, held prejudices against Chinese migrants. The older generation especially were "apt to underestimate mental abilities of Asian migrants," she said. But with growing economic interdependence has come an acceptance that, like it or not, China has come to play a central role in the future of the Far East. Marina said, "Most Russians, thinking rationally, would reject the total absence of China in the life of the Russian Far East."

Maria Lebedko, a professor of English at the university who also teaches courses in inter-cultural communication as part of an arrangement with universities in Japan, China, and other neighbouring countries, told me the region had no choice but to come to terms with its geographic reality—something she tried to impart to her students. "We are in Asia. ... We are not in Europe," she said. "I think we have to know each other better."[16]

Scene II

The Arctic

Russia's Maritime Doctrine 2020 underlined the fact that being in Asia or Europe was not enough for Russia. The importance of history and geography set the Russian priorities in the new millennium—i.e., in the northern maritime sector, which is the Arctic shelf. The Doctrine reiterated the leading role of Russia in charting the Northern Sea Route and the founding of the Arctic ice-breaker fleet. The experience of building major cities and industrial zones was also unique, according to the Doctrine. The major thrust of the doctrine was Russian style Arctic planning. How that very idea affected the Arctic climate seems to be the guideline of the numerous reports that have appeared so far.

Flag Planting in the Arctic

On August 2007, a slightly eccentric entry was made by a Russian nuclear ice-breaker *Rossiya* and research ship *Akademik Fedorov* that reached the North Pole where two deep-water submersibles, *Mir-I* and *Mir-II* were launched and some nine hours later, safely retrieved after reaching the seabed at about 4,300 m. The veteran explorer Artur Chilingarov made a risky expedition—his submersible reached the Arctic seabed (the Amundsen Basin squeezed between the Lomonosov and Gakkel ridges) for collecting what was dramatically announced as "geological evidence" and planted the Russian flag there. Chilingarov remarked, "We have exercised the maritime right of the first night."

The symbolic planting of the Russian flag made from corrosion-resistant titanium at the highest latitude point has received significant media coverage. Triumphant statements by the Russian leadership about Russia's historic ownership of the Arctic seabed and Chilingarov's statement aroused international criticism. Most of them are openly contemptuous of Russia's proactive policy, especially since the launching of the Russian flag in a rather dramatic way on the Arctic seabed in August 2007. The Canadian Foreign Minister MacKay retorted—"This isn't the fifteenth century—you can't go around the world and just plant flags and say 'We're claiming this territory.'"[17] The fact is that the first claim was made by Russia (of 460,800 square miles of territory) in a "thin ice" oceanic environment of drifting ice chunks which made the rest of the Arctic Five worry about the fate of their control in a roughly circular territory in the extreme north that was recognised by the UN Convention on the Law of the Seas. The issue in question was connected to their own continental shelf even as Russia extended its claim on its continental shelf which is connected to the North Pole via the Lomonosov Ridge, which bisects the Arctic Ocean, stretching between Siberia and Canada's Ellsemere Island.[18] Such options sounded music for Russian ears but were a source of concern for the rest of the Arctic Five. In Soviet maps, the USSR borders were shown as going along straight longitudinal lines of 32 degree east from the Kola Peninsula and 180 degree east from the Bering Strait towards the Pole, so that a huge sector of the Arctic Ocean was designated as territorial waters. The new Russian claim is slightly more ambitious—it seeks to expand its 230-mile Exclusive Economic Zone (EEZ) a million square kilometres beyond the Chukotka Sea and the East Siberian Sea, with the argument that underwater ridges like the Lomonosov Ridge and the Mendeleev Ridge are continuations of the continental shelf. As Russia laid claims on the Arctic seabed, the Arctic Five became proactive in an effort to securitise the potential hydrocarbon and mineral wealth of the region.

Russia's Arctic Past

Russia's association with the Arctic is almost five centuries old. Its history with the region forms an important component of its reasoning behind its current assertions that "the Arctic is ours."[19] Since the sixteenth century, explorations under the auspices of the Imperial Russian Geographical Society (now Russian Geographical Society) were conducted. Russia's involvement with the Arctic was also studied extensively in Soviet accounts that narrated boastfully how Russian sailors (*pomory*) sailed the Barents and Kara Seas and discovered the islands of *Novaya Zemlya* (New World), much before the Great Northern Expedition of the eighteenth century by the influential Danish explorer, V. Bering (1733-1743).[20] According to Soviet accounts, the Russian interest in new circumnavigating trade routes between Europe and Asia over the Arctic Ocean was already felt. In pre-revolutionary historiography, the colonial plans for the New World and the Pacific Ocean have been attributed to private individuals while in Soviet historiography the expansionist exercise has been attributed to the Tsarist government. By the beginning of the eighteenth century, the Governor Generalate in eastern Siberia had begun to report on valuable information about the unknown lands (and islands) lying to the east of Chukotka, i.e., Alaska. The grandiose plan which culminated in the annexation of the Amur is the subject of research by Mark Bassin. Bassin argues that the Amur region, despite its local Siberian profile, became "intertwined" with other issues of the day. The framework of "contact" with the regions around speak about a geographical vision which is also a cultural enterprise because there is an element of "perception" of the people who belong to this region and how they are turned into objects of "representation."[21] The circumnavigating voyages were made under the auspices of Imperial Academy of Arts and the Academy of Arts (when Alexander I was the Russian Emperor, i.e., from 1801 to 1825). Participants in around-the-world voyages went on to play a leading role in shaping Russian imperial discourse. The general impression is that the plan was to convert the northern part of the empire in the New World into a "Russian Sea"—a venture that was actively promoted by the Tsarist government as well as private individuals. The "exclusive plan of merchant circles" was studied by Soviet and post-Soviet authors.[22]

Bering's expedition, conceived by Peter the Great, was the first one to devise the strategy of cartographic mapping of the northern shores of both Europe and Asia from the White Sea to Kolyma, the Okhotsk Sea, Kamchatka, the southern and eastern limits of Siberia. "It was the first nationally directed, long term sustained effort in Arctic exploration, carried out to a large extent in a scientific manner. It had been costly, both in lives and money. But it was extraordinarily successful."[23] The scientific nature of the expedition that was partly funded by Lomonosov, the founder of the Moscow State University, was acclaimed.

In the nineteenth century, Russian explorers led special expeditions to the Arctic to build a powerful fleet of ice-breakers to tap the Arctic's resources for Russia's economic development. In the early twentieth century, especially after the Russo-Japanese War of 1905, the Tsarist government decided to explore the possibility of moving Russian naval vessels along Siberia's northern coastline. Before the outbreak of World War I, Russia confirmed its 12-mile territorial waters. The Arctic Ocean Flotilla was created under Russian supervision in response to both German naval activity and British "fluctuating" exercises in the region. Subsequent Soviet "scientific expeditions" indicated the growing Russian military as well as diplomatic interests in the Northern maritime theatre. The approbation by the *Sovnarkom* of the Northern Sea Route agenda is a subject that has been analysed by modern-day Russian authors. The Northern Sea Route was a strategy that would allow the safe and quick transfer of ships from West to East in the direction of the Pacific Ocean. Except for the World War II period, Soviet Russia continued to alert the world of its "breakthrough expeditions" (e.g., the discovery of the Lomonosov ridge).[24] Soviet writings tend to dramatise the scale of Russian penetration into Arctic waters.

The historical interest in Russian imperial consciousness about the Pacific, therefore, never waned. Arctic explorers are not only Arctic heroes but also readers and writers of a supposedly empty space, imagining or articulating the unknown. So, there is a vast spectrum of writings about the imagined and the real that the Arctic represents—approaches that are so central to the understanding of the "unknown."[25]

So, if the contemporary debate about "who owns which part of the Arctic" is to be taken seriously, Russia does have its own story to tell. The Arctic zone, according to "the UN law of the sea," encompasses a massive span of "continental shelf" including a vast coastal area of about 3.1 million square kilometres (about 18% of the landmass of the Russian Federation)—a sizeable physical land reserve (*prostranstvenniyrezerv*) with a huge amount of hydrocarbons, natural gas and other raw materials, which Russia is in no position to give up. Contemporary debates about the Arctic as the scene of Russian "action" have led to deliberation among Arctic Five-turned Arctic Eight-turned Arctic Council in an effort to securitise the potential hydrocarbon and mineral wealth of the region.

NSR Debates

Russia's Arctic strategy of developing new oil and gas fields has come under the scanner. First and foremost, it appears that Russia is trying to camouflage her military intentions in the Arctic as a "gas business." The rationale for development in the North served as a catalyst for Putin's third term win in the Presidential elections. Moreover, the Arctic engagement is pretty expensive, Pavel Baev feels, especially on the part of the Russian military and the Russian navy. The military reforms since 2008 have called for downsizing its military apparatus for massive and specialised mobilisation. At the same time, modernisation of the strategic capabilities would be necessary which would mean removal of the previous submarines. The costs would go up and so modernisation of the conventional facilities of the Northern Fleet would go down. The ice-breaker fleet would strengthen Russia's maritime power but its deployment to secure the NSR would be immensely expensive. Added to this is the growing frustration about federal governments in the Arctic North (Murmansk or Karelia) as security provider. Such contradictions are practically damaging Russia's image as the ice-breaker in the Arctic.[26]

There is speculation whether the much talked of reserves at all have any significance. The cost of extraction is indeed one factor of concern. Baev also indicates that the estimates of resources in the North, coming from geologists, need to be verified. It seems there are inflated perceptions about Arctic hydrocarbon resources which are completely disconnected from Russia's energy policy. Interestingly, the Gazprom and Rosneft, which have exclusive offshore oil and gas rights, are in no hurry to incur investments in such costly projects. They have even cut down their exploration budgets. The development of the Yamal gas field has been stalled for a while. The situation is also difficult for the Shtokman project, which is a know-how generating project for Gazprom, and seems to be maintaining a low profile. So, the "Go-North" policy does not seem prospective enough, though it does make good sense in the context of images, discourses and other intangibles.[27]

The economic viability of access, let alone extraction, of the reserves is questionable which tends to make Russia "open" to options. So, it is not entirely out of context if Russia sees herself as a global competitor in terms of the Northern Sea Route which, as the former President Medvedev asserted, could link the European and Far Eastern maritime and water transport system and also enhance business links between Russian and foreign business partners. The most publicised affairs are the St. Petersburg-Vladivostok route via NSR as well as the Murmansk-Yokohama route via NSR. But to make these routes viable, investment in local infrastructure (especially nuclear-powered ice-breakers) should be substantial. Even about that investment, one has to be realistic. The NSR agenda, or the system of shipping lanes, is not a sudden appearance. There have been annual "trips" on this sector since the beginning of the twentieth century, but much of that was given up when the Transsib became more attractive for the shipment of military freight during the War years.

What happened in the post-Soviet period was a complete breakdown—the period of reforms in the 1990s had resulted in a curtailment of the traditional economic production of Northern Russia. The centralised economy collapsed and the NSR movements ceased for some time. Only in the last decade was there improvement with some prospects of federal programmes in the Arctic. But the emphasis here was on the nationalistic agenda of a "Russian Eurasian transport corridor" rather than internationalising the Northern Sea Route (NSR). The NSR is at the centre of a political gamble—it is seen as a prestige issue for Putin and Medvedev in the run-up for the Presidential elections in the 2000s.

Some are actually critical of the hype about a battle for the Arctic. For Baev, the much-hyped "competition" between Russia and the West is *a virtual battle* for non-existent resources. In his words—"the far north, is still closed to development: not a single resource deposit of any kind has been discovered there, and plans to expand shipping in the region have been dashed by shipping's overall decline caused by global recession. There are a lot of parallel jokes about Chilingarov's expedition to plant a Russian flag into the Arctic seabed which trivialised the scientific value of Russian exploration. Chilingarov's action brought certain theatricality to the event but has produced a lot of emotional reaction."[28] But the most interesting twist to the Arctic story is given from a geopolitical angle whereby the Arctic has been projected as the new geopolitical pivot. Titles like "Arctic Meltdown," "Arctic Land Grab" focused on Russian activities in the Arctic and articulated a sense of competition and crisis. In the twenty-first century, the increased accessibility of the Arctic is prompting Russia to become a maritime state. So, as Russia's geographic isolation or continental encirclement ends in the Far North, it is only natural that Russia and its Western neighbours will feel the necessity to devise a new geostrategy that will be conducive to the global business atmosphere, global financial and commercial networks, etc.

Hope and Despair

According to reports, there is both hope and despair about the new business environment in the Arctic region:

> In a small fishing village with a smattering of wooden houses in the Nenets Autonomous Region, Yuri Tyulyubayev, a travel company owner, says many local residents agree with the government.

"People are happy that we have oil because ... we have more work, we have more profit, we have everything," says Tyulyubayev.
In many ways, Tyulyubayev is a poster child in Russia's campaign for Arctic energy. He arranges travel for the oil industry. So his small company stands to profit if foreign energy companies flock here. His native land of north-central Russia is largely unspoiled.
"It's a very, very reindeer region," he says. "We have more than 150,000 reindeer for 40,000 people."

The environmentalists have voiced their sentiments too:

Nadezhda Lyashenko is a spiritual leader in the Saami tribe, indigenous people who live in Russia's northwest Arctic region. As Russia and other world powers search for oil in the Arctic Ocean, she worries about the environmental consequences.
And now, a lot of oil and gas companies. There are Russian firms, but also companies from the US and Vietnam, all exploring for oil and gas onshore. And if Russian leaders have their way, exploration will begin in the Arctic Ocean itself as early as this winter. Tyulyubayev says the more money and business that come to this region, the better.
But what about the risks to the environment?
"Of course we worry. But I would not say that this is the first worry in our life," he says. "Economic life is much more important for people."

The scars of history have not faded, some reports point out:

The Russian Arctic has the scars of history. The northwest, around the port city of Murmansk, was pummelled by Adolf Hitler's forces during World War II. The Arctic was also one of Soviet dictator Josef Stalin's favourite places to send his perceived enemies, with gulags that dotted the snowy landscape.
The indigenous people of this region bore much of the brunt. The Saami tribe, for one, has lived centuries in Russia's northwest, near the Norwegian border. Saami people were forcibly collectivised on farms under Stalin. Nadezhda Lyashenko, the Saami woman singing

> traditional tribal music here, can recount the horror stories. Her grandfather, a reindeer shepherd, was shot in 1937, accused of being a spy after he crossed into Finland chasing a reindeer herd.
>
> After decades of relative peace, Lyashenko says, trouble seems to be returning to her native Arctic lands. She sees Russia and other world powers in a race for oil and gas, ignoring the potential impact to a part of the Earth that's been rarely touched.
>
> "The Arctic is just so fragile," she says. "This time, it's a research boat going out there. It's like the prick of a needle, and the land will heal. But if they go with knives, with spears, they could break everything. And then what?"

There is weariness about Putin's "gift"—i.e., about the business environment in the Arctic:

> Russia has signalled that it means business. The government seems determined to militarise the Arctic, announcing recently that two army brigades—several thousand troops—will soon be patrolling there.
>
> Konstantin Simonov, who heads the National Energy Security Fund, a Russian think tank that consults with oil and gas companies, says the Arctic is a political gift for Putin. As Soviet power fades into memory, Putin can say this is one part of the world where Russia still calls the shots.
>
> "With the help of Arctic, Putin can show to people that Russia is still a serious power," Simonov says.
>
> The risk, Simonov says, is exaggerated expectations. Many of the offshore oil and gas projects are at least a decade away from bringing economic benefit—assuming they succeed.
>
> Yet Russians who live above the Arctic Circle are growing excited. They look to neighbouring Norway, or to Alaska, where citizens share in oil profits. And they believe their time has come. Simonov thinks about one desolate village, Teriberka. It's on the coast near the Norwegian border. People there were told that as soon as a new offshore gas deposit, known as the Shtokman field, is explored, the community will get a natural gas processing plant and plenty of jobs.

There is both belief and disbelief:

> To reach the village of Teriberka requires driving 100 miles across empty tundra. It's a place that's struggling. It has dirt roads and maybe 700 residents who live in old Soviet housing that's crumbling.
>
> According to 33-year-old Andrei Udin, life in Teriberka is depressing. He has tried for years to find real work. Udin likes the tough talk from Putin, the promise to fight for Arctic territory. "What's ours should be ours," Udin says. But after years of delay, he's beginning to wonder if that natural gas processing plant is really coming to Teriberka.
>
> "If I don't have a job, natural gas does nothing for me," Udin says. "I can't exactly use the gas for food." Frustration is growing around this village. People are beginning to say that unless the oil and gas riches will be shared, maybe it's best to leave nature alone.

Conclusion

Historical perspectives and contemporary observations have added new dimensions to the study of Russia's policies in the Far East and the Far North. Resource potential has made Siberia and the Russian Far East the centre of gravity for Soviet and post-Soviet planners. Russia's quest for hydrocarbon resources in the Arctic seabed has not only aroused a lot of sentiments but also camouflages a lot of other factors, for example, Chinese intentions. China's interests in Russia's Arctic programme are not very clear, though one cannot ignore China's strong desire to be part of the Arctic Council (as observer) for which it is wooing Canada.[29] Even though it is not an Arctic country, China is the single Asian country facing the stake of immediate supply of raw materials from the Arctic ports of Russia via the Northern Sea Route. Since its trade is shipping dependent, any change in global shipping routes would affect its import and export trade and hence its economy as a whole.[30] Another unspecified link is Japan.[31]

Russia on the other hand has begun playing a long waiting game in the Arctic. It is in no hurry to give up its business-related interests, as the National Maritime Doctrine 2020 (approved by Putin much earlier).

There are graver issues at stake—in the deliberations of the Arctic Council, there have been talks about the newly emerging Arctic security environment. The "hotting up" of the Arctic signifies new security relationships among Arctic states. But it is also time to think beyond the bigger picture of Russia in the Arctic or how the Arctic Five can be expanded into an Arctic Eight with observer status to long-distance partners like India and Singapore. There are more nuanced issues like a Trans-Pacific Partnership that is juxtaposed to a newly restructured APEC. In terms of Asia-Europe connectivity, more promising and realistic at present seems to be the Eastern reach via railway corridors across Russia and the Baikal-Amur Railroad is showcased as one big option. It is time to address some of these issues and not get carried away by the big picture.

Notes

1. Anthony Bubalo and Malcolm Cook, "Horizontal Asia," *The American Interest,* May-June 2010.
2. Mark Adomanis, "Why Russia's 'Pivot to the East' is not going to work in one chart," *www.forbes.com,* June 8, 2013.
3. Iwashita Akihiro, "Primakov Redux? Russia and the 'Strategic Triangles in Asia,'" http://src-h.slav.hokudai.ac.jp/coe21/publish/no16_1_ses/09_iwashita.pdf
4. Fiona Hill and Bobo Lo, "Putin's Pivot: Why Russia is Looking East?" July 31, 2013. http://www.brookings.edu/research/opinions/2013/07/31-russia-china-pacific-pivot-hill
5. Stephen Blank, *Russia's Far East Policy: Looking Beyond China* (Paris: IFRI Russia/NIS Center, 2010).
6. "Going East: Russia's Asia-Pacific Strategy," Russian National Committee of the Council for Security Cooperation in Asia Pacific (CSCAP), *Russia in Global Affairs,* December 25, 2010.
7. Victor Sumsky, "Modernization of Russia, East Asia Geopolitics and the ASEAN Factor," *International Affairs,* Special Issue, 2010.
8. Elizabeth Wishnick, "Russia in Asia and Asians in Russia," *SAIS Review* 20.1 (2000): 87-101.
9. The enthusiasm about a Pacific gateway is sharpened by the ongoing talks about the forthcoming APEC summit in Vladivostok in 2012. http://apec2012.ru/en/content/?s=176
10. Natalia Ryzhova, "Informal Cross border exchanges: reaction to institutional transition (Russian-Chinese Border case)," Suchandana Chatterjee and Anita

Sengupta (eds.), *Communities, institutions and transition in post-1991 Eurasia,* (Delhi: Shipra Publications, 2011), p. 213.

11. Details of the pipeline layout is as follows: the ESPO, which was initiated in 2004 and is being built by Transneft, Russia's state-owned oil pipeline company, is intended to open the Asia-Pacific markets for Russian oil—notably both China and Japan. Currently, most Russian oil is produced in Western Siberia and transported through pipelines to Western Europe. However, the eventual 4,188-kilometre (2,602-mile) pipeline will transporting oil from western and central Siberian oilfields to the Sea of Japan, creating a significant shift in the direction of oil exports. The first stage of the pipeline will flow from Taishet to Skovorodino along with the port facility at Kozmino Bay. Oil is due to be shipped via rail to the Pacific coast until the second stage of the pipeline is constructed. Interim negotiations resulted in creating a spur line (Daqing) from the original track, which is being built in China's territory with Chinese finance. The second stage of the pipeline will run from Skovorodino to the Pacific Coast.The construction of a gas pipeline from the Kovykta field near Irkutsk through Mongolia to northeastern China was also a subject of negotiation between Russia and China since 2005. The gas field operators along with the Government of Buryatia recommended a gas line along the south of Lake Baikal, a proposal that was opposed by environmentalists. The plan was revised and the pipeline has been shifted 50 kilometres north of Lake Baikal. Gas would be transferred in two routes—via northeast China and via Siberia.
12. Natalia Ryzhova, "Informal Cross border exchanges …"
13. T. D. Wilkinson, "The other Far East," *Prospect Magazine,* May 9, 2011.
14. Sergey Guneev, "Russia's Far East Envoy Unveils Giant Sakhalin Bridge Plan," *RIA NOVOSTI,* July 18, 2013.
15. President Putin criticised the bridge collapse in Russkiy Island due to heavy rains on the eve of the APEC summit of 2012. The bridge was to connect the island with Vladivostok airport.
16. Sebastian Strangio, "As Asia Rises and Europe Declines, Russia Invests Its Hopes in Its Far East," *The Atlantic.com,* October 27, 2011.
17. "Russia Plants Flag under N. Pole," *BBC News*, August 2, 2007, http://news.bbc.co.uk/2/hi/europe/-6927395.stm
18. Vsevolod Gunitsky, "On Thin Ice: Water rights and resource disputes in the Arctic Ocean," *Journal of International Affairs,* vol. 61, no. 2, 2008.
19. Former President Medvedev's statement in September 2010.
20. Reconnoitring Nansen's expedition in the Central Arctic, Soviet explorers have tried to gain experience by setting up Arctic stations on the eve of the World War II. Clifford J. Webster, "The Soviet Expedition to the Central Arctic, 1954," http://pubs.aina.ucalgary.ca/arctic/Arctic7-2-58.pdf
21. Mark Bassin, *Imperial Visions: Nationalist imagination and geographical*

expansion in the Russian Far East, 1840-1865, Cambridge University Press, 1999, Introductio: 6-7.

22. Andrei V. Grinev, "The plans for Russian Expansion in the New World and the North Pacific in the Eighteenth and Nineteenth Centuries," *European Journal of American Studies,* Special Issue—The North-west Pacific in the 18th and 19th Centuries, 2010.
23. D. Mountfield, *A History of Polar Exploration* (London: Hamlyn, 1974), 47.
24. Reconnoitering Nansen's expedition in the Central Arctic, Soviet explorers have tried to gain experience by setting up Arctic stations on the eve of the World War II. Clifford J. Webster, "The Soviet Expedition to the Central Arctic, 1954," http://pubs.aina.ucalgary.ca/arctic/Arctic7-2-58.pdf
25. Anka Ryall, Johan Schimanski and Henning Howlid Waerp, "Arctic discourses—an introduction," in Anka Ryall, Johan Schimanski and Henning Howlid Waerp, *Arctic Discourses* (Cambridge Scholar Publishing, 2010).
26. Mentioned in Introduction, Pavel Baev, *Russia's Arctic Policy and the Northern Fleet Modernization* (Paris: IFRI Russia/NIS Center, August 2012).
27. Pavel Baev, "Russia's Arctic Policy: geopolitics, mercantilism and identity-building," *The Finnish Institute of International Affairs,* Briefing Paper 73, December 17, 2010.
28. Pavel Baev refers to the feminists' challenge. Pavel Baev, "The turnaround in warming political relations," in Dmitri Trenin and Pavel K. Baev (eds.), *The Arctic—A view from Moscow* (Washington: Carnegie Endowment for International Peace, 2010).
29. Mia Bennett, "Facing Cold Shoulder from Oslo, China Turns to Ottawa for Support in Arctic," *Foreign Policy Association,* February 2, 2012. foreignpolicyblogs.com/
30. Margaret Blunden, "Geopolitics and the Northern Sea Route," *International Affairs*, 88:1, 2012.
31. Eric Pardo, "Northern territories and Japan-Russia relations: will the knot ever untie?" *UNISCI Discussion Papers,* no. 28, January 2012.

3. The Northern Periphery of the Great Silk Road

Vladimir A. Lamin and Yanina A. Kuznetsova

Silk not the only Factor in Europe's Expansion in Asia

One of the earliest written evidence of the idea of silk in Europe dates back to the seventh century BC. However, that does not mean that the interaction between the West and the East of the Eurasian continent was lined with silk fabric and silk trade reached high values and was a determining factor of ongoing traffic between Western and Eastern civilisations.

The Great Silk Road is an artistic image to some extent. In fact it was India which played a stimulus for the movement of Mediterranean States towards Asia. The historical processes show that even during interactive phases especially trade contacts, military clashes between the West and the East erupted at short intervals. The transcontinental movement of goods, especially silk from China, took place in the Mediterranean through sale and resale of Chinese silk products. Taking into account the isolated and closed nature of the "Celestial Empire" and its contrasting ideology that symbolised divine superiority over the rest of the world, it was unlikely that silk trade would be limited to China as a sporadic phenomenon. The general objective of the European movement to Asia was India and this seems to be a more acceptable argument.

It all began when the army of Alexander the Great reached the banks of the Ganges but was forced to retreat. Despite the retreat, the advance from the northerly direction was more decisive.[1] After Alexander's death and the collapse of the Macedonian Empire, the energy of military expansion in Asia was reduced and the Macedonian initiative subsided for a long period of time. Moreover, the influx of nomadic peoples across the Dardanelles and Gibraltar towards southern Europe and over the East

European plain in the north practically altered the demographic balance. The process of settlement of the Asiatic war tribes to the European territories to the level of state entities and their relative pacification lasted for about 1,000 years. The result of this process, where a considerable role was played by the warlike tribes with the Roman Empire, was the state-political structure of Europe, the concept of which quite clearly can be detected in the modern national state form of Europe. One of the remarkable effects of the great migration of peoples testifies to the fact that it brought to Europe evidence, confirming ancient myths and legends of the fabulous wealth of the country, of the miracles of India and mysteries of China.

The major initiatives of trade relations with India and China were concentrated in Spain and Portugal. In the end of the Reconquista, success in shipbuilding, navigation and in the development of problems of the global mapping the discovery of India by the Europeans became possible. The Portuguese court was destined to have the biggest success to the extent that in 1451, Portugal by a special decree of Pope Nicholas V, had obtained the right to discover and possess all lands to the South and East of Cape Bojador. The Portuguese court was enthusiastic about exploring India and protested the discovery of West Indies (in fact, America) by Christopher Columbus. To safeguard its right to possess at least Eastern India, Portugal sent a flotilla under the command of Vasco da Gama to India by taking the route around Africa in 1497. Unlike the first expedition of Columbus that was considered to be a divine phenomenon and was greeted with enthusiasm by the indigenous people of America, the first contact of the Portuguese with India was not a very friendly one. The Mission of Vasco da Gama, sent to the Indian coast for trade negotiations, was asked a question: "What the devil has brought you here?" Later, American natives interpreted this as the devil's thirst for enrichment of unwelcome invaders.[2]

Russia's Trade Motives

The first active Russian attempts to establish trade relations with India were made in the reign of Peter I, nearly 200 years after the Portuguese expeditions in the Orient. The exploration of a possible route of trade communication began in 1692 from the Siberian city of Tobolsk. Formally it was a diplomatic mission that was sent to Turkestan for negotiations about the conditions of the release of Kazakh Khan Tauke's noble tribesmen from Russian captivity. Actually this Embassy headed by S. A. Nepripasov was meant to compile a complete description of physical-geographical and other features of the trade route to India through the Kazakh steppe. Instead of successful negotiations, what happened was completely different—the Khan ordered the imprisonment of a Russian diplomat. He let the Cossacks accompanying the ambassador go home with a charter as an ultimatum demanding the release of imprisoned princes and persuading the Russian side of sincere efforts to develop friendly relations. The next Russian mission went from Tobolsk in April 1694, and three months later reached Turkestan. It was headed by F. Skibin who was put into the same prison as Nepripasov. The latter died soon and Skibin managed to escape to Khiva, where he spent three months collecting information about the links of the Khiva khanate with the neighbouring countries. In July 1696 Skibin returned to Tobolsk and described his experiences in Turkestan, Khiva and the routes that he passed.

In 1699 according to the Decree of Peter the Great, work on the map description of the Caspian Sea started. The aim was to explore the use of its water area for trade communication with India. The expedition studies of the western coast of the Caspian Sea were complicated by military-political relations with Turkey and were soon discontinued. In the next 15 years the Indian expedition was left without any changes. However, in 1714 Captain-Lieutenant Prince A. Cherkassky arrived in Astrakhan with the Tsar's secret Directive. The Astrakhan administration was ordered to provide Cherkassky with a troop of 1,500 people and all other resources necessary for mapping the Eastern coast of the Caspian Sea. The ultimate goal of cartographic studies was to find the sea route or the land road for the establishment of trade relations with Khiva khanate and henceforth with India. The end of the military-trade expeditions under the command of Prince A. Cherkassky proved to be dramatic. In 1717 the Khan of Khiva pretended to submit to the Tsar and agreed on the accommodation of three thousand people in the Russian Diplomatic

Mission. But on the first night after the entry into the city all the soldiers and about two hundred Russian merchants engaged in profitable trade with Khiva and India were killed. Prince A. Cherkassky was killed in that night's massacre.

One more attempt to establish trade relations in the direction of India took place almost 100 years later after the Khiva tragedy.[3] In 1814 the Georgian nobleman Madatov organised a caravan for trade with India. But due to a number of obstacles the caravan was able to reach only till Kashmir. However, the merchants participating in the caravan purchased 200 shawls made of goat fur and a half *pood*[4] of Kashmir goat wool. A large profit from their sales in Russia aroused a considerable interest in the trading community. It was supposed to organise a caravan to Tibet and Kashgar for delivery of fine-wool goats to Russia and extending of trade relations. The idea of this project was discussed and approved at the governmental level. Academician Baron Meyendorff was at that time in Semipalatinsk and actively supported the initiative. But the leaders of the trading community were of the opinion that this kind of trade relations would be under the high risk of plunder of caravans by thieves and robbers without military support. The merchant community agreed to join the trade enterprise with a trade route directed towards Tibet and India, but only under the protection of a military detachment at public expense. The Russian government could not afford such military engagement in the territories that were in British military and political interests. As a result, such an initiative that had the possibility of establishing trade relations between Russia and the countries of South Asia had to be discontinued.

Russian Expeditions

The Russian Emperor Peter the Great continued to nurture the desire of finding a trade route to India. In 1724 he gave an instruction about the necessity to organise an expedition for establishing a strait between Asia and America. The expedition headed by W. Bering was not only meant to build the strait, but to investigate the conditions of navigating it. That was extremely important in view of the future feasibility of the arrangement of the shortest sea route from Europe to India along the Arctic coast of Russia. Success in this field had the brilliant prospect of Russia's monopoly in the system of commercial maritime communications with the countries of eastern and southern Asia. Scientific confirmation of the existence of a Strait between Asia and America discovered by S. Dezhnev in 1649 strengthened belief in the possibility of realisation of Peter the Great's initiatives.

The second Kamchatka expedition aimed to investigate the conditions for navigation in Arctic waters from the mouth of the Pechora to an intercontinental Strait and it was started by V. Bering immediately after his return from the first expedition. The results of a decade's work for investigating the feasibility of navigation along the Arctic coast of Siberia were not very promising. The immense prospects of a northern transoceanic trade route faded away. But the scientific importance of the results of the activities of the northern troops had a lasting value. The knowledge about Arctic waters and territories has advanced from cosmographical notions of antiquity and speculative hypotheses to a scientific approach. The Northern troops of the Kamchatka expedition initiated the entry of Russia into the ocean waters despite the icy conditions of the Arctic. However, the successful continuation of this initiative did not happen. The initiatives of Vitus Bering, who narrated in his account of the first expedition that the Pacific coast of Siberia was very suitable for shipbuilding, were not heard by the Russian Admiralty. The reasons for this aloofness had historical origins. Moreover, after the death of Peter I naval initiatives began to fade quickly. So his grandson Peter II, crowned Tsar in 1727, said: "I do not want to walk on the sea like my grandfather."[5] Peter's endeavours to explore the possibilities of commercial navigation on the northeast passage were supported and developed later by academician M. V. Lomonosov.[6] By means of his energetic and assertive efforts a secret expedition was organised under the command of Chichagov during the reign of Catherine II. A squad of three sailing ships was instructed to pass from the Atlantic Ocean to the Pacific Ocean directly through the North Pole. This route was based on the hypothesis that behind the zone of ice must be an ice-free Polar Basin. The assumptions did not materialise. After two attempts in 1765 and 1766 the squad of Chichagov broke through the ice to 90° 30' north latitude and had to abandon the venture.

One of the last initiatives of Russia in transport breakthrough in the South Asian countries that belonged to the trading network of the so-called Silk Road was by Badmaev, the family physician of Tsar Nicholas II. In particular, one of his projects suggested the possibility of building a railway line from the district of Nizhneudinsk (Ulan-Ude) to Lanzhou, the midpoint of the Great Silk Road.

Siberian Railways

The study of the history of ideas, initiatives and realities of transport development in Siberia in the pre-Soviet period of Russian history would be incomplete without the accounts of those kinds of activity which, even without much technological breakthrough in transport communications, were considered relevant and practically important. First, the Moscow-Siberian horse-drawn path which was a major transportation artery until the construction of the Siberian Railway (Transsib) needs to be examined more closely.[7] It is no exaggeration to say that the Siberian highway despite its primitive technical arrangement was of economic significance and was for more than a century linked firmly with the account of Russian territorial acquisitions in North Asia. An equally important role that the Transsib played was in establishing trade relations with China and transforming it from a distant caravan spot to a border hub with tendencies of extensive network. However, some of those trends such as the Russian tea trade were not well developed.

It is worth mentioning the so-called *Sibrechputi* project, in which it was proposed to connect the river basins of the Volga and the Kama rivers, the Ob and the Irtysh, the Yenisei, the Lena, the Amur by canals and locks into an overall network of inland waterways.[8] The opponents of that project not without reason called it a water extravaganza. According to their calculations a steamer from the Volga following through canals and locks—dug through the Urals and Siberian rivers watersheds—could, only in extremely fortunate circumstances, reach the mouth of the Amur during a single navigation because of the short period and different times of the navigation on the rivers of the empire. Despite this objective criticism, the project of an artificial correction of the wrong flow of Siberian rivers was zealously initiated by the Russian Ministry of Transport Communications and the Ob-Yenisei Canal was built. But transportation on it did not happen. The first demonstration steamer voyage was made in 1897, the second and the last was made in 1914. The digging of the canal and the construction of locks cost the Treasury 20 million roubles. Commercial efficiency was less than zero. However, even nowadays there are some active supporters of the continuation of this senseless plan.

The construction of the Trans-Siberian railroad put an end to this monument of Russian mismanagement. The construction of the Great Railway track across Siberia (Transsib) begun in 1891 doomed the Ob-Yenisei canal to desolation, oblivion and extinction. The start of the construction of the Transsib was preceded by a lengthy debate in which one side argued that the colossal construction and maintenance expenses would never pay off. On the other hand, another side argued that all European freight traffic to the Asia-Pacific region would flood the Trans-Siberian Railway and, as a result, shipping through the Suez Canal would stop and the companies that built the Panama Canal would go bankrupt. But the decision of Emperor Alexander III about the urgent need to build a railway line across Siberia superseded all these debates about the controversial project. The purely commercial prospects of non-profit of the Siberian Railway, as well as forecasts of its devastating impact on the global system of transport communications, were minor and insignificant.

The main reason for the final decision of constructing the Transsib was the difficult economic and political situation in the Asia-Pacific region.[9] Britain and France forced China to open the domestic market to free trade. Russia actually supported those Western demands, hoping to get their share of the Chinese market for the future. Unlike France and Britain, which had a vast merchant navy, Russia, despite its long border with China, had no reliable transport communications necessary for cross-border trade. Military and diplomatic tension in the region was heightened by the Eastern gaze and China's technical equipment and new naval construction were sponsored by England to the extent of increasing expansionist ambitions of Japan leading to a military confrontation with Russia.

The fortress city of Vladivostok was the only strength of Russia on the Pacific coast but it had no reliable transport links with the rest of Russia. It was believed that the defence capabilities of the fortifications, much due to the will power and courage of the forces there, would provide a scope for Vladivostok to withstand a long siege. The decision on the forced construction of the railroad across Siberia to Vladivostok had important political implications. The Russian government agreement on the construction of the eastern part of Transsib on China territory (CER), renting ports on the Liaodong peninsula and the construction of the railway line (SER) to them, was intended to demonstrate the steadfastness of Russian positions in the APR.[10] This agreement with China definitely outlined the Russian economic and political interests in East Asia. The entry of Russia into the ice-free Yellow Sea significantly changed the value of Transsib. As the English political commentator in Shanghai, Kolhun, concluded: "While Siberian railway was being built to the freezing port of Vladivostok, it did not threaten British interests. Now, when it is directed toward the warm seas, it would be extremely dangerous for the English world trade and transoceanic strategic communications." Japan reacted with equal alarm to the new and obviously political geography of the railway construction. In particular, the editor of one of metropolitan newspapers Takuchi wrote that it was necessary to prevent the prospect of Russian transport monopoly in the trade between Asia and Europe by all means. For that he proposed the urgency of designing the cross-border railway track of what was once the Great Silk Road.

However, these and other threats, dangers and risks derived from Russian, English, French, German and Japanese political disposition in East Asia, were eliminated by the Russo-Japanese War of 1904-1905. Japan, about which the Russian Emperor Nicholas II said that in the case of an attack on Russia, Russian Cossacks "would shower it with hats" (indicative of their confidence of an easy victory), dealt a stunning blow to the realities, especially about prospects of the Russian presence in the APR. As a result, Russia had to retire from Port Arthur, withdraw from the Korean peninsula, cede to Japan the southern half of Sakhalin and, in view of the growing threat of the loss of CER, start in 1907 the construction of the railway to Vladivostok on its own territory. The high hopes that Transsib would become a thoroughfare of global significance waned.

Most of the Russian railway construction projects in the Asiatic region of the empire did not materialise. However, during 1905-1907 the Siberia-Alaska project, which was even more ambitious than the Transsib, was discussed in governmental, engineering, commercial-industrial and military circles. Its initiator was Frenchman Loic de Lobel, who called himself an engineer-entrepreneur, but some participants of the discussion considered him to be a crook, businessman, trickster, an agent of major American capitalist corporations aimed at economic and subsequent political separation of significant parts of Siberia.[11]

The basic idea of the project, as it was interpreted and promoted by de Lobel, was to create a united global railway system. To implement that plan it was enough to build a tunnel under the Bering Strait and railroad lines from Transsib near Irkutsk to the strait and from the Canadian-American railway system to the strait. As a result, two separate railway systems of two subcontinents would make up a whole, beyond the economic impact of which would remain only Australia and the Antarctic. After the defeat of Russia in the war with Japan, de Lobel assured sincere love for the Russian people and the equally deep antipathy toward Japan with these words—"the eternal enemy of the Russian empire"—emphasising the urgency of the Siberia-Alaska highway project. To this main project he added proposals about projects on railway arteries connecting Kamchatka and several points on the coast of the Sea of Okhotsk. In other words, the system of seaports, supported by transport links to the hinterland of Siberia rich in various natural resources, opened up opportunities for a wide outlet of Siberian goods to the Pacific market. This very system in the case of war with "insidious" Japan would make the Russian Pacific coast impregnable. At the same time the benefactor of Russian interests in the Pacific region consistently emphasised that in case the Alaska-Siberia Railway was constructed on the terms of 99-year concession and for the funds of the Franco-American syndicate, Russia actually would be free from worries connected with the security of its eastern areas. In addition, de Lobel assured the Russians that the government of the

North American United States would never allow anyone to threaten and encroach on the legitimate interests of their citizens in Russia.[12]

Some high-ranking Russian officials and the great princes of the Romanov family reacted more than favourably to such alluring prospects. For example, the Grand Duke Nicholas N., who was responsible for the defence, was committed to securing the Pacific borders of the empire at the expense of the USA. Metropolitan news media were bought off by de Lobel and were directed to praise the Alaska-Siberia project, as a result of which Russia would become a focus of cargo passenger traffic between Eurasia and America, i.e., in fact almost of all world trade.

Divergent Views

However, alongside the energetic voices that praised the project and its unprecedented pace, there were divergent views, too. The initial opponents of the Paris-New York railway project were entrepreneurial communities of Transbaikalia, the Trans-Amur Territory and the Maritime Territory. Their negative evaluation of the grand railway enterprise project was not surprising, because its implementation under the flag of American syndicate would cause total land concession of the size of the territory of France. The most striking case of the Siberian entrepreneurial public was, as people say, the foolish enthusiasm of metropolitans for the excellent future of Siberia at the expense of American benefactors.

Under the pressure of critics de Lobel had to retire from a number of positions that were initially meant for him in the concession contract. So he agreed with the requirement that the construction of the Russian part of the railway should be carried out by Russian labour force and not imported from France, the USA and other countries. The possibility of a redemption of the concession company by the Russian side not in 35 years after its commissioning, but 10 years earlier was also admitted. But he emphasised that it would be more profitable for Russia to get a totally free highway after a 99-year concession in 2003-2004. Theoretically he had nothing against the Russian engineering supervision of the construction and the subsequent operation. However, in spite of all that, he assured that the syndicate had a highly qualified and very experienced staff to ensure a proper quality of construction and efficient operation of the railways. De Lobel agreed with the fact that the Siberian part of the track line would pass across the territories poorly supported with reliable cartographic materials, but ensured that the syndicate had the best opportunities in the world to solve that problem as soon as possible. It was planned to carry out full-scale, field engineering, geological and other preparatory studies for a maximum of five years. De Lobel did not deny that the construction of a tunnel under the Bering Strait, despite the existing world experience of sinking of large mountain tunnels, would entail the solution of unprecedented complex engineering problems. But his argument was that the undersea part of the tunnel would be at least two times less than the width of the Bering Strait, as a part of the transport connection of Eurasia and America would be built on the Diomidov islands. The opponents incriminated the project initiator in the absence of ideas about the geography of the Diomidov islands, the actual width of the Bering Strait, and claimed that the construction of an undersea tunnel was de Lobel's imagination about an ice-breaking train ferry. Due to criticism of the project, de Lobel put forward arguments that were mutually beneficial.

However, in 1907 the Russian government decided to build the Amur railway line connecting Vladivostok with the rest of Russia on its own territory. This decision and its quick implementation were uniquely timed. During World War I the vast majority of goods imported from Canada and the United States was delivered by the port of Vladivostok and the Amur railway line. Transportation by the CER was under Japanese control after the Russo-Japanese War.

On the eve of the Soviet period of Russian history the transport system of the country in all its structural and technical components lagged far behind its West European counterparts, and even more the United States. The devastating consequences of World War I and the Civil War were overcome only by the end of the 1920s. Technical reconstruction and modernisation of the transport system, the main components of which were railroads, and river steamer communications comprised the lion's share of transport investments.

Logistical support of large-scale construction of a new railway was formed in the first half of the 1930s. Planning, surveying and building preparations for the erection of the Baikal-Amur Mainline (BAM) began in 1933. Its accelerated construction as well as at the time of Transsib was dictated by the Japanese military threat. Unlike the Trans-Siberian railroad a new railway line was to go a considerable distance from the border with China, the northern territories of which were under Japanese occupation. Another significant difference was that a large complex industrial centre in Komsomolsk-on-Amur was being built together with the railroad. The third difference was that the eastern end-point of BAM was to be Sovetskaya Harbour, i.e., an ocean port on the Pacific coast of Russia. In other words, the lessons of the Russian-Japanese War of 1904-1905 proved to be very instructive. By the time that Nazi Germany attacked the Soviet Union, it was possible to realise only the priority objectives of the project, i.e., mainly to build industrial enterprises in Komsomolsk-on-Amur and connect the city with the Trans-Siberian railway. During the war after the Tehran conference, as a result of which the Soviet Union agreed to take part in the Allies' war with Japan, a railway line from Komsomolsk-on-Amur to Sovetskaya Harbour was built. In the post-war period the construction of BAM Far-Eastern branch line slowed down and then stopped at the Duque station. Priority efforts were concentrated on the construction of the line Tayshet-Ust-Kut, providing a rail link to the Lena River basin in Yakutia. After this, the construction of BAM came to an end.

Field studies data show that the construction of the central part of the BAM line would have involved the penetration through many kilometres of tunnels into large mountain barriers with an unexplored geology. Time and cost of the construction could increase to a considerable extent. Leading experts offered to bypass the mountain barriers by the far northern route across the low hills of Yakutia. There was intense debate on this as other experts believed that the field survey of the new northern route alternative would take many years and the results were unpredictable.

The debate was solved in an unexpected way. In February-March 1947, in accordance with a Soviet decree, the majority of experts joined the Northern Plan and survey expedition of the USSR Ministry of Internal Affairs[13] (Documents, 2005). Initially the expedition was expected to carry out an urgent field work on the site selection on the western bank of the Gulf of the Ob for the construction of a naval base, dockyard, a residential village and the railway to it and to Salekhard from the area of Vorkuta.

Preliminary studies indicate that the area set by the USSR Resolution was not suitable for the planned objectives. In this context and on the initiative of the chief of the expedition P. K. Tatarintsev, the construction of a seaport and the plant with a village was moved to the district of the deep-water Yenisei Gulf. The designed railroad track went towards Salekhard-Igarka with a prospective development to Yakutsk (figures 1 and 2).

In 1947 the USSR Council of Ministers decided to build a Polar railway from the region of Vorkuta to Norilsk. The railway was traced across today's diamond mining area and was supposed to go to Chukotka with the branches to the ports of the NSR, Kamchatka and the Okhotsk coast of Siberia. The construction of the Polar railway line was proposed by military strategists who also emphasised the economic importance of such a project. The lessons of World War II became evident when the residents of Dixon had to fend off the German battleships. Also during the Crimean War the garrison of Petropavlovsk-on-Kamchatka repulsed the Anglo-French squadron. Fortunately, the Germans, as well as the French and the British more than 100 years ago, were stunned by the resistance of the indigenous people of the island, and unaware of the forces of combat they retreated (as pointed out in the five-volume *The History of Siberia*, 1968). Of course, it was a battle of immense local importance. The main point of justification of the Polar railway was the military-strategic factor and concomitant naval bases on the Arctic and the Pacific coast that were premised on the possibilities of a future war. Some of those premises took shape in the 1930s. In particular, it was assumed that the rapid development of air battle would turn the Arctic into a strategic region of paramount importance because the shortest routes between America and Eurasia went across this particular region.

Russian activity spread in the Arctic region during the 1930s-1950s. At that time the former hypothetical track of the Northern Sea Route became a significant transportation artery. However, its practical value was determined not so much by the dominant idea of access from Europe to East and South Asia by the shortest transoceanic route, but rather by the plans of economic growth of Arctic territories of the Soviet Union. Until the mid-1950s, the economic development of the North of the USSR progressed systematically. The natural resources deposits ranging from gold and "cannon" to rare earth metals were developed on a large scale. The capacity of transport ice-class vessels and ice-breakers was increased. Frontal geological exploration and diamond mining determined the future of the north of Siberia. The 1,470-km long railway line Chum-Salekhard-Igarka with ferries on the Ob and Yenisei was planned to be put into regular operation in 1955. The ferrying capacity of Chum-Salekhard-Igarkaline was estimated at 1.5 million tonnes per year. However, in reality not even a tonne of goods, unless absolutely necessary for its construction, was transported. At the end of March 1953 a decision of the Presidium of the USSR Council of Ministers was adopted. According to L. P. Beria memorandum, road construction, the remains of which the locals still call "Stalinka" was stopped. The same fate befell another 20 objects mainly related to transport construction. Among them there was also a railway tunnel on the island of Sakhalin, with a total length of 13.4 km and an underwater part under the Tatar Strait of 7.3 km with a depth of 35 km from the bottom of the Strait in order to ensure a reliable operation in the event of bombing. In the 1950s when the construction of the tunnel was being carried out, the Cold War heightened, especially in the Japanese island of Hokkaido where the US had its strategic aviation base.

L. P. Beria's offers to stop the construction of 20 objects, "the implementation of which in the coming years is not caused by the urgent needs of the national economy," in March 25, 1953 were approved by the Decree of the USSR Council of Ministers and for more than 20 years firmly broke the railway network development in Siberia. That cost the national economy a lot and till today the amount is yet to be recovered.

It was difficult to defend the projects for geological surveys for oil, gas and diamond. The debate was about recovery of costs despite the discovery of those untapped resources in northern Siberia. It was a time when the state officials were governed by the so-called macro-economists and this was inimical for the future of Northern Siberia. Their narrow mercantilist minds were incapable of generating quick and large revenue. The ideologues of that concept neglected the immutable truth, which is—he who does not invest in the future, always stays in the past.

Figure 1. The railway line Chum-Salekhard-Igarka // V. Lamin, V. Plenkin, V. Tkachenko. Global track. The development of the transport system in the east of the country. Schematic maps of the construction of railways USSR.Yekaterinburg, 1999. No. 5. (Please refer colour map on page 249).

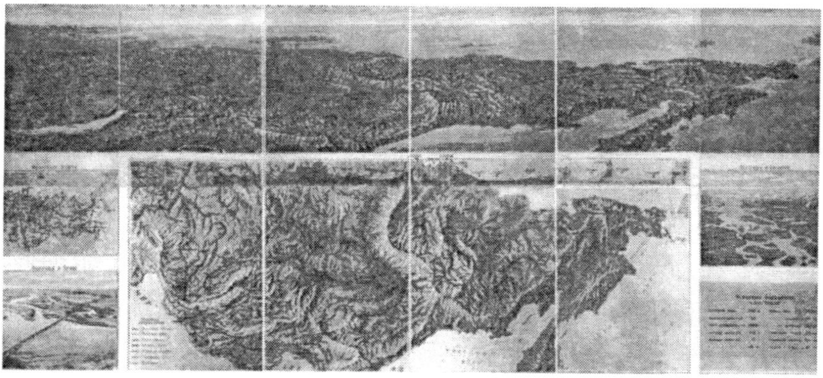

Figure 2. The railway line Yakutsk-Chukotka // V. Lamin, V. Plenkin, V. Tkachenko. Global track. The development of the transport system in the east of the country. Schematic maps of the construction of railways USSR.Yekaterinburg, 1999. No. 6. (Please refer colour map on page 249).

Notes

1. F. Shahermayr, *Alexander of Macedon* (Moscow: Nauka, 1986). /F. Shahermajr, *Aleksandr Makedonskij*, Moskva: Nauka, 1986.
2. I. P. Magidovich, V. I. Magidovich, *Essays on the history of geographical discoveries*. In 5 volumes. Moscow: Prosveshchenie, 1986. /I. P. Magidovich and V. I. Magidovich, *Ocherki po istorii geograficheskih otkrytij. V 5-ti tomah.* Moskva: Prosveshhenie, 1986.
3. I. V. Shcheglov, A chronological list of the most important data from the history of Siberia. 1032-1882. Surgut: Severny Dom, 1933. /I. V. Shheglov, *Hronologicheskij perechen vazhnejshih dannyx iz istorii Sibiri.1032-1882 gg.* Surgut: Severnyjdom, 1933.
4. A Russian unit of weight equivalent to about 16.4 kilograms (36.1 pounds).
5. V. O. Klyuchevskiy, *The course of Russian history*, vol. 4, p. 4. Moscow: Mysl, 1989. /V. O. Klyuchevskij, *Kurs russkoj istorii*. T. 4. Ch. 4. Moskva: Mysl, 1989.
6. D.A. Shirina, *Russia: the scientific study of the Arctic. XVIII century—1917*. Novosibirsk: Nauka, 2011; S. I. Boyakova, *The exploration of the Arctic and the peoples of Northeast Asia.* Novosibirsk: Nauka, 2011. /D. A. Shirina, *Rossiya: nauchnoe issledovanie Arktiki. XVIII v. – 1917 g.* Novosibirsk: Nauka, 2011; S.I. Boyakova, *Osvoenie Arktiki i narody Severo-Vostoka Azii.* Novosibirsk: Nauka, 2011.
7. O. N. Kationov, *Moscow-Siberian highway and its inhabitants in the XVII-XIX centuries*. Novosibirsk, 2004. /O. N. Kationov, *Moskovsko-Sibirskijtrakt i ego zhiteli v XVII-XIX vv*. Novosibirsk, 2004.
8. V. Lamin, V. Plenkin and V. Tkachenko, Global track. The development of the transport system in the east of the country. Yekaterinburg, 1999. /V. Lamin, V. Plenkin and V. Tkachenko, *Globalnyj trek. Razvitie transportnoj sistemy na vostoke strany.* Ekaterinburg, 1999.
9. V. Averin, *The struggle for the Pacific Ocean. Japanese-American contradictions.* Moscow: OGIZ, 1947. /V. Averin, *Borba za Tihij okean. Yapono-amerikanskie protivorechiya.* Moskva: OGIZ, 1947.
10. *The history of Siberia from ancient times to the present day.* In 5 volumes. Leningrad: Nauka, 1968. *Istoriya Sibiri s drevnejshih vremen do nashih dnej. V 5-ti tomah.* Leningrad: Nauka, 1968.
11. The trajectories of the projects in high latitudes. Collect. Monograph. Novosibirsk: Nauka, 2011. *Traektorii proektov v vysokix shirotah. Kollekt. Monografiya.* Novosibirsk: Nauka, 2011.
12. Meeting in 1906 in Irkutsk on Siberian lines of communications. Part 1. Irkutsk. Part 2. Irkutsk, 1907-1908. /*Soveshhanie 1906 g. v Irkutske o putyah soobshheniya Sibiri. Ch. 1. Irkutsk. Ch. 2. Irkutsk, 1907 – 1908.*
13. Documents. Stalin's Gulag construction.1930-1953. Moscow, 2005. /*Dokumenty. Stalinskiestrojki GULAGA.1930-1953.* Moskva, 2005.

Space, Memory and Identity

4. Dugin's Early Eurasianism and the Problem of Recycling Ideology

Dmitry Vladimir Shlapentokh

Certain ideological paradigms can have a long life and be resurrected many times to justify a particular political move. Historians of ideas, in this case, have to be cautious and never forget that each round of ideological recycling changes ideology, adjusts it to the present reality even if the external façade seems to be the same. The new elements can be integrated into the narrative with all old shibboleths and for this reason overlooked by researchers. This, for example, was the case with Eurasianism, the creed quite popular in early post-Soviet era.[1] While the popularity of Eurasianism in early post-Soviet era demonstrated certain nostalgia for the past, it also pointed to new elements in Russian politics—desire to follow West/Central Europe despite all conflicts/friction with the West, caused not much by "conflict of civilisations" in the Huntingtonian interpretation, but by *raison d'état.* These pro-European feelings had a different manifestation, including appeal to National-Socialism, and were due to a different and controversial process. In some cases, the interest in National Socialism sans imperialism was due to increasing demographic pressure and general "decline of the West"—if one would use Spenglerian terminology—where Russia experienced the same problems as the rest of the Western world. However, this paradoxical defensive racism was not the only reason why National Socialism became popular in early post-Soviet era and after. For many Russian intellectuals and, in a way, some segment of the general public, it was mostly due to a desire to demonstrate the attachment to Europeans and protest against despiritualising cynicism of robber baron capitalism. For them the ideological fabric of Asiatophilia was a form of anti-Americanism which had Nazi symbols woven in, though it did not necessarily mean any fascination with Nazi atrocities. Alexander Dugin, prominent Russian intellectual and supporter of Eurasianism in early post-Soviet era, demonstrates this intellectual trend clearly.[2]

Eurasianism: the Origin

Why did Eurasianism emerge? Present-day intellectuals and historians of culture believe that the origin of a particular idea can be found in other cultures and the origin of one discourse can be found in the context of another discourse. They also believe that it is this discourse that ultimately defines political and social realities. Still others hold an opposite view. Indeed, while the relationship between ideology and political reality is often complicated, it is the political reality that constitutes the foundation of political thought. One should apply this model in the study of Eurasianism and the way how it emerged among the Russian émigré community in the 1920s. It reflects not so much what happened outside the country but inside the country.

Eurasianism: from the Origins to Post-Soviet Era

After the Bolshevik victory, Russia, and later the USSR, whose borders roughly coincide with the borders of the Russian empire, became almost completely isolated from both East and West. Even the Slavic countries, usually seen by traditional Russian nationalists as their ethnic, cultural and religious kin, became the country's enemies. At the same time, the hope for worldwide revolution—the Bolshevik's early dream, that should have put any notions of nationality and ethnicity, as it is usually understood, to an end—did not materialise. The Bolshevik Revolution not only isolated Soviet Russia/the USSR from Russian elite but also elevated minorities—many of them Muslim by their historical faith—to the position which they had never occupied before.[3] Bolsheviks, who originally appealed to the grassroots support of the workers and poor peasants, soon discovered that with a well-organised system of control and repression, they actually could lead society to whatever direction they wanted. Eurasianists responded to these new geopolitical and ethno-political realities.[4] Eurasianists were émigrés; however, these émigrés were the spokespeople for a much broader group of people inside the

USSR, people who could not voice their views because of censorship. Eurasianists were, in a way, one of the first European post-modernists and also crypto-Bolsheviks. This was not due to their political beliefs but because they were aware of the absolute power of the Soviet Government, which could create whatever it wished in reality.

While acknowledging the importance of the strong and, as they put it, "ideocratic" government, it was not that which made Eurasianists unique, or at least different from the majority of émigrés. Eurasianists proclaimed that division between Europe and Asia was artificial. This was at least true of Russia/the USSR, which should be regarded as part of Eurasia where the differences between Asiatic and Eurasian parts shall be ignored. Secondly, Eurasianists stated that the old ethnic/cultural definition could well be replaced by a new one. In the past, it was assumed that from an ethnic point of view, Russians were closer to the Slavs of East Southern Europe than to any other ethnicity. The proponents of Slavophilism, one of the leading creeds in late imperial Russia, proclaimed that East European Slavs, especially those who were historically Orthodox, had a natural gravitation to Russia and if they were excluded from the Russian Commonwealth, it was due either to alien force, e.g., Austro–Hungarian and Ottoman Empires, or because of a sort of cultural/ethnic treachery as was the case with Poles. Eurasianists rejected this notion and created a new cultural/ethnic reality. They proclaimed that Russians, historically Orthodox, are closer, from a cultural perspective, to Muslims, mostly Turkic, who live inside Russia/the USSR rather than to the Slavs outside of Russia/the USSR borders.

Thirdly, Eurasianists completely reshaped Russian history, transforming the villains, i.e., Mongols who invaded Russia in the thirteenth century, into heroes, as true demiurge of Russian statehood. The destructive aspect of Mongol invasion was downplayed and Mongols were seen as the force which forged Russian mighty multiethnic empire.[5] Eurasianists created a quasi-party that fell apart in 1929 after the Left Eurasianists split from the more conservative mainstream. Eurasianism re-emerged as a viable creed by the late Soviet era and was related with the name of Lev Gumilev (1912-92). In Gumilev's view, the people of Eurasia/the USSR are bound together by a common geographical space, as in the case of pre-WWII Eurasianists, but by a quasi-mystical cosmic force.[6] On the one hand, it was a response to calamities which befall the majority of Russians in late Soviet/early post-Soviet era. The changes had led to a catastrophic decline in the standard of living for the vast majority, wide social polarisations, spread of crime and prostitution as well as the gamut of other ills. All of this was reinforced by divisions of the country with millions of people having personal ties all over Soviet space. In addition, millions of Russians became discriminated minorities in many republics of the former USSR. The negative implications of these catastrophic developments cannot be fully understood unless one remembers the view of the USSR and East European empires by the majority of ethnic Russians in the last years of the Soviet regime. On the one hand, most ethnic Russians, even those who were critical toward the regime, were proud of the great Soviet Union which they saw as basically a great Russian state. On the other hand, this pride in the Soviet state was, in a way, an abstract phenomenon and in no way related to their daily activities. Most would hardly engage in any activities aimed to increase the power of the state unless they were compelled to do this. The majority would avoid service to the army. Moreover, even on an abstract level, the image of the empire was not absolutely positive among the average ethnic Russians. Indeed, most ethnic Russians who were proud of the empire span also believed that their low standard of living was directly related to their "help" to ungrateful "brothers." Russians believed that it was the generous help to the people of East Europe and residents of the republics of the USSR which prevented them from having a much better standard of living. This assumption was not absolutely groundless as the Kremlin provided a generous investment for economic development of outskirts of the empire which Moscow regarded as the integral part of the state. Russians and the Russian Federation were, of course, more important than other parts of the state. Finally, in the early post-Soviet era, Eurasianism's popularity reached its peak, and it is Alexander Dugin's (1962-) teaching that should be credited with the spread of Eurasianism albeit in specific form where the nostalgia for Soviet empire and hatred of the USA had been combined with peculiar Europhilia. These peculiarities were due to the condition of early post-Soviet society where the rejection of the changes had been interwoven with acceptance of the changes.

Contradictory Aspects and Perceptions of Post-Soviet Experience

From this perspective, the arrangement was quite different from those of traditional European empires where divisions between metropolis and colony was quite sharp and where the lion's share of investment went to the metropolis. Soviet arrangements were different from that of traditional European empire from another perspective as well. European metropolis had never provided the raw materials for colonies. Rather it was the colonies that played the role of raw material appendix to the metropolises. In USSR, it was Russia which provided the gas, oil, and other raw materials to East Europe. One might also add here that the standard of living of most of the republics of the USSR and satellite states of East European empire was, in most cases, higher than that of ethnic Russians in the Russian Federation. All of these feelings—deep alienation from the state and the sense of being exploited by other ethnic groups and states of Soviet empire—was as strong or even stronger than Russians' pride in the might of Russia/Soviet state. All of this contributed to their desire to shed the empire as the way of improving their living conditions. This vision of the empire as a liability was also related with the belief that Soviet planned economy is abnormal and inefficient, and Western market capitalism is the best economic arrangement. One shall, of course, also note that many members of numerous ethnicities of the former USSR and, of course, residents of East European satellite states were convinced that it was the exploitive nature of the USSR, its imperial domination and artificial social/economic arrangements imposed by Moscow that prevented them from enjoying high standards of living.

All of this contributed to speedy disintegration of East European empire and the USSR itself. As a matter of fact, the disintegration of the East European empire and the USSR itself was almost bloodless, at least in comparison to that of disintegration of Yugoslavia. The sense of liability of the empire had corresponded with the sense of belief in the West. It was assumed by the majority of Russians, both members of the elite and the populace, that conflict between the USSR and the West was due to ideological reasons and the end of the regime would result in a harmonious relationship between the West and Russia. Soon however this belief disappeared. "The end of history" prophesied by Francis Fukuyama in his famous essay—here the Western, mostly American capitalism, had replaced the Soviet Communism, the omega of world history—was a great catastrophe for the majority. The disintegration of the USSR had led not to improvement of living conditions; rather there was a dramatic fall of living standards. The West, with the USA at the spearhead, immediately took advantage of Russia's predicament and NATO, or actually the USA, expanded eastward. The resentment caused by tragic events where the economic/social breakdown was related to the demise of the USSR led to re-emergence of neo-imperial ideologies where comparative prosperity and stability was related not with the collapse of the empire, as it was the case before, but with its resurrection. This aspect of the early post-Soviet nostalgia is well known[7] and often noted to explain the rise of the popularity of Eurasianism and similar doctrines in early post-Soviet Russia when discussion on applicability of Eurasianism to Russia's reality became quite a popular subject of not just numerous articles but also scholarly and quasi-scholarly publications.[8]

It is clear that nostalgic pro-Soviet feelings were quite strong in early post-Soviet era. As a matter of fact, post-socialist nostalgia spread not only among Russians but even some East Europeans whose expectations of post-socialist and post-imperial past were dashed by the harsh realities of capitalism.[9] Still the desire to go back was not total and, in fact, it was interwoven with desires, at least among the residents of big cities, to preserve what they regarded as the positive results of the changes. It is true that residents of the countryside and small cities, as well as those who were totally impoverished by the changes, hated the West completely. Still, considerable numbers of urban dwellers, especially those who started to adjust themselves, at least somewhat, to changes had a more complicated and often contradictory view. These peoples' vision of the changes and of the West was contradictory. On the one hand, they bemoaned the collapse of the USSR, the resultant economic collapse and emerging huge differences between the impoverished majority and emerging groups of superrich, who often behaved brazenly. On the other hand, they did not want complete restoration of late Soviet arrangements. They wanted to preserve private property rights, especially on their apartments which made rich those who lived in the big cities. They wanted to have access to high-quality goods and remembered well the endless Soviet shortages. Many of them also wanted to preserve the right to travel abroad and read whatever they wanted.[10] The USA and Europe, mostly what Donald Rumsfeld, Bush's Secretary of Defence, called "Old Europe" became demarcated from the USA which could suffer dramatic changes from what it was just a few years ago.

Before the Gorbachev era and during the first years of *perestroika*, the USA emerged as the embodiment of goodness. It was a paradise or omega of history place not in future—as it was promulgated by the official Soviet propaganda whose adept prophesy of Communism as point of omega for the USSR and ultimately for the entire humanity—but in space. America was a place of immense wealth, easy living and all imaginable pleasures for the Soviets. The USA's glossy journals, occasionally smuggled to the USSR, were the story about real life and not the mirror image of the reality. It was the image of the USA as the place of plenty and easy life which was one of the reasons why post-WWII Soviet ideologists presented the USA—the mortal threat for the people in Moscow—as the embodiment of evil. This was especially the case in early Cold War era.[11] At the same time, these positive images in the minds of Russian population were reversed soon enough and the image of the USA became in a way quite similar to those in official Soviet propaganda or, one could suggest, even worse. It emerged as a cynical predatory country which was primarily responsible for the collapse of the USSR, robber baron privatisation, and spread of corruption, prostitution and similar ills. On the other hand, Europe or more precisely West/Central Europe were a quite different land; East European "brothers" were discarded as ungrateful traitors and US stooges.[12] One might also add here that many East Europeans—for example, Poles have historically quite negative a view of their huge neighbour on the East[13]—emerged as geographical symbols of all the good stuff which changes brought to considerable numbers of urban dwellers. Their ideal society was often not much related to Soviet regime but to a peculiar authoritarian regime with strong ties to Europe. Their admiration for Europe had a variety of manifestations, including the appreciation of National Socialism. Still it would be wrong to see in this use of Nazi symbols just the desire to follow Hitler's footsteps in their totality. It was mostly a symbol of their desire to join Europe. Dugin's Eurasianism could be here a good sort of pseudo-Nazism as the symbol of love for Europe. Indeed, Dugin's peculiar philo-Europeanism and philo-Semitism indicated the beginning of the acceptance of new reality by considerable numbers of Russian elite and the masses, and implicitly moving away from traditional Eurasianism which was nothing but a peculiar form of ideological Sovietism.

Dugin's Eurasianism as a Manifestation of Philo-Europeanism

The interest in Eurasianism which emerged in early post-Soviet Russia was directly related to the deep disappointment which followed the collapse of the USSR and socialist system. Indeed, nostalgia for the USSR was quite strong in the very beginning of post-Soviet era. All of this had led to the nostalgia for the USSR and this provided the ground for the re-emergence of Eurasianism, which was a rather marginal teaching in the beginning of Perestroika, as one of the leading political/ geopolitical creeds. And it was Alexander Dugin who must be credited for the interest in Eurasianism, or actually neo-Eurasianism. Duginian Eurasianism incorporated the notions of the old Eurasianism and brought to it the new elements which were related to the social, political and geopolitical realities of post-Soviet Russia.

There were unmistakable signs of the old Eurasianism in the Duginian construction. It was an assumption that the USSR was not traditional European empire destined to disintegration but an organic entity where people of different ethnicities, cultures and religions were living in the condition of happy symbiosis. The USSR was destroyed by the treachery and conniving work of the foreign enemies, mostly the USA.[14] Secondly, Dugin followed the other route of previous Eurasianist thinking. He believed that Eurasian civilisations are absolutely different from the West in social and political arrangements. He accepted that traditional, classical pre-WWII Eurasianist notion that Russia is "ideocracy," i.e., the country which lived for the highest goal which transcended economic prosperity and, even more so, narrow personal interests. Dugin brought new aspects into his Eurasianism and it was related to the new realities of post-Soviet Russia. To start with, Dugin reflected the peculiar anti-westernism which had emerged in post-Soviet Russia. In his narrative, the West became divided. While the USA became the embodiment of evil and the civilisation absolutely opposite to that of Russia/Eurasia, West/Central Europe emerged as natural country of Eurasian civilisation and which could be allies with Russia/Eurasia. In his positive view of Central/Western Europe, Dugin was especially fond of Germany. Pro-German attitude was related with Dugin's positive views of National Socialism. Consequently, he believed that the conflict between National Socialist Germany and Stalinist USSR was a great tragedy in the sense that it was a conflict between two Eurasian powers whose political and social culture were quite close to each other. The conflict in many ways was manufactured by "Atlantists"—the USA and the UK—the mortal enemies of the Eurasian powers. Dugin's positive approach to National Socialism in the 1990s—he later tried to move away from his earlier pronouncement—led to the view that Dugin was nothing but Nazi and thus he would approve all Nazi monstrosities. But this was not the case. One should remember that Nazism and especially anti-Semitism—Jews here, of course, were seen as ethnic and a not religious group—was the cornerstone of Nazi philosophy. It was hardly the case with Dugin, even in the early 1990s when he was quite fascinated with National Socialism. In his construction of National Socialist Germany, he saw basically two brands of elite. On the one hand, in his view, there was the narrow-minded racist segment of Nazi elite who defined the elite in narrow ethnic/racial terms. It was these peoples' rabid anti-Semitism and Russophobia—in their view Russians were the members of an inferior race—which helped conniving "Atlantists" to drive two friendly Eurasian nations ruled by wholesome corporate/totalitarian regimes to the fraternised conflict. On the other hand, there was the other group of Nazi leaders. They understood that Aryanism was not the racial, biological category but spiritual one. It implied that while a biological/racial Aryan could degenerate to subhumans, i.e., a person who was driven just by the narrow interests, the member of any ethnic group could well lift himself to "Aryanism" by spiritualising himself and becoming the member of the elite, if not by official but informal stratification. To emphasise his point, Dugin cited the example of ancient India.

Ancient India had attracted considerable attention of a host of Russian intellectuals since the nineteenth century. Russians here follow the model of European intellectuals; one might state here that Russian Orientalism or precisely, "Indophilism" of sorts was a peculiar westernism. Some ideas of Buddhism/Hinduism had percolated to Russian thought by European thinkers who, while still convinced of European military might, increasingly questioned intellectual and implicitly political traditions of Enlightenment. It was Arthur Schopenhauer's (1788-1860) *The World as Will and Representation*[15] which blamed human suffering on blind drives of the flesh that influenced Ivan Turgenev (1838-1883), the seminal Russian classical writer. Nietzsche's ideas of "endless return"—quite possibly borrowed from Hinduism/Buddhism—quite likely influenced Fyodor Dostoevsky, also a classical Russian writer with global influence. Indeed in his novel, *The Brothers Karamazov*, the Devil complained that he saw his Universe emerging and disappearing an endless number of times and this bored him. In the beginning of the century, the search for mystical ultimate knowledge transcended the narrow confinements of rationalism of Enlightenment, the general political and geopolitical instability of fin de siècle influence of Europe, and percolated to Russia whose intellectuals, the elite in general, increasingly saw themselves as part of Europe. One might state that paradoxically enough, Russian anti-westernism and Orientalism with anti-western tinge was a peculiar form of westernism. This would explain the emergence of such Russian intellectuals of the late nineteenth/early twentieth century as Elena Blavatsky (1831-91)[16] and Nicholas Roerich (1874-1947). While Blavatiskaia was a well-known Russian occultist with European influence, Nikolai Roerich was the painter and philosopher who actually lived in India.[17] Their and other Europeans' interest in ancient Indian culture had some influence on India. Indeed, it was Indian mysticism which encouraged such Indian intellectuals as Vivekananda to venture to the West to enlighten westerners in Indian wisdom. The interest in India as source of mysterious knowledge had flared up anew in the beginning of post-Soviet era when traditional Soviet scientism and the entire ideological construct of the regime collapsed. While some Russians appealed to Indian tradition to find the revelations and answers to questions raised by life, others appealed to Indian history/tradition to buttress their racist views. Their approach to Akraim could be an example.

Arkaim—a Bronze Age settlement in southern Urals—was discovered in the late 1980s. In the beginning the importance of the discovery was overlooked and the site had barely escaped from being flooded; the dam was planned to be built nearby.[18] Later however Arkaim attracted considerable attention of Russian Nationalists. Some archaeologists suggested that Arkaim was a place from where Aryans started the conquest of India in the second millennium BC. For scores of Russians, Arkaim's existence provided the ideological ammunition to assert that Russians are pure "Aryans," the members of "master race" and the assertions of their critics, for example, Ukrainian Nationalists, that they—Russians—are Asians and thus inferior, are groundless. Dugin, following the prevailing mood also appealed to Indian past and this interest was incorporated in his fascination with Nazi legacy in the early 1990s; one might add here that Nazis themselves were much fascinated with India and its past for here they wished to find the origins of the "Aryan" race, the global masters, the cornerstone of their racist Social Darwinism philosophy.

Following this template, Dugin saw the future post-Yeltsin Russia as imitating, in a way, ancient India social structure. Brahmins, the wise philosopher priests were on the top of social pyramid. The noble kshatriya warriors would defend and expand the state whereas the representatives of the low classes/castes toiled for the benefit of the state and consequently, two higher castes. One might assume that Dugin had followed the design seen in Nazi interpretations of Indian past where the elite represent "Aryan" supremacy, whereas the low classes were the representatives of the "inferior" races. A close look at Dugin's formulations revealed the complexity of the picture. In some cases, Dugin seems to be following the racist/biological definition of Aryans and equated them with people who lived in the North, though it is not so much a physical/geographical

North but a peculiar cultural/spiritual dimension. Moreover the narrative often implied "Brahmanism" or "Kshatriyanism" as the spiritual category. Brahmans and kshatriyas are those who think and live for lofty ideals and are ready to fight and die for them, whereas "shudras"/"vaishyas" were those who are selfish and despiritualised. Moreover, in some of Dugin's narrative, the workers/proletariat were part of the "Aryanism" and, implicitly, elevated to the position of higher caste because they worked for public good and individual workers were not obsessed with possessive individualism. Here Dugin, in a peculiar way, blended his visions of Indian caste system with not just transmogrified National Socialism but with Marxism where workers were lionised as demiurges who, while forsaking personal narrow interests, build the ideal society of Communism. And while the noble labourers were placed on the same level as "Brahmans" and "Kshatriyas," this "holy trinity" was quite similar to Soviet official images of workers, peasants, and intellectuals as wholesome groups of Soviet society; it was the money-making class, the emerging *nouveau riche* of post-Soviet era, who was placed at the very bottom of the social order. As a matter of fact, as Dugin implied in his early texts, this sort of parasite should be mercilessly exterminated. Here Dugin was clearly influenced by Soviet ideology. One, of course, could argue here about the building blocks of Dugin's ideological construction. Still, anti-racism of general ideological construction is clear. The lack of anti-racist overtones, at least as it is usually understood, could be also seen in Dugin's view on Jews. And here he was different from both classical pre-WWII Eurasianism as well as that of Lev Gumilev.

Jews in Dugin Discourse: Heroic "Eurasians" and Disgusting "Atlantists"

Jews played comparatively little role in early Eurasianist narrative. In classical, pre-WWII Eurasianism, Jews as an ethnic and religious category was just one among many peoples of Russia/Eurasia and not the most important ones. Here, Eurasianists pretty much ignore the considerable role played by Jews in early Soviet Russia where they were well represented in all segments of society from culture to secret police. Still they were not ignored completely. The major attention was paid here to Khazaria, Turkic state in the early Middle Ages at the territory of present-day European Russia. The specificity of Khazaria lies in the very fact that the elite had professed Judaism. Due to philo-Semitism of the early Soviet regime, Khazaria was seen rather positively in early Soviet historiography. This was, for example, the case with classical works on Khazaria written by Mikhail Artamonov (1898-1972).[19] After WWII, the approach to Jews, once again seen here as ethnic group—and since the 1930s, the ethnicity of each Soviet citizen was fixed in internal passport—changed dramatically. There were several reasons for this. To start with, it was increasingly due to the spread of Russian Nationalism which had replaced the official cosmopolitan "internationalism" by the early 1930s. It was Russian Nationalism, in its idiosyncratic form, which became the functional ideology of the regime. It was, in most of the cases, tempered by residual trans-ethnic imperial identity of "Soviet people." Secondly, Israel, originally thought to be a Soviet satellite/ geopolitical friend, started to drift toward the West led by the USA which emerged as the USSR's major geopolitical adversary. Through most of late Soviet era, Israel's image in official Soviet discourse was extremely negative.[20] Due to these reasons, the state changed the approach to Jews markedly. One of the major changes in approach was to emphasise Jews' artificiality in Russia. In the past, the Soviet ideologists/scholars emphasised Jews integration in Russian history and constructed their images as noble sufferers. On the one hand, the state emphasised that Jews were the victims of the endless waves of pogrom and suffered discrimination at the hands of the tsarist state. On the other hand, Jews were presented as progressive ethnic groups who joined revolutionary movement en masse. The narrative was changed in post-WWII USSR. Jewish role in the revolutionary movement or any contributions in Soviet and Russian culture disappeared from official narrative. More important was implicit presentation of Soviet Jews as "rootless cosmopolitans" who had no roots/indigenous territory in the USSR and who implicitly had no attachment to Russia or any other constituted republic of the Soviet Union.[21] The "cosmopolitanism," the absence of affiliation with any state/territory was negative recasting of "internationalism," praised as the positive characteristic in the early years of Soviet history. Here, of course, Soviet ideologists noted the famous Marxian statement that "Proletariat has no motherland!" One shall be clear here: the negative image of Jews in official discourse and practices in post-WWII USSR had never reached the intensity of National Social Germany or even tsarist Russia. There was no violence or any other direct coercion against Jews, though Stalin seemed to be planning to deport Jews to "Jewish Autonomous Regions," the enclave in Russian Far East created in the 1930s. One, however, should note that Stalin had deported scores of other ethnicities from Russian Germans to Russian Koreans to the distant heartland of the empire for geopolitical/national security reasons as it had been done by others; one should remember here that Roosevelt did the same with Japanese Americans, and all western allies saw no wrong in ethnic cleansing after WWII when millions of Germans were forcefully removed from the land where they lived for centuries on the grounds of "collective responsibility" for Nazi war crimes. Soviet Jews continued to work in the Soviet Union as other ethnicities, though the state tried to limit their access to the most prestigious universities and jobs; in some of the professions they were excluded almost completely. In any case, Jews, totally assimilated/Russified by the late Soviet era, became transformed from privileged minority, Janissaries of Soviet Regime in the early years, to second-class citizen and alien body among the other ethnicities; Jews were singled out even in comparison to that of other "rootless" ethnicities such as Soviet Germans and Koreans who had no indigenous territory in the USSR and who, as in the case with Germans, took advantage of Soviet/the USA, West détente, started to emigrate from the USSR since the early 1970s en masse. The official latent/or not so latent anti-Semitism influenced public opinion and Russian intelligentsia, official and dissident/semi-dissident. It was clear here that some of them, even those who were at odds with the regime, had accepted the anti-Semitic stand of the authorities. This was, for example, the case with Lev Gumilev, "the last Eurasianist," as some people called him.

Gumilev regarded all peoples of Eurasia/Russia as living in the condition of happy symbiosis. Even Mongols who swept through Russia/ Eurasia were viewed as rather positive force. Their destructive energy was downplayed and they were credited with unifying Eurasia/Russia and thus leaving the rest of people of Eurasia in peace. In Gumilev's presentation, Khazars were full-fledged Jews and their Turkish ethnicity was ignored. In Gumilev picture, they were the lords of pathetic Slavic population. Khazaria, in Gumilev's view, looked as Soviet Russia in the very beginning of its history as it was visualised by monarchists and their ideological allies. For them, Soviet Russia, at least in the early 1920s, was a country ruled by "Yids" and here he noted the very fact that Jews played an important role in early Soviet elite, including the repressive machinery of the regime. Dugin's approach for Jews was different and reflected the approach of many members of Russian intelligentsia.

Some of the members of Russian intelligentsia had resented Jews, especially those who emigrated. They regarded them as people who were indeed rootless, especially if they went to the USA but not to Israel, their "historical motherland." Upon the end of the regime and the beginning of robber baron privatisation, they became outraged by the role of Jews in the process. Indeed, Jews were prominently present among robber barons of the first wave of privatisation. They saw those Jews who stayed in Russia as the organic part of Russian society and history, especially if they were involved in privatisations, money making and bemoaned the collapse of the state and political/ideological milieu. Moreover, even some of Russian Nationalists expressed their admiration for those Russian Jews who forsook the USA—the place of cynical individualism and disregard of anything but filthy lucre—and went to the land of their forefathers despite all the hardships which they might face. Even some of the Western liberals expressed their respect for these Russian Jews. Dugin's view on Jews represented the peculiar and controversial feeling which post-Soviet society entertained in regard to West, particularly Europe, where the views of Jews and Israel played an important role in intellectual discourse. Dugin rejected the notion that Jews are a unified ethnic/religious or cultural entity and he divided them into two categories. The first represented "Atlantic" Jews. They represented the United States, the civilisation absolutely alien to Russia/Eurasia. The second was Eurasian Jews. These Eurasian Jews need not necessarily come from Eurasia. Eurasianism here was not directly connected with geography, e.g., the former USSR and related Asian/European countries. "Geography" here was "desacrilised." "Eurasianism" in this reading was more a spiritual make-up and, in a way, it was the same as "Brahmanism," "Kshatriyanism" and "Aryanism." It implied spiritualisation and noble bellicosity and willingness to die for the high goal, for Jewish state and Jewish people or, in the case of Soviet Jews, for great USSR/Eurasia.[22] And it was this that defined early post-Soviet Dugin's generally positive view of Israel, especially the early periods of Israel's history. Dugin saw this early Israeli society as quite similar to the National Socialist state in Germany. Paradoxically enough, at least at first glance, this was seen not as a liability, as it was in the case of those who usually made such a comparison, but as advantageous since it provided the ground for Israel's potential alliance with Russia. Of course, in this case, both Russia and Israel would have to clean themselves from "Atlantist" malady.

Elaborating on this early Israel's make-up, Dugin noted that many westerners who praised Israel stated that it was born as a truly democratic state, the only true democratic state in the Middle East. This assumption is absolutely wrong. Israel, Dugin noted, had a corporate economy, gave citizenship only to Jews defined by blood, and glorified ruthless warriors from the Old Testament as role models. It was that which made Israel much closer to National Socialist Germany than to modern Western democracies. It is, of course, obvious to Western observers. The comparison between Nazi Germany and newborn Israel, who emerged as the direct result of Jewish Holocaust, was seen as blasphemous by Europeans. But Dugin held that the comparison was clear and Israel should not be ashamed by this for National Socialist state was the same spiritualised/ideocratic country which could have struck an alliance with equally wholesome Stalinist USSR. The conflict between Nazi Germany and the USSR was artificial in the same way as the alliance between early Israel and the USA was artificial.

Conclusion

Eurasianism emerged in the 1920s as the result of the USSR separation from both West and East Europe. Kremlin's increasing flirtation with Asia and the big role played by minorities—mostly Asians—in early

Soviet history indicated that Eurasianism was not just an intellectual artefact of a small émigré community but a reflection of the ideological trends in the USSR. Later Eurasianism re-emerged in early post-Soviet era and usually was seen as the ideology of imperial nostalgia and as anti-western creed. Some critics noted the similarities between some variations of Eurasianism and National Socialism and proclaimed that Eurasianism was just a transmogrification of National Socialism. This, however, is a one-sided view as the philosophy of such prominent Eurasianists as Alexander Dugin demonstrated clearly. In the 1990s/ early 2000s, Eurasianism was a core of Dugin philosophy which included not just appreciation of Asia and hatred of the USA but also a peculiar philo-Europeanism and philo-Semitism usually associated with Russian liberals. His use of National Socialist symbols played here a peculiar role. On the one hand, it reflected his and an increasing numbers of emerging Russian middle class's fascination with Europe, and at the same time the disgust with cataclysms of post-Soviet era and, especially with de-spiritualising crass materialistic ethos of that time when everything was clearly for sale. This pro-European trend is related to the evolution of Russian elite and formation of Russia as a nation-state in its European meaning. As time progressed, it became more and more close to nation-states of European powers in the nineteenth/early twentieth century. These states approach Asia not just for the sake of imperial expansion for its own sake but with designs to get economic benefits. Consequently the early post-Soviet Eurasianism, with its residual Asiaphilism mixed with its fascination with Europe, started to change its inner core regardless of the appearance of continuity with Gumilevian and pre-WWII version. And one shall look at Putin's pet project—Eurasian Union—from this perspective.

On the eve of his third term, Putin proclaimed that he was planning to create a Eurasian Union. This idea seems to be fully supported by Nursultan Nazarbayev, who put forward similar ideas already in 1994, and Alexander Lukashenka whose Belorussia was supposedly in close union with Russia for more than a decade. One could assume that ideas of Eurasianism had finally triumphed; at least they provided the framework for unification of the USSR in a new form. However, a closer look reveals that the proposed union has little in common with the USSR or even the tsarist empire. The designs, at least on the Russian side, are more reminiscent of the old traditional imperial policy of nineteenth/ early twentieth-century European imperialism. One must remember here that traditional Eurasianism emerged as the result of particular social-political arrangements of the USSR and the states which preceded it. First it was the power of the state which pulled together and homogenised the various peoples of Eurasian space. Secondly, Eurasianism implied generous economic/military help as payment for geopolitical loyalty. Neither this nor that exists in Putin project. Putin elite see in Europe or "Asian Europe"—such as Japan and South Korea—its major role model if not allies as even early Duginian Eurasianism demonstrated clearly. Therefore it would try to get as much economic benefits from its potential Eurasian Union members as possible. At the same time, Russia hardly had enough economic clout to make Eurasian Union/Russia centred geopolitical universe. The same could be said by other great powers that competed for influence in post-Soviet space and Northern Eurasia in general. Most likely the Eurasian Union would just be a part of the complicated and quite unstable geopolitical and economic *ménage à trois* as was the case with many areas of Asia in the late nineteenth/ early twentieth century where Europeans compete for influence or, as was the case with Iran/Persia, share in a way the geopolitical space and its benefits. Thus the appeal to Eurasianism in present-day Russian policy emerges more as ideological mimicry than the resurrection of past arrangements. It demonstrated Russia's elite and middle classes in general continuous gravitation to Europe, or at least transformation along European capitalist model. Russia's flirtation with Asia is not designed as a way of separating from Europe, or to be precise, European model of development for internal Europisation could well coexist with geopolitical friction or even hostility. This could be seen even in early post-Soviet era when a nostalgic feeling for the past was especially strong as early Dugin's Eurasianism clearly demonstrated. And here, the appeal to old ideology attempt to "recycle" already existing creed revealed different meanings and implications.

Notes

1. On Eurasianism, see Dmitry Shlapentokh, *Russia between East and West: Scholarly Debates on Eurasianism* (Leiden, Boston: Brill, 2007); Marlene Laruelle, *Russian Eurasianism: An Ideology of Empire* (Washington, DC: Woodrow Wilson Centre Press, Baltimore, MD: Johns Hopkins University Press, 2008); Patrick Seriot, *Structure et totalite: les origins intellectuelles du structuralisme en Europe central et orientale* (Paris: Presses Universitaires de France, 1999).
2. For one of the best accounts of Dugin's ideas and biography until 2000, see Stephen Shenfield, *Russian Fascism: Traditions, Tendencies, Movements* (Armonk, NY: M. E. Sharpe, 2001). On Dugin's later works and their place in the intellectual discourse of present-day Russia, see Edith W. Clowes, *Russia on the Edge: Imagined Geographies and Post-Soviet Identity* (Ithaca, NY: Cornell University Press, 2011). While Dugin's views are often mentioned in the works dealing with Russian nationalism and related subjects, some of the scholars dedicated comprehensive monograph articles related to Dugin's views. See, for example, Dmitry Shlapentolkh, "Alexander Dugin's Views on the Middle East," *Space & Polity* 12, issue 2, August 2008; Dmitry Shlapentokh, "Dugin Eurasianism: a window on the minds of the Russian Elite or an intellectual ploy?" *Studies in East European Thought* 59, issue 3, September 2007; A. Hollwerth, "Alexander Dugin and the Extreme Right-Wingers Networks, Facts and Hypotheses about the international ramifications of the Russian New Right," *Osterreichische Zeitschrift fur Politikwissenschaft* 37, no. 1, 2008: 129-31.
3. Terry Martin, *The Affirmative Action Empire: Nations And Nationalism in the Soviet Union, 1923–1939* (Ithaca, London: Cornell University Press, 2001).
4. For a long time, Eurasianism was basically ignored by not just émigré scholars in post WWII period but for the western scholars as well and only one monograph was published for several decades. See Otto Boss, *Die Lehre der Eurasier; Ein beitrag Zur russischen Ideengeschichte des 20. Jahrhunderts* (Wiesbaden: O. Harrassowitz, 1961). Since the late 1980s and especially the 1990s, the interest in Eurasianism started to pick up in the USSR/Russia and then in the West. For recent works on Eurasianism both in its classical and more recent modifications, see Marlene Laruelle, *Russian Eurasianism: An Ideology of Empire* (Washington, DC: Woodrow Wilson Centre Press, Johns Hopkins University Press, 2008); Dmitry Shlapentokh, *Russia between East and West: Scholarly debates on Eurasianism* (Leiden, Boston: Brill, 2007).
5. Nikolai Sergeevich Trobetskoi, *The Legacy of Genghis Kahn and Other Essays on Russia's Identity* (Ann Arbor: Michigan Slavic Publications, 1991).
6. L.N. Gumilev, *Ot Rusi k Rossii; ocherk letnicheskoi istorii,* Moscow: Ekopros, 1992; L.N. Gumilev, *Searches for an Imaginary Kingdom: The Legend of the Kingdom of Prester John*, Cambridge, New York : Cambridge University Press, 1987;

L.N. Gumilev, *Poiski vmyshlennogo tsarstvo. Legenda o gosudarstve presvitera Ioanna*, Moscow: "Nauka," 1970; L.N. Gumilev, *Drevnie tyuri*, Moscow: "Nauka," *Glav. red. vostochnoi lit-ry*, 1967; L.N. Gumilev, *Otkrytie Khazarii: istoriko – geograficheskii etiud*, Moscow: Izd-vo "Nauka," *Glav. Red. Vostochnoi lit-ry*, 1966; L.N. Gumilev, *Etnosfera: istoriia liudei i istoriia prirody*, Moscow: Ekopros, 1993; L.N. Gumilev, Drevniaia Rus' *i Velikaia step'*, Moscow: Mysl', 1989; L.N. Gumilev, *Ritmy Evrazii: epokhi I tsivilizatsii*, Moscow: Ekopros, 1993.

7. Maria Todorovol and Zsuzsa Gille (eds.), *Post-communist Nostalgia* (New York: Berghahn Books, 2010); Otto Boele "Remembering Brezhnev in the New Millennium: Post-Soviet Nostalgia and Local identity in the City of Novorossiisk," *Soviet & Post-Soviet Review* 38, issue 1, 2011; Moonyoung Lee, "Nostalgia as a feature of 'glocalization': use of the past in post-Soviet Russia," *Post-Soviet Affairs* 27, issue 2, April-June, 2011; N. P. Popov, "Nostalgia for Greatness—Russia in the Post-Soviet Space," *Sociological Research* 47, issue 5, September/October 2008; Elena Pourtova, "Nostalgia and lost identity," *Journal of Analytical Psychology* 58, issue 1, February 2013.
8. I. A. Isaev, *Puti Evrazii: russkaia intelligentsia i sud'by Rossii*, Moscow: Russkaiakniga, 1992; L. I. Novikova, Irina Nikolaevna Sizemskaia, *Rossiiamezhdu Evropoi i Aziei: evraziiskiisoblazn: antologiia*, Moscow: Nauka, 1983.
9. Grzegorzi Ekiert, "The Illiberal Challenge in Post-Communist Europe Surprise and Puzzles," *Taiwan Journal of Democracy* 8, issue 2, December 2012.
10. Jennifer Patico, *Articulating Middle Class Culture, Consumption, and Post Socialism; Consumption and Social Change In Post-Soviet Middle Class* (Stanford, CA: Stanford University Press, 2008).
11. Sh. B. Lif, *Polozhenie proletariata v SShA: stenogramma publichnoilektsii, prochitannoi v Moskve*, Moscow: Pravda, 1949; B. P. Vronskii, *Bor'baprogressivnykh i reaksionnykhsil v SShA*, Moscow: Gosdarstvennoe izdatel'stvo politicheskoi literatury, 1949.
12. Ludmilla A. Beckett, "Appraisal in the Russian Press: The Characterization of the Ukrainian Leaders," *Revista Electronica de Linguisitic Aplicada,* December 1, 2009.
13. Anna Misiak, "Don't Look to the East: National Sentiments in Andrzej Wajda's Contemporary Film Epics," *Journal of Film & Video* 65, issue 3, Fall 2013: 26.
14. Aleksandr Dugin, *Konspirologiia: nauka o zagovorakh, tainykhobshchestvakh i okkul'tnoivoine*, Moscow: Arktogeia, 1993; Aleksandr Dugin, *Giperboreiskaiateoriia: opytariosofskogo issledovaniia*, Moscow: Arktogeia, 1993.
15. Sigrid McLaughlin, *Schopenhauer in Russland: zurliterarischenRezeptionbei Turgenev* (Wiesbaden: O. Harrassowitz, 1984).
16. For examples of Blavatsky's work see H.P. Blavatsky, *Teosofskiislovar'*, *Izd-vo*

"Sfera" Rossiskogo teosofskogo obshchestva, Moscow, 1994; H. P. Blavatsky, *The Secret Doctrine: The Synthesis of Science, Religion and Philosophy*, Theosophical University Press, 1977; H. P. Blavatsky, *Isis Unveiled: A Master-Key to the Mysteries of Ancient and Modern Science and Theology* (Calif.: Theosophical University Press, 1977).

17. Nicholas Roerich, *Altai-Himalaya: a travel diary* (New York: Frederick A. Stokes Company, 1929); Nicholas Roerich, *Heart of Asia* (New York: Roerich Museum Press, 1930).
18. Aleksandr Kaunov, "Ne vsenaprodazhu," *Izvestiia*, 31 October 1990.
19. Artamonov's innovative work on Khazars was translated into French. M. I. Artamonov, *Etudes d'histoireancienne des Khazares* (Leningrad: Editions d'Etat, 1936).
20. T. J. Tyssovskii and L. S. Oriova, *Ochagsionizma i agressii* [Sbornikstatei], Moscow: Politizdat, 1971; F. S. Maiatskii, "*Prorocheskiisotsializm*" i sionistskii variant "sotsializma," Kishenev : "Kartiamoldoveniaske, " 1973.
21. Andrei Aleksandrovich Zhdanov, O. V. Selin, Georgii Maksimillianovich Malenkov, *Stalin i kosmopolity,* 2012.
22. On Dugin's and similar minded intellectuals such as Mikhail Agurskii, see Dmitry Shlapentokh, "The fate of Jews in post-Soviet Russia," *Word & World J* 15, issue 4, April, 2000.

5. Turkey in Eurasia: Identity and Foreign Policy

Anar Somuncuoğlu

In the beginning of the 1990s, Central Asia was accepted as Turkey's cultural neighbourhood. This followed the introduction to Turkish official discourse a wider understanding of Turkish identity, according to which all Turkic peoples in the world are parts of a Turkish nation. It should be noted that in Turkish, there is no difference between the terms "Turkish" and "Turkic," and the Turkish word Türk refers to both. The vast geographic area populated by various Turkic peoples was named the Turkic World and the republics of Azerbaijan, Kazakhstan, Kyrgyzstan, Turkmenistan and Uzbekistan were known as Turkic Republics. Thus, through the incorporation of the idea of Turkic unity into the official discourse, Turkish politicians redefined Turkey as a country destined to be an important player in Eurasia.

The aim of this paper is to scrutinise the impact of official attempts to redefine Turkish identity on Turkish foreign policy discourse regarding "Turkic Republics" of Central Asia and the Caucasus during the last decade. Adalet ve Kalkinma (AKP) leadership has supported the religious basis of national identity and has challenged the official Turkish identity conception by defining Turks not as a nation, but only one of ethnic groups in Turkey. The study is based on Turkish Prime Minister Recep Tayyip Erdogan and Turkish Foreign Minister Ahmet Davutoğlu's writings and speeches, since they are considered to be the principal protagonists of the internal and external dimensions of the new official discourse. It seems that despite the new official discourse on Turkish identity at home, there has not been much change in the discourse on Turkish identity directed to the Central Asian Turkic countries. In spite of novelties in practice, Turkish officials still lay emphasis on unity of Turkic language, culture and history while conducting relations with Turkic countries and regions. Thus in these relations the persistence of

Turkist (pan-Turkist) understanding of Turkish identity which became a part of official national identity conception can be easily explored. The study tries to identify some causes of this contradiction between the official discourses. It is being argued that the ambiguity of Turkish national identity conception in foreign policy was used for some practical reasons by the Adalet ve Kalkinma Partisi (AKP) leadership. The paper questions the widespread description of Turkish foreign policy towards Central Asia and Azerbaijan of the 1990s as "romantic" or "irrational."

The Discourse of the 1990s

During the early 1990s the whole complex of Turkish foreign policy activities in Turkic Republics was dominated by the discourse of common language, religion and history. Common identity became the most important explanation of Turkish motivations in Turkic Republics and particularly in Central Asia. Not only the official discourse, but the activities of such profound religious networks as Fethullah Gülen's network were based on Turkic understanding of Turkish identity.[1]

Since the establishment of the Republic of Turkey, the term Türk has had different meanings in official discourse. Nevertheless, by the beginning of the 1990s in official discourse and language of the mainstream media the term referred to any citizen of Turkey, regardless of his/her religious and/or ethnic roots. From the constitutional point of view the Turkish nation consisted of its citizens. The cultural foundation of Turkish identity, as can be understood from the Constitution of Republic of Turkey, is the Turkish language. In practice, in the 1990s the influence of the Ottoman understanding of "millet" ("nation" in modern Turkish) as a confessional community was still partially in place. Thus cultural Islam was another cultural component of Turkish identity.

Yet, there was wider understanding of the Turkish nation, which includes all Turkic peoples in the world. This Turkist, or pan-Turkist understanding, which was the predecessor of the official national identity conception, emerged in the nineteenth century and despite the official definition of Turkish identity after the foundation of the Republic of Turkey, survived among Turkist circles in Turkey. By the beginning of the 1980s in Turkish politics Nationalist Movement Party (MHP) was the main advocate for this Turkist understanding of Turkish identity. According to Turkist understanding, all Turkic peoples around the world were parts of one Turkish nation and their languages were only the dialects of the Turkish language.

International realities at the end of the 1980s and the beginning of the 1990s had a profound impact on the official understanding of Turkish identity where a broader understanding of it was called for. There is a stereotype that Turkey was unprepared for the collapse of the Soviet Union and the emergence of independent Turkic states. In reality, official Turkey was unprepared. But Turkish Turkist politicians and intellectuals who were dreaming of times when the Turkic World would become independent long before 1991 had advocated special ties between Turkey and Turkic communities abroad. Many of Turkish historians and linguists belonged to this Turkist circle. In fact, Turkist intellectuals invented the very term "Turkic World" and established the foundation of researches on Turkic peoples in Turkey.

Of course it is not a coincidence that the official understanding of Turkish identity revealed a capacity to embrace a broader understanding of Turkish identity at the beginning of the 1990s. After all, originally Turkish nationalism was born as a Turkist idea. Although pre-AKP official Turkish identity conception is inclusive it is based on Turkish culture, with roots in Central Asian geography. Thus, unlike the official historiography of many countries, a significant part of Turkish historiography is devoted to the history of Central Asia. Official Turkish historiography established a direct connection between present-day Turkey and various historical states of Eurasia on the basis of Turkic/ Turkish culture. Turkish historical thesis and Turkish linguistics were established in accordance with Turkist understanding. Thus, from the founding of the republic researches in humanities in Turkey were influenced by Turkism.

In the 1990s the understanding of common Turkic roots between Turkey and the Turkic Republics was embraced at the state level as a natural part of Turkish identity and was promoted officially not only while conducting relations with Turkic countries, but also at home. Important examples of this promotion is renewing of textbooks to contain such notions as "Turkic World" and organising celebrations of Navroz in Turkey to emphasise common historical and cultural legacy of Turkic countries. Thus, Turkist understanding of Turkish identity became a natural part of official understanding of Turkish identity much more than it was before the 1990s.

The other important component of the official discourse towards Turkic Republics was based on the westernisation of Turkish identity. The importance of Turkish experience of liberalisation and westernisation was in Turkey's identity as a Muslim and Turkic country. Because of this fact the Turkish case was differentiated from other liberal transformation stories by the very name "Turkish Model." According to this model Turkish experience proved that a Muslim and a Turkic country can undertake a successful liberal transformation and integrate with the world. Although some Turkish economists participated as advisers in the economic transformation of Central Asia, the main role of Turkey was more like a personification of successful liberal economic transformation and its promotion through diplomatic relations.

In many works on the Turkish Model it is stated that secularism was a part of this model. It was, but in a manner that enabled Turkish assistance for the revival of Islam in traditional Muslim areas of the former USSR. This new role of Turkey as a poster child of modern secular Muslim country was promoted by the Western leaders.[2] It can be said that because of the nature of Turkish secularism by the beginning of the 1990s Turkish as well as Western officials could present Turkey as a part of the Muslim and the Western worlds simultaneously. Thus, positioning itself as a secular country with a Muslim majority, Turkey provided official assistance in religious education of clerics and masses, as well as restoration and construction of mosques.[3] In addition various Turkish religious communities have actively participated in the process of the so-called rebirth of Islam in Eurasia. The most influential of them is Fethullan Gülen's religious community (*jamaat*) which established dozens of schools in the post-Soviet area in the 1990s. Although Turkish bureaucracy and especially diplomats kept their distance from these schools, the same cannot be said about politicians. There is evidence of the crucial political support of then President, Turgut Özal, to the

Fethullah Gülen's religious community in Central Asia in the early 1990s.[4] This support continued with other prominent Turkish decision-makers of the 1990s, such as Süleyman Demirel, Tansu Çiller and even left-wing politician, Bülent Ecevit, who served as a prime minister in 1999-2001. Bülent Ecevit expressed his support of the schools on the ground that they prevent Iranian and Saudi Arabian influence in Central Asia.[5] The other widespread motivation behind political support was the schools' contribution to establishing Turkish influence.[6]

The Turkish Model lost its attraction by the mid-1990s, due to Turkish economic problems, the international and regional situation and change in American foreign policy towards the region. Turkey itself lost its enthusiasm towards Turkic World and Central Asia by that time. Nevertheless, Turkist discourse of Turkish foreign policy towards Central Asia and Azerbaijan, as well as institutional structure of the Turkic World policy survived.

Re-conceptualising of Turkish Identity in the Last Decade

The 2000s brought about major changes in Turkish political life. Accession to power of the Justice and Development Party (AKP) with outright majority in the 2002 general elections and a crushing defeat at the ballot box of other right-wing parties, as well as restructuring of the Middle East initiated by the US, contributed to the second birth of the Turkish Model. The essential part of the recent studies on Turkish foreign policy is concentrated on the relationship between Turkish identity and foreign policy, trying to establish a connection between the recent re-conceptualisation of Turkish identity (embracing of Ottoman past and stressing the Muslim part of Turkish identity) and Turkish active foreign policy in its neighbourhood. Many see the changes in Turkish identity as the main cause of the Turkish deep involvement in the Middle Eastern problems.

Indeed, today the main area of Turkish foreign policy activity is the Middle East. There is a consensus that the Muslim part and the Ottoman past of Turkish identity have become one of the main themes in the Turkish official discourse directed to the Middle East. Nevertheless, Turkish Government also champions such Western ideals as liberal democracy, free market and human rights. The promotion of this "Western" part or democratic part of Turkish identity in the new official discourse is also well documented.

Although Turkish Prime Minister Erdoğan had to adjust many of his ideas throughout his political career, there is one persistent idea which has not changed much despite political needs and different circumstances. It is an idea about the basis of the nation of Turkey. Unlike other issues, he seems to be quite consistent regarding the issue of "millet" (nation). On many occasions Erdogan explained in detail what he understood about the concept of "millet." In fact, even the famous turn of his political career—his speech in Siirt in 1997, due to which he was sentenced—was dedicated to his understanding of the pillar of Turkish national identity. During his speech he claimed that currently the national identity of Turkey is based on race, while "our reference is Islam." He also accused authorities of trying "to silence the azan" in Turkey.[7]

During the anti-government Taksim Gezi mass protests in summer 2013 Erdogan used the term "millet" only for his own supporters, distinguished by their piety and support of the ruling party.[8] Although it can be claimed that at that time Erdogan had been influenced by the unusual atmosphere of agitation during the Taksim Gezi protests, a number of his speeches about the "nation" demonstrate that by "national values" he understands only religious values. For example, Erdogan's address at the AKP Congress on September 30, 2012 clearly reveals his seriousness about associating nation with Muslim values. Erdogan explained that AKP conducts politics in accordance with "national values." As an example of these "national values" he put forward the case about bringing back the *azan* in Arabic instead of the *azan* in Turkish in 1950s.[9] Other examples of "national values" are of a similar sort. He also clearly explains how the democratisation process facilitated the embracing of "national values" by the state.

Another dimension of Erdoğan's discourse on nation is that Turks are not a "nation," but only one of the ethnic groups in Turkey. He frequently reiterates that there are many ethnic groups in Turkey (he has used different numbers), Turks being one of them. Although he admits that Turkish language will continue to be used as the only official language, from his point of view the concept of Turkish national identity has to be reconsidered. First of all, the new national identity cannot be even named as "Turkish identity," since in this case it bears an ethnic meaning, and may cause a reaction from other ethnic groups. Hence, there is a need to re-conceptualise Turkish identity. To be clear, Erdoğan always uses the term "millet," which means "religious community" in Ottoman Turkish, but means "nation" in modern Turkish. Nevertheless Erdoğan prefers not to pronounce the name of this "millet" clearly, which is an unusual rhetoric for a Turkish politician. While it is not clear what would be the new name of this nation according to Erdoğan, it is being stressed by him that citizenship, not ethnicity, is the pillar of the new national identity.[10] To compare, both main opposition parties preserve the view that Turks are not an ethnic group, but a nation, the cultural basis of which is Turkish history, Turkish language and Turkish culture; and other ethnic groups in Turkey are historically and sociologically parts of this Turkish nation.

Ahmet Davutoğlu, who is known as an architect of AKP foreign policy, outlined his views on Turkish foreign policy in his famous book "Strategic Depth" (*Stratejik Derinlik*) first published in 2001.[11] According to the book, embracing long rejected historical heritage and cultural affinities will make Turkey an influential power. By accepting its Muslim and Ottoman roots, Turkey will forge solid relations with surrounding nations as well as the Western world. This process, called by Erdoğan as convergence of state and nation, adds new dimensions to Turkish foreign policy, but does not question Turkish alignment with the West in general and the US in particular.

The ongoing turmoil in the Middle East provided a background for the new official discourse on democratic and Muslim nature of the national identity of Turkey. After the beginning of the Arab Spring in 2010, Turkey appears as the supporter of democratisation and the enemy of authoritarian governments. There was an initial hesitation about the situation around Lybia, which was quickly forgotten after Turkey decided to side with the US. Generally, during the Arab Spring, AKP officials presented Turkey as a champion of democracy and human rights. This discourse was radicalised dramatically during the turmoil in Syria and especially after the military coup in Egypt in 2013. Erdoğan and Davutoğlu's discourse on the Arab Spring sometimes resembles American official discourse based on the "end of history" understanding. For example Davutoğlu defends Turkish stance to support the "epic democratic struggle" simply by stating that Turkey decided to position itself "on the right side of the history."[12]

AKP officials and many Turkish scholars suggest that close involvement of Turkey in the Middle East does not mean that Turkey is drifting apart from the West. In addition, as Graham Fuller suggests, with its "moderate Islamist" party, which came to power through elections, Turkey is the model of modernisation for the surrounding nations. The attractiveness of "Turkish Islam" to the Arab countries may harm short-run American interests, but will benefit American long-run interests in the region.[13] Erdoğan himself is a supporter of this idea.[14] This common American-Turkish vision of the Turkish role in the Middle East was proclaimed in July 2006 in a document signed between the US and Turkey which states that Turkey will "promote peace and stability in the broader Middle East through democracy."[15]

The AKP government of Turkey has not used the definition "Turkish Model" or "Turkey's Model" in its official discourse actively, but the official foreign policy discourse since the beginning of the 2000s has experienced a change in line with the propositions suggested in this model. Presenting the case of Turkey as the proof that "in a country with Muslim people, democracy can be sustained in the most advanced way," Erdoğan suggested that "this understanding is the example for all Muslim countries."[16] It is natural that in such society as Turkey, with Christian minorities and a long tradition of secularism, the ruling party still preserves the discourse about secularism. Nevertheless, in Erdoğan's interpretation the meaning of secularism is to provide a guarantee to the non-Muslims in Turkey. Erdoğan also likes to stress that tolerance towards different ethnic groups is rooted in his devotion to God, as his frequent use of famous Turkish Sufi poet Yunus Emre's "We love the created/For the Creator's sake" words clearly shows.

In sum, during the AKP period such prominent Turkish officials as the Prime Minister Erdoğan and Foreign Minister Davutoğlu have actively propagated the re-conceptualisation of national identity in Turkey (if to follow Erdoğan's discourse, it cannot even be called as "Turkish national identity"). According to the supporters of "Davutoğlu vision," the embracing of Muslim and Ottoman cultural and historical legacies made possible Turkish growth as an influential international actor and broke Turkish estrangement from its neighbourhood. It also helped to redefine Turkish-American and Turkish-European relations on more favourable terms for Turkey. According to this understanding Turkey became the independent international player by the redefinition of its identity, no more being stuck to the European choice. Nevertheless, this redefinition does not mean cold relations with the Western world. Quite the contrary, according to the AKP supporters it means that by asserting its cultural and historical identity Turkey questioned its subordinated status of dependent ally and presented itself as an independent partner of the West. In other words, according to the AKP discourse, furthering away from Turkish identity based on Turkish culture and secularism did not bring estrangement from the West, but added Middle Eastern, Balkan, Caucasian and Central Asian dimensions to Turkish foreign policy. This discourse explains how being at the centre of all of these regions, Turkey became a central country, which was made possible only because of the redefinition of "Turkish identity."

Impact on Turkish-Central Asian Relations

Despite attempts to reconstruct Turkish identity and the fact that Islam and democracy became the prevailing themes in the Turkish foreign policy discourse especially since 2007, Turkey-Turkic republics relations do not seem to be influenced from these developments. Despite being countries with undemocratic regimes and overwhelmingly Muslim populations, neither democratic nor religious parts of the "new Turkish identity" are being extensively used in the official discourse directed to the Turkic republics. To be sure, Turkish officials, as well as Erdoğan himself, use the discourse of democracy and common religion. But common religion and liberalism are parts of Turkish official discourse towards Turkic republics since the establishment of relations between the parties. It is a usual practice for a Turkish official to state that Turkey and Turkic republics share "common language," "common religion," "common roots" and "common historical past." The general words about desirability (from Turkish point of view) of integration to the world, liberalisation and democratisation, are also usual. Despite the changes in overall Turkish official discourse in Turkish foreign policy discourse concerning Turkic Republics, common religious ties and democratisation are not being stressed more than they were before the AKP.

As for the real activities on the ground, it can be said that the AKP government has supported Turkish schools established by the Fethullah Gülen religious network more than previous governments. Nevertheless, the activities of these "Turkish schools" that were sponsored by the official bodies are Turkish Olympiads, which aim to show the success of these schools in spreading Turkish language and Turkish culture abroad. Both Erdoğan and the Turkish president Abdullah Gül paid their visits to the so-called "Turkish schools" in Turkic republics during their foreign policy trips. But when they praised these schools' activities, they praised Fethullah Gülen's schools as the disseminating centres of Turkish language.

While in "internal discourse," or "Turkish electorate-oriented discourse," Erdoğan himself and other AKP officials present Turks as only one of the constituent ethnic groups of the nation of Turkey, in the official discourse of AKP directed to Turkic states, we see different Turks. While apparently it is not useful from Erdoğan's point of view to identify Turks as a nation, in Turkic geography it continues to be actively used as such. In fact, the degree of Erdoğan's expressed emotions about Turkic republics can be compared only to the language of Turkish politicians in the early 1990s. For example, his address to the National Parliament of Azerbaijan in 2009 was completely based on common identity and Turkish-Azerbaijani understanding of bilateral relations as "two states, one nation." While common religious roots between two countries were stated only once, the whole speech was dedicated to explaining the special nature of Turkish-Azerbaijani relations based on common identity. According to Erdoğan, such kind of relationship "is not present in international relations," "is not present between any other two countries."[17]

One of the recent examples is Erdoğan's rhetoric during his visit to Turkmenistan, right after the summit of the Turkic Council in Gabala, Azerbaijan in August 2013. While inviting Turkmenistan President to the next summit of the council, which is to be held in Turkey, Erdoğan described Turkey-Turkmenistan relationship as a "two states, one nation" relationship. This description, completely in line with the Turkist discourse, was coined by Haydar Aliyev, the former president of Azerbaijan, and used by Turkish officials to describe Turkish-Azerbaijani relations.[18] During the AKP period this approach was put into service to describe not only relations between Turkey and Azerbaijan, but also between Turkey and Turkmenistan. According to Erdoğan, "we have to develop the consciousness of 'two states, one nation.'" He stressed that Turkey will always support Turkmenistan in international organisations, but also asked Turkmenistan to be more active in such organisations.[19] In addition, on the website of the Foreign Ministry of the Republic of Turkey, it is clearly stated that "two states, one nation" understanding is the basis of Turkey-Turkmenistan relations.[20]

In his book "Strategic Depth" first published in 2001, Davutoğlu defines Turkish foreign policy towards Central Asia in the 1990s as "abrupt," "nostalgic," "emotional" and "irrational."[21] While it is not clearly written what he means by these definitions, it can be anticipated that he implies (1) the ambitious aims of Turkish foreign policy towards Central Asia, proclaimed at the beginning of the 1990s, such as economic integration; (2) the Turkist discourse of commonalities between Turkey and Turkic Republics; (3) both of them. This opinion is actually the stereotype which is present in almost every study about Turkish foreign policy towards Central Asia in the 1990s.

Most works dedicated to praising AKP policy in Central Asia try to demonstrate how Turkish foreign policy became pragmatic with the AKP's accession to power. In these articles, as well as in many other works by Turkish scholars, "emotional" policy of the early 1990s has been opposed to "rational" policy during the AKP period.[22] Yet, in these very articles it is clearly seen that ideational basis of Turkish foreign policy and officially proclaimed aims of foreign policy towards Central Asia have not changed at all. Speeches delivered by Davutoğlu as a Foreign

Minister reveal a high degree of emotions and identification with Turkic republics. He even suggested that Turkic republics as well as Tajikistan can use Turkish embassies as their own.[23] During the 4th summit of the Turkic Council Davutoğlu claimed that all Turkic communities, even if they live in different countries, belong to one nation.[24]

The analysis of the AKP official discourse reveals that AKP government's proclaimed ideational basis of Central Asian policy remains the Turkist one. Neither Erdoğan nor Davutoğlu rejected this ideational basis. They preferred to conduct their foreign policy towards Central Asia in accordance with principles that emerged under the "romantic" atmosphere of the early 1990s. Such expressions as "Turkic/ Turkish Republics," "Turkic/Turkish World," "two states, one nation," "sister countries" and even "unity in language, idea and action"—the words of prominent Turkist ideologue Ismail Gasprinskiy (Gaspirali)—are still being used actively.

The same can be said about the institutional basis of Turkish-"Turkic World" relations. The names and the discourses of such institutions as TÜRKSOY (International Organisation of Turkic Culture) and TIKA (Turkish International Cooperation and Development Agency) remain in their place. Moreover, new institutions have been founded. They are the Turkic Council—an intergovernmental organisation of Turkic speaking countries, the Parliamentary Assembly between the Turkic Countries and The Department of Turks Abroad and Relative Communities under the prime ministry of Turkey. The language used by Turkish politicians during the summits of the Turkic Council reveals the preservation of Turkist understanding of Turkish identity while conducting relations with Turkic republics.

Of course, Turkish foreign policy towards Central Asia or towards Turkic republics is not as active as it was in the early 1990s. AKP's foreign policy during its first term was concentrated on the EU dimension, and has concentrated on the Middle East since 2007-8. Nevertheless, proclaimed objectives of Turkish foreign policy in Central Asia, such as cultural and economic integration as well as Turkish official discourse on Turkic republics, remain the same. This discourse was neither influenced by the new official discourse on Turkish identity nor by the "multidimensional foreign policy," based on the new interpretation of Turkish cultural heritage.

The continuation of the Turkic ideational basis of relations between Turkic countries does not mean that nature of Turkish foreign policy in the Turkic countries has not changed. It is a well-known fact that many Turkish entrepreneurs in Central Asia had close ties either with AKP or with the Fethullah Gülen's religious network. That until 2013 Gülen's network was considered as a hidden partner of the AKP rule is also well-known. Thus the situation around Turkish schools in Central Asia during the first decade of the 2000s was completely different from what it was in the 1990s. All in all, close affiliation of Turkish entrepreneurs and schools with Turkish Government reveals an emergence of different foreign policy on the ground, although the proclaimed ideational basis of this policy has not changed.

Possible Explanations

There is a persistence of the so-called "irrational" and "emotional" discourse towards Central Asia, despite the fact that Davutoğlu and other insiders such as Undersecretary of MIT (National Intelligence Organisation) Hakan Fidan had expressed a critical view about this discourse in their academic works and despite the fact that it contradicts Erdoğan's vision of the nation of Turkey. I argue that the reasons of this are partly internal and partly international.

On the one hand Erdogan tries to transform the official understanding of Turkish nation which is being supported by the so-called Atatürk nationalists or Kemalist nationalists, as well as Turkist-nationalist circles; on the other hand he extensively uses the nationalist discourse. Here we are dealing with the phenomenon which was called an "AKP paradox" by Burhanettin Duran. According to Duran, AKP uses the discourse about "Ghazi Mustafa Kemal" to justify the rejection of the very values on which Mustafa Kemal founded the Turkish republic.[25] Similarly, Erdoğan frequently uses works of Turkists and Turkish official nationalists, albeit not to sustain their ideas. Since in Turkey religious values are a part of what can be called "national culture," even some works of such prominent ideologues of Turkish official nationalism as

Ziya Gökalp (who is also considered by Turkists as an ideologue of Turkism) can be useful for Erdoğan.

Erdoğan's efforts to attract votes of the so-called "nationalists," who are traditional electorate of Nationalist Movement Party (MHP), are well documented. One of the prominent examples is his citing of the poems of nationalist poet Arif Nihat Asya[26] (those poems in which Asya describes "Turkish nation" just as "nation" are useful for Erdoğan's discourse) or Erdoğan's emotional reading of the last letter written by a young MHP supporter just before his execution in the aftermath of the military coup in 1980.[27] Just as understanding of Turkishness as an ethnic group is deeply internalised by Erdoğan, the wider understanding of Turkishness as a nation, but a nation with Central Asian roots, is deeply internalised by traditional nationalist voters, many of whom vote for AKP. The same can be said about the conservative electorate generally. Turam's interviews with Gülen schools' supporters and teachers in her study about Gülen community clearly show how Turkist discourse plays the role of self-motivation for participators. Indeed, various studies demonstrate that behaviours of many Turkish entrepreneurs of conservative background and teachers of Gülen's schools cannot be explained without feelings of commonality between Turkey and Turkic Republics.[28] So Erdoğan balances between his reconstruction of nation and traditional nationalist discourse.

Not only the conservative electorate, but the general public as well positively react to Turkist discourse on special relations between Turkey and the Turkic World. As Davutoğlu put it, "It is impossible to avoid or turn one's back on these regions when one considers the strong public opinion."[29] The popularisation of Turkist discourse and practices related to the Turkic World concept in the1990s had more profound effect on Turkish society than on the societies of Central Asia. Indeed, the majority of activities were directed to Turkish society itself. The effect was especially clear when domestic opposition arose against the Turkish-Armenian protocols in Zürich in 2009. Opposition parties successfully built their campaign against the accords on emotional appeal to Turkic ties between Turkey and Azerbaijan. As a result of this campaign the ruling party refrained from ratification of the accords.

Another explanation is that Turkist discourse in Turkish foreign policy is not and never has been based only on emotions. After all, ethnic, religious or ideational commonalities are being considered as the legitimate basis of close relations, cooperation or even integration between different countries. In fact, the Turkist discourse in Turkish foreign policy is so rational, that even AKP government which strives to introduce a new understanding of nation in Turkey still has to use the term "nation" when they speak about Turkishness/Turkicness abroad. Central Asian republics' demand for special relations based on understanding of common identity proves the rationality of Turkic identification. If the Turkist discourse in Turkish-Turkic republics relations is the basis of the special role of Turkey in Central Asia, then looking from Central Asia the same discourse can be the basis for special relations with Turkey. Turkist discourse is being used in Central Asian countries' foreign policy as well as internal politics. Central Asian countries themselves called for Turkish role in Central Asia at the beginning of the 1990s, possibly with the pragmatic aims to balance against Russian influence. The discourse of Turkic ties with Turkey is being used by Central Asian countries to promote partnership with Turkey and to guarantee Turkish support in the international arena. Even the mobilisation of Turkist discourse and establishment of new institutions based on this discourse after 2006 was not in reality a Turkish initiative, but a Kazakh one.

These explanations demonstrate that Turkish foreign policy discourse on the Turkic World has emotional as well as rational motivations. The fact that this discourse survived even during the re-conceptualisation of Turkish identity at home proved its durability as the ideational basis of special relations between Turkey and Turkic republics. This phenomenon is different from AKP's recent foreign policy towards the Middle East, which is also partly based on emotions and even on identification with some Middle Eastern political groups. Unlike the latter case, all Turkish major political groups seem to share a view that it is the national interest of the Republic of Turkey to be emotional towards Turkic republics, thus recognising the unity of interests and emotions in this case.

Notes

1. Berna Turam, "A Bargain between the Secular State and Turkish Islam: Politics of Ethnicity in Central Asia," *Nations and Nationalism,* vol. 10, no. 3 (2004): 353-74.
2. Idris Bal, *Turkey's Relations with the West and the Turkic Republics: The Rise and Fall of the "Turkish Model"* (Hampshire: Ashgate, 2000), pp. 114-15.
3. For Turkish official religious activities in Central Asia see Şenol Korkut, "The Diyanet of Turkey and Its Activities in Eurasia after the Cold War," *Acta SlavicaIaponica,* vol. 28: 117-39.
4. Fethullah Gülen's website, "Deceased Turgut Ozal" (in Turkish "Merhum Turgut Özal"), Fethullan Gülen's website, http://tr.fgulen.com/content/view/9897/13/, April 17, 2012, retrieved on October 27, 2013.
5. Zaman, "Ecevit: Where is a Reaction Here?" (in Turkish, "Ecevit: "İrtica Bunun Neresinde?"), *Zaman,* March 30, 1998, from http://tr.fgulen.com/content/view/3518/12/, retrieved on August 8, 2013.
6. Bayram Balci, "Turkish Islamic Movements and their Contribution to the Islamic Revival of Central Asia," in Suchandana Chatterjee and Anita Sengupta (eds.), *Communities, Institutions and "Transition" in Post-1991 Eurasia* (New Delhi: Shipra Publications, 2011), p. 411.
7. Milliyet, "10 Months Sentence for Erdogan" (in Turkish, "Erdoğan'a 10 Ay Hapis"), *Milliyet,* April 22, 1998.
8. See for example AKP, "Only Nation Can Direct Turkey's Path" (in Turkish, "Türkiye'nin Rotasını Sadece Millet Çizer"), http://www.akparti.org.tr/site/haberler/turkiyenin-rotasini-sadece-millet-cizer/50391, August 4, 2013, retrieved on August 24, 2013.
9. AKP, "Full Text of Prime Minister Erdoğan's Address during the 4th Regular Congress of AKP" (in Turkish "Başbakan Erdoğan'ın AK Parti 4.Olağan Kongresi Konuşmasının Tam Metni"), the official website of AKP, September 30, 2012, retrieved in August 5, 2013.
10. AKP, "Our Thesis is Citizenship of the Republic of Turkey," (in Turkish, "Tezimiz Türkiye Cumhuriyeti Vatandaşlığıdır"), http://www.akparti.org.tr/mobil/haberler/tezimiz-turkiye-cumhuriyeti-vatandasligi/36643, January 19, 2013, retrieved on August 13, 2013.
11. Ahmet Davutoğlu, *Stratejik Derinlik: Türkiye'nin Uluslararası Konumu* (Strategic Depth: International Position of Turkey), İstanbul: Küre Yayınları, 30th edition, 2009: 90-95, 263.
12. Ahmet Davutoğlu, "Principles of Turkish Foreign Policy and Regional Political Structuring," *Turkey Policy Brief Series,* third edition, Ankara: TEPAV, 2012 : 6.
13. Graham Fuller, *Yeni Türkiye Cumhuriyeti: Yükselen Bölgesel Aktör,*Mustafa Acar (trans.), İstanbul: Timaş Yayınları, 2008, p. 319. Originally published as *The New*

Turkish Republic: Turkey as a Pivotal State in the Muslim World (Washington DC: US Institute of Peace Press, 2007).

14. AKP, "Prime Minister Erdoğan Delivered a Speech at AEI Think-Tank: Turkey's EU Membership is a Meeting between Civilizations," ("Başbakan Erdoğan, Düşünce Kuruluşu AEI' da Konuştu: Türkiye'nin AB Üyeliği Medeniyetler Arası Buluşma"), the official website of AKP, January 29, 2004.
15. Pinar Tank, "Dressing for the Occasion: Reconstructing Turkey's Identity?"*Southeast European and Black Sea Studies*, vol. 6, no. 4, 2006: 473.
16. AKP, "Full Text of Prime Minister Erdoğan's Address during the 4th Regular Congress of AKP."
17. AKP, "AK Party Chairman and Prime Minister Erdoğan Addressed Azerbaijan National Assembly" (in Turkish "AK Parti Genel Başkanı ve Başbakan Recep Tayyip Erdoğan Azerbaycan Milli Meclisi'ne Hitap Etti"), http://www.akparti.org.tr/site/haberler/ak-parti-genel-baskani-ve-basbakan-recep-tayyip-erdogan-azerbaycanmilli-me/6360, May 12, 2009, retrieved on August 15, 2013.
18. See, for example, AKP, "Press-Conference of Prime Minister Erdoğan and Aliyev" (in Turkish "Başbakan Erdoğan-Aliyev Basın Toplantısı"), official website of AKP, May 12, 2009, retrieved in August 15, 2013.
19. R. T. Erdoğan, "We Have to Strengthen the Consciousness of the One Nation" (in Turkish, "Tek millet bilincini güçlendirmeliyiz"), http://www.akparti.org.tr/site/haberler/tek-millet-bilincini-guclendirmeliyiz/50779, August 15, 2013, retrieved on August 20, 2013.
20. Republic of Turkey Ministry of Foreign Affairs, "Political Relations between Turkey and Turkmenistan (in Turkish "Türkiye-Türkmenistan Siyasi İlişkileri"), http://www.mfa.gov.tr/turkiye-turkmenistan-siyasi-iliskileri.tr.mfa, retrieved on August 21, 2013.
21. Davutoğlu, *Stratejik Derinlik*, 487.
22. Bülent Aras and Hakan Fidan, "Turkey and Eurasia: Frontiers of the New Geographic Imagination," *New Perspectives on Turkey,* no. 40, 2009: 195-217; Hakan Fidan, "Turkish Foreign Policy toward Central Asia," *Journal of Balkan and Near Eastern Studies*, vol. 12, no. 1, 2010: 109-21.
23. Ahmet Davutoğlu, "Opening Speech" (in Turkish "AçılışKonuşması"), in *Bağımsızlıklarının 20.Yılında Türk Cumhuriyetleri: Uluslararası Toplantı*, 5-6 Ekim 2011, *Konuşmalar,* Ankara: AhmetYeseviÜniversitesiMütevveliHeyetBaşkanlığı, 2011: 31.
24. Republic of Turkey Ministry of Foreign Affairs, "Speech of Minister of Foreign Affairs Ahmet Davutoğlu Delivered at the Meeting of Council of Foreign Ministers Held within the Scope of the Fourth Summit of Cooperation Council of Turkic Speaking States (Turkic Council), July 4, 2014, Bodrum" (in Turkish "Dışişleri Bakanı Sayın Ahmet Davutoğlu'nun Türk Dili Konuşan Ülkeler İşbirliği Konseyi

IV. Zirvesi Kapsamında Gerçekleştirilen Dışişleri Bakanları Konseyi Tolantısında Yaptığı Konuşma, 4 Haziran 2014, Bodrum"), http://www.mfa.gov.tr/disisleri-bakani-sayin-ahmet-davutoglu_nun-turk-dili-konusan-ulkeler-isbirligi-konseyi-iv_-zirvesi-kapsaminda-gerceklestirilen.tr.mfa, retrieved on June 25, 2014.

25. Burhanettin Duran, "Understanding the AK Party's Identity Politics: A Civilization Discourse and Its Limits," *Insight Turkey,* vol. 15, no. 1, 2013: 100.
26. AKP, "Full Text of Prime Minister Erdoğan's Address during the 4th Regular Congress of AKP."
27. "Teary-eyed PM Erdoğan Appeals for 'Yes' in National Vote," *Today's Zaman*, July 20, 2010.
28. Anita Sengupta, "Models in Transition: The Turkish Model and Central Asia Twenty Years After," *Contemporary Central Asia,* vol. 15, no. 3, 2011: 8.
29. Ahmet Davutoğlu, "Turkic Republics since Independence: Towards a Common Future," Vision Papers No. 5, Centre for Strategic Research (SAM), January 2013: 3.

6. Siberian Regionalism in the Second Half of the Nineteenth to the Early Twentieth Centuries: Views in Historiography

Denis Ananyev

The modern world is often described in terms of globalisation, integration of various countries and regions, greater transparency of borders arising from the exchange of views, technologies, products, etc. Growing interdependence of various regions can dramatically affect their current status and future development. Siberia is often viewed as a distant periphery of this globalising world. Due to remoteness from major political, technological and financial centres, Siberia's social and economic future remains unclear. This paper attempts to study the intellectual transition in Siberia, reflecting on ideas of regionalism and globalisation.

According to Siberian philosopher, Vyacheslav Kudashov, the best way for his native region to become prosperous and play an important role in the future globalised world was to be able to become "a bridge between Europe and Asia" using the unique human, scientific and cultural potential of its population. Such ideas are by no means new. More than a hundred years ago they were frequently discussed by the Siberian regionalists. The principal advocates of regionalism (*oblastnichestvo*) were N. M. Yadrintsev and G. N. Potanin who argued in favour of full-scale autonomy for their native region and its liberation from "colonial dependence" on European Russia and hoped for Siberia's democratic development in the future.

Siberian Regionalism in the Second Half of the Nineteenth Century

The ideology of *oblastnichestvo* originated in the late 1850s and early 1860s. The ideas evolved among young intellectuals of Siberia who studied at the universities of Moscow, St. Petersburg and Kazan. The pioneering role was played by the so-called "Siberian students fraternity" in St. Petersburg in 1859-1863. Its members were N. S. Shchukin, G. N. Potanin, N. M. Yadrintsev, N. I. Naumov, S. S. Shashkov and others. At first their meetings did not have a clear ideological orientation. However, over the course of time they started discussing a wide range of topical issues connected with Siberia's "colonial status" and the future of the region within the Russian empire.

Siberian regionalists (*oblastniki*) perceived their native region as Russia's colony and interpreted its development as a result of mass activity, especially of their most energetic and freedom-loving elements. However, from the standpoint of Siberian *oblastniki,* the results of such activities had not led to Siberia's prosperity as they were appropriated by the autocratic Russian state and the region became the land of exile and penal labour. The ideologues of Siberian regionalism believed that the only way out of this situation would be promotion of the people's "spirit of enterprise," freedom to migrate, development of Siberian trade and industries and improvement of the workers' conditions of life. They also wanted to do away with the exile system, promoted the development of education and culture, and were among the first to raise the question of establishment of the first Siberian University.

In 1863 after their return to Siberia they brought their ideas to public attention in Tomsk, Omsk, Krasnoyarsk, Irkutsk. In 1865 some of them were arrested following an enquiry in Omsk about the authors of leaflets titled "To the Patriots of Siberia". Only after G. N. Potanin's "frank avowal of guilt" were the members of this movement accused of separatism and preparation for Siberia's secession. G. N. Potanin was sentenced to five years of penal labour, while the majority of the others were exiled to the remote areas of the Arkhangelsk and Vologda Governorates.

After the amnesty in the 1870s the *oblastniki* returned to propagate their ideas in newspapers as "Siberia," "Eastern Review," "Siberian Newspaper." They published theoretical work, organised the celebrations on the occasion of the 300th anniversary of Siberia's accession to Russia and N. M. Yadrintsev's book "Siberia as a Colony" was published at this time. In their analysis of the history of Siberia's colonisation, the ideologues of *oblastnichestvo* argued that the exile system and corruption of bureaucratic officials were the real reasons behind the lack of development of their native region Siberia, compared to other European nations.

Soviet and Russian Historiography of Siberian Regionalism

Soviet historians have long neglected the problems of Siberian regionalism due to the fact that this social and political movement was viewed by the Marxist ideologues as "bourgeois" and "reactionary" and as an obstacle in the path of the revolutionary process of Soviet development involving all regions of Russia. Despite the fact that during the first years of the Soviet period there were attempts to revise the role of *oblastnichestvo* in Siberian history, the general attitude towards Siberian regionalists remained negative. Interest in this topic grew after Stalin's death, in the middle of the twentieth century. Various aspects of the theme were investigated by I. M. Razgon, M. G. Sesyunina, L. M. Goryushkin and M. V. Shilovskiy.[1]

There was a renewed interest in these writings in the post-Soviet period. Summarising the results of these historical studies, in 1990, L. M. Goryushkin[2] pointed out that the economic conditions of *oblastnichestvo* were "rooted in the situation of Siberia as a colony especially in the economic sense of the term; that is, as territory specialising in the production of agricultural goods and raw materials but depending on the centre for the supply of manufactured and industrial products." All profits earned in Siberia for the most part went outside the region which made the Siberian merchants and entrepreneurs demand more rights in their struggle with competitors from other parts of the empire.

The political and philosophical ideas of the *oblastniki* had much in common with the views of political exiles in Siberia, especially the Decembrists like D. I. Zavalishin who considered Siberia a colony of European Russia, and V. I. Steingel who addressed the role of voluntary peasant migration in the settlement of Siberia and wrote about the "injustice and oppression" of the Tsarist administration. It was V. I. Steingel who formulated the notion of "Siberian patriotism" as a means of recognising the "needs" of Asiatic Russia and for that reason later was regarded by the Siberian regionalists as "the first patriot of Siberia." L. M. Goryushkin also mentions the Siberian historian A. P. Shchapov among those who deeply influenced the regionalist theories of self-government and economic independence. N. M. Yadrintsev and G. N. Potanin adopted his ideas of popular colonisation, the role of the commune in the development of peasant democracy and of the federative principle of state organisation.

The fundamental argument of the *oblastniki* was that Siberia was a colony of Russia. According to Potanin, the Siberian region had been annexed after the formation of the Russian state; and in relation to Siberia, the central government had a colonial approach of aggrandisement and control. However, the Siberian regionalists believed that the colonisation of Siberia was carried out in competition with that of the government aimed at establishment of the crown and state ownership of the land and enforcement of the rule of the Tsarist administration. P. M. Golovachev testifies by saying that "the Tsarist government was able to gain upper hand, and in the interest of centralisation … began to control popular initiative in Siberia." While the historians of the official-conservative school declared that the manufacturing industry in Siberia was underdeveloped due to the poor communication links, the *oblastniki* argued against the disastrous consequences of the Tsarist policy for the economic and socio-political development of the territory.

One of such measures taken by the government and attacked by the Siberian regionalists was the so-called "Chelyabinsk tariff barrier," which enabled the central government to extract considerable sums of money from the Siberian peasant economy. Trying to protect the private landowners of European Russia, the government artificially increased transport charges for the cheaper Siberian grain, which obviously reduced its competitiveness. Goryushkin's data substantiates the argument that the state extracted up to forty million roubles per year from the economy of Western Siberia alone, strengthening the foundations of agricultural production there.

The *oblastniki* countered this policy by demanding the establishment of a free port at the mouth of the Ob and the Yenisei rivers and the opening up of the Northern Sea route. At the same time they strongly opposed the construction of the Trans-Siberian railway considering it an instrument of enslavement and subjugation of Siberia to the central government. D. N. Collins observed certain variable trends—for instance, Yadrintsev might at first have had some positive feelings about the concept, but he soon realised that talks about trade, progress and development in the East often masked a complete indifference to the real needs of Siberia's inhabitants, whether indigenous people or Russian settlers. He feared that each railroad town would become a slum like London's Whitechapel: cosmopolitan, bustling, and competitive. Economically Siberia would face ruin as competition from more developed regions bit into the traditional markets.[3]

Like other regionalists N. M. Yadrintsev was in favour of liquidation of the system of exile of criminals to Siberia, as it "hampered the economic and social life of Siberian population," "spoiled the morals" and "led to increase of crime." According to Yadrintsev, its abolition would be as historic as the abolition of serfdom.[4] During the 1870s and the first half of the 1890s, following the democratic traditions of the previous period, the Siberian regionalists paid much attention to the indigenous people's question. Their proposals were directed towards the Russification policy of the autocratic state. The *oblastniki* wrote about the progressive character of interrelations between the Russian and aboriginal population, their mutual enrichment with economic practices and objects of material culture. Potanin saw the future of mankind in synthesis between Asiatic and European forms of culture which would lead to resurrection of Asian nations. He thought that this could be achieved through science, education and trade, and Siberia would play the role of intermediary in this process.[5]

N. M. Yadrintsev was emphatic about Siberia's European way of development. At the same time he pointed to the desperate situation in which many aboriginal peoples lived in Siberia. On this issue, M. V. Shilovsky disagreed with many researchers who believed that Yadrintsev wrote only about the negative effect of Siberia's annexation by Russia which resulted in the subjugation of the indigenous population. In reality, even though Yadrintsev admitted the decrease in the number of indigenous people, he considered it an exceptional situation rather than a logical consequence of contact with the Russians. N. M. Yadrintsev also expressed the view that the successful acquisition of Siberian lands and settlement in Siberia was only possible under conditions of friendship and interdependence between the settlers and the aboriginal peoples.

Western Historiography on Siberian Regionalism

In Western historiography the regionalist discourse was the subject of analysis in the writings of G. Hanson, D. Watrous, N. Pereira, D. von Mohrenschildt, A. Wood.[6] Notable contribution to the historiography of *oblastnichestvo* was also made by German historian W. Faust.[7] The text of Faust's dissertation (1980) was entitled "Russia's Gold Mine: Siberian Regionalism in the Second Half of the 19th century." W. Faust turned to the history of Siberian *oblastnichestvo* when problems of regionalism had created considerable interest among European scholars. Till the works by D. Gerhard in the 1950s, the majority of Western scholars had never questioned the idea that Russian autocracy always sought to suppress a region.[8] According to W. Faust, such interpretations of Russian history were biased and unfair. In response to C. Goehrke's[9] appeal, Faust attempted to study the phenomenon of "regionalism" as applied to the history of Siberia.

Unlike D. Watrous, whose research was not based on West Siberian periodicals belonging to the second half of the nineteenth century, W. Faust used in his research a wide range of historical sources including numerous publications by prominent "regionalists" like Yadrintsev, G. N. Potanin, S. S. Shashkov in Siberian newspapers and journals. In historical studies, the analysis of certain problems and ideas of regionalists is possible after thorough investigation of their biographies—a methodology that has allowed this author to better understand many pivotal moments in the evolution of regionalist ideology. W. Faust also analysed the history of regionalists' contacts with revolutionary democrats and "populists" (*narodniks*), in particular, "ideological proximity" with A. I. Herzen, M. A. Bakunin, N. G. Chernyshevskiy, N. A. Dobrolyubov, D. I. Pisarev, P. L. Lavrov; underlined the links that existed between some ideas of Siberian regionalists and views of the French socialists, American, British and German economists and historians. All these aspects have had limited attention among Soviet researchers as well as that of Western experts like Watrous. For Faust the struggle for Enlightenment, belief in science and education brought Siberian regionalists and socialists and radical thinkers on the same platform.

Following the argument of Soviet historians, Faust attributes the origins of Siberian regionalism to the works by Shchapov and the federal principles of N. I. Kostomarov. The views of regionalists on peasant commune and industrialisation have been taken into account by Faust. His conclusion is that this social and political ideological movement does not fit into the simplified categories of either a populist or a bourgeois or a liberal ideology. He believes that Siberian *oblastnichestvo* cannot be divided into separate categories (political, economic, cultural) and that all of these elements are well connected with each other and in various periods of history could have played a significant role in the social and political scene.

Faust considers *oblastnichestvo* a separatist movement (at least at an early stage of its history, during the 1860s), however, this separatism was rather due to "the lack of self-confidence and political immaturity" than a strategy of their fight against autocracy. In contemporary Russian historiography such an assessment was in fact disputed by M. V. Shilovsky who believes that "Siberian separatism" in the 1860s was synonymous with the term "Siberian patriotism." It appeared as a self-definition of a group of young people in Siberia who did not belong to the nobility category. Having dedicated their lives to the Siberian cause, they later came to be called *oblastniki*. According to Shilovsky, the *oblastniki* were later accused of separatist tendencies by some historians.[10]

L. M. Goryushkin also agreed that there had been much discussion in Soviet historical literature about the regionalists' proposal for separation of Siberia from Russia and formation of a democratic republic. As a result, the *oblastniki* were indiscriminately labelled as "separatists." However, the demand for complete separation appeared on only one occasion and is not to be found in the later documents. Moreover, as G.

N. Potanin testified, the *oblastniki* themselves looked on separatism "not as an end, but as a means of stimulating regional patriotism."[11]

It is worth mentioning here another conclusive statement by Faust—that without studying the history of Siberian regionalism one cannot understand the history of "modernisation" and "Europeanisation" (or rather "colonisation") of Siberia. German historians believe that it was the idea of "Siberian patriotism" that played a key role in cultural, political and economic integration of the region in the imperial space, as it helped overcome "colonial past," created a desire among the Siberian people to catch up with European Russia ("the mother country") and a predetermined entry of Siberia into the modern age and its future universal importance. Many questions raised by W. Faust in his dissertation became a subject of discussion in the field of Russian historiography. However his work should not be underestimated as it helped to draw the attention of Western scholars to the problems of social and political development of Siberia in the post-reform period.

The *oblastniki's* activities of the early twentieth century were studied by Stephan Stuch, a graduate of Cologne University.[12] He admitted that researchers of Siberian regionalism have not made a clear distinction between *oblastniki* and representatives of other political movements and groups (e.g., Kadets or the SRs, i.e., Social Revolutionaries) or have neither proved that *oblastnichestvo* was identical to "regionalism" or "separatism." The German historian refers to the terms "region" and "regional consciousness" as key elements to the study of the history of regionalist movements. "Region" (a "mental construct") is defined as a territorial and social structure located between an individual's living space and a larger political entity (nation state). Region is a space on which certain views and desires of the people are projected even if they are not necessarily implemented in practice.[13]

The acceptance of originality and integrity of a region as well as its opposition to a larger territorial entity with a higher status are possible within the "regional consciousness." Stephan Stuch identifies major factors that determined regional consciousness in Siberia in the early twentieth century. Among them the very name "Siberia" spread to all newly acquired territories in Asia; and the creation of the administrative system whose representatives viewed the region as an organic whole; various representations (mental images) of Siberia (especially those formed in European Russia and then carried beyond the Ural). Stuch notes that by the end of the nineteenth century practically all inhabitants of Siberia shared a common vision of the region as a "colony" of European Russia.

Siberian Regionalism at the Beginning of the Twentieth Century

Issues that acted as a catalyst for the emergence of regionalism in the first decades of the twentieth century are: the idea that Siberians had a unique character that was different from the people in European Russia as well as exaggerated notions of uniqueness of "Siberian culture." However, the most decisive factor was the awareness of discrimination. From the Siberian intellectuals' point of view there was an infringement by the mother country on legitimate rights of the colony in many ways, especially when the government restricted the pace of reforms of Alexander II in Siberia. The urban councils (*gorodskie dumy*) had only limited rights and were largely dependent on the authority of the governors, while the rural councils (*zemstvos*) were not established in Siberia at all and judicial reforms started only in 1897, thirty years after their implementation in European Russia. All this allowed S. S. Shashkov to characterise the state of Siberian government as "administrative lawlessness and absence of rights." The *oblastniki* also believed that Siberia was harmed by the state resettlement policy and suffered from the economic dependency on European Russia.

According to M. V. Shilovskiy, during the revolution of 1905-1907 the *oblastniki* claimed to be a political force representative of the interests of the entire population of Siberia. Their dream of Siberian autonomy was embodied in the project of creation of the Siberian Regional Duma. By the beginning of the February Revolution of 1917 the Siberian regionalist movement merged liberal ideas of accelerated capitalist development (with attraction of foreign investments and opening the free ports in the mouths of the Ob and Yenisei rivers) and the neo-populist illusions of creating the new economy based on widespread cooperative societies.

During 1917-1920 the *oblastniki* were on the extreme right-wing of the liberal movement without a single leadership or political organisation. Many of them united with the SRs against the Bolsheviks, supported the West-Siberian Commissariat, the Provisional Government of Autonomous Siberia, the Provisional Siberian Government. When Kolchak came to power many of them disappeared from the political stage, although their slogans and ideas (especially their demand for autonomy of Siberia) were used by participants of various anti-Communist movements (including the territories of the Far Eastern Republic) during 1920-1922.

In October 1922, before the evacuation of the anti-Bolshevik troops from Vladivostok and the advent of the Red Army, a group of regionalists (A. V. Sazonov, V. I. Moravskiy, M. P. Golovachev and others) declared formation of the Siberian Government which soon emigrated to Japan. Later many adherents of the *oblastniki's* ideology surfaced in Harbin, Prague and other émigré centres where they published numerous books and periodicals drawing the attention of the foreign audience to Siberia's past and present.

Siberian Regionalism in the Late Twentieth–Early Twenty-first Century

The last decade of the twentieth century was marked by revival of many ideas expressed by the leaders of *oblastnichestvo*. In 1990 this tendency led to the creation of the Interregional Association of the Economic Cooperation of the Constituent Entities of the Russian Federation—i.e., the Siberian Accord (IASA). The legal basis for the IASA activity was formed by the resolution of the Supreme Soviet of the RSFSR dated March 4, 1991, "On the interregional association of the *krais*, *oblasts* and autonomous *okrugs* of Siberia" and by the federal law dated December 17, 1999, "On the general principles of organising and working of interregional associations of the economic cooperation of the constituent entities of the Russian Federation." IASA comprises 15 Constituent Entities of the Russian Federation (various krais, oblasts and republics within Siberia) and aims at sustainable development of the Siberian region in the market economy.[14]

The supreme body of "Siberian Accord" is the Council of the Association which consists of the heads of the republics' governments, *krais*', oblasts' and autonomous *okrugs*' administrations and chairpersons of legislative bodies. The Council of the association focuses on the issues of investment policy; support for small business; local self-government; energy resources, food security and environmental issues; healthcare; cultural development, etc. During the political crisis of 1993 some members of the Siberian Accord (e.g., A. Tuleyev, the governor of the Kemerovo oblast) even proposed the idea of an independent Siberian Republic.

M. V. Shilovskiy characterises the contemporary situation in Siberia as "Renaissance of regionalist ideas" including the demands for regional and territorial independence.[15] He believes that this tendency should be viewed as a combination of two alternate trends. On the one hand, under the flag of de-ideologisation, economic and legal nihilism, populist manipulations and utopian hopes for "prosperity" (at the expense of monopolistic use of oil, gas, timber, coal, non-ferrous metals, diamonds, etc.) one can notice restoration of old slogans and theses that had been in use during 1917-1920. These ideas have "added to the armoury" of the technocratic intelligentsia lacking human feelings and of local authorities and top bureaucracy striving to keep its control over the region by any possible means. These circles are trying to use the trump card of "protection of regional interests." However, the bureaucratic model of Siberian autonomy is opposed by the desire of certain territories within Siberia to survive and prosper on their own.

On the other hand, in its search for the efficient model of evolutionary transition from totalitarian system to democracy and multi-sectoral economy our society, having outgrown the radical-democratic period of the 1990s, is facing the need for administrative decentralisation, that is, less centralised grip over huge territories beyond the Ural mountains. There are two models of governing such huge territories. The first is based on federative principles with strong local self-government elected by the people and partially controlled from the centre. The second model is based on the highly centralised system of government that was established in Siberia in full measure in the course of Peter the Great's modernisation. Despite all democratic reforms this system de facto has not undergone any significant changes. However, one should support M. V. Shilovskiy's main idea that decentralisation of the regional system of administration seems to be an inevitable and logical stage in the future development of Siberia.

Such decentralisation will provide better adaptation of Siberia to the new globalised world. Regional authorities, state and private companies as well as individuals will be more flexible in reacting to new challenges and using new opportunities connected with modernisation of the Trans-Siberian Railroad and BAM, construction of new highways and high-speed railways, building of gas and oil-pipelines, handling of migration flows, development of economic ties with the growing markets of Korea, China, Japan, India and other regions of Eurasia. This implies development of human capital with large-scale subsidies for education and job skill training within Siberia. In fact, many of these objectives were formulated by Siberian regionalists in the second half of the nineteenth century and still remain unachieved. Their theoretical and conceptual heritage should be taken into account when we are re-addressing these problems in the context of globalisation.

Notes

1. Israel Razgon. *Sibirskoye oblastnichestvo v 1917 godu: programma I kratkoye soderzhaniye* (Siberian Oblastnichestvo in 1917: Programme and a Short Summary). Tomsk: University Press, 1964; Israel Razgon and Yelizaveta Babikova, "Ob evolyutsii sibirskogo oblastnichestva v 1917 godu," in *Nekotoryye voprosy rasstanovki klassovykh sil nakanune I v period Velikoy Oktyabrskoy sotsialisticheskoy revolyutsii* (On the Evolution of Siberian Oblastnichestvo in 1917, in *Some Questions of Alignment of Class Forces on the Eve and during the Great October Socialist Revolution*). Tomsk: University Press, 1976: 55-82; Marina Sesyunina. *K voprosu o vozniknovenii sibrskogo oblastnichestva* (On the Question of origins of Siberian Regionalism), Trudy Tomskogo gosudarstvennogo Universiteta (Works of the Tomsk State University), vol.158. Tomsk: University Press, 1965, pp. 20-36; Leonid Goryushkin. *Oblastniki o khozyaystvennoy samostoyatelnosti Sibiri vo vtoroy polovinye XIX –nachale XX v.* (Regionalists on Economic Independence of Siberia in the Second Half of the 19th-early 20th century), *Izvestiya SO AN SSSR* (Bulletin of the Siberian Branch of the Academy of Sciences of the USSR), 1, 1988: 37-44; Mikhail Shilovskiy. *Sibirskiye oblastniki v obshchestvenno-*

politicheskom dvizhenii v kontse 50-60-kh gg. XIX v. (Siberian regionalists in the social and political movement in the late 1850s-1860s). Novosibirsk: University Press, 1988; Mikhail Shilovskiy. *Obshchestvenno-politicheskoye dvizheniye v Sibiri vtoroy poloviny XIX–nachala XX v.* (Social and Political Movement in Siberia in the Second Half of the 19th-early 20th century). Novosibirsk, 1995.

2. Leonid M. Goryushkin, "Late Nineteenth-Century and Early Twentieth-Century Siberian Regionalists' Views on the Economic Independence of Siberia," *Sibirica: A Journal of North Pacific Studies,* vol. 1, no. 1, 1990: 153-68.
3. David N. Collins, "Plans for Railway Development in Siberia, 1857-1890 and Tsarist Colonialism," *Sibirica: A Journal of North Pacific Studies,* vol. 1, no. 1 1990: 128-50.
4. Mikhail Shilovskiy, *Sibirskoye oblastnichestvo v obshchestvenno-politicheskoy zhizni regiona vo vtoroy polovine XIX–pervoy chetverti XX veka* (Siberian Regionalism in the Second Half of the XIX–First Quarter of XX Century). Novosibirsk: Sova, 2008: 101.
5. Mikhail Shilovskiy, *Sibirskoye oblastnichestvo v obshchestvenno-politicheskoy zhizni regiona vo vtoroy polovine XIX–pervoy chetverti XX veka* (Siberian Regionalism in the Second Half of the XIX–First Quarter of XX Century). Novosibirsk: Sova, 2008: 115.
6. Gary A. Hanson. *Afanasii Prokofevich Shchapov (1830-1876): Russian historian and social thinker*: PhD diss., University of Wisconsin, 1971; Stephen D. Watrous, *Russia's land of the future: regionalism and the awakening of Siberia, 1819-1894*: PhD diss., University of Washington, 1970; Stephen D. Watrous, "Regionalist Conception of Siberia, 1860 to 1920," in G. Dimant, Y. Slezkine (eds.), *Between Heaven and Hell: The Myth of Siberia in Russian Culture* (New York: Palgrave Macmillan, 1993), pp. 113–32.
7. Wolfgang Faust, *Russlands Goldener Boden: Der sibirische Regionalismus in der zweiten Haelfte des 19 Jahrhunderts* (Wien: Boehlau, 1980).
8. Dietrich Gerhard, "Regionalismus und staendisches Wesen als ein Grundthema europaeischer Geschichte," *Historische Zeitschrift, Bd.* 174, 1952: 307-37.
9. Carsten Goehrke, *Zum Problem des Regionalismus in der russischen Geschichte. Vorueberlegungen fuer eine kuenftige Untersuchung*, Forschungen zur osteuropaeischen Geschichte, Bd. 25. Berlin, 1978: 75–107.
10. Mikhail Shilovskiy, *Sibirskoye oblastnichestvo v obshchestvenno-politicheskoy zhizni regiona vo vtoroy polovine XIX–pervoy chetverti XX veka* (Siberian Regionalism in the Second Half of the XIX–First Quarter of XX Century) (Novosibirsk: Sova, 2008).
11. Leonid M. Goryushkin, "Late Nineteenth-Century and Early Twentieth-Century Siberian Regionalists' Views on the Economic Independence of Siberia," *Sibirica: A Journal of North Pacific Studies,* vol. 1, no. 1, 1990: 153-68.

12. Stephan Stuch, *Regionalismus in Sibirien im fruehen 20 Jahrhundert.* Koeln, 2003.
13. Stephan Stuch, *Regionalismus in Siberien in fruehen 20. Jahrhundert*, Jahrbueher fuer Geschichte Osteuropas, Neue Folge, Bd. 51, H.4, 2003: 549-63.
14. http://www.sibacc.ru/en/
15. Mikhail Shilovskiy, *Sibirskoye oblastnichestvo v obshchestvenno-politicheskoy zhizni regiona vo vtoroy polovine XIX–pervoy chetverti XX veka* (Siberian Regionalism in the Second Half of the XIX–First Quarter of XX Century) (Novosibirsk: Sova, 2008), pp. 266-67.

Globalising Political Geographies

7. China's Security Governance of Central Asia

Emilian Kavalski

Thoughts about the contexts of international relations in Asia gravitate easily towards the realms of fiction and fantasy. This seems to be particularly the case when grappling with the nascent international agency of China, an actor whose conceptualisation in world politics often straddles the invention/reality divide. Beijing's enhanced confidence and ability to fashion international relations has been most pronounced in its regional environment. In particular, post-Soviet Central Asia (encompassing Kazakhstan, Kyrgyzstan, Tajikistan, Turkmenistan, and Uzbekistan) seems to attest to the transformations in, and the transformative potential of, Chinese foreign policy attitudes—that is, while at the beginning of the 1990s Beijing was still described as a "regional power without regional policy."[1] By the beginning of the 2000's it had already gained significant beachhead in the region, made conspicuous by the institutionalisation of the Shanghai Cooperation Organisation (SCO).

In this respect, an ungainly but important task is to distinguish between the phantoms and substance in China's involvement in Central Asia. The analytical synthesis of this investigation is assisted by the emergent literature on "security governance." As will be explained, its approach both (i) reflects the suggestion that regions do not exist merely as material objects indicated by their behavioural dimension, but also as constructs that are imagined and can bend to the efforts of political entrepreneurs;[2] and (ii) acknowledges that regional international relations need to be understood as fractures into spaces whose ramifications are delineated not only by territorial boundaries, but also social relations and their sociological, cultural, and (eco) historical nexus of reference.[3]

Thus, by synthesising the literature on Asian international relations and, in particular, by contextualising its insights to recent trends in Central Asia, this article identifies the main elements of China's involvement in the region, that is, Beijing's "normative power" and its "socialising" propensities. These processes suggest the interpretative modes of China's security governance of Central Asia through SCO. Such a focus has not only brought attention to the norms and values of China's foreign policy, but has also provoked a reconsideration of the cognitive structures of the field of international relations.[4]

The Notion and Practices of Security Governance

The emergent literature on security governance has asserted itself within the intersections between security and globalisation in the articulations of global governance. It suggests that although contending discourses, the simultaneous dynamics of globalisation and localisation should not necessarily be interpreted as conflictual.[5] Instead, as James Rosenau points out, the pervasive interaction between fragmenting and integrating processes in the post-Cold War period has prompted "new dimensions of security." As such, the *fragmegration* of security "serves as a constant reminder that the world has moved beyond the condition of being 'post' its predecessor to an era in which the foundations of daily life have settled into new and unique rhythms of their own."[6] Reflecting these tendencies, Thomas Moore notes that discourses of "globalisation (*quanqiuhua*)" have replaced the narratives of internationalisation in Chinese diplomatic parlance. Thus, the then Foreign Minster, Tang Jiaxuan, declared that "the question of security [is] becoming increasingly globalised."[7] In this context, the notion of security governance has been promulgated as a heuristic tool advancing the analysis of the transformations in security threats and the dynamics that these changes bring about in the management and implementation of security. Such a shift from epistemology (where everything that is known depends on perspectives) to ontology (where what is known is also being *made* differently) is central to the discourses of complex security governance. This consideration discerns the uncertainty, cognitive challenges, complex risks and exaptation underlining the security governance of world affairs.[8]

The conceptual origins of security governance reflect that (i) states are no longer the single most important source of threat to international security; (ii) the nature of security threats both strains state-capacities and indicates the inadequacy of sovereignty-bound policymaking; (iii) state legitimacy is no longer premised on the monopoly over the provision of security, but on the cost-efficient delivery of security.[9] Thereby, the notion of security governance suggests a system characterised by heterarchy (the existence of multiple centres of power), the interaction of a large number of state and non-state actors, the formal and informal institutionalisation of these relations, their ideational character as well as their collective purpose.[10] In this setting, China's subscription to the ideas of "multipolarisation" (*duojihua*) indicates a normative conviction that it is the multilateral forms of security governance that can contribute to global peace, stability, and economic growth.[11]

It has to be noted that unlike the dominant (western) understanding of security governance, the Chinese one is prompted by a sense of insecurity that is driven not by "security dilemmas," but "security predicaments"—insecurity complexes generated and compounded by pervading and penetrating domestic social experiences (revolution, war, and reform), which accentuate the vulnerability of the Chinese state.[12] In this setting, the management of diverse security predicaments—socio-political, socio-economic, and socio-ecological challenges—at home underwrites China's involvement in security governance practices internationally. These idiosyncrasies notwithstanding, the patterns of security governance reflect the socialising capacities and the normative power of the participating actors. The following section elaborates these tendencies in China's external agency.

Elements of China's Nascent Security Governance

Grasping the nascent international agency of regional actors with global aspirations has become a key element of contemporary world affairs. Facilitated by the end of Cold War order, such proliferation of actors reflects the emergent complexity of global life. China has probably become the most prominent actor that has availed itself of the disintegration of the bipolar world and has proceeded to advance its distinct attitudes in international life. Such setting, therefore, beckons the discussion of the "socialising" propensities and the "normative power" underwriting China's emergent security governance practices. It has to be acknowledged at the outset that the content and intentions of China's practices in international life might not necessarily be that different from those of other international actors. However, owing largely to the non-western provenance of China, its international agency acts as "a metaphor for 'difference'" to the seeming hegemony of western international society—thence, "what the China model *is* is less important than what it *is not*."[13]

In this respect, one of the central claims of this study is that normative power emerges as a *power in context*—it is not entirely an intrinsic property of an actor, but depends on the kind of interactions it has in specific contexts. Hence, the security governance practices of normative power are not necessarily only about affecting the perceptions of other actors (which tends to outline a rather limited scope of action), but mostly about framing the responses of those other actors. As Erik Ringmar cogently observes, the "reaction [of other actors] is far more important than the action itself and their reaction is what the exercise of power ultimately seeks to influence."[14] This suggestion draws attention to the performative qualities of normative power, which are revealed in the socialising practices of security governance.

Dynamics of China's International Socialisation

By acknowledging the complexity of China's relations with Central Asia, the intent of this investigation is to sketch a prolegomenon of Beijing's agency in the region. In this respect, most commentators acknowledge the transformative potential implicit in China's involvement in Central Asia. Usually, in the same breath they also point out Beijing's objectives of creating an environment conducive with its (economic and energy) interests in the region.[15] These analyses, however, often tend to overlook the dynamics of international socialisation which their explorations infer—a neglect that beckons the conceptual probing of China's socialisation of Central Asia.

Traditionally, the literature on world affairs considers the meaning of international socialisation as the "experience and exercise of political responsibility [that] operates to keep states in touch with the facts of life, to practise them in reading their meaning, and to make them responsible for giving effect to the lesson."[16] The actual mechanisms of socialisation reflect both the instructive and coercive aspects of that experience. Thus, in itself, socialisation is defined as a process that is directed toward states' internalisation of the constitutive beliefs and practices institutionalised in their international environment.[17] In this respect, China's engagement of Central Asian states in various collaborative initiatives during the 1990s and the subsequent institutionalisation of SCO indicate the socialising propensities of Beijing's security governance. In this regard, trade (as well as the promise of an enhanced trade relationship) has become China's "most important" conditioning carrot.[18] China's "rhetoric governing"[19] of regional interactions, therefore aims not only at educating neighbouring states about what Beijing perceives as appropriate behaviour, but also at their adoption of the Chinese "perspectives toward themselves" and, thus, importing the process of "conditioned foreign policy reflexes." It is in this setting that China has promoted itself as a model of a state that "'behaves' in a certain way domestically, and in some particular way internationally."[20] The contention, therefore, is that the dynamics of international socialisation are *driven* by specific international actors that have the *ability to condition* the conceptions of what is acceptable and what is unacceptable behaviour. Such logic is instrumentalised in the rules and norms that underwrite the identity of socialising agents.

Some have even argued that China's socialisation aims at "sinicising" its neighbours by resurrecting the age-old idea of acculturation-through-exposure or "*laihua*" (come and be transformed).[21] China's socialisation practices, therefore, suggest the dynamics of "converting others" to Beijing's stance. For instance, Beijing's enunciation of the "new security concept," "strategic partnerships," and other initiatives intimate its fashioning of the security governance of regional interstate relations by socialising neighbours into a set of norms of appropriate behaviour.[22] At the same time, however, such perceptions accentuate the expectations that these actors might hold about the pattern of international politics. Beijing has succeeded to ensure that all Central Asian states subscribe to its "One

China" policy, which has prevented Taiwan from gaining a diplomatic leverage in the region.[23] In this respect, Central Asian states have been described as "more convenient targets" for analysing the dynamics through which China moulds the behavioural norms of neighbouring countries.[24] To borrow from a different context, the normative power of China's socialisation of Central Asia suggests that its "conception of its foreign policy role and behaviour is bound to particular aims, values, principles as well as forms of influence and instruments of power in the name of a *civilisation of international relations*."[25] Thus, concurring with Lucian Pye's poignant observation, this study proposes that China's socialisation of Central Asia reflects the normative agency of a *civilisation pretending to be a state*.[26] Such understanding of socialisation requires detailing both the notion of "normative power" and its Chinese characteristics.

China's Normative Power

The socialising dynamics animating China's security governance posit that in its international relations it tends to act as a *normative power*. Being distinct from the notions of civilian or soft power, the application of this term to the study of world affairs accentuates an actor's ability to "shape what can be 'normal' in international life."[27] The claim is that when applied to Beijing's security governance practices, the concept of normative power denotes a particular kind of actor, a framework for its external relations, and means for involving others. Therefore, in terms of the Central Asian agency of China, the notion of normative power suggests that its international behaviour is not only preconditioned by a particular kind of self, but also that its foreign policies to the region indicate that other states *should* behave according to these principles. The proposition, therefore, is that owing to the specificities of its historical trajectory, its idiosyncratic polity, and its power constellations, China advances a particular understanding of what is appropriate in international life that predisposes it to act in a normative way in its relations with Central Asia.

In this setting, a number of commentators have prompted assessments that portray Beijing's outreach on a continuum from a cuddly "panda" to a fire-breathing "dragon."[28] The claim here is that these images of

China's external relations represent distinct (but not mutually exclusive) aspectual contexts of the composite normative power underwriting China's "*zhoubian*, or 'omni-directional' foreign policy initiatives."[29] Thus, while China's foreign policy calculus has earned it the label of the "high church of *realpolitik*"[30] such depiction does not negate that despite the huge spillover effects of its economic growth on the rest of the world Beijing "will still on some levels be uncomfortable internationally."[31] The complexity of such characterisations conveys China's self-identification as an "excluded" or "isolated" state.[32] This perception reflects the structural dynamics in post-Cold War world politics, which have left China out as a "deviant" state representing one of "the last bastions of communism" challenging the practices and the propagation of liberal democratic values.[33]

In this respect, Beijing's "charm offensive" reflects China's attempt to construct itself as a responsible as well as a reliable international player that offers an alternative to Western actors and organisations. At the same time, Beijing has generally resisted engaging in direct subversion of established institutions and regimes, and has more often than not complied with their standards and/or sought inclusion through membership of their organisational clubs. Therefore, some commentators have claimed that China's international relations are informed by an analytical two-step involving a "system of symbols" about what is acceptable in international life and an understanding of "the most efficacious policies" for pursuing and ensuring the maintenance of such acceptability.[34]

It has to be noted, however, that the identification of an international actor as a normative power does not imply that it is a "force for good."[35] Thus, although the entire logic of normative power is about the spread of particular norms and values, this acknowledgement does not deny the strategic rationale of such socialisation.[36] In this respect, even when the norms diffused by international actors may very well be considered legitimate and valid, this need not occlude the realisation that the motivation for diffusing such norms is self-regarding and is oftentimes triggered by strategic considerations.[37] Thus, China's socialisation of Central Asia is consistent with claims of *normative rhetorical masquerade* of ulterior power manipulation.[38]

In this respect, while some commentators would argue that China has always been (or has always had) a normative power (in the sense that its socialising agency was devised to foster an environment consistent with Chinese interests), this study posits that the normative power of China's security governance can be read through the interaction between three foreign policy values: "peaceful rise" to international status, non-interference in the domestic affairs of states, and maintaining Chinese national values. The normative three-step provided by China's foreign policy discourse reflects the interaction between contending normative and strategic cultures. Such conceptualisation intimates the perplexing phenomenon of its security governance—the "union of subconscious rationality and conscious irrationality" that brings together "moral internationalism and selfish nationalism" within Beijing's socialising rhetoric.[39] Undoubtedly the picture that emerges is more complex and perhaps less amenable to models of predictability required by policy-planners; yet, the contention is that such analysis makes possible the conceptual and contextual examination of China's security governance of Central Asia.

The Shanghai Cooperation Organisation and China's Security Governance of Central Asia

The region of Central Asia provides the contexts instantiating China's nascent security governance practices.[40] Traditionally, Beijing's foreign policy interests in the region are grouped into four dominant narratives: (i) diversifying and ensuring China's access to energy resources; (ii) cutting any international links between Muslim Uyghur separatists in the province of Xinjiang and their ethnic and religious kin across Central Asia; (iii) encouraging economic and trade relations between China's western provinces and Central Asian states; (iv) indicating China's preparedness to become a global actor.[41] From these four discursive contexts, the stability of Xinjiang seems to have been of central concern to Beijing. For instance, China's ability during the 1990s to convince Central Asian states through different confidence and security building measures to sign treaties demarcating their joint border has been specifically linked to the issue of Uyghur separatism.

Yet, Beijing's rapid movement from the difficult task of delineating and disarming its borders with Kazakhstan, Kyrgyzstan, Russia, and Tajikistan to promoting a multilateral organisation and establishing growing economic and security ties attest to more than just the conventional power politics of national self-interest. Instead, the creation of the "Shanghai Five" in the mid-1990s promoted a climate that managed to alleviate Central Asian suspicions about China's intentions. Thus, the accession of Uzbekistan and the transformation of the "Shanghai Five" into SCO in 2001 seem to implicate regional susceptibility to Beijing's power of attraction. On a pragmatic level this development reflects the strategic contexts and has facilitated China's security governance of Central Asia: (i) the post-Cold War vacuum in the region in the aftermath of Russia's retreat owing to the complexities of its post-Soviet transition; and (ii) the post-2003 diversion of the USA from the region because of its preoccupation in Iraq/Middle East. Thus, SCO has become the epitome of China's socialising propensity, which suggests its uniqueness in terms of the patterns of China's security governance: (i) it is probably the first instance where China takes the lead to develop a regional regime; (ii) it allows Beijing to address critical security concerns on the basis of multilateral cooperation rather than through formal alliances or unilaterally; (iii) bearing in mind China's lack of experience in framing multilateral institutions, it has successfully become a significant regional institution.[42] In fact, Beijing itself has indicated that it perceives SCO as a "major innovation in the history of China's diplomacy and in the international relations of the Central Asian region."[43] As SCO's first Secretary-General asserts, "it is not an ordinary organisation of cooperation. On the one hand, the SCO cooperation on security is not carried out in the way of a traditional military bloc such as NATO; on the other hand, its economic cooperation is not aimed at closer integration as in the EU."[44] In this respect, through SCO's diplomatic rhetoric and policy-practice of peace-building, development, and economic integration, Beijing signals its willingness to share with Central Asian states the opportunities associated with China's "peaceful rise" within the context of compliance with promoted rules.[45]

Although its main goal is defined as the "strengthening of peace and ensuring the security and stability in the region," both the 2001 SCO Declaration and the 2002 SCO Charter emphasise the normative rather than military rationale of SCO's security governance (it has to be reiterated that the reference to *normative* does not negate that it could be *strategic*). In this regard, the security predicaments posed by the prospect of "splittism"—a term describing a violent secession of Chinese territory—motivates Beijing to experiment with novel arrangements for ensuring predictable Central Asian attitudes. Thus, by striving to "preserve and safeguard regional peace, security, and stability," SCO intends to assist in the creation of a "fair and rational political and economic order" premised on "the goals and principles of the Charter of the United Nations, other commonly acknowledged principles and rules of international law related to the maintenance of international peace, security and the development of good-neighbourly and friendly relations, as well as the cooperation between states."[46]

Promoted as an organisation for Central Asian cooperation that seeks to maintain regional stability and advance economic relations, SCO not only reiterates Beijing's increasing clout in international life, but also boosts its credentials by emphasising China's peaceful foreign policy intentions.[47] Yet, attesting to the normative politics of Beijing's involvement in Central Asia, SCO has been promoted as the embodiment of the "Shanghai Spirit" of partnership, which "speaks for mutual respect and seeks commonalities while preserving differences."[48] The reference to the "Shanghai Spirit" has become shorthand for the observance of "mutual trust, mutual benefit, equality, consultation, respect for multi-civilisations, and striving for common development." To that effect SCO has established a permanent Secretariat (inaugurated on January 15, 2004) headquartered in Beijing. Moreover, in order to further "coordination of efforts for the maintenance of peace and enhancing security and confidence in the region,"[49] SCO has instituted a set of issue-specific dialogues under the so-called "mechanism of meetings."

In this respect, China's evolving socialisation of Central Asia has led Beijing to take the initiative in fostering a security environment that, while consistent with its interests also, engages its neighbours in cooperative initiatives. These dynamics are evidenced through the Regional Anti-Terrorist Structure (RATS). It builds upon the work of the 1999 Joint Control Group which verified compliance with the 1996 Agreement on Confidence Building in the Military Field along the Border Areas and the 1997 Agreement on the Mutual Reduction of Military Forces in the Border Areas signed by the members of the then "Shanghai Five." RATS is a multilateral security arrangement that establishes precise security commitments between SCO Member States.[50] It confirms their subscription to what China perceives to be the "three evil forces"—separatism, extremism, and terrorism.[51] Such form of international socialisation promotes rule-conformity both as a rhetorical practice and operational mechanism. The establishment of RATS has urged a number of commentators to declare that China is gradually becoming the key security provided in Central Asia.[52] Confirming such claims, under the RATS aegis there have been several cross-border military and counter-terrorism exercises attesting to "the highly unusual—even unprecedented—for China participation in organisation whose primary purpose is security cooperation."[53] In this respect, China's participation in the security infrastructure of Central Asia reflects its more confident perception of its identity in regional and global politics.

In this context, the SCO framework—which Beijing views as the instrumentalisation of the "Shanghai spirit"—outlines the normative patterns of China's security governance of Central Asia. In this respect, China's security governance of the region confirms Beijing's insistence on its peaceful rise to international prominence. SCO, therefore, provides both a confirmation of this claim as well as an institutional infrastructure for pre-empting the turbulence on China's periphery. As Zhang Deguang points out, "SCO does not bear a gene of confrontation … [It] emerged on the basis of generalisation of the historical experience of the Cold War period and fits the demands of our time: aspiration towards peace and cooperation, anchoring stability and development in the region."[54] At the same time, Beijing's socialisation of Central Asia suggests "China's fundamental interest in the establishment and maintenance of a new regional security order."[55] Thus, in a comment on China's role in the region, the current SCO Secretary-General has attested to socialising capacities by acknowledging that "only the tree which bears fruit attracts attention."[56] Beijing's conditioning propensity, therefore, attests to its ability to project coherent (and contextualised) policies for the security governance of the region.

Conclusion

Roger Beaumont has quipped, there is something quite paradoxical implicit in any attempt to "conclude" the observation of a complex and constantly moving target—especially, one as dynamic as China and its expanding international relations.[57] The reason being that the sequential unfolding of uncertainties, dilemmas, and contingencies works against focusing analysis and drawing neat conclusions on a research subject that keeps on evolving and altering the patterns and trajectories of its international outlook, as well as the contexts to which it is being applied. Having in mind the international interactions of rising actors such as China, Donald Puchala has drawn attention to the difficulty of framing the "unobservable wholes" that these constantly moving targets represent, which invariably reveal "considerable uncertainty about whether the parts observed are actually elements of the wholes inferred."[58]

Thus, by indicating the overlapping contexts of China's normative power, the analytical synthesis of this study has suggested that the institutionalisation of SCO affords Beijing an opportunity to project itself as a blueprint for the future trajectories of Central Asian states. Consequently, China's involvement in the region has exhibited the socialising effects of Beijing's security governance. In this setting, China's influence in the region has been assisted by its ability to articulate self-reflexive security governance policies premised on the centrality of sovereignty and the economic benefits of its "peaceful rise."

Beijing's security governance of Central Asia, however, is also an instance of its emergent *global* foreign policy strategy "to secure and shape a security, economic, and political environment that is conducive to China."[59] The task, then, for policy-planners, analysts, and scholars of both Central Asia and China's external relations remains ambiguous.[60] On the one hand, the complexity of regional interactions is too precarious to simply be discarded. On the other, the projection of Beijing's values and rules needs to be continuously re-assessed through the exposition of contradictions within this discourse, and between this discourse and China's other foreign-policy practices. Thus, the conceptualisation of the international role of China as a shaper of norms intimates procedural socialisation mechanisms and practices. The elaboration of China's involvement of Central Asia through the contexts of its security governance, therefore, attempts to suggest not only that Beijing's emergent *global* foreign policy is underwritten by normative premises, but also that it predisposes China to act in a normative way in world politics.

Notes

1. Bin Yu, "China and Russia: Normalizing Their Strategic Partnership," in *Power Shift: China and Asia's New Dynamics*, D. Shambaugh (ed.) (Berkeley, CA: University of California Press, 2005), p. 228.
2. Peter Katzenstein and Rudra Sil, "Rethinking Asian Security: A Case for Analytical Eclecticism," in J. J. Suh, Peter Katzenstein and Allen Carlson (eds.), *Rethinking Security in East Asia* (Stanford: Stanford University Press, 2004), p. 24.
3. Muthiah Alagappa (ed.), *Asian Security Practice* (Stanford, CA: Stanford University Press, 1998).
4. Amitav Acharya and Barry Buzan, "Why Is There No Non-Western International Relations Theory," *International Relations of the Asia-Pacific,* vol. 7, no. 3, 2007: 287-312.
5. Anthony Reid, "Global and Local in Southeast Asian History," *International Journal of Asian Studies* 1, no. 1, 2004: 20.
6. James Rosenau, "New Dimensions of Security," *Security Dialogue,* vol. 25, no. 3, 1994: 255-81.
7. Thomas Moore, "Chinese Foreign Policy in the Age of Globalization," in Yong Deng and Fei-ling Wang (eds.), *China Rising: Power and Motivation in Chinese Foreign Policy* (Lanham: Rowman and Littlefield, 2005), p. 135.
8. Emilian Kavalski, "Partnership or Rivalry between the EU, India, and China in Central Asia: The Normative Power of Regional Actors with Global Aspirations," *European Law Journal*, vol. 13, no. 6, 2007: 839-56.
9. Elke Krahman, "American Hegemony or Global Governance," *International Studies Review*, vol. 7, no. 3, 2005: 537.
10. Mark Webber, Stuart Croft, Jolyon Howorth, Terry Terriff and Elke Krahman, "The Governance of European Security," *Review of International Studies*, vol. 30, no. 1, 2004: 5-9.

11. Niv Horesh and Emilian Kavalski (eds.), *Asian Thought on China's International Relations* (Basingstoke: Palgrave, 2014).
12. Chengxin Pan, *Knowledge, Desire and Power in Global Politics: Western Representations of China's Rise* (Cheltenham: Edward Elgar, 2012).
13. Shaun Breslin, "The 'China Model' and the Global Crisis," *International Affairs*, vol. 87, no. 6, 2011: 1324.
14. Erik Ringmar, "Performing International Systems: Two East-Asian Alternatives to the Westphalian Order," *International Organization*, vol. 66, no. 1, 2012: 19.
15. Emilian Kavalski, *Central Asia and the Rise of Normative Powers: Contextualizing the Security Governance of the EU, China, and India* (New York: Continuum, 2012).
16. Emilian Kavalski, "From the Western Balkans to the Greater Balkans Area: The External Conditioning of 'Awkward' and 'Integrated' States," *Mediterranean Quarterly*, vol. 17, no. 3, 2006: 86-100.
17. Frank Schimmelfennig, "International Socialization," *European Journal of International Relations* 6, no. 1, 2000: 109-39.
18. Marc Lanteigne, *China and International Institutions* (London: Routledge, 2005), p. 119.
19. Arano Yasunori, "The Formation of Japanocentric World Order," *International Journal of Asian Studies* 2, no. 2, 2005: 185.
20. Shih Chih-yu, *The Spirit of Chinese Foreign Policy* (New York: St. Martin's Press, 1990), pp. 21-25.
21. Yongjin Zhang, "System, Empire and State in Chinese International Relations," *Review of International Studies*, vol. 27, no. 1, 2001: 55.
22. Emilian Kavalski (ed.), *The Ashgate Research Companion to Chinese Foreign Policy* (Farnham: Ashgate, 2012).
23. Lanteigne, *China and International Institutions*, p. 119.
24. Shih, *The Spirit of Chinese Foreign Policy*, p. 21.
25. Thomas Diez, "Constructing the Self and Changing Others: Reconsidering 'Normative Power Europe,'" *Millennium*, vol. 33, no. 3, 2005: 617.
26. Lucian Pye, "China: Erratic State, Frustrated Society," *Foreign Affairs*, vol. 69, no. 4, 1999: 58.
27. Ian Manners, "Normative Power Europe: A Contradiction in Terms," *Journal of Common Market Studies*, vol. 40, no. 2, 2002: 253.
28. Randall Peerenboom, "The Fire-Breathing Dragon and the Cute, Cuddly Panda: The Implications of China's Rise for Developing Countries, Human Rights, and Geopolitical Stability," *Chicago Journal of International Law*, vol. 7, no. 1, 2006: 17-50.
29. Lanteigne, *China and International Institutions*, p. 2.
30. Thomas Christensen, "Chinese *Realpolitik*," *Foreign Affairs*, vol. 75, no. 5, 1996: 37-52.

31. David Lampton, "Alternative Security and Foreign Policy Futures for China," *Asia Policy,* vol. 4, 2007: 8.
32. Yong Deng, *China's Struggle for Status* (Cambridge: Cambridge University Press, 2008), p. 55.
33. Yongjin Zhang, "Problematizing China's Security: Sociological Insights," *Pacifica Review*, vol. 13, no. 3, 2001: 247.
34. Alastair Johnston, *Cultural Realism: Strategic Culture and Grand Strategy in Chinese History* (Princeton, NJ: Princeton University Press, 1995), p. 222.
35. Helene Sjursen, "The EU as a 'Normative' Power: How Can This Be," *Journal of European Public Policy,* vol. 13, no. 2, 2006: 235.
36. Emilian Kavalski, "The Struggle for Recognition of Normative Powers: Normative Power Europe and Normative Power China in Context," *Cooperation & Conflict*, vol. 48, no. 2, 2013: 247-67.
37. Sjursen, "The EU as a 'Normative' Power ..." 239.
38. Shih, *The Spirit of Chinese Foreign Policy,* p. 2.
39. Shih Chih-yu. *China's Just World* (Boulder: Lynne Rienner, 1993), p. 35.
40. Kavalski, *Central Asia and the Rise of Normative Powers.*
41. Kavalski, "The Struggle for Recognition of Normative Powers."
42. Lanteigne, *China and International Institutions*, p. 116.
43. Emilian Kavalski, "Chinese Normative Communities of Practice: Comparative Study of China's Relational Governance of Africa and Central Asia," in Li Xing (ed.), *China-Africa Relations in the Era of Great Transformations* (Farnham: Ashgate, 2013).
44. Zhang Deguang, "Generalizing Experience, Deepening Cooperation," http://www.sectsco.org/html/01007.html, May 14, 2006.
45. Zhang Yunling and Tang Shiping, "China's Regional Strategy," in David Shambaugh (ed.), *Power Shift: China and Asia's New Dynamics* (Berkeley, CA: University of California Press, 2005), p. 55.
46. Shanghai Cooperation Organization Declaration. Available at: http://www.sectsco.org/html/00088.html, 2001.
47. Russell Ong, "China's Security Interests in Central Asia," *Central Asia Survey*, vol. 24, no. 4, 2005: 436.
48. Chung Chien-peng, "The Shanghai Cooperation Organization," *China Quarterly*, vol. 44, no. 180, 2004: 991.
49. Shanghai Cooperation Organization Charter. Available at: http://www.sectsco.org/html/00096.html, 2002.
50. Shanghai Cooperation Organization Concept on Combating Terrorism, Separatism, and Extremism. Available at: http://www.ecrats.com/ru/docs/read/conception_shos_members, 2005.
51. Chung, "The Shanghai Cooperation Organization," 991.

52. Zhao Huaseng, "The Shanghai Cooperation Organization," *China and Eurasia Forum Quarterly*, vol. 4 no. 3, 2003: 106.
53. David Shambaugh (ed.), *Power Shift: China and Asia's New Dynamics* (Berkeley, CA: University of California Press, 2005), p. 31.
54. Zhang Deguang, "Interview with the *Oriental Weekly*." Available at: http://www.sectsco.org/html/01008.html, September 6, 2006.
55. *White Paper on China's National Defence*. Available at: http://www.china.org.cn/english/2791.htm, October 16, 2000.
56. Bolat Nurgaliev, "Interview with *Wenhuibao*." Available at: http://www.sectsco.org/html/01203.html, January 22, 2007.
57. Roger Beaumont, *War, Chaos, and History* (Westport, CT: Praeger, 1994), p. 145.
58. Donald Puchala, *Theory and History in International Relations* (London: Routledge, 2003), pp. 21-22.
59. Zhang Yunling and Tang Shiping, "China's Regional Strategy," p. 48.
60. This paragraph benefits from Kavalski, "The Struggle for Recognition of Normative Powers."

8. Daydreams and Nightmares: Dreaming of Al-Qaeda and the Once and Future Caliphate—Extremist Narratives on Globalised Islam

Michael Fredholm

All societies include extremists. While Islamic extremism, as exemplified and inspired by Al-Qaeda, in the second half of the twentieth century grew into jihadism and became a threat to security in much of contemporary Eurasia, other types of extremism caused problems too. With globalisation followed large-scale migration and the Internet revolution, which enabled extremist ideologies and narratives of all kinds to transcend national borders. Globalised Islam has thus become a source of narratives which has more to do with the dreams and nightmares of its various proponents and opponents than with any theological developments.

Most of those who dream of Al-Qaeda are Sunni Islamic extremists. Such extremists can be defined as believers who (1) reject the basic Islamic traditions, that is, the four legal schools of Sunni Islam and Shia Islam; (2) claim the right to brand as "non-Muslims" traditional believers who happen to disagree with their interpretation of Islamic law; and (3) claim the right to kill "infidels" including traditional Muslims who fail to side with them.[1] Closely linked to this religious view is Islamism, a radical political ideology based on the belief that Islam is the only solution to society's shortcomings. Extremist religious views are not always translated into political actions—and even if they are, engaging in terrorism is not necessarily the automatic response. As long as somebody with religious inclinations sits at home thinking of the divine, his opinions, however extreme they might be, are a matter of theology, not political acts that affect the society in which he lives and the life of his fellow man.

However, if the extremist turns to preaching hatred, incites others into taking up arms, or himself grabs a gun or a suicide vest with the intention to kill, then his beliefs have been translated into political acts. His views then become the cause of Islamist terrorism, that is, jihadism. Needless to say, not all Islamists turn to violence. However, many do choose to engage in what they refer to as armed jihad or global jihad. When jihad is in support of Islamism, it will here be referred to as armed or global jihad or indeed jihadism, the proponents of which are described as jihadists, in order to distinguish the activity from the Islamic theological concept of *jihad*.

Al-Qaeda constitutes a prime example of jihadism. Since Osama bin Laden established Al-Qaeda as an organisation in Peshawar, Pakistan, at some point between August 1988 and late 1989, it has grown into something more than a mere terrorist group. Al-Qaeda can presently be defined as no less than four quite different phenomena. These are:

- A formal organisation, in which members swear loyalty (*bayah*);
- An ideology, with religious leaders advocating global jihad;
- An idea and inspiration for those who want to take action, particularly since 2001;
- A loose network of sympathisers and self-professed members.

On August 23, 1996, Osama bin Laden issued his first *fatwa*, a declaration "to His Muslim Brothers in the Whole World and Especially in the Arabian Peninsula: Declaration of Jihad against the Americans Occupying the Land of the Two Holy Mosques; Expel the Heretics from the Arabian Peninsula." This has since been regarded as Osama bin Laden's formal declaration of war against the United States. In this, he also outlined the means he wished to use to defeat the superpower: "fast-moving light forces that work under complete secrecy. In other words to initiate a guerrilla warfare, where the sons of the nation, and not the military forces, take part in it."[2] What Osama bin Laden did was not only to issue a declaration of war; he also stated his intention to use civilian terrorists, not formal military forces. The eventual result was the terror attacks on the United States on September 11, 2001, which in turn led to wars in Afghanistan, Iraq, and elsewhere.

In late 2001, Al-Qaeda escaped into Pakistan, where Osama bin Laden rebuilt his organisation. It has since acquired affiliates in many countries. Formal affiliates are Al-Qaeda in Iraq (AQI), the North African Al-Qaeda in the Islamic Maghreb (AQIM), Al-Qaeda in the Arabian Peninsula (AQAP), Al-Shabaab in Somalia and East Africa, and Al-Nusrah Front in Syria.[3] Numerous other jihadist groups look up to Al-Qaeda and wish to join its growing rank of affiliates. Al-Qaeda is approaching its 30-year anniversary, which is a mature age for a terrorist group and sadly makes it a lasting and exceedingly brutal source of influence in world affairs.

Yet, even more Islamic extremists dream of the Caliphate than about joining Al-Qaeda. For them, the idea of a re-established Caliphate is a potent source of inspiration. It reminds them of the time when Muslim society was strong, not weak, fragmented, and often backward as today. However, the contemporary extremist or jihadist as often as not lives outside mainstream Muslim culture and society, in fairly secular environments such as those which exist in the European Union, the Russian Federation, and many parts of Central Asia. Many are second-generation immigrants or converts who feel culturally more tied to an imagined, "pure" Islamic society elsewhere. The contemporary jihadist often knows little or no Arabic, and is not an Islamic scholar. For him, religion and ideology are primarily used as an after-the-fact justification and legitimisation for violent acts and could more accurately be referred to as the effect rather than cause of jihadism. For those who wish to take action, indignation over perceived injustice and the decision to engage in jihadism often precede both ideological awareness and religious justification. Far more important to the jihadist is the narrative: a conviction that a worldwide struggle between good and evil, between justice and injustice, and between true Muslims and enemies of Islam is taking place.[4]

Since many jihadists know little or no Arabic and many lack theological knowledge, it is not the Koran or Islamic theology which is the source of their dream, but the narrative. And this narrative is eloquently described in jihadist publications such as *Inspire*, published online by Al-Qaeda in the Arabian Peninsula since June 30, 2010. As a source of propagandistic knowledge of religion and international affairs, heavily biased in favour of Al-Qaeda's struggle against Western and any other non-Muslim civilisation, indeed any civilisation beyond the desire to fight and die in the global jihad, such publications disseminate simplistic solutions and easy-to-digest knowledge for those idealists who wish to take action in the name of God. And the solutions presented are extremely attractive. Indeed, many of these publications readily affirm their readers that the Caliphate, once re-established, will immediately solve all problems and bring a new world—paradise on Earth.

Russian-speaking Jihadist Networks and the Dream of a Caliphate in the Caucasus

A key principle for those who dream of the Caliphate is the refusal to assimilate with mainstream culture and society, unless the mainstream does not first side with them. For if assimilated into mainstream society, the extremists correctly conclude that their cause is irrevocably lost. The potent source of inspiration which is the idea of the once and future Caliphate and global jihad becomes clear when investigating Russian-speaking jihadism. The emergence of and further developments among Russian-speaking jihadist groups illustrate the turn from secularism to jihadism that often characterised non-Arabic-speaking Islamic extremists. In particular the rise and fall of the Chechen Republic of Ichkeria,[5] so called after the traditional name for the Chechen highlands, the core region for Chechen culture as it is perceived today, display the ideological slide which has characterised the struggle for Chechen independence.

With the decline and fall of Soviet power, several North Caucasian republics, most of them nominally Muslim and all part of the Russian Federation, declared sovereignty. Chechnya's first president, Dzhokhar Dudayev, went further and in 1991 declared independence under the name of the Chechen Republic of Ichkeria. The Russian leaders could accept the break-up of the Soviet Union—but not the Russian Federation. The opposing Chechen and Russian policies ultimately led to the First Chechen War which lasted from 1994 to 1996. Although unrecognised by the international community, Chechnya successfully defended its independence. The formation of the Chechen republic was inspired by separatism, not jihadism.[6]

However, the economic decimation brought about by the war caused the new Chechen president, Aslan Maskhadov, to lose control over parts of Chechnya that subsequently fell under the sway of Islamic extremists and jihadists. Jihadism had arrived in Chechnya in 1995. Already before the war began, well-funded missionaries from the Middle East, so-called Wahhabites,[7] had operated in the Caucasus. The missionaries typically began by setting up mosques and Islamic boarding schools (madrasahs), often for orphans. Next the Wahhabites began to send young people abroad to study, with groups of between 15 and 30 young men going to, for instance, Turkey, the United Arab Emirates, or Jordan. Upon their return, the students would drive from one village to another to propagate the faith among other young people. They distributed the appropriate literature, and called upon Muslims to fight for the purification of Islam and evict the unbelievers from the villages. The Wahhabites then set up local communities that banned music as well as traditional celebrations, weddings, and funeral practices. After war had broken out, the most notable among the Middle Eastern Wahhabites was the commander known as Khattab. He arrived in Chechnya with a small group of foreign jihadists in the spring of 1995. Members of the Khattab group had already fought in places as diverse as Afghanistan, Tajikistan, and Bosnia as well as Abkhazia, Nagorno-Karabakh, and Ingushetia in the Caucasus. Khattab himself claimed to have fought in Afghanistan, Nagorno-Karabakh, and Tajikistan for eight years. In Chechnya, he became the main commander of foreign Islamic extremists.[8]

The Second Chechen War began in 1999 when Khattab and his Chechen associate Shamil Basayev assumed control over and spearheaded an uprising in neighbouring Daghestan, another Russian North Caucasian republic with a Muslim population. This soon turned into a full-scale invasion of Daghestan. The resulting fighting ultimately provoked a Russian invasion of Chechnya and the Second Chechen War, which independent Chechnya lost.[9] The Chechen Republic of Ichkeria collapsed and since then only remains as a government in exile. Although at first largely secular, the perceived lost cause of the Chechen Republic of Ichkeria caused many of its former supporters to abandon the lost, secular struggle for independence and instead turn towards the cause of radical Islam.

Because of the dissolution of the Soviet Union in 1991 and the two subsequent Chechen wars, many Chechens and other North Caucasians moved to Europe and further afield in search of asylum. Many had combat experience, and several were engaged in organised crime, jihadist groups, or both. Over time, many of the originally quite secular-minded North Caucasians radicalised and, like several leaders of the Chechen Republic of Ichkeria government in exile, adopted increasingly extreme forms of Islam, including the agenda of global jihad of Al-Qaeda. The development was particularly striking among the younger generation, which had grown up within the Diaspora and retained few if any links to their former homes. A case can be made for including in this group Rustam Gelayev, son of the late Chechen warlord Ruslan "Hamzat" Gelayev. The younger Gelayev moved from Russia to Georgia, where he married. When a child was born, the young family moved to Belgium. After a few years, young Gelayev decided to learn about Islam, so he moved to Egypt, from which he went to fight in Syria from June to August 2012, when he was killed.[10]

Thus emerged a number of Russian-speaking jihadist networks, consisting primarily of Muslims from the North Caucasus, Urals, Azerbaijan, and Central Asian countries such as Uzbekistan, Kyrgyzstan, Kazakhstan, and Tajikistan, who to a certain extent still rely on Russian as a *lingua franca*.[11] The networks maintain links to one or several of the following terrorist groups: The Islamic Emirate of the Caucasus (*Imarat Kavkaz*), Islamic Movement of Uzbekistan (IMU), Islamic Jihad Union (IJU), and Jund al-Khilafah, of which the latter two are less prominent and arguably may no longer exist in their original forms. In addition, jihadist groups in Syria maintain close links to the Russian-speaking jihadist networks, in particular the Jaish al-Muhajireen wa'l-Ansar, which is close to the Al-Qaeda affiliate Al-Nusrah Front.[12]

In the Caucasus, the Russian-speaking jihadist networks grew into prominence as a result of the failure of the Chechen separatist movement. For this reason, their cause was by many widely but mistakenly regarded as purely separatist in nature, unconnected to the more familiar Al-Qaeda-style, Arabic-speaking brand of jihadism. Not so. Previously, the Chechens and other North Caucasians who constitute a major part of the Russian-speaking jihadist networks, unlike the Central Asian members, primarily supported the struggle in Chechnya. Many had participated in one or both Chechen wars. However, during the 2000s, many North Caucasians too acquired an interest in the war in Pakistan and Afghanistan. From 2012, both categories of Russian-speaking jihadists became heavily involved in Syria as well, as was exemplified by the aforementioned Gelayev case and frequently documented by jihadist websites.[13]

Furthermore, many of the Russian-speaking jihadists also belonged to networks and gangs engaged in organised crime. This entailed further experience in violent activities as well as assured access to weapons and explosives.[14] Many Russian-speaking Muslims, both those within Muslim regions in Russia such as the Caucasus, Tatarstan, and Bashkortostan, and within the refugee Diaspora in Europe, became radicalised during the 2000s. The war itself radicalised many Chechens, pushing some so far as to engage in suicide bombings.[15] In particular the younger generation increasingly often chose radical forms of Islam which sympathise with the global jihad of Al-Qaeda. There is little doubt that for them, the ethnic origin of their associates was unimportant, so whether they focused on Chechnya, Pakistan, or any other place with ongoing jihadism mattered little. Indeed, since the opportunities for successful armed jihad looked more promising in places such as Syria, they may no longer be that much concerned with the situation in the Caucasus. Besides, among recent asylum seekers to Europe from the Caucasus and Central Asia, a growing number are connected to Islamic extremist and jihadist groups.[16] This is hardly surprising; since Islamic extremists for obvious reasons are prone to be regarded as sympathisers of terrorist groups which claim their cause to be Islam, they no doubt feel persecuted in their native countries to a higher degree than others.

The online presence and impact of Russian-speaking jihadist networks have grown considerably since jihadism in 1995 emerged as a disruptive political force in Chechnya. Besides, spillover effects from the Chechen wars in time grew increasingly obvious, including in the Diaspora in the European Union and North America where many integrated poorly into local society. By the early 2000s, French jihadists trained with Chechens in Georgia, constituting what became known as a Chechen network.[17] Members of the Chechen Diaspora too began to take up arms, and their activities were not limited to Russian targets. In September 2010, Lors Doukaiev, a Belgian citizen of Chechen refugee origin, detonated a bomb in Denmark.[18] In April 2013, the two brothers Tamerlan and Dzhokhar Tsarnayev bombed the Boston Marathon, killing several.[19] That radical jihadists played a significant role in the Chechen wars was a historical fact. The Doukaiev case proved that individuals with a history of personal trauma in the Chechen wars could turn into jihadists even outside the Caucasus region, while the Tsarnayev case showed that even those without such a history but with an interest in Russian jihadism could turn to violence.

The slide from secularism to radical jihadism has been particularly obvious online. A key example is provided by the Kavkaz Centre website, founded in 1999 by Movladi Udugov who himself is an example of this ideological slide. Udugov was first press secretary of the separatist government. In 1996, he was appointed First Deputy Prime Minister for state policy and information by Zelimkhan Yandarbiyev, a radical promoter of Islamic extremism. Then, in 1999, Udugov created Kavkaz Centre, Chechen Times, and several other websites. Shortly thereafter, at the outbreak of the 1999 war, he left Chechnya for Turkey but retained control of the websites.[20]

Udugov has since remained a promoter of jihadism. The Kavkaz Centre website is a fairly large jihadist site. It is frequently updated with news and professionally designed so as to be easy to navigate. The web domain name was first registered in Udugov's name through an address in Turkey. Originally based in Chechnya, the site moved when the Chechen separatist government lost control of its capital, Grozny. The website first relocated to Estonia, then in 2003 Lithuania. In September-October 2004, the website was briefly based in Finland. On November 13, 2004, it reopened from Sweden. By then, it had become devoted to armed, global jihad. The Kavkaz Centre website is published in five languages:

Russian, English, Ukrainian, Arabic, and Turkish. The content differs depending on language chosen, but all its sites promote hatred to Russia and often serve as platforms for communiqués from international jihadist groups, in particular the Caucasus Emirate for which the website operates as a dedicated news agency. It has also featured extensive translations from the works of Al-Qaeda's *Inspire* online publication.

Traffic data from websites are routinely collected by numerous commercial actors, since they have an interest in determining the commercial value of advertising on any given website. Analysing the data, one can determine the number of unique users and from which countries they access the website. In 2011, before Russia began to block the website, such an investigation showed that the Kavkaz Centre website then had a daily total of approximately 7,000 unique users. The result suggests the following rough number of unique visitors who on an average day actively searched out the Kavkaz Centre website in each given country (rounded to the nearest whole tens):[21]

Table 1. Daily Unique Visitors Per Country

Country	Unique Visitor
Russia	2,010
Sweden	670
Ukraine	660
Denmark	590
Georgia	360
France	260
Poland	260
India	240
Norway	240
Turkey	230

The Kavkaz Centre also appears on Twitter. Traffic data from 2013 shows that its tweets are followed by more than 8,000 people. While this number may not appear shockingly high, it still suggests the existence of quite substantial numbers of Russian-speaking jihadists in the Diaspora countries. That secularism in time grew into jihadism is indeed also shown by the example of Doku Umarov, the very leader of the Caucasus Emirate. Born in 1964 in Chechnya, he was involved in racketeering around 1990. He once described how he first joined the war for Chechen independence: "When war began ... I arrived ... in a Mercedes, wearing shoes and with a cigarette in my mouth … did I perform Islamic prayer? I answered that I did not."[22] Following this decidedly non-jihadistic beginning, Doku Umarov served as a Chechen commander in both Chechen wars. Meanwhile, he became increasingly extreme in his religious views. When he announced the formation of the Caucasus Emirate in October 2007, he implicitly declared war on the United States, Britain, Israel, and their allies as well by announcing that "[o]ur enemy is not Rusnya [Russia] only, but everyone who wages war against Islam and Muslims."[23] On July 3, 2013, in a public message he confirmed that his organisation had joined the Al-Qaeda-style global cause: "Caucasus Emirate is only a part of the global Jihad."[24]

Russian-speaking jihadist websites, chat rooms, and social networking sites have become increasingly prevalent as inspirers of terrorism. Technical and tactical innovation and adaptability followed, often more so than in other terrorist networks due to the interconnectedness among separatists, jihadists, and organised crime. The separatists sustained a tradition of connections with the Western world, while the jihadists maintained links to Al-Qaeda and global jihadism. Organised crime, finally, contributed technical and logistical capability in violence, tradecraft, and the provision of weaponry. The Russian-speaking jihadist networks can thus be characterised by having support networks in the Western and Islamic worlds, links to organised crime, and an extensive online presence.

The Counter-Jihad Narrative

The growth of jihadism, especially but not exclusively in Diaspora countries, was not only a source of danger in itself. The phenomenon also resulted in the formation of another extremist narrative, in effect a counter-narrative. Claims to cultural and legal autonomy among Islamic extremists, such as took place in the Caucasus in the 1990s and in cities of the European Union today, ignited existing but until then largely dormant nationalistic, extreme right sentiments and created grounds for anti-immigration and anti-Muslim movements and political parties to gain popularity in hitherto moderate or predominantly secular host countries.[25] Sharing the jihadist conviction that a worldwide struggle between good and evil, between non-Muslims and Muslims, was taking place, but regarding the jihadist dream as a nightmare, some far-right extremists decided to take action. One of the most extreme proponents of this narrative was Norwegian national Anders Behring Breivik, who on July 22, 2011 took his conviction to its ultimate and bloody conclusion. He first killed eight people with a car bomb in Norway's capital Oslo, and then shot 69 youngsters to death in a summer camp set up by the ruling party. On the same day, shortly before the attacks, he published a manifesto of some 1,515 pages called *2083: A European Declaration of Independence*, which he distributed electronically. From his manifesto, it became clear that Breivik regarded his action as a protest against multiculturalism and a grand conspiracy to allow a Muslim takeover. He claimed that his victims were accomplices in the conspiracy and that he had to take action to prevent it.

Breivik was not part of any group or movement when he carried out his acts of terrorism. Yet his online manifesto attracted considerable attention and found him an audience. As of July 2012, the imprisoned Breivik had received almost six hundred letters from sympathisers. Breivik continued to write, and planned to set up an organisation called the Conservative Revolutionary Movement.[26] The cases of Al-Qaeda, the Caucasus Emirate with Kavkaz Centre, and Breivik suggest that there indeed seems to be such a phenomenon as a generic extremist's creed. A team of psychologists, Saucier et al., have studied patterns of thinking in militant extremism and concluded that all types of extremist narratives, regardless of professed ideology, can be summarised as follows:

> We have a glorious past, but modernity has been disastrous, bringing on a great catastrophe in which we are tragically obstructed from reaching our rightful place, obstructed by an illegitimate civil government and/or by an enemy so evil that it does not even deserve to be called human. This intolerable situation calls for vengeance. Extreme measures are required; indeed, any means will be justified for realising our sacred

> end. We must think in military terms to annihilate this evil and purify the world of it. It is a duty to kill the perpetrators of evil, and we cannot be blamed for carrying out this violence. Those who sacrifice themselves in our cause will attain glory, and supernatural powers should come to our aid in this struggle. In the end, we will bring our people to a new world that is a paradise.[27]

The extremist's creed is indeed generic and such sentiments can be found in different cultural and religious contexts. Psychologists and social scientists have investigated whether there are cultural factors that can be shown to link to terrorist activity more than others. One such study by Gelfand et al. suggests that cultural factors do play a role. In their research, societies with belief systems that one's destiny and life events are predetermined (fatalism) have strong punishments for deviation from norms (cultural tightness) and markedly different gender roles (low gender egalitarianism) have higher terrorism rates than those that have low scores on these dimensions, even when accounting for other factors that might lead to terrorism. But of possibly higher interest, the results of this study show that of these factors, cultural tightness—defined as higher ethnocentrism, a low tolerance for deviance, a belief that one's way of life must be protected against foreign influences, and justification for strong punishments—stood out since it was related to higher number of fatalities per incident of terrorist activity.[28] In other words, while fatalistic societies and societies with low gender egalitarianism produced a somewhat higher number of terrorist incidents than many others, it was in the culturally tight societies that most people were killed when an act of terrorism took place. Al-Qaeda and jihadism fit this pattern, but also the anti-Islamic ideology of Breivik.[29]

Estimated Number of Extremists

Can we estimate the number of extremists in any given population? Sociological surveys indicate that some conclusions can indeed be drawn. According to the results of a sociological survey carried out by Anatoliy Kosichenko and his team among students and religious experts in Kazakhstan in 2005, madrasah students in the southern Kazakhstani city of Shymkent believe that all acts of terrorism attributed to Muslims were in fact the work of the United States and the Western countries, in a plot to stop the development and spread of Islam. Indeed, the very term Islamic extremism has been made up by the enemies of Islam, they argued, since such terms cause disrespect for Islam and, in their opinion, Islam and extremism are incompatible phenomena (a common enough conclusion in the Islamic world, since extremism would never be referred to as such by those who believe in it as they believe that what they preach is true Islam). Others believed that the United States was using the Muslims as weapons against Russia and Russian Orthodox civilisation. When Russia is destroyed, the West will destroy the Muslims, they argued. Perhaps more worryingly, 22.2 per cent of the students polled (who in most but probably not all cases were Muslims) believed that the values of Islam completely contradict the liberal values of Western civilisation. Another 36.1 per cent found the question difficult to answer, which also gives cause for concern. In comparison, only 40.7 per cent of the students polled thought that these values were compatible, partly compatible, or complemented each other.[30]

When religious experts (clergy, religious teachers, and activists from religious groups) were polled in the same survey, about the same share, 22.7 per cent were found to believe that the values of Islam completely contradict the liberal values of Western civilisation. Even among the experts, another 20.5 per cent found the question difficult to answer. As compared with the students, 52.3 per cent of the experts thought that these values were compatible, partly compatible, or complemented each other.

Both Muslim students and Muslim experts were quite tolerant of Islamic suicide bombers in Central Asia. A total of 48.5 per cent of Muslim students characterised them as people who deliberately sacrifice their lives for their faith, as opposed to 16.2 per cent who saw them as terrorists who cannot be condoned by any religion. Among Muslim experts, the corresponding figures were 46.2 and 11.5 per cent, respectively.[31] While a number of other opinions were also expressed about suicide bombers, it would seem clear that almost half of the polled Muslims were disposed to see them as deeply religious martyrs for the faith. In other words, the suicide bombers are seen as Muslims, pure and simple, regardless of whether one supports their activities or not. This would seem to belie the often expressed statement that Islamic extremism has nothing to do with Islam. In this case at least, almost half of the polled Muslims clearly identified the suicide bombers with religious beliefs.[32] However, when faced with the question of whether any religion could cause social tensions in their country, both Muslim students and experts stated their belief that Islam is more prone to cause social tensions than other denominations. No less than 37.3 per cent of Muslim students and 23.1 per cent of Muslim experts believed this, and this was far in excess of how they rated the risk that other denominations would do so (from 6.2 to 8 per cent, depending on denomination in question and polled group).

Since Kosichenko concluded his survey, the issue of support for tactics such as suicide bombings has been surveyed in other countries as well. The Pew Research Centre conducted surveys on popular views in many countries, and several of their surveys include data on support for extremism and terrorism, and on levels of support for suicide bombing. The following table gives the results for some countries covered in the survey.[33]

Table 2. Levels of Support for Suicide Bombing over Time

	Percentage of Muslims saying suicide bombing is often/sometimes justified							
	2005	2006	2007	2008	2009	2010	2011	2013
Pakistan	25	14	9	5	5	8	5	3
Indonesia	15	10	10	11	13	15	10	6
Jordon	57	29	23	25	12	20	13	12
Turkey	14	17	16	3	4	6	7	16
Egypt	-	28	8	13	15	20	28	25

To summarise, the levels of support for tactics such as suicide bombings have fallen since the Afghan and Iraq wars began; but young people remain especially susceptible. Levels of support for suicide bombing are roughly 3-16 per cent, with populations in some countries and under certain conditions swinging towards higher levels, such as those in southern Kazakhstan in 2005.

The Pew Research Centre also conducted surveys on popular views of Al-Qaeda. The results are, perhaps unsurprisingly, roughly comparable to those for the support for suicide bombings.[34]

Table 3. Views of Al-Qaeda Percentage of Muslims holding favourable and unfavourable views, respectively, of Al-Qaeda

	Favourable	Unfavourable	Do not know
Lebanon	1	96	2
Jordan	13	81	6
Turkey	7	73	20
Egypt	20	69	11
Nigeria	9	62	29
Senegal	9	57	34
Tunisia	15	56	29
Indonesia	23	53	23
Palest. ter.	35	53	12
Malaysia	20	48	32
Pakistan	13	46	41
Median	13	57	23

The results indicate that roughly 7-20 per cent of Muslims have favourable views of Al-Qaeda. It is perhaps significant that most favourable views are typically held by those populations without direct exposure to Al-Qaeda and its activities, such as in Indonesia and Malaysia. Yet another method of estimating extremist beliefs is to assess election results in countries where democratic elections are held in which militant extremist parties take part. A relevant case study may be Pakistan, where extremist religious parties from time to time have participated in elections. The Jamiat Ulema-ye Islam-Fazlur Rehman Group (commonly known as JUI-F) is a particularly interesting case, since it had links to the Afghan Taliban since the very beginning of this movement. The JUI ("Society of Islamic Scholars") in 1981 split into two main factions, the largest of which was led by Fazlur Rehman.[35] The party remained politically isolated until Pakistan's 1993 elections, when it became part of the ruling coalition under Prime Minister Benazir Bhutto. The JUI then established close links with the army, the ISI, and the Interior Ministry. By 1994 the JUI was closely involved in Afghanistan, guiding and nurturing the emergence of the Taliban movement. Fazlur Rehman organised the initial bustard hunting trips for Gulf Arab princes and in the process established the first direct contacts between the Taliban and their Arab sponsors. Dozens of luxury jeeps were flown in on huge transport planes to be used while hunting and many of these remained as gifts from the Arabs for their Taliban hosts. JUI leaders were accordingly directly involved in the financing and support of the Taliban. In 1996, the Taliban in return handed over control of a number of training camps to the JUI and several of its many breakaway factions. These factions became the chief recruiters of Pakistanis and others for the Taliban forces.[36] Fazlur Rehman also became one of the leaders of the Council for the Defence of Afghanistan, a public charitable organisation established in Pakistan in January 2001 in response to the imposition by the United Nations Security Council of sanctions on Afghanistan and with the task of protecting the Taliban government and Osama bin Laden, in particular from the United States.[37] While the factions of the JUI operated in support of violent activities, the party's election results can be summarised in the following table.[38]

Table 4. Election Results of JUI

Year	Percentage
1988	1.8
1990	2.9
1993	3.2
1997	1.7
2002	11.3
2008	2.2

Consistently strong in the southern part of the north-western province of Khyber Pakhtunkhwa and the northern parts of Baluchistan, the party in 2002, inspired by feelings of support with the ousted Taliban government in Afghanistan, allied with other religious parties to form the Muttahida Majlis-e Amal which gained power in Khyber Pakhtunkhwa and governed it from 2002 to 2007. The party's close links with the army, the ISI, and the Interior Ministry no doubt helped as well, but it is significant that there were strong feelings in favour of Taliban-style extremism in Pakistan at the time. According to the Pew study, in 2002 no less than 33 per cent of Pakistani Muslims supported suicide bombing, and it would be surprising had these feelings not affected the election results.[39] Yet, fewer people voted for the JUI than supported suicide terrorism. The results accordingly indicate that even in Pakistan, where there is strong support for militant extremism, extremist support still fluctuates between roughly 2 and 11 per cent.

Another way of attempting a survey of extremist beliefs is to use the methodology of the Gallup study *Views of Violence*. Among other related topics this study sets out to measure public attitude towards individual or small group violence aimed at civilians. The questions posed specifically addressed the "targeting" of civilians, rather than any unintended harm caused by other actions such as those aimed at military targets. The respondents were asked to choose between absolutely rejecting the targeting of civilians as "never justified" and conditionally accepting such targeting as "sometimes justified."[40] The results in the survey are inconclusive and at times hard to assess. For instance, popular rejection of deliberate attacks on civilians is generally strong in stable societies with a low risk of social conflict and high level of human development, yet it remains unknown whether the popular perception of the illegitimacy of violence produces these outcomes, or whether the favourable societal conditions produce non-violent social norms, or whether the process indeed works both ways.[41] Even so, the data shows that regardless of society, those who see religion as important in their lives do not *per se* regard the targeting of civilians as more acceptable. In fact, religion has a neutral to positive effect on the likelihood of rejecting violence, although those who do not want to know about other religious faiths and neither have respect nor feel respected by those of other religious faiths in many countries display a greater sympathy for attacks on civilians regardless of which religion is prevalent in the country.[42] A comparison can presumably be made with the results produced by the aforementioned study by Gelfand et al. on culture and extremism, and particularly the role played by cultural tightness.

Even so, the individual country assessments as recorded by the Abu Dhabi Gallup Centre give certain hints. The percentage of the population that believes that individual attacks on civilians are "sometimes justified" range from 2 per cent (in Finland and Egypt[43]) to 35 per cent (in Congo Brazzaville, Djibouti, and Haiti). The median value is 13 per cent, and this particular percentage applies to a healthy range of countries on several continents and in different regions of the world: Belgium, Colombia, Czech Republic, Iran, Ireland, Kenya, and Palestinian Territories. If we remove those countries with a percentage of 5 per cent and less and of more than 25 per cent, respectively, we find that four-fifths (78 per cent) of all countries fall between a value of from 6 to 25 per cent.[44]

The Abu Dhabi Gallup results thus correspond fairly well with the results of other surveys. In most populations, 6-25 per cent support targeted violence by civilians against civilians, with a median value of 13 per cent, which exactly corresponds to the median value of support for Al-Qaeda. The range of support for Al-Qaeda found in the Pew survey to be 7-20 per cent was also quite comparable.[45] This figure also corresponds roughly to the election results of religious extremist parties. It can then be concluded that every population, regardless of cultural or religious background, includes a minority of extremists and their relative numbers are not that different from those in other populations.

Extremists and Freedom of Expression

One should of course not forget that those who in these various surveys come out in support of violence are sympathisers, but not necessarily terrorists. Typically only some of the sympathisers decide to take action and engage in violence. Of the more than eight thousand followers of the Kavkaz Centre, only some choose to participate in fighting. Having determined that in all populations there is a small but statistically significant core of individuals who support violence, and that cultural tightness, defined as higher ethnocentrism, a low tolerance for deviance, a belief that one's way of life must be protected against foreign influences, and justification for strong punishments, stands out as related to higher number of fatalities per incident of terrorist activity, how should society address the slide in ideology from secularism to jihadism as experienced by significant numbers of Muslims, including those who live outside mainstream Muslim culture and society? Few would agree with Breivik's extreme conclusions and violent actions; yet assertive Muslims demand exemptions from the common norms of Western society. One rather obvious example was the "defamation of religions" issue which was first introduced to the United Nations Commission on Human Rights in 1999 by Pakistan on behalf of the Organisation of Islamic Conference (OIC) under the agenda item on "racism." The draft resolution, in its original form, was introduced with the title "Defamation of Islam." Pakistan suggested that "[t]here was a tendency in some countries and in the international media to portray Islam as a religion hostile to human rights, threatening to the Western world and associated with terrorism and violence, whereas, with the Quran, Islam had given the world its first human rights charter. No other religion received such constant negative media coverage. That defamation campaign was reflected in growing intolerance towards Muslims."[46] This draft resolution led to a campaign to introduce legislation against the defamation of religions which continued for more than a decade. Yet, a basic difficulty always remained in that the concept of defamation, as defined by Pakistan, the OIC, and others, conflicted with the right to freedom of expression. The concept of defamation of religions could simply not be reconciled with the right to freedom of expression, and in March 2011, the OIC ceased their demand that such protection against defamation was essential to defend Islam, and other religions, against criticism that caused offence to ordinary believers.[47]

In July 2011, the United Nations Human Rights Committee indeed noted that "[f]reedom of opinion and freedom of expression are indispensable conditions for the full development of the person. They are essential for any society. They constitute the foundation stone for every free and democratic society." In paragraph 48, the Human Rights Committee concluded that "[p]rohibitions of displays of lack of respect for a religion or other belief system, including blasphemy laws, are incompatible with the Covenant, except in the specific circumstances envisaged in article 20, paragraph 2, of the Covenant. Such prohibitions must also comply with the strict requirements of article 19, paragraph 3, as well as such articles as 2, 5, 17, 18 and 26. Thus, for instance, it would be impermissible for any such laws to discriminate in favour of or against one or certain religions or belief systems, or their adherents over another or religious believers over non-believers. Nor would it be permissible for such prohibitions to be used to prevent or punish criticism of religious leaders or commentary on religious doctrine and tenets of faith."[48] As for the reference to article 20, paragraph 2 in the International Covenant on Civil and Political Rights of December 19, 1966, the text states: "Any advocacy of national, racial or religious hatred that constitutes incitement to discrimination, hostility or violence shall be prohibited by law."[49] In other words, the right to freedom of expression continued to be paramount, but it nonetheless remained unlawful to advocate hatred. This resolved the issue of defamation of religion, yet it offered no real guidelines on how to address minorities such as those Islamic extremists who dream of Al-Qaeda. Since their spiritual and political leaders in most cases, online or in real life, advocate hatred and prohibit their followers from assimilating into majority, non-extremist culture, the issue thus boils down into the following one: Should mainstream society aim to protect the unassimilated extremists, *or* their chosen narrative? The former might be necessary to prevent, for instance, extremist parents from indoctrinating and sending their offspring to die in religious wars, such as can be seen among the young followers of the Caucasus Emirate who fight in Syria. The latter, however, would be in line with the right to freedom of expression. Is it an inalienable right to harbour extremist views? Yes, according to the United Nations Human Rights Committee. Is it also an inalienable right to translate these views into actions? No, according to the same institution. In that case, criminal law will take precedence.

The distinction is an important one, since extremists of all hues tend to identify with the clash of civilisation thesis. They do it because it confirms their beliefs and accordingly their view of the world as a Manichaean struggle between good and evil, in which they inevitably see themselves as on the side of good. Would a modern society by suppressing such self-proclaimed fighters against evil thereby in itself turn to evil? Not so. Ishtiaq Ahmed has argued that it is important that secular and democratic states do not surrender, in the name of multiculturalism—the concept so hated by Breivik—by offering exemptions that conflict with the overall inclusive and equal citizenship that applies to the very idea of a secular and democratic state to Muslim or any other communities within its borders. Ahmed also emphasised that vigilance and surveillance of extremists including Muslims must be maintained and improved but without jeopardising the rights of the Muslims in general to equal treatment under the law. Immigrant communities should be informed about not only their rights but also their obligations. Any exemptions by which immigrant and other minority communities are allowed to violate the law will only create grounds for anti-immigration and anti-Muslim movements and parties to gain popularity. In the long run, Ahmed argues, integration that in time results in voluntary assimilation into mainstream society is the answer, not the offering of exemptions that only serves to alienate population groups from mainstream society.[50]

A few concluding remarks may be in order. Globalisation is unavoidable and overall has resulted in increased prosperity and positive developments in the dissemination of science, arts, and culture. Unfortunately, fuelled by the Internet revolution and large-scale but increasingly unassimilated population groups as a result of migration, globalisation has also resulted in increased opportunities for the proponents of extremisms of various shades. In much of Europe and Eurasia, there has been hesitation to address extremism, in particular when its ideologues framed themselves as leaders of religion or culture. Calls have been made for criminalising the expression of ideas that could be deemed offending to religious or cultural beliefs. However, as noted, the United Nations Human Rights Committee has argued that freedom of opinion and freedom of expression are indispensable conditions and essential for any society; and the OIC has ceased claiming that such protection against defamation is essential to defend Islam, and other religions, against criticism that causes offence to ordinary believers.

Besides, the singular importance of an exclusive narrative for the extremists reinforces the conclusion that extremism should not be more protected than mainstream religion. Extremist views will have to be addressed, and in this endeavour the right to freedom of expression is of key importance. Arguments to limit the right to freedom of expression in an attempt to protect the religious and cultural sentiments of minorities will only serve to protect the extremist viewpoints and its proponents, not the silent mainstream.

For this reason, secular Eurasian states should remain steadfast in their support of secularism, inclusive and equal citizenship, freedom of expression, and pluralism. In the arena of ideas, globalisation has so far failed to contain extremism. Yet globalisation could also lead to a deeper commitment within Eurasia to the principles of secularism, pluralism, and the free exchange of ideas. Unfortunately, it is always likely that there will be extremists. A number of sociological surveys, when taken together, suggest that some 5-15 per cent of any given population hold extremist views. They will no doubt continue to voice opposition to mainstream society and in some cases promote violence. To hold extremist views is within their rights, yet society should never fear to exercise the right to expose the voices of extremism. And as for those who advocate "national, racial or religious hatred that constitutes incitement to discrimination, hostility or violence," in the words of the International Covenant on Civil and Political Rights of December 19, 1966, society has every right to prosecute them and should do so, not least in order to protect other vulnerable individuals who are at risk of falling victim to extremism but who have not yet entered that path.

Notes

1. Definition of Islamic extremism by the Council of the Muftis of Russia, June 30, 2000. See also Michael Fredholm, *Islamic Extremism as a Political Force in Central Asia: A Comparative Study of Central Asian Extremist Movements*, Stockholm: Stockholm University, Asian Cultures and Modernity 12, 2006, p. 5; Michael Fredholm, "Pustyye dushi: ziyaniye, kotoroye dolzhno byt' zapolneno," *Idei i idealy,* vol. 3, no. 13, 2012: 74-91.
2. "Declaration of holy war against the United States and the West, 23 August 1996," statement by the London-based Saudi dissident organisation, the Committee for the Defence of Legitimate Rights (CDLR), posted at http://msanews.mynet.net. Quoted in Yonah Alexander and Michael Swetnam, *Usama bin Laden's al-Qaida: Profile of a Terrorist Network* (Ardsley, New York: Transnational Publishers, 2001).
3. See, for example, Yonah Alexander and Michael S. Swetnam, *Al-Qa'ida: Ten Years after 9/11 and Beyond* (Arlington, Virginia: Potomac Institute Press, 2012).

4. Michael Fredholm, "A Narrative of Heroes: In the Head of the Contemporary Jihadist," *Terrorism: An Electronic Journal and Knowledge Base* 1, 2012; Fredholm, "Pustyye dushi."
5. In Russian: *Chechenskaya Respublika Ichkeriya,* ChRI.
6. The literature on the Chechen wars is vast. See, for example, Carlotta Gall and Thomas de Waal, *Chechnya: A Small Victorious War* (London: Pan, 1997); Anatol Lieven, *Chechnya: Tombstone of Russian Power* (New Haven: Yale University Press, 1998); Stasys Knezys and Romanas Sedlickas, *The War in Chechnya* (College Station: Texas A & M University Press, 1999).
7. Wahhabism is the dominant Islamic sect in Saudi Arabia, from which many of the missionaries came. In Russia and Central Asia, the term Wahhabite came to be used fundamentally as a synonym for Islamic extremist.
8. Igor Dobaev, "Islamic Radicalism in the Northern Caucasus," *Central Asia and the Caucasus* 6, 2000: 76-86. Dobaev refers to newspaper articles including one by Umar ben Ismail, Amir of the Wahhabite Jamaat of Urus-Martan.
9. See, for example, Michael Fredholm, "The Prospects for Genocide in Chechnya and Extremist Retaliation against the West," *Central Asian Survey,* vol. 19, no. 4, 2000.
10. NewsRu.com, August 23, 2012.
11. Because of the influx of Central Asians in the jihadist networks, many of whom are Turkic-speakers, Turkish too is sometimes used as a working language.
12. See, for example, Michael Fredholm, "From the Ferghana Valley to Waziristan and Beyond," *Islam, Islamism and Politics in Eurasia Report* 22, Monterey Institute for International Studies, 2010; Michael Fredholm, "The Role of Uzbek Islamic Extremists in the Civil Wars of Tajikistan, Afghanistan and Pakistan," in Anita Sengupta, Suchandana Chatterjee and Susmita Bhattacharya (eds.), *Eurasia Twenty Years After* (Delhi: Shipra, 2012); jihadist website Kavkaz Centre, www.kavkazcenter.com.
13. Jihadist websites Kavkaz Centre; Fisyria.com.
14. On contemporary Chechen organised crime, see Tomáš Šmíd and Petr Kupka, "Eastern Outlaws: Chechen Organised Crime in Europe," *Jane's Intelligence Review,* vol. 24, no. 4, April 2012: 36-41. On links between jihadists and Russian-speaking organised crime including Chechen groups, see Colleen M. Traughber, "Terror-Crime Nexus? Terrorism and Arms, Drugs, and Human Trafficking in Georgia," *Connections*, vol. 6, no: 1, 2007: 47-63. On the links between Chechnya and Chechen organised crime during the 1990s, see Louise I. Shelley et al., *Methods and Motives: Exploring Links between Transnational Organized Crime & International Terrorism,* NCJRS, 2005: 68-75; Thomas M. Ross, *Wolves in Wolves' Clothing: The Role of the Chechen Mafia in the Formation of an Independent Chechen Republic*, dissertation, Naval Postgraduate School, Monterey, California, 2011.

15. Michael Fredholm, "The New Face of Chechen Terrorism," *Central Asia-Caucasus Analyst*, September 24, 2003, www.cacianalyst.org
16. See, for example, *Kleine Zeitung* (Austria), December 6, 2010, www.kleinezeitung.at
17. Secretary of State Colin L. Powell, Address to the United Nations Security Council, New York, Transcript, February 5, 2003; Andrew McGregor, "'The Chechen Network' on Trial: Terrorist Prosecutions in Paris," *North Caucasus Analysis,* vol. 7, no. 18, May 4, 2006, www.jamestown.org. McGregor is overly critical of the French court case but provides a useful summary.
18. See, for example, *BT* (Denmark), September 15, 2010, September 21, 2010, www.bt.dk.
19. See, for example, RFE/RL, April 19, 2013.
20. The Kavkaz Centre websites are most easily accessed through the web address, www.kavkazcenter.com.
21. Data from Alexa.com, September 23, 2011. For a discussion, see Michael Fredholm, *Media in Defense against Terrorism: European Perspectives* (Stockholm: Team Ippeki, 2013).
22. The Daghestani jihadist website Hunafa.com, May 18, 2009. See also Kevin Daniel Leahy, "From Racketeer to Emir: A Political Portrait of Doku Umarov, Russia's Most Wanted Man," *Caucasian Review of International Affairs*, vol. 4, no. 3, 2010: 248-70.
23. Kavkaz Centre, November 22, 2007, www.kavkazcenter.com. The context makes it clear that Umarov also spoke of the United States, Britain, Israel, and no doubt their allies as well. The Caucasus Emirate's official translation says, "Today in Afghanistan, Iraq, Somalia, Palestine our brothers are fighting. Everyone who attacked Muslims wherever they are, are our enemies, common enemies. Our enemy is not Rusnya [Russia] only, but everyone who wages war against Islam and Muslims."
24. Kavkaz Centre, July 3, 2013, www.kavkazcenter.com. Umarov spoke Russian, and this point was particularly highlighted in the English summary of his statement provided by the Kavkaz Centre's English-language site.
25. Extremisms feed on animosities, with each atrocity carried out by one group usually inspiring a similar act of evil committed by the other, so it is often quite futile to attempt to determine which extremist group took to violence first. One could just as easily argue over what came first, the bird or the egg, a question which has been with us since the time of Aristotle. Nationalism and racism certainly existed in Europe by the second half of the twentieth century, but so did very similar sentiments as well as jihadism in the Islamic world. Any attempt to apportion blame in relations between Islam and Christianity would take us back to the very origin of contacts between the two belief systems. From a historical point of view, this would be another exercise

in futility, since strife is as old as humanity itself. Al-Qaeda claims to fight against Western crusaders, to take revenge for aggression during the Middle Ages and to recover territories lost then and later. Yet the crusades were to a comparable extent the result of a perceived need to re-conquer territories lost to Islam during the early Arab conquests and to halt the ongoing expansion of Islam. Similar struggles for territory and souls can easily be found between other world religions, as well as between various sects within them.

26. *Verdens Gang* (Norway), July 26, 2012.
27. Gerard Saucier, Laura Geuy Akers, Seraphine Shen-Miller, Goran Knežević and Lazar Stankov, "Patterns of Thinking in Militant Extremism," *Perspectives on Psychological Science*, vol. 4, 2009: 256-71.
28. Michele J. Gelfand, Gary LaFree, Susan Fahey and Emily Feinberg, "Culture and Extremism," *Journal of Social Issues*, vol. 69, no. 3, 2013: 495-517, especially 511-12.
29. The data available cannot be used to determine whether cultural factors cause terrorism or whether ongoing terrorism causes this very type of cultural factors. Gelfand et al., "Culture and Extremism," 512. Again one is reminded of the question of what came first, the bird or the egg.
30. V. D. Kurganskaya, A. G. Kosichenko and V. Yu. Dunayev, *Nauchno-analiticheskiy otchet po rezul'tatam sotsiologicheskogo issledovaniya-Ekstremizm v Tsentral'noy Azii: Otsenki tendentsiy (na primere Kazakhstana)*, Almaty: Tsentr gumanitarnykh issledovaniy, 2005.
31. Certain groups of Muslims in southern Kazakhstan, where Islamic sentiments generally are stronger than in other parts of the country, displayed yet higher levels of identification of religious values in suicide bombers. See V. D. Kurganskaya and A. G. Kosichenko, *Islam i islamskiye lidery v Yuzhnom Kazakhstane: Nauchno-issledovatel'skiy otchet*, Almaty: Tsentr gumanitarnykh issledovaniy, 2005: 44.
32. For more on the interpretation of the surveys, see the discussion in Michael Fredholm, *Islam and Modernity in Contemporary Central Asia: Religious Faith versus Way of Life*, Stockholm: Stockholm University, *Asian Cultures and Modernity* 14, 2007: 42-3.
33. *Muslim Publics Share Concerns about Extremist Groups* (Washington, DC: Pew Research Centre, 2013), p. 4.
34. Pew Research Centre, *Muslim Publics Share Concerns* ... p. 6.
35. Muhammad Amir Rana, *A to Z of Jehadi Organizations in Pakistan* (Lahore: Mashal Books, 2007), pp. 157, 160-67.
36. Ahmed Rashid, "The Taliban: Exporting Extremism," *Foreign Affairs*, November/December 1999: 22-35; Ahmed Rashid, *Taliban: Islam, Oil and the New Great Game in Central Asia* (London: I. B. Tauris, 2000), p. 201; Ahmed Rashid, *Descent into Chaos: The United States and the Failure of Nation Building in Pakistan,*

Afghanistan, and Central Asia (New York: Viking, 2008), pp. 53, 158, 159, 240, 242-43, 249-50, 276.

37. See Rana, *A to Z of Jehadi Organizations* ... pp. 475-78.
38. Election Commission of Pakistan website, www.ecp.gov.pk
39. Pew Research Centre, *Muslim Publics Share Concerns* ... p. 4. The results on the Pakistani public's view on Al-Qaeda in 2002 were not published.
40. Abu Dhabi Gallup Centre, *Views of Violence: What Drives Public Acceptance and Rejection of Attacks on Civilians 10 Years after 9/11,* Abu Dhabi Gallup Centre, 2011: 2.
41. Abu Dhabi Gallup Centre, *Views of Violence* ... 14.
42. Abu Dhabi Gallup Centre, *Views of Violence* ... 8-10.
43. The result for Egypt may possibly be atypical, when seen in comparison with the already reported levels of support for Al-Qaeda and suicide bombing.
44. Abu Dhabi Gallup Centre, *Views of Violence* ..., 21-22.
45. Pew Research Centre, *Muslim Publics Share Concerns* ... p. 6.
46. United Nations Economic and Social Council, Commission on Human Rights, Draft Resolution: Racism, Racial Discrimination, Xenophobia and all Forms of Discrimination, UN Doc. E/CN.4/1999/L.40 (April 20, 1999), cited in United Nations Economic and Social Council, Commission on Human Rights, Summary Record of the 61st Meeting, E/CN.4/1999/SR.61 (May 3, 1999).
47. Reuters, March 25, 2011.
48. United Nations, International Covenant on Civil and Political Rights, Human Rights Committee, 102nd session, Geneva, July 11-29, 2011, CCPR/C/GC/34 (September 12, 2011).
49. International Covenant on Civil and Political Rights. Adopted by the General Assembly of the United Nations on December 19, 1966.
50. Ishtiaq Ahmed, "Muslim Immigrants in Europe: The Changing Realities," *India Quarterly* 69, no. 3, 2013: 265-82.

9. Afghanistan and Central Asian Security: Strategies for Global Concern

Arpita Basu Roy

Central Asian states have expressed a wide range of security concerns in relation to the withdrawal of International Security Assistance Force (ISAF) from Afghanistan, including the possibility of greater volatility both within Afghanistan itself and in the wider region. The drawdown of troops portends an alteration of the geopolitical balance as declining interest on the part of the USA and EU member-states, combined with a heightened sense of vulnerability due to a potentially worsening security situation—both within Afghanistan and across the region—has the potential to create a new geopolitical situation, with a greater role for regional powers such as China, Iran, India and Russia. Central Asian policymakers and experts also believe that a complete withdrawal of ISAF forces from Afghanistan will lead to a new phase of instability in the country. The Afghan Government and the Afghan armed forces are not seen as capable of independently confronting a Taliban insurgency and there is also a general agreement that the situation in Afghanistan has serious security implications for Central Asian states. However, the degree of an individual state's concern depends on its level of exposure and perceived vulnerability to security challenges coming from Afghanistan, with Tajikistan being viewed as the most fragile and Kazakhstan as the most remote and, therefore, the most secure.[1] The paper discusses the concerns and policies of the Central Asian states in the backdrop of the complexities within Afghanistan, the global narratives on the country concerned and the likely scenarios in the post-2014 phase.

Complex Milieu

Contemporary Afghanistan is a complex environment characterised by powerful and competing agendas. While there have been development successes, most notably in health and education, the optimism that was witnessed in the few years after 2001 has much diminished.[2] While building Afghan institutions constituted the core task of state-building and democratisation in Afghanistan, the donors and agencies seeking to establish institutions and programmes tried to find clients and linked up directly with a de facto power on the ground. This in turn undermined the democratic process. The country's newly-established democracy has already been weakened by widespread vote rigging, and the conflict is causing increasing numbers of civilian and military deaths each year.[3] Afghanistan remains one of the poorest countries in the world, one that will be dependent on international aid for years to come. An autonomous and modernising Afghan state requires governance systems that are effective and accountable. While there has been heavy investment in building a strong centralised state, this has not been complemented by commensurate attention to local government at the provincial and district levels. As a result of this neglect the separation of powers between the executive, legislature and judiciary is not clear at a local level; local governance is too complex, local representative bodies fail to devolve power or responsibility in any meaningful way; donor policies have contributed to the lack of coordination of government structures.[4] Afghanistan is today marked by an absence of proper post-conflict peace building and an emphasis on "democracy" without consolidation of the institutions of representative government. The state and non-state agencies have been admitted with little knowledge of local conditions and there has been a certain degree of wastage of aid funds and misdirection of activities. Insurgency is on the rise and national security forces are weak. There has been a failure to secure a peaceful geopolitical space in which good governance could take place.

It is extremely difficult to exactly prognosticate how the chain of events will unfold in Afghanistan as intervening variables may suddenly appear to morph the scenarios. The volatility of Afghanistan is engrained as "the Taliban still remains entrenched, negotiations have not taken off, the Afghan government suffers from a profound legitimacy crisis and Afghanistan's economic future seems fraught with instability. At the time of writing, one crucial question about the survival of the political system in Afghanistan after the Presidential elections and the hotly-disputed run-off to the election though an audit to the votes have been agreed upon after timely intervention by John Kerry.[5] Latest reports have suggested that neither former Afghan Finance Minister Ashraf Ghani and former Foreign Minister Abdullah Abdullah, the two Presidential contenders can agree on the technical details of the current ballot audit being conducted by Afghanistan's Independent Election Commission leading the nation to a brink of collapse.[6] The possibilities of the return of the Taliban leading to another round of ethnic mobilisation and proxy war fuelled by Afghanistan's neighbours are other major concerns. The issue of whether the Afghan forces would prove effective in the face of insurgency or whether the US will continue maintaining its bases are other critical issues that are debated and discussed.

Global Impressions on Afghanistan

The narratives on Afghanistan seem to have both varieties—a narrative of anxiety and a narrative of opportunity as the international community does not want to see itself as a loser. All these narratives leave a confused impression to any analyst. While the anxiety is all about the uncertainty and instability in a politically volatile and insecure Afghanistan, there are other questions related to the resource decline and developmental issues. While questions about political transition and its outcome are puzzling, the apprehensions related to continued conflict and conflicts of various forms including ethnic tensions and associated casualties remain foremost. Interference of the regional actors—both state and non-state—continue to impede chances of regional cooperation on Afghanistan.

On the other hand what we witness is the parallel narrative of opportunity being offered by a variety of actors in the international community. The purpose is to ensure stability and security in Afghanistan as preparations begin for the withdrawal of US-led NATO forces in 2014. Several conferences on Afghanistan have offered possible ways out of the impasse. For example, the Bonn (December 2011) and Istanbul (November 2011) meets were about political stability, Chicago Conference was about security in Afghanistan while the Delhi Investment

Summit (July 28, 2012) was about private investment in the country. The Tokyo Summit (July 2012) was all about economic stability and financial commitments to the country.[7]

The New Silk Route project establishes Afghanistan as a regional trade and transit hub.[8] Dubbed as a vision to integrate Afghanistan into the regional economy and boost for all Afghan neighbours it aspires to transform Afghanistan into the "Asian Roundabout." There are also initiatives to promote Afghanistan's resource potential and attract new investments. Besides several strategic partnership agreements have been signed between Afghanistan and several crucial states—for example, the Strategic Partnership Agreement between the Islamic Republic of Afghanistan and the United States of America (May 2012), the Strategic Partnership Agreement between India and Afghanistan (October 4, 2011), the Strategic Partnership Agreements with China (September 2012), Agreements covering Aid Diplomacy and Security and with Russia (Agreements on trade and Economic Cooperation) and so on.

An Integrated regional framework was initiated in Istanbul in November 2011 called the "Heart of Asia" Process and developed in Kabul in May 2012. The process framed seven major CBMs that would make the countries of Afghanistan's wider neighbourhood major stakeholders in its stabilisation. The aim was to minimise regional security dilemmas and develop mutually beneficial economic ties that will have large security and political dividends. The assumption behind this initiative was that stability in Afghanistan should be addressed in a regional context. It was imagined as a kind of holistic space connected by shared religion and cultures, social and trade networks, common identities and history that transcend national borders.[9]

The Likely Post-withdrawal Scenarios (2014)

Barring any major untoward incident which could subvert the time table, drawdown of US-led forces shall be completed by the end of 2014 as planned. On the non-withdrawal scenario, the National Intelligence Estimate (NIE) classified report[10] has outlined the differences that could jeopardise Obama Administration's planned withdrawal of most of US troops and start handing over responsibility to the Afghan government by 2014.[11]

One view holds that the Taliban is gaining influence in eastern Afghanistan and lot of territory is under their control. They are still a force to be reckoned with. On the other hand, Pentagon and military commanders think that the above intelligence estimates may not be based on sound premises. Also detractors hold that NIE estimates proved wrong in Iraq. Building up 400,000 Afghan troops and police will make possible a phased withdrawal. The Obama Administration is positive of "substantial progress" in Afghanistan and his military commanders foresee post-2014 commitment to that country.[12] Moreover, the drone attacks were quite successful against militants and some sanctuaries in Pakistani soil.

Both views may border on the extreme: the truth, to be sure, lies somewhere in-between. But the harsh fact is that the deteriorating US economy, fatigue of decade-long war, stalemate in Afghanistan and the resulting public disenchantment together with coming US presidential elections argue for a drawdown of forces. Different scenarios are being conjured up after US-led NATO forces withdraw from Afghanistan.[13] They range from the optimistic to the pessimistic and with a mixture of both. Although the US dominated ISAF views the process of transferring security to the Afghans with calculated optimism and suggests that the transition process is on the right path, an unbiased analysis would suggest that any optimism is based on unfounded assumptions.

Scholars and observers predict varying scenarios in the aftermath of international withdrawal from the region. Citha D. Maass and Thomas Ruttig suggest that four scenarios may evolve in the period up to 2014 and beyond.[14] First, the current power oligarchy could continue to consolidate without the Taliban participation until the completion of the transition process in 2014 or a later date. Again there can be an integration of the opposing Taliban by the current power oligarchy as part of the previously initiated dialogue by sharing power with them. Another probable scenario is that despite economic and profit interests, the ethno-political polarisation intensifies to such an extent that the army and police as well as the Karzai government collapses. Local warlords and armed insurgents battle each other leading to crime spiralling out of control. This happens when negotiations with the Taliban totally fail and a local power struggle would be enough to spark widespread violence across Afghanistan. The fourth scenario is the establishment of the "Islamic Emirate of Afghanistan" established by taking advantage of the drawdown of the NATO troops, where Taliban take control of Kabul and large parts of the country, the Karzai government, army and police disintegrate. Western military trainers and the majority of civilian aid workers leave the country and a few anti-Taliban factions wage guerrilla warfare.

Therefore speculations about emerging scenarios vary according to the variables that seem to have emerged in Afghanistan. Some feel that the Afghans with the harrowing and exhausting experience of more than thirty years of conflict could cooperate on a pluralistic arrangement created in the aftermath of exit of ISAF forces from Afghanistan where there is a general tendency to coexist and power-sharing by different ethnic groups. Also, in a world where interdependence is the norm no one group can dominate Afghanistan as did the Taliban from 1996 to 2001. The view is also supported by the fact that fast-track economic development should take place once a professional Afghan National Army (ANA) is operational. This could be an ideal dispensation in which the Taliban are delinked from Al-Qaeda; a regional consensus of immediate neighbours emerges; a minimum protective security cover of foreign forces is available; and strong national and police forces are raised to maintain national integrity and sovereignty. In other words, an Afghanistan at peace with itself and with the outside world would be a boon for the region and the international community.

Again, a neutral Afghanistan is an excellent proposition[15] but based on wishful thinking.[16] The ground reality is that neighbours could favour their own ethnic group/groups and proxies (Uzbeks, Tajiks). Iranians, Indians and Pakistanis have done so in providing weapons, training and logistics to their favoured groups. None of the big powers such as the US, China and Russia may tolerate a neutral Afghanistan. Each has a stake in that country. It is questionable what incentives all of these could provide to keep Afghanistan neutral.

An extremely negative scenario could emerge according to speculation about an all-out civil war in Afghanistan once NATO-led ISAF forces leave and create a vacuum of sorts. All regional players would like to protect their regional interest and support ethnic kinsmen/allies against the Taliban. This includes China, Central Asian states, Iran, India and Russia. Some analysts think that setting a deadline for NATO forces' withdrawal is a mistake: this will instigate sectarian and ethnic forces and internecine wars could erupt in the post-withdrawal stage.[17] The Taliban is the most aggrieved party and could make a bid for a war of vendetta and revenge against the Northern Alliance now in power, and finally take over. ANF comprising 300,000 troops is ill-equipped, ill-trained and not professionally competent to control the country, and there could be a replay of the 1992 scenario when the US departed in haste.[18] This could lead to rise in militancy, influx of refugees in Pakistan and further souring of relations with Afghanistan. While the situation is qualitatively different from the 1990s when the Taliban ruled they could stage a comeback still. One would agree that the country is exhausted after decades of fighting, and that a new Taliban leadership has emerged, different from yesteryear and more pragmatic and aware of living in a globalised and interdependent world. Yet their tribal culture of revenge and retribution and overvaulting ambition to control Afghanistan still exists. Moreover, if they are supported by external powers through ideological and financial props they could attempt to capture Kabul, the capital in establishing an "Islamic Emirate of Afghanistan." Of course, this scenario will be anathema to all regional neighbours of Afghanistan as they do not want the Taliban to stage a comeback in any form and consequently infect adjoining borders by their radical ideology. That is one reason these countries shall exert to the hilt by arming their respective ethnic/ideological groups/proxies in resisting the menace of the Taliban. Sustained commitment of the international community in Afghanistan is likely to mitigate tensions in the region and increase prospects for regional cooperation, but that withdrawal of international community support is likely to have consequences up to and including a renewed civil war in Afghanistan and increased instability in the region.[19]

There is a possibility that the withdrawal of forces would not be completed unless some NATO residual forces are left to man some nodal installations and bases in Afghanistan. This option is not liked by any regional country as it could release dangerous forces and trends. This thesis has been propounded by former US Ambassador to India, Robert Blackwill, to break up the country on ethnic lines to stop internal fighting and make it manageable for the outside world. As ethnic identities of Tajiks, Hazaras and Uzbeks have become stronger over the years and the danger of civil war exists, the debate on limiting violence through separation of territorial units is in vogue in some quarters.

Break-ups and disintegration of national units has taken opposing arguments. Disintegration of any nation is not liked as such by any nation or by its central leadership or the international community due to setting up a wrong precedent, and emotional and physical suffering caused to that country's population. States do not like changes in borders and birth of new units: Chechnya in Russia, Tibet in China and Kashmir in India. But in the last few years the break-up of Sudan, Kosovo and East Timor took place. Chronic political instabilities in Africa, rise in ethnicities, high levels of poverty, crumbling infrastructures, ethnic and sectarian polarisation render many as "failing states" with added cartographic stresses.

Some observers foresee the break-up of some nation-states by 2030.[20] Protagonists of such theories argue that national integration can be promoted only on interconnectivity through infrastructure-building, end to violence (e.g., lingering or perpetual conflict or long civil wars) through speedy, quick divorce and sometimes fractionating the state for better integration with the world.[21] However, many countries have not still disintegrated despite these factors, namely, Congo, Yemen, Iraq, Afghanistan and Iraq. An equally unwelcome scenario envisages that no major change would come about after US/NATO start exiting after 2014. Although the US has some plans of building and reviving the famous Silk Route craft integration plans in the region, this is going to take time and effort. Given the latest Doha initiative and the US-Taliban talks, there is scepticism that prolonged negotiations and the "New Great Game" will persist in the foreseeable future—and could even flare up with intensity once the US forces leave.

Unlike the "Great Game" of former Great Britain and Russia in the early nineteenth century now it is not a bipolar competition of ISAF versus the Taliban only. A number of actors are vying for a greater share of the Afghan pie and old rivalries and animosities are surfacing: China vs. India, Saudi Arabia vs. Iran, Pakistan vs. India, China against Russia and Taliban vs. Non-Pashtuns.[22] Pak-US relations have come under strain after the US attack on three check-posts on November 26, 2012 killing and wounding many of its soldiers. Ever since, Pakistan has stopped the passage of logistical supplies through Pakistan destined for US-ISAF forces in Afghanistan. This has sent a strong message of protest to the US and the international community about Pakistan's central role in any future settlement of Afghanistan. The region's interest resides in a stable, sovereign and integral Afghanistan. But historical fact and current realities dictate that external interference in Afghanistan's polity is difficult to stop. In fact, Afghanistan as a state has always acted as a buffer with constant meddling from outside powers. It can only become a "roundabout" of commercial traffic when trade and commerce flourish with the cooperation of its neighbours.

Central Asia and Afghanistan: Critical Dynamics

Central Asia, which includes the countries of Kazakhstan, Kyrgyzstan, Tajikistan, Turkmenistan, and Uzbekistan, is on the frontlines of the war in Afghanistan. Three of the five countries share a long and porous border with Afghanistan, and the region is bound to its southern neighbour by ties of ethnicity, culture, history, politics, and language. Its shared history with Afghanistan is evident by the fact that northern Afghanistan (Maimana, Mazar-i-Sherif, and Kunduz) was part of a Central Asian polity ruled by Uzbek Emirs.[23] They are also connected by flows of militant groups and illicit narcotics. As the United States plans for the 2014 transition, Central Asia will continue to play a critical role in stabilisation efforts and the broader regional strategy. In this regional matrix involving Afghanistan, the Central Asian states remain crucial, not only because of the its threat perceptions *vis-à-vis* Afghanistan but also because the region can act as a vital route for any military or commercial activity within Afghanistan and may be used by major powers like Russia, China or the USA for their geopolitical and geostrategic objectives. Despite its partial oil and gas wealth, politically Central Asia remains one of the most neglected regions of the world. The states remain deeply suspicious of outsider intentions where the Americans are disliked, the Russians are not trusted and overwhelming Chinese influence is feared.[24]

Today Central Asia perceives Afghanistan as a base for terrorism, crime, drug trafficking and have assisted the international coalition in operations in Afghanistan—transit and troops supplies along the Northern Distribution Network. Uzbekistan and Tajikistan have long supported the Northern Alliance's combat against the Taliban. The US has also wanted to maximise the cooperation of the states of the region for counter-terrorism efforts.The US operated from an important base at Manas airport outside Bishkek, the capital of Kyrgyzstan, which it used as a stage-post to ship equipment and soldiers into Afghanistan.[25] The Central Asian states, particularly Tajikistan, Turkmenistan and Uzbekistan also now face the threat from Islamic militancy and will be directly affected by instability in Afghanistan. Apart from the connections related to shared history and porous borders, there is an urgency on their part to ensure that their territory is not used as safe havens by the Taliban and that there is no possible spillover of instability from their south.

Complementarity in the Security Interests of India and Central Asia

There is a fair degree of complementarity of Indian and Central Asian interests and concerns on Afghanistan. There is an urgency not to allow Afghan territory to be used for the destabilisation of India. In the past Afghan territory was used to train groups operating in Kashmir. The idea being that radical ideologies should not threaten regional stability and Afghanistan should not emerge as a major theatre for geopolitical contest. But since Afghanistan is yet to have a well-trained army and police force, India has concerns about the post-US withdrawal situation that may emerge in Afghanistan in which India's engagement and investment is likely to be challenged. India is rethinking how best to protect its strategic stakes and enhance connectivity with Central Asia.[26]

New Delhi's ability to influence the outcome is limited as it is unlikely that the present regime or one of its successors will undertake any such expeditionary venture in the form of a military role. India's developmental activities remain dependent on the presence of a viable security umbrella. In the absence thereof, barring a dramatic improvement in Indo-Pakistani relations, India's aid workers would be acutely vulnerable to possible attacks. It can ill-afford to see Afghanistan become a haven for Islamist forces yet again. Consequently, any regime in New Delhi will make concerted efforts to try and fend off the re-emergence of such elements. Beyond this strategic goal it would like to have a substantial diplomatic presence in a stable Afghanistan to enable it to pursue commercial and economic interests in the states of Central Asia.

India shares collective commitment of the international community to the unity, integrity and prosperity of Afghanistan and has the capacity to help the Afghan economy through both export markets and reconstruction. It seeks to work with other states which also do not wish to see Afghanistan plunge into a renewed vortex of internecine conflict. It is also in their interests to remain engaged with key regional states including India, Russia and even Iran to ensure that Pakistan's security and intelligence establishments do not enjoy a *carte blanche* to pursue their parochial and myopic policies and interests in the country in the wake of NATO's withdrawal. Thus threats emanating from Islamic extremism and radicalism remain crucial to both India and the Central Asian Republics.

Threat Perception and Strategies of Central Asian States

While the Central Asian states feel politically slighted by the US and Kabul governments they are themselves deeply at odds with each other as they cannot agree on a common post-2014 regional plan. However, most experts in Central Asia have a pessimistic assessment about the political transition and the capabilities of Karzai's successor to tackle the insurgency. They believe that the Taliban has the potential to deeply influence the political process leading to the patterns of civil war to re-emerge. They also fear that the international community is not seriously discussing an alternative plan to address the potential failure in Afghanistan. Just like Russia, the Central Asian Governments are critical of the West, in particular the US, for having committed multiple strategic errors. At the same time, however, they complain about the West's departure, which they see as another error, given that "the work is not finished.[27] Some states have already started depending on Russia. Tajikistan, for example, ratified a treaty with Moscow to extend by three decades Russia's bases and troops in Tajikistan. Russia has 6,000 troops stationed in three cities to defend Tajikistan's border with Afghanistan.[28]

With regard to opium trade, the most vulnerable countries are Tajikistan, Uzbekistan and Turkmenistan, which share over 1,200 miles (1,900 km) of borders with northern Afghanistan. Narco-traffic is already a major cause of domestic tensions within Tajikistan.[29] Tajikistan is already the weakest state in the region, with an untrained army and facing a severe economic crisis—and corrupt state institutions resulting from their involvement in the opium trade coming out of Afghanistan.[30] The main spillover threats and a renewed civil war that would involve Afghan Tajiks is a major concern for the Tajiks.[31] The Taliban/Pashtun attacks against Tajik symbols of power would have a negative impact on official relations between Dushanbe and Kabul. Another primary concern is that the Islamic Renaissance Party (IRPT), the only legal Islamic opposition in Tajikistan, could find itself confronted with Salafist movements, especially if these movements receive additional foreign support.

Islam Karimov's regime has historically been the main target of the region's Islamic insurgency and this has been the primary challenge of the Uzbek government. The jihadists Islamic Movement of Uzbekistan (IMU) have been trained in Afghanistan and Waziristan.[32] These fighters have maintained close connections with the Taliban, and could therefore benefit from their return to power. But the Uzbek army is better prepared than its Tajik or Kyrgyz counterparts.[33] Also, unlike the situation in the two neighbouring countries, drug-trafficking in Uzbekistan does not directly contribute to state failure. It seems to be better monitored by law enforcement agencies and is protected by some high-level senior officials who have links to the security services.

Among the neighbours, the stakes are higher for Tajikistan and Uzbekistan. Turkmenistan is most likely to cite its "perpetual neutrality," as it did in the 1990s, and will cooperate with the regime in Kabul, whatever its ideological orientation.[34] Both President Nizayov and his successor President Gurbanguly Berdymuhamedov have had a good relationship with Afghan President Hamid Karzai. Turkmenistan intends both to move forward on its energy projects with Afghanistan and to remain hermetically sealed against any kind of "spillovers."

It is generally believed that Kazakhstan had no direct security concern related to Afghanistan apart from some soft security threats. But it is now understood that the country is not completely immune to security threats. Kazakhstan has promised to step up its financial and political commitments to Afghanistan in an effort to counter any threats to regional security that might stem from the withdrawal. Astana's main challenges are the need to address home-grown Islamisation[35] among impoverished young people, especially in Western Kazakhstan, and ensuring the continuous improvement of living standards so as to avoid political protest. Although Kazakhstan is not a major donor to Afghanistan, Astana's new commitments to Afghanistan would include funding for the Afghan National Security Forces and other programmes to educate Afghan students in Kazakhstan, as well as supporting international efforts to halt drug-trafficking and arms trading.[36]

Kyrgyzstan could be affected indirectly by Islamic insurgency and drug-trafficking It has no borders with Afghanistan and very few co-ethnics live there. But in recent years, local Islamic insurgents, mostly Uzbek and Kyrgyz young men from the southern part of the country, have been training in Afghanistan. The Kyrgyz armed forces do not have the capacity to manage sustained attacks from insurgents. However, the major actors involved in the Islamisation of Kyrgyzstan—Hizbut-Tahrir and Tablighi Jamaat—are home-grown and have no connection with Afghan issues. Social tensions in the country are expressed primarily through ethnic rather than radical Islamic violence. As in Tajikistan, a reduction in drug-trafficking is likely to trigger increased conflict over the control of routes, especially among southern elites; an increase would provide criminal organisations with new financial benefits and create incentives to keep the country's institutional capacity weak. Again, Kyrgyz politicians are concerned about Afghanistan and see the Manas Transit Centre helping to counter a common threat. But some Russian and Kyrgyzstani officials have alleged that Manas is connected to drug smuggling, without presenting evidence, which Americans deny. The Kyrgyz government, in the process, have lost $60 million annual lease payment, as well as tens of millions more in parking fees, landing rights, and local contracts.[37]

Central Asian states also fear soft security risks like uncontrolled migration and refugee flows should there be a civil war situation. Central Asian states remember the difficulties they faced in the first years of independence, when they had to cope with flows of Tajik refugees fleeing the civil war. The three neighbouring states of Uzbekistan, Tajikistan and Turkmenistan are particularly likely to have to deal with refugee inflows. Kazakhstan too could attract a growing number of Afghans, in particular graduates who have worked for the international community during the last decade and who might be drawn to the country's regional power status and economic dynamism. Although the issue of the Uzbek refugees following events in Andijan was handled appropriately initially, the handing over of four refugees to the Uzbek authorities in August 2006 raised the concerns of the international community. The risks of violent political conflicts and of a large refugee crisis remain.[38] The refugee problem is the only soft security issue on which official Central Asian actors request greater foreign involvement. Major gas, electricity and transportation projects could be partially stopped or impeded, and the growing private businesses in cement, food, chemicals and fuel to Afghanistan could be disrupted.

Given the negative assessment of Afghanistan's future predominant in Central Asia, preparations for the post-2014 situation are mostly defensive. Tajikistan, Turkmenistan and Uzbekistan plan to reinforce security at their southern borders.[39] They present themselves as fortresses under siege. This perception will probably have repercussions for the transit of people and goods likely to reinforce domestic control over the population. It is also largely felt that in the garb of the struggle against terrorism, the authorities will probably increase the already numerous mechanisms limiting public freedoms and increase the discretionary powers of law enforcement agencies.

Strategies of the Major Powers and Central Asian Concerns

Afghanistan's vulnerability to major power competition really does make a difference to Asia's wider order and Central Asian States as well as India are wary on that count. The most significant players of any such geopolitical competition would include Russia, China and the USA. Russia is dissatisfied with both Western security's presence in and its departure from Afghanistan (2014) but whether Western departure can be seen more as a win or a loss for Moscow depends on how Moscow assesses and balances its own security concerns in the region: instability, extremism and narcotics.[40] The fight against drug-trafficking routed through Central Asia from Afghanistan is one of Moscow's security priorities and the other is the control of labour migration from Central Asia. Russia fears the dangers of interaction between its own Islamic networks and those in Central Asia and Afghanistan. Russia is prioritising the creation of a Eurasian Economic Space and promoting greater regional coordination in key sectors such as hydrocarbons, electricity, transport and cereals production with its partners in the region.[41] Russia may partially retract its interest in states that resist its influence, such as Uzbekistan and Turkmenistan. Instead, it will privilege regional structures with fewer members—Kazakhstan, Kyrgyzstan and Tajikistan. Examples of this include the Collective Security Treaty Organisation (CSTO) and the yet incomplete Customs Union/Eurasian Economic Space. There is a possibility that there is a large gap between Moscow's power projection and its actual political will and capacities on the ground. Whether the CSTO can really guarantee Tajik and Kyrgyz security or whether it is only useful for Moscow, as Moscow becomes more and more hesitant about any military intervention in Central Asia, is a crucial question. The Central Asian governments are not sure whether the answers to all these questions would favour them and are uncertain about Moscow's role in post-2014 regional security.[42] Affected by the Soviet intervention in Afghanistan, the Central Asian elites are sceptic that Russia is ready to replace the international coalition.

China is likely to play a "huge" commercial role in helping rebuild the country in post-2014 Afghanistan.[43] The Chinese stance on the post-2014 situation is confusing to the Central Asian authorities. China's investments throughout the region and in the northern provinces of Afghanistan are appreciated, although Beijing is also criticised for targeting only minerals and hydrocarbons. China has promised to work with Afghanistan on the construction of the Silk Road Economic Belt and has an ambitious vision for linking China to Europe via Central Asia and the Middle East.[44] On security, the majority of the Central Asian elites are either sceptical or actually afraid of China's involvement on the ground. China is even less involved in military issues in Afghanistan and tries to avoid making definite commitments in terms of security engagement as requested by Kabul. It is largely believed that the Chinese authorities are not interested in developing the security aspect, which could turn out to be a quagmire. China has also recently increased its involvement in other, more security-minded forms of cooperation, including the training of Afghan police and security forces. China's commitment to Afghan reconstruction since the ouster of the Taliban in 2001 has been a relatively paltry $250 million and its security support has been mostly limited to counter-narcotics training. But a consortium of Chinese investors was involved in a landmark $3 billion deal to produce copper in Afghanistan although work on the deposit, among the world's largest, has been largely halted by insurgent attacks.[45] As confirmation of this trend, US State Department officials told *The Guardian* that "concerns on terrorism" rather than economic concerns are now "driving Chinese policy in Afghanistan."[46]

The decision by the US to commit 9,800 troops with the assumption that the legal framework, or bilateral security agreement, will be in place shortly after the inauguration of the soon-to-be-elected Afghan president attempts to eliminate uncertainty as NATO Allies and partners finalise planning for the Resolute Support mission to train, advise and assist Afghan security forces from the beginning of 2015 to cement coalition gains made during the previous 13 years.[47] Previously, the US has made a ten-year financial commitment to Afghanistan for the period 2014-2024, and has signed a Strategic Partnership with Kabul, which includes a military presence in Afghanistan for the next decade, in the form of intelligence operations, special forces and training activities. In May 2014, Obama with about 32,800 US troops in Afghanistan announced a drawdown to 9,800 by the end of the year and withdrawal of virtually all by the end of 2016 and the conclusion of his presidency.[48] But this continued involvement cannot mask the US's expected future disengagement. US priorities in international security have clearly been reoriented toward the Asia-Pacific region and the "Greater Middle East." The sense of future American disengagement is also visible in the State Department's 2011 "new Silk Road" narrative. No specific budget has been allocated, nor have any commitments been made in terms of diplomatic personnel. The launching of the Northern Distribution Network was supposed to be accompanied by a revival of American investments in the Central Asian economies, but this has not been the case. There is no hard commitment to improving economic conditions and good governance in the region.

Conclusion

Even after years of international intervention, Afghanistan remains at the vortex of security implications for the region and beyond. The question of the survival of the political system in Afghanistan or the possibilities of the return of the Taliban leading to another round of ethnic mobilisation and proxy war fuelled by Afghanistan's neighbours are other major concerns. These issues amidst apprehensions have added a new dimension to interstate relations in Afghanistan's neighbourhood and calls for evaluation of the contingencies and preparing beyond. Failure in Afghanistan, nevertheless, would mean common security challenges (terrorism, radicalism) for both India and Central Asia. From a regional perspective, Russia, China and the US have demonstrated inadequate commitment to post-2014 security which is marked by a complex environment characterised by powerful and competing agendas. It is more or less understood that there can be no short cuts in the case of Afghanistan and a total withdrawal, in fact, would be catastrophic for the country and would mean a reversal of all the achievements of the last decade. The Central Asian states are not satisfied with the current commitments and fear disengagement by the main external actors in preparing for the post-2014 situation. Central

Asia and Afghanistan are the victims of the multiple grand narratives and grand geopolitical designs that have framed the involvement of external actors in the region, from the "war on terror" to "nation building" to the New Silk Road Strategy. Cooperation between India and Central Asian States like Uzbekistan on Afghanistan is essential and a dialogue among the main stakeholders in Afghanistan's future could be initiated. A failure of the Afghan project would also be a jolt to regional cooperation involving South and Central Asia. Regional peace building is the ideal approach but given the difference in interests and policies of the various states involved, a comprehensive regional policy is a challenge. Iran, China, Pakistan, India and other regional actors will have to resolve their differences to play a significant role as well. However, much international cooperation will depend on the outcomes of political transition under way in Afghanistan, as well as on the results of various related economic and security transitions that are currently evolving.

Notes

1. Nargis Kassenova, *Relations between Afghanistan and Central Asian States after 2014: Incentives, Constraints and Prospects* (Sweden: Stockholm International Peace Research Institute, May 2014).
2. Arpita Basu Roy, *Human Security in Afghanistan: Reconstructing An Alternative Notion of Security for Afghanistan in the South Asian Security Paradigm* (New Delhi: Pentagon Press, 2014).
3. "Afghanistan: At Least 21,000 Civilians Killed," *Costs of War*, www.costsof war.org/articles/afghan-civilians
4. Douglas Saltmarshe and Abhilash Medhi, "Local Governance in Afghanistan: A View from the Ground," *AREU Synthesis Paper* (Kabul: AREU, June 2011).
5. Matthew Rosenberg and Carlotta Gall, "Kerry Pushes for Solution to Afghanistan Election Crisis," *New York Times*, July 11, 2014.
6. Sara Carter, former Afghan Official: John Kerry Has "Prepared the Ground for Absolving the Obama Administration" on Afghanistan, *The Blaze*, August 1, 2014.
7. Kenneth Katzman, *Afghanistan: Post-Taliban Governance: Security, and U.S. Policy*, CRS Report, Washington: Congressional Research Service, US Department of State, July 11, 2014, www.crs.gov, accessed on August 8, 2014.
8. *US Support for the New Silk Road*, US Department of State. http://www.state.gov/p/sca/ci/af/newsilkroad/ accessed on August 1, 2014.

9. Marissa Quie, "The Istanbul Process: prospects for regional connectivity in the heart of Asia," *Asia EurJ*, Springer, www. Springerlink.com
10. NIE report is more than 100 pages and represents the consensus view of CIA and 15 other intelligence agencies. Like previous ones it challenges the Pentagon's view of US/ISAF military's stalemate in Afghanistan. It underlines rampant corruption, incompetence of Afghan national forces and Taliban controlling the southern Afghanistan. Consult, "US intelligence report on Afghanistan sees stalemate," *Los Angeles Times* (California), January 11, 2012. This is at odds with the Pentagon's assessment of progress being made by NATO forces in Afghanistan and recommends against any hasty withdrawal of troops.
11. In late 2009 President Obama agreed to deploy 33,000 additional troops commonly termed as "surge" in Afghanistan in a bid to defeat the Taliban and start negotiations. This peaked to 100,000 in summer 2011 and since then the number is 91,000 troops with the remaining scheduled to withdraw by 2014. The US-led NATO forces have three broad options in Afghanistan: to fight and destroy completely Taliban insurgent forces; to negotiate with the Taliban; and ultimately withdraw leaving behind Afghan forces to deal with them.
12. For example, General John Allen, the commander of US-led coalition remarked: "... we don't want December 31, 2014 to become the end of history. It isn't. In fact it's the beginning of history of Afghanistan." On another occasion, he remarked: "There will be US military presence [after 2014]. This is work in progress, we're not going to be done at the end of 2014." As quoted in Kevin Baron, "US Military Wants Troops in Afghanistan Beyond 2014." http:news//.yahoo.com/u-military-wants-troops-afghanistan-beyond.../ accessed on December 20, 2011.
13. Lt. General (Retd.) Kamal Matinuddin, "Possible Post-Withdrawal Scenarios," Paper presented at an International Conference: *Transition in Afghanistan: Post-Exit Scenarios*, Jointly held by IPRI and HSF, October 5-6, 2011, Islamabad. Cited in a presentation by Dr. Maqsudul Nuri, Acting President, IPRI, in a Seminar organised by Maulana Abul Kalam Azad Institute of Asian Studies entitled *Bonn '01 to Bonn'11: Debating the Political Future of Afghanistan*, February 8-10, 2012, JMIU, New Delhi.
14. Citha D. Maass and Thomas Ruttig, "Is Afghanistan on the Brink of a New Civil War? Possible Scenarios and Influencing Factors in the Transition Process," *SWP Comments 21*, German Institute for International and Security Affairs, August 2011.
15. Karl F. Inderfurth and Chinmaya R. Gharekhan, "Afghanistan Needs a Surge of Diplomacy," *The New York Times,* January 20, 2010.
16. C. Raja Mohan, "Afghan Neutrality," *The Indian Express*, August 11, 2010.
17. Cowper, *Daily Times*, Lahore, December 9, 2011.
18. Maqsudul Hasan Nuri, "Military Withdrawal: Prospective Scenarios for Afghanistan and the Region," Arpita Basu Roy et al. (eds.), *International Intervention in*

Afghanistan: Motives and Approaches (New Delhi: Shipra Publications, 2012), pp. 61-77.

19. Jonathan Schroden et al., *Summary of Independent Assessment of the Afghan National Security Forces*, Summary Report for the US Congress (Washington DC: CNA Strategic Studies, 2014).
20. Parag Khanna, "Breaking up is good to do," *Daily Times*, Lahore, January 15, 2011, p. A8.
21. Parag Khanna, "Breaking up is good to do," *Daily Times*.
22. Brian M. Downing, "Negotiations and Great Games in Afghanistan," *Daily Times*, Lahore, January 14, 2012: A8.
23. *Afghanistan's Other Neighbors: Iran, Central Asia, and China*, Conference report, Istanbul: American Institute of Afghanistan Studies and the Hollings Center for International Dialogue, July 24-26, 2008. http://www.bu.edu/aias/reports/aon_conference.pdf accessed January 18, 2014.
24. Ahmed Rashid, "Central Asia concerns over US pull-out from Afghanistan," *BBC News-Asia*, October 5, 2013.
25. The Manas Air Base which was unofficially called the Ganci Air Base is a former US military installation at Manas International Airport, near Bishkek, Kyrgyzstan. It was primarily operated by the US Air Force and the primary unit at the base was the 376th Air Expeditionary Wing. On June 3, 2014 American troops vacated the base and it was handed back to the Kyrgyzstan military. The US lease officially expired in July 2014.
26. Arpita Basu Roy, "Afghanistan Beyond 2014: Regional Security Concerns For India and Central Asia," P. L. Dash et al. (eds.), *Central Asia and Regional Security* (New Delhi: Knowledge World, 2014), p. 139.
27. Such inference has been largely drawn from the author's interactions with analysts in Tajikistan and Uzbekistan.
28. Ahmed Rashid, "Central Asia concerns over US pull-out from Afghanistan," *BBC News-Asia.*
29. *Tajikistan and Afghanistan*, Institute for the Study of War, Washington, http://www.understandingwar.org/tajikistan-and-afghanistan
30. Ahmed Rashid, "Central Asia concerns over US pull-out from Afghanistan," *BBC News-Asia.*
31. "TAJIKISTAN: UNHCR concerned over deportation of Afghans," http://www.irinnews.org/report/18687/
32. Jacob Zenn, *IMU Re-establishes Bases In Northern Afghanistan*, Central Asia Caucasus Institute, Central Asia-Caucasus Institute & Silk Road Studies Programme, Paul H. Nitze School of Advanced International Studies, The Johns Hopkins University Washington, DC, USA. August 2, 2012.
33. Marlene Laruelle, Sebastien Peyrouse and Vera Axyonova, *The Afghanistan-*

Central Asia Relationship: What role for the EU?, Working Paper 13, EUCAM, February 2013. www.EUCENTRALASIA.EU accessed January 3, 2014.

34. Turkmen President, Niyazov pursued a policy of strict neutrality in international affairs. This to a great extent shielded the Turkmen state from the unrest in neighbouring Afghanistan, and thus the country has been spared the regional trends such as armed separatism and Islamic extremism. While the Niyazov regime generally had a positive relationship with the Taliban in the 1990s, it was supportive of the US-led intervention and maintains a good relationship with the government of Hamid Karzai (Institute for the Study of War).
35. *Fight against terrorism and extremism in Kazakhstan*, Ministry of Foreign Affairs Republic of Kazakhstan. http://mfa.gov.kz/...
36. Selina Williams, "Kazakhstan Sees Threat from Afghan Instability: Regional Security a Concern as NATO-led Troops Prepare to Leave Afghanistan," *The Wall Street Journal*, January 20, 2014.
37. Davis Trilling, "Kyrgyzstan: Afghanistan Drawdown Puts Manas in Reverse Gear," *EurasiaNet*, September 21, 2012 www. Eurasianet.org
38 *Regional Strategy Paper for assistance to Central Asia (CA RSP)*, European Community, 2007-13 http://eeas.europa.eu/central_asia/rsp/07_13_en.pdf accessed March 2, 2013.
39. Marlene Laruelle, Sebastien Peyrouse and Vera Axyonova, *The Afghanistan-Central Asia Relationship: What role for the EU?*, Working Paper 13, EUCAM, February 2013. www.EUCENTRALASIA.EU accessed January 3, 2014.
40. Ekaterina Stepanova, *Afghanistan After 2014: The Way Forward for Russia*, IFRI Russia/NIS Centre, May 2013. www.ifri.org accessed on July 25, 2014.
41. Russia, Belarus and Kazakhstan signed the historic Eurasian Economic Union which will come into effect in January 2015. Cutting down trade barriers and comprising over 170 million people it will be the largest common market in the ex-Soviet sphere. See "Russia, Belarus, Kazakhstan sign 'epoch' Eurasian Economic Union," *RT*, May 2014. http://rt.com/business/162200-russia-bealrus-kazakhstan-union/
42. Marlene Laruelle, Sebastien Peyrouse and Vera Axyonova, *The Afghanistan-Central Asia Relationship: What role for the EU?*
43. Michael Martina, "China will not fill US void in Afghanistan," *Reuters*, July 21, 2014. http://www.reuters.com/article/2014/07/21/us-china-afghanistan-idUSKBN0FQ12I20140721 accessed on August 5, 2014.
44. Shannon Tiezzi, "Xi, Karzai Discuss the Future of China-Afghanistan Ties," *The Diplomat*, May 21, 2014. www.the diplomat.com
45. Michael Martina, "China will not fill US void in Afghanistan," *Reuters*.
46. Michael Martina, "China will not fill US void in Afghanistan," *Reuters*.
47. "US announces commitment to Afghanistan," *ISAF News*, May 28, 2014. http://

www.isaf.nato.int/article/isaf-news/u.s.-announces-committment-to-afghanistan.html

48. Luke Johnson, "Obama Announces Post-2014 Force for Afghanistan," Radio Free Europe: Radio Liberty, May 27, 2014. http://www.rferl.org/content/obama-to-announce-post-2014-force-for-afghanistan/25400633.html

Globalising Cultural Geographies

10. The Point of Convergence: Reasons for New Age Spirituality in Kazakhstan

Alexey Zelenskiy

In the recent five years the Kazakh state made a certain revision with regard to religion that immediately faced a comprehensive criticism from the liberal opposition and freedom defenders. It was mentioned that religious freedom in Kazakhstan was essentially curtailed and religious diversity was reduced. Further, for a shorter expression I suggest calling that complex transformation of the State's attitude towards religion as "religious turn." So, this religious turn of 2008-2013 for the first time in the history of the Kazakhstan's independence was a cause of great concern which was almost unthinkable before.

There used to be two "protected" topics in the public discourse in Kazakhstan that were free from negative attributions: (a) personality and activities of President Nazarbayev and (b) religious world views. While the personality of the President enjoys such immunity due to an authoritarian political regime, a censure regarding religion was commonly explained via the notion of "political correctness." Nevertheless, I would like to make a few observations in addition in order to question probable deeper ties between attitudes towards the regime and attitudes towards religion in Kazakhstan, because such questioning reveals how and why ideology in Kazakhstan works.

As will be shown further, these two attitudes partially overlap in a specific appropriation of the New Age culture in this Central Asian country. The name "New Age" is usually synonymous with "New Paganism," which has also a larger meaning—"New Age obscurantism." However it is interpreted, it is in addition to political and economic modernisation and has to be considered.

A metaphor of "the point of convergence" in the title is to point to a place of an imaginary though impossible spiritual unification in the real social and political construction of Kazakhstan. I am going to show that the New Age way of thinking corresponds to a split within secular spirituality, which provides a minimum of reflexivity needed for inducing a sort of reactive ideology in religiosity. The nature and the structure of this split are to be discussed too in order to localise New Age spirituality in socio-political symbolical space of Kazakhstan.

Insofar as the subject of my inquiry belongs to the domain of the imaginary rather than a domain of facts, this text will progress through three main points which are inspired by major concepts of the psychoanalysis of Jacques Lacan. The first point corresponds to the concept of "symptom" and gives an idea of how Kazakhstan's ideological issues and New Age culture can be effectively put together. Other two points are inspired by the concepts of "The Mirror Stage" and "The Big Other." Thus the section "The Point of Convergence and the 'Religious Turn'" discusses the topic of a self-image in ideology, and the last section questions the imaginary instance, which corresponds to a self-image from the previous section.

New Age in Kazakhstan: Brief Introduction

"The Heart of Eurasia" is an officially promoted identification of the capital Astana and metonymically of Kazakhstan itself.[1] This title corresponds to an often heard ideological claim that Kazakhstan is the cradle of all civilisational connections between the East and the West, and between the North and the South of the country. The country is populated by the representatives of 130 national minorities except the Kazakh majority. A great variety of religious affiliations are also represented. For two decades of independence President Nazarbayev did not cease to mention that Kazakhstan is either one of the few countries, or perhaps the only multinational and multi-confessional country, unfamiliar with interethnic or religious conflicts due to its tolerant and peaceful traditions. Thus one can assume that some eclectic and pluralistic spirituality must come along, and it apparently does.

The New Age spirituality is often referred to and probably in accordance with the current global spiritual trend. A common psychological interpretation explains the rise of the New Age as a response to global challenges and threats of the late twentieth century, such as ecological crisis, the discrediting of Christian values, social disintegration, existential uncertainty and others. An impact of New Age values on secular spirituality as well as on social institutions and state decision-making is unambiguously detectable in Kazakhstan in particular. Just after its "official inauguration," New Age culture promptly reached Kazakhstan in late Soviet times in the 1970s-1980s. A decade later it was already widely represented on the ruins of the USSR by plenty of extrasensory, astrologers, theosophists, UFO enthusiasts, cryptologists, zoologists, messiahs, occultists and so on. Today similar to Western societies and due to commercialisation New Age is organically integrated into the Kazakhstani popular culture.[2] Thus, it may seem that this trend remains independent or even indifferent to all kinds of ideological challenges and political catastrophes in the post-Soviet space. Due to its very presence, regardless of transformations in symbolical space, it deserves special attention.

The outburst of New Age mentality of the late 1980s and early 1990s was accompanied by a "religious renaissance" of Christianity and Islam in Kazakhstan, when taboo on religion was suspended and official ideology was such that it appreciated religion and mutual respect. Atheism of Marxism and communism lost favour and ceased to conduct a secular spirituality by default. Later, due to the sweeping criticism of Marxism it mostly degenerated into a reactionary agnosticism. However, despite highly plausible prognoses that were popular among the Kazakhs, Islam did not find official favour, and the new State declared itself secular. Meanwhile the vacant place left by atheism was immediately occupied by a sort of eclectic attitude, the conceptual origins of which are still unknown. One could univocally recognise the typical New Age trend of respect for religion and spirituality reflected in attitudes like assumption of a convergence of all religions, distrust of organised forms of religion, praise for human moral and intellectual potencies, etc. In other words, the secular spirituality in the proclaimed secular State revealed ambiguous non-secular traits or at least traits of obscure nature.

In this case the current popularity of New Age ideas among people in Kazakhstan seems reasonable or even natural. However, I am going to question the presumed links between psychological issues, geographical, cultural and historical facts on the one hand and the necessity of domination of the New Age way of thinking on the other. I argue that there is a need to analyse a real function of this sort of spirituality beyond its imaginary (including an ideological) recognition, which can be achieved through special analysis.

My first objection to the aforementioned determination is that they in a certain way ignore political and ideological factors. As I have already mentioned, New Age attitudes occupied the place of dialectical materialistic atheism in popular recognition of religious values and institutions. This has happened during the political catastrophe, the collapse of regime. Hence this initial inscription of such attitudes into symbolical order must not be disregarded.

The second objection points to a more general and all-round impact that hardly takes into consideration spirituality and is much more related to the symbolical space. The fact that beliefs in poltergeists, extrasensory perception, UFO, astrology, etc., were present long before the political collapse can become evidence of rigidity or indifference to spirituality in respect of political and social transformations. The closest example is the image of "eternal values" and "traditions," which survive any historical perturbations. Although such an idea effectively means fantasy at an ideological level, its real function is different.

However, all this does not mean that we deal with a case of implementation of what was called "New Age Politics" in Kazakhstan. Neither is Nazarbayev a New Age politician nor are New Age political attitudes worth examining by any state at all. The relationship between the Kazakh State and New Age culture is rather complex and not one-dimensional or univocal. While certain trends and concepts are favoured and promoted, there are also persecuted manifestations of that complex movement.

A good example of the former, besides "ecumenical" projects of President Nazarbayev, which I will discuss in the last section, is the activity of the First Lady, the President's wife, Sara Nazarbayeva. She is well known as a disciple of *Detka* ("Babe"), a Russian mystic, Porfiriy Ivanov, and is a student of the Indian guru, the Late Sathya Sai Baba. She enforced propagation of Ivanov's teaching in state clinics and, according to rumour, of Sathya Sai Baba's teaching in governmental organisations. Recently she developed and introduced a discipline called "Self-Knowledge"—inspired by what is called "Religion of the Self"—to secondary school education.

A more obvious case of official sentiments and the New Age culture is the architectural design of the capital Astana and National symbols.

On the other hand along with privileging a set of definitely foreign trends, in terms of the official ideology, one can notice, for instance, a certain hostility of the official authorities to both domestic and foreign messianic sects, like *Ata Zholy*, *Allya Ayat*. None of these has got official registration in 2012. Another feature is that the State recognises Islam as a traditional religion of Kazakhs instead of shamanism or religion of Tengri. Although this can be identified as an indication of setting apart such ideology and New Age favouring non-traditional and pagan religions, one should not forget the place of shamanism and Tengri on the level of traditions and customs, and that those traditions and customs have an ideological priority before Islam.

To be more precise, for integrating New Age values into the culture of Kazakhstan, it is worth distinguishing rural traditions and urban subculture. Though rural traditions influence urban Kazakhs up to a certain degree, an urban subculture as such is considerably autonomous and self-sufficient due to its complex ethnical composition and modern attitudes. People in cities prefer to believe in undefined complexities (political, scientific, religious, etc.), in infinite capacities of human brain and body, in mantras, Feng-Shui and so on. Books on "Philosophy/Psychology/Culture," "Medicine and Health/Love, Sex and Erotic," "Home and Garden" and "Business" has a definite New Age content.[3]

From this, I conclude that ideological construction of Kazakhstan reveals a New Age content. To point to some of the most important aspects of this structure:

- New Age values and principles affect disciplinary spaces (schools, clinics, and also perhaps the army);

- Those values are integrated into everyday practices and in the discourses of self-identification and belonging;
- Though the State sympathises with multiculturalism or multi-confessionality, it also posits itself as a "strong State," which distances its methods from the New Age priority of decentred network-like forms of cooperation and organisation;
- New Age has spread into the institutions of consumer society.
- At last, certain New Age "brand names" (Sathya Sai Baba, Norman Foster) are associated with Kazakhstan's elite and symbols.

The Point of Convergence and the "Religious Turn"

Kazakhstan inherited the idea of convergence from the late Soviet period. It is well known that Mikhail Gorbachev was a great enthusiast of the liberal-democratic market and the convergence of political and economic systems of the socialist order. Kazakhstan became independent exactly in the middle of the process of such convergence and had to complete it in its own way. Unsurprisingly the need of building new nationalism stimulated a more general vision of a character and outcomes of this process.

It is important that on the level of fantasy (to be precise, on the level of the Lacanian Imaginary) an idea of convergence projects a Subject (of a nation, a people) in the final point of a process, on the place of a centre of gravitation or, in terms of Lacan, on the place of an *objet petit a* (object-cause of desire). From the analytical point of view it is a narcissistic fantasy par excellence. Thus, when a nationalistic ideology represents a nation as the highest state of integrity of values and world views, as it is with nationalism in Kazakhstan, it just operates with the same imaginary scenario.

However, this position in the centre, in the point of convergence is not safe for a Subject. A narcissistic approach of being the focus of attention perpetually turns into an anxiety and despair due to the impossibility of leaving that place. In this respect every nationalistic figure reveals ambivalence: although being in the centre or in the point of convergence (in the "Heart of Eurasia" for instance) means having a privileged position, it also means that there is no escape (being in the centre of Eurasia means that wherever you look or go from that point you see and reach the same Eurasia and nothing else; no wonder that the idiom "in the middle of nowhere" is so popular among Americans or Europeans referring to Kazakhstan in particular). Nevertheless, such analysis provides us with a good perspective on the "Religious Turn."

After two decades of praise and celebration of cultural and confessional diversity (in 1991-2008) the official ideology in Kazakhstan has swiftly converted into a sort of anxiety with regard to religion, which after a short period of project formulation (2008-2010) transformed into a new policy of 2010-2012. The Annual Report of the US Commission on International Religious Freedom states:

> By October 2012, when the year-long re-registration period ended, the number of registered religious organisations fell from 46 to 17, *EurasiaNet* reported. The number of registered faith-based civic groups fell from 4,551 to 3,088. The ARA director said in Almaty that of 666 registered Protestant religious associations, 462 were re-registered and the remaining 204 "will be liquidated." He also said that out of 48 "non-traditional" religious organisations—whose identity he did not specify—only 16 were registered.[4]

Officials in the person of the chairman of the 2011 Agency for Religious Affairs, Lama Sharif, pointed to a number of reasons to justify that new policy, such as promotion of a secular State, the need to create a well-administered confessional space, prevention of religious extremism, control over activities of foreign actors and at last getting a realistic idea of what is going on. Nevertheless, those reforms, which by the way remained unnoticed by most people, in general were estimated as reducing freedom and religious diversity and met with little support and understanding from religious communities.

What has happened to the widely promoted self-image of a multi-confessional and tolerant country? Why does the "Heart of Eurasia" hesitate to be open for religious freedom and diversity?

Let us look closer into the data. According to the 2009 year census, 96% of people in Kazakhstan were either Muslims or Christians.[5]

This means that the President's speeches are less categorical about multi-confessionalism in this country implying it to be a minor factor unless one recognises the heterogeneity among Muslim and Christian communities. Does it not show, above all, that the "Religious Turn" can be considered as an attempt to tell the truth about the real confessional situation? In order to reconstruct this event, it must be noted that this involuntary "confession" happened three years before re-registration and the criticism that followed. If the new politics of 2010-2012 has reduced the strength of religious diversity, there have been other factors due to which the confessional space had already lost its relevance by 2009.

There can be at least two explanations for this turn of attitude—before and after 2009. One of them assumes that the events of the last few years revealed or confirmed once again the true nature of the political regime in Kazakhstan, that Kazakhstan is not a free democratic country, while the previous prosperous freedom of religion and multi-confessionality was a sham. This is the position of the opposition and can also be found in the report by the Norwegian Helsinki Committee titled *Broken Promises: Freedom of Religion or Belief issues in Kazakhstan and Kyrgyzstan*.[6] Another way of establishing the link is to say that both the states are complementary components of a cycle of institutional and spiritual development of the State and the society, i.e., that both are the moments of one truth. So, while the first explanation asserts that Kazakhstan has serious problems with freedom of religion, the second one tells us that the Kazakh government is neither repressive nor does it unconditionally provide such freedom. But the problem is that both versions push us to overlook one subtle feature.

In order to notice this feature, it is necessary to go one step further in the same direction as does the opposition and point to the conservative character of these reforms. In his last annual *Message to the People of Kazakhstan*, Nazarbayev unambiguously urges the nation to turn back to traditions in order to withstand the "foreign,"[7] and Lama Sharif does not hesitate to respond to this call in the context of his Agency's activities.

There is no need to explain in detail why the deviation to the conservative pole means for the State not only a way of defending Kazakhstan from religious extremism or foreign influence, but also a way to immobilise the long-standing traditionalists' pressure on State authority. This second vector immediately comes to light if one attempts to figure out what that tradition, to which Nazarbayev refers, is. Actually, no such certain tradition exists. As always happens, real traditions differ from place to place and contradict each other. For instance, regardless of what Nazarbayev suggests, there is no traditional consensus regarding women's freedom. There are plenty of Kazakh traditionalists dreaming of women's submission or of polygamy, for example. Nazarbayev hardly has in mind something of that kind. Instead, he speaks about traditions as a remedy for foreign cultural influence and gives an example of what counts as foreign:

> Today, the issue of non-traditional for our people religious and pseudo-religious trends is sharp. A part of the young people blindly assimilates that foreign vision of life, because a part of our society has weak immunity against foreign pseudo-religious influence … The inner "filter" must ask questions: whether we need our mothers, sisters and daughters wearing clothes of other nations, wrapping themselves up in kerchiefs? No taking food at one table with us? Driving no cars? These are all the established traditions of other nations, but none of such customs ever existed in our steppe. Read the classics, watch the movies.[8]

And compare it to a quote from an interview with Lama Sharif discussing a problem of "harmful religious trends":

> Besides increasing people's religious literariness, it is necessary to take a complex of steps including those outside properly religious sphere. Young people should see a clear perspective for themselves, should have an opportunity to study, to find a job, to build a family. In short, to live with dignity. Also, a positive part in this process, I believe, is to be played by a revival of our culture and historical self-consciousness. A person, who deeply respects a native culture and holds traditions of the wise ancestry, has a natural immunity from all that.[9]

An ambitious notion of "pseudo-religion" in the President's speech is striking. And the combination of this notion with the foreign is scandalous. However, the message is clear: pseudo-religions and harmful cults always come from outside and reveal themselves in disturbing *our* liberal secular traditions. The truth is that one way or another it is precisely traditions and traditional religious acts that cause anxiety in this "witch-hunt" on religions.

Surprisingly, above all, in this xenophobic form one can see a word in defence and support of secular freedoms. Then, what is wrong in this case? An obvious answer to that would be biased views about civil liberty.

However, let us find out what a liberal way can offer.

Once again: the fact is that the "Religious Turn" affects, reduces religious freedom. But do religious communities and believers exactly look for that kind of freedom which critics are talking about? If we look closer to religious thinking, we find that it is in several ways hostile to the secular idea of freedom. First of all, almost every such community thinks in a particular manner, regarding its way and belief as the ultimate truth. This means that they would hardly wish others to have the same amount of freedom as they wish to have themselves. Secondly, there are beliefs that are indifferent to official recognition. So, that civil, liberal kind of freedom is obtruded and cannot satisfy believers.

This uncovers a trivial truth about demands of religious freedom: freedom defenders do not worry about believers and religions as such. But, most likely, this estrangement is the only normal way to support liberal values in the society. The opposite is different—an interest and a sincere concern. That is why one can get a weird feeling about public manifestations of that concern and the excessive eagerness demonstrated by the Agency (they visit worship centres, connect with members of congregations, request declarations of donations, etc.). This performative interest is juxtaposed to the liberal silent disinterest and denotes that subtle feature, which has been dropped out from liberal or institutional discourse. So that is the liberal paradox: ignoring religious attitudes and values is the way of providing religious freedom, and every interest in religion tends to become an intervention.

This leads us to a special case of queer tensions between the Agency and the Church of Scientology. A registration as a religious organisation was refused to Scientologists, because Scientology was not accepted as a religion. In this the Agency manifests itself as a police of religious purity, which is aware what religion is and what it definitely is not. But this is only half of the story. Having refused registration to the scientific association, the Agency also suspended its activities on grounds of suspicious religious activity.[10] In order to be just I have to claim that this aberration in behaviour must be considered not as a petty tyranny of bureaucrats, but as an objective quality of religion in the contemporary symbolical universe. It is obvious here that a bureaucratic imagination keeps detecting something religious even after its symbolical discharge. Thus, religion here clearly reveals the qualities of the imaginary *objet petit a,* which remains in the core of a subject after its full symbolical disintegration.

This is why the Agency is still able to operate by binary opposition of "true and false" with regard to religion. This opposition of "true and false" either in the form of "true" (traditional) religions and (foreign) pseudo-religions, or as an opposition to authentic secular traditions to non-traditional religious customs, functions as a mirror-image in which one should re-establish one's identity and thus dignity. This "true," "integral," "authentic" image is perceived from a distance and as alienated so far among "false" shadows, which are to be overcome. It is very easy to notice that the mentioned ambitions of Nazarbayev and the Agency are extremely close to the most popular New Age attitudes towards religion: both are suspicious about organisational forms of religion, both favour "natural" spirituality and both pretend to have an actual and true knowledge of the nature of spirituality and religion. This particularly stimulates a reactive religiosity in a form: there are religions and *my* religion, which is better.

Besides the unprecedentedly large attention paid by Nazarbayev to religious issues in his 2013 "Message," this year is significant for two other events. One of them is the Fourth Congress of Leaders of the World and Traditional Religions, which recently took place in Astana. This Congress is a personal initiative of Nazarbayev, which was institutionalised ten years ago. It is worth mentioning that traditionally this Congress is held in a special building designed by the New Age architecture icon Norman Foster—that is, the Palace of Peace and Reconciliation (unofficially also called "The Temple of All Religions"). The Palace offers a variety of rooms and halls for art, concerts and worships as well. According to Nazarbayev's idea, the Congress provides leaders of world and traditional religions with opportunity to discuss and bring common decisions about urgent issues of political and religious agenda.

Another notable event of the year is just one fine part of Nazarbayev's speech on his meeting with businessmen. In his speech he declared revolutions no less worthless in the context of the twenty-first century. This last note is important for a comprehensive reconstruction of an imaginary addressee of the official ideology. Besides an absorbing self-image provided by the New Age there is a self-propelling refusal of antagonistic Subject to any place in a symbolical universe in the centre of an ideological node. Although there is nothing new in the idea that authorities always hide and mask contradictions, it is worth knowing that public discourse alone is not the only centre of gravity and there are other "scenes" where an ideological activity of cleaning up takes place. A suppression of political opposition by the State is not the only outcome of such activity, but rather a supplementary one, because in the opposition, the authorities always confront a certain perceived either as integral or as multiple other, while the main aim is the confrontation, i.e., antagonism itself. Whether it is or is not symbolically neutralised, antagonism disintegrates as a self-image, which makes it incommunicable. That is why a "revolutionary," antagonistic Subject exorcised by official ideology happens to be rejected at the everyday level and in private life too. However, there is one symbolical level more between the pure Lacanian barred Subject $\$$ and the level of a rejected "revolutionary" Subject, that is a level of denied (symbolical) interpellation.

While the New Age vision of an authentic spirituality and religiosity beyond institutionalised forms provides Kazakhstanis with an imaginary scenario of the "true" Self, what is unnoticed by the majority "Religious Turn" represents the impasse of that imaginary construction. In general in the "Religious Turn" we deal with a hysterical image of the Subject due to forced suppression putting it in the place of the object-cause of desire: a spirituality/religiosity beyond symbolical determinations, an excessive exhibition of the figure of the President ("the Leader of the Nation") and the narcissistic nationalism point on the permanent anxiety and despair.

Ingratiation besides Flattery

The public space and discourse in Kazakhstan are affected by authoritarian rule and are reduced in terms of freedom. The common discourse is especially flattering in terms of the President. It reminds us of what Hegel called "the heroism of flattery" regarding monarchy. In the short section on *flattery* in his famous "Phenomenology of Spirit" he wrote:

> It is the point of the self into which the many points or selves through renouncing their own inner certainty, are fused into one. Since, however, this Spirit proper of state power consists in its obtaining actuality and nourishment from the sacrifice of action and thought by the noble consciousness, it is an independence that is self-alienated ...[11]

So, the public discourse in Kazakhstan is organised as flattery.

In short, this organisation means that individuals have to look for their self-realisation as socially recognised subjects via, by definition, this outer and insincere form, regardless of what they really think and do.

From a structural point of view, that flattery can be regarded as a reply to the President's *Messages*, which provide it an agenda. However, a position of identification in symbolical order, i.e., a position from which a subject of flattery is seen and constituted, does not seem to be necessarily provided by *Messages* as a reflection of a message is presumed, but flattery is an expression of excess. So, from which point of view can flattery be an attractive option? It would be perhaps so if Kazakhstan was a monarchical system.

One should not forget that contemporary authoritarianism exists in the context of its well-articulated criticism. So, a flattery is not only a gesture addressed to authority as the ultimate Other, but to some "outer" more powerful Other. It says: "Look at what I have to say and to do though I realise it's silly." Here acts the well-known denial mode in postmodern culture among those who study a rejection of one's interpellation, i.e., of a symbolical mandate in a society. But, let us look closer at what is happening here in terms of the Hegelian evolution of the political Subject. Actually "the heroism of flattery," this "extraverted" form for Hegel is a more advanced stage of subjectivity than the "noble consciousness" with its moral dignity, because it is a step away from an illusion of mysterious inner truth and substantiality of a Self. Flattery presumes discourse and symbolical universe as the Self's substance. Hence, paradoxically, the context of liberal criticism pushes an authoritarian subject to a less advanced stage condemning this subject to perpetual fluctuation between the two poles.

It was mentioned above that besides the politics of the head of the State there is arguably another subject of flattery, religious beliefs but not religions as such! It is almost impossible to overlook that New Age offers the same dialectic of inner truth and outer hypocrisy. That is why every precedent of implementation of New Age values in education or other social institutions has a character of ideological propaganda. Unsurprisingly, the first topic in the mentioned school textbook on "Self-Knowledge" is concerned with the individual "inner world."

Nazarbayev's rhetoric rich in New Age figures sounds as a promise of a happy solution in a deadlock of discredited ideologies. It performs as a sober, wise and reflective attitude to the mainstream: there is neither ruthless fight against the now defunct Marxism, nor naive enthusiasm about capitalism and democracy. So, the New Age way of expression provides, first of all, a safe distance from common positions in ideological space, an illusion of being an outsider. It also helps one to avoid identifying oneself in common language in the post-modern times. The same is true on the individual level of attitude towards religion.

One of the outcomes of such symbolic universe is that critical attitudes along with honesty and scholarship turn to a private idiosyncratic marginality. Sometimes one can hear intelligent people with a Soviet background comparing themselves with ignorant but ideologically cultivated youth and saying: *I am ashamed to know it!*, meaning an awareness of facts or possession of literary abilities. This is a shame, a frustration of lacking abilities, of being depreciated due to having higher intellectual and moral attitudes. Actually, such feelings are not what make current conditions different from the Soviet past, when one could not be simultaneously intelligent and honest, so the grounds for hysteria remain. Today the public discourse interpolates a flatterer, official ideology challenges a "barred" revolutionist and popular culture promotes cynical distancing from symbolical mandates.

Notes

1. Nursultan Nazarbayev, *V serdtse Yevrazii* (In the Heart of Eurasia) Almaty, Astana: "Zhybek Zholy," 2010.
2. It must be noticed, though, that the title "New Age" is still not well known among Kazakhstanians and almost no New Age phenomena are identified as such (as pertaining to New Age).
3. Based on the catalogues of the two biggest bookstores in Kazakhstan.
4. The Annual Report of the US Commission on International Religious Freedom. April 2013, 244.
5. Agentstvo Respubliki Kazakhstan po statistike, *Itogi natsionalnoy perepisi naseleniya 2009 goda* (The Agency for Statistic of the Republic of Kazakhstan, *National Census 2009 Results*) http://www.stat.kz/news/Pages/n2_12_11_10.aspx
6. Norwegian Helsinki Committee, *Report: Broken Promises: Freedom of Religion or Belief Issues in Kazakhstan and Kyrgyzstan*, 1: 2010 http://www.nhc.no/filestore/Publikasjoner/Rapporter/2010/Report_1_2010.pdf
7. Nursultan Nazarbayev, *Strategiya "Kazakhstan 2050"* (Strategy "Kazakhstan 2050"), 2012 // http://www.stat.kz/Pages/poslanya_2013.aspx
8. Nursultan Nazarbayev, *Strategiya "Kazakhstan 2050"* (Strategy "Kazakhstan 2050"), 2012 // http://www.stat.kz/Pages/poslanya_2013.aspx (My translation, AZ)
9. Altaynews, "Kayrat Lama Sharif: o religii i otvetstvennosti" ("Kayrat Lama Sharif: On Religion and Responsibility") http://altaynews.kz/9515-kayrat-lama-sharif.html, August 24,2012
10. Zayavleniye po povodu informatsii v brifinge predsedatelya Agentstva RK po delam religiy Kayrat Lama Sharif (Statement on account of the Information in the Briefing of the Chair of The Agency for Religious Affairs of the Republic of Kazakhstan Kayrat Lama Sharif) by the deputy director of the department for public relations of

"The Centre for administration of Dianetics and Scientology propagation agency" Yuriy Ivanovich Maksimov http://www.religiopolis.org/publications/6281-otvetit-za-sharifa.html

11. Hegel, *Phenomenology of Spirit*, 1977, p. 311.

11. The Silk Route in Mustafo Bafoev's Imagination

Diloram Karomat

The Great Silk Route or Caravan Route[1] which played an important role in economic and cultural development among people of the East and West was an immense source of inspiration for Mustafo Bafoev, the Uzbek composer who was optimistic about cultural dialogue among the regions. As a good musician-performer who learnt music first of all as a traditional musician and played on the *ghidjak,* he has a deep feeling for the musical tradition of neighbouring countries and shows amazing intonations, which characterise a particular country. His musical caravan, representing the journey of music, passed through medieval China, Tibet, India, Turkey, Iran and the Arab countries. The national musical instruments like Jew Harp (*Chang-qobuz*), Flute (*Nai*), Lute (*Ud*), a type of large Zither (*Qanun*) became the symbols of his caravan. The three Great persons Alexander Great,[2] Prophet Muhammad[3] and Amir Timur[4] became symbols of unity and promotion of development along the Caravan route. Mustafo Bafoev's grandiose composition *Buyuk Ipak Yo'li* (The Great Silk Route) was composed in 1996.[5] It was staged in Abror Hidoyatov's theatre[6] in 1997 and the same year was shown in the First Festival of *Sharq Taronalari.*[7] Mustafo Bafoev's music has challenged the compositions of the stage director, B. Yuldashev and artist, G. Brim, whose compositions about the medieval world are shown through fine arts, dance and special effects of light. Exotic shows indicate the technical possibilities of the modern stage in representing the rich heritage of traditional culture. This article seeks to analyse the music of Mustafo Bafoev's *Buyuk Ipak Yo'li* through the lens of geography, globalised space and symbolism in the composer's imagination.

Mustafo Bafoev and the Silk Route

Prof. Mustafo Bafoev[8] belonged to the middle generation of the composers of Uzbekistan. He was born in 1946 in a small village Ganchkash near Bukhara and belongs to a simple family. In private conversation he joked that his grandfather had only *arba* and horse. He began his musical career at the age of fourteen. First of all he learnt music as *ghidjak* player in Bukhara. After that as a *narodnik* (musician of national musical instruments) he studied at Tashkent Conservatory. In 1979, he was awarded a diploma as master of composition when he was 33 years old in the class of Boris Giyenko.[9] Nowadays he is considered to be a talented composer and master of different genres, including opera,[10] ballet,[11] musical drama,[12] symphony,[13] and oratory,[14] vocal[15] and instrumental composition,[16] etc. His works represent a unique fusion of the very best of the European and Asian musical traditions. He has given particular attention to melody, by following the traditions of a thousand years old national art music (*maqamat*).[17]

He has several musical compositions dedicated to the Silk Route, e.g., *Buyuk Ipak Yo'li* (1996), *Silk Road in my imagination* (2000)—for chamber orchestra and *Shyolkoviy piut* (2007)—which is an ensemble of ten piano compositions. These compositions were released when the UNESCO initiative of the Silk Route was launched in 1988.[18] It is well known that UNESCO organised a wide range of activities in close cooperation with a number of prestigious international partners. All projects are aimed "to enhance our understanding of the dynamic cultural interaction that brought together diverse identities and heritage of the people."[19] As a result, the Silk Route projects facilitate dialogue and exchange among officials and scholars, educators, tourism professionals, students and youth as well as among artists, composers and musicians. Within these projects several of Mustafo Bafoev's compositions have been compiled in compact discs (CDs). For example, one of them is the Silk Road Project Workshop Readings of the concert in Tanglewood (2000),[20] where *Bukhara concert*[21] was staged (as cello and six national musical instruments) and *The Silk Route in my imagination* by the famous Silk Road chamber orchestra of acclaimed cellist Yo-Yo Ma.[22] Mustafo Bafoev has remembered Tanglewood as a place where came together talented Central Asian composers, and in an informal creative atmosphere were realised many interesting ideas. From several sources we learn that The Silk Road Ensemble (Silk Road Project Inc.) initiated by Yo-Yo Ma in 1998, has been characterised as "arts and educational organisation that connects musicians, composers, artists and audiences around the world" and "an initiative to promote multicultural artistic collaboration."[23] Remembering the Tanglewood performance, Mustafo Bafoev recalls the well-known American ethnomusicologist Theodore Levin.[24] Levin asked him to create composition-imitation of Sufi *Zikr.* Levin knew Bafoev's Bukhara background and his personal experience of the *Zikr.* Like Bafoev, in the middle of the 1970s he was an intern in Tashkent State Conservatory. In one night the composition *Al-Haq* was created[25] which was performed without any instrumental accompaniment and with the help of Alisher Latif-zade[26] and other young composers from Central Asia. This example testifies to the fact that the compositions of Mustafo Bafoev originate from Tajik-Uzbek art music and personify the cultural identity, heritage and thousand years' historical legacy of Bukhara.

Bukhara and Samarkand, the important cities of Silk Route, not only preserved memories of Caravan Route and restored former Caravanserais for tourist gatherings today, but also have immense value for their contribution in the field of historical study.[27] Bafoev is one of those composers who have a great interest in the history of the region. The conception of *Haft Iqlim* (Seven Climates), which was spread across medieval times in Persian and Turkic manuscripts, exists in Mustafo Bafoev's grandiose composition *Buyuk Ipak Yo'li.* This conception symbolised the vast area, regions and countries and every "kingdom of the earth" that had its own peculiarities in the eyes of human beings. But most significant is the mystery of the Universe.

Buyuk Ipak Yo'li

The ballet-show *Buyuk Ipak Yo'li*[28] consists of 16 episodes (musical suites).[29] The blurred sounds are lifting the veil of the ballet-show. The Triton interval[30] is given to drop-down musical sounds which have a mystical effect. The *first episode* is named "Mysteries of the Space" (*Tainy kosmosa*), which are dedicated to Space, Caravan and Great personalities. The mysteries start with the tune (leitmotif) of space, which is mainly characterised by beautiful sounds of bells. The drop-down melody of stars symbolises the Holy Light and Spiritual knowledge, which are coming down from the Heavens. According to legend, Alexander the Great, Prophet Muhammad and Amir Timur were born under one Star and they were aimed for greatness. All of them have musical image (leitmotif) in Bafoev's composition and these tunes (first time has been given in first episode) have come forward at particular places (Alexander the Great in Central Asia and India, Prophet Muhammad in Arab countries and Turkey, Amir Timur in almost all countries). The leitmotif of Prophet Muhammad is very calm and beautiful. It starts as a distant note and then bit by bit it seems that the entire universe is refilled with the enigma of Prophet Muhammad. Unlike him, the musical leitmotifs of Alexander and Timur, who conquered large territory by force, are full of thunderstorms (the piano being the solo instrument). In the leitmotif of Amir Timur, which comes after the tune of The Prophet, the composer has used the traditional rhythm and intonations of *Gardun*,[31] related to cycle *Shashmaqom*.[32] The melodies of great personalities are mixed with the themes of the Universe and stars and this brings the listeners to the next episode named "Caravan."

"Caravan" (Episode Two) is much smaller than the first one and shows the merchants on horseback and travellers, who swing from one side to another as they move with the caravan. The tune of Caravan plays a great role in the ballet-show as a main tune, which brings together all parts of the composition. Moreover, the composer uses this tune as a keeper of the main intonations on the one hand, but from the other side it changes as the location changes—i.e., from one country to another (which also transfers the listener from one country to another) with the help of musical instruments which are common for the particular country and region. In Mustafo Bafoev's imagination, musical Caravan starts its journey from *Turan* (Transoxiania) and then comes to China. The audience finds itself in the *Third Episode,* which is named "In Emperor's garden" (*V imperatorskom sadu*). The composer has used the pentatonic scale[33] and musical elements (rhythm and intonations) which are very much common to China. The music has helped to draw the image of the Emperor's Palace, which is full of intrigue. The poisoning of a victim in the Emperor's garden occurs as the final effect of the plot. The nervous sound of the flute has mixed with the tune of the Caravan, which is performed on Jew Harp (*Chang-qobuz*) and Bells.

Caravan (Episode Four) is enriched with new intonations and brings us to another locale, i.e., India.[34] The drop-down musical sounds, which are commonly used by musicians who play on Indian musical instrument *Sitar*,[35] has an effect of coming down from the Himalayas. The suite (Episode Five), which is named "The dream of the holy cow" (*Son sviashchennoy korovy*) shows the rich inner and outside world of medieval India by using the musical intonations, rhythm and modes of Indian music. If inner philosophical world and the beauty of the land are shown mainly with the help of the *sitar*, then the brisk trades in *bazaars* are displayed through electronic sounds in musical instruments. The tune of the *bazaar* is mixed with the tune of the Caravan. The philosophical monologues and trade in *bazaars* are shortly interrupted by the leitmotif (on piano) of Alexander the Great, who many centuries ago came to India. The listeners again are dipped and dissolved in an atmosphere of *bazaars*, philosophy and nature. The Caravan is further enriched by Indian tunes (the musical instruments being the *Sitar*, *Chang-qobuz*, Flute and electro-orchestra) and bring us to Tibet. In Bafoev's imagination Caravan is not only a trader's caravan, but also a symbol of cultural and spiritual exchanges between countries.

One of the secret places of Asia, i.e., Tibet (Episode Seven) is named by the composer "The Temple of Thousand Bells" (*Khram tysiachi kolokol'chikov*). The episode is filled with meditation, sacred knowledge and philosophy of the Lamas. It has been suggested that the origins of the famous emblem (three circles inside a big circle) on the *tamga*[36] of Amir Timur is associated with the journey to Tibet. In a private conversation Bafoev explains his feelings for Tibet and its temple of a thousand bells, where people who fall ill are treated by using the sound of the bells. So, the musical pattern of the episode is mainly based on the sound of bells, pentatonic scale. The tune of Caravan is mixed very carefully in this composition. An important role is given to mystical leitmotif of Stars from Episode One, as a symbol of spirituality and the holy kingdom Shambhala.[37]

Caravan (Episode Eight) leads us further—this time to Turkey. We are entering West Asia and the patterns of Islamic culture become visible. Musical instruments *Ud* and *Qanun* become the leaders in performing the melodies. The calm leitmotif of Prophet Muhammad is used by the composer as a main tune, which characterises the region.

Turkey (Episode Nine) is a meeting point of travellers and with grand buildings (the episode is named *Aya Sophia*[38]), the Black Sea and flying seagulls. Bafoev has used a few musical citations in this episode: modern Turkish tune, recitation of *Azan* and the famous *Ave Maria* (Bach-Gounod).[39] Besides that, similar to previous episodes, the composer has used the musical modes and rhythm which are common to Turkish music. *Azan* in Turkish cities is often mentioned by travellers[40] as one of the mystical moments in their lives. In the beginning, reciting of *Azan* is given by the composer in total silence; gradually various musical instruments have been included. Then, the sound of the *Azan* is mixed with tunes of Stars (Triton), Prophet Muhammad and Amir Timur. The last two leitmotifs appear in this episode several times, even mix with each other and probably indicate the historical conquest of regions of Turkey by Amir Timur (he invaded Anatolia) under the legacy of Islam. He was often praised by European rulers,[41] because they believed that his victory at Ankara allowed Christian merchants to remain in the Middle East, allowed for their safe return home and also helped to restore the right of passage for Christian pilgrims to the Holy Land. In this context the citation of *Ave Maria* by the composer, as a symbol of Christianity and tolerance, is very important. In Bafoev's imagination Turkey is a country which is historically a place of Christianity and Islam. It is well-known that one of the greatest surviving examples of Byzantine architecture, the legendary *Aya (Hagia) Sophia*, has served as an Eastern Orthodox cathedral (dedicated to the *Wisdom of God* [the Logos], the second person of the Holy Trinity) and later as Imperial Mosque. The Black sea as a witness of historical changes and symbol of eternity is framed as "episode."

Caravan (Episode Ten) leads us further into Iran. This *Episode* is based on earlier Turkish melody and performed on piano and *Ud*. Episode

Eleven is about Iran and contains two parts: "Fire spell" (*Zaklinaniye ognia*) and "Dedication to Hafez" (*Posviashcheniye Khafizu*).[42] The melody performed on Flute and leitmotif of Timur are given at the outset in this episode. The ancient and early medieval Iran first of all is associated with Zoroastrianism[43] and fire worship. "Fire spell" is a very rhythmic music, which shows the "dance" of fire and fighting of two polar deities *Ahura Mazda* (Illuminating Wisdom) and *Ahriman* (Angra Mainyu as Destructive Principle/Spirit) in the dualistic doctrine of Zoroastrianism. Unlike the first part, "Dedication to Hafez" is very calm and performed on the piano. The composer has used musical tunes, which are very close to folk songs. Many legends and mythical tales were woven around Hafez's name. One of the most famous legends is connected with following verses:

> If that Shirazi Turk would take my heart in hand, I would remit Samarkand and Bukhara for his/her mole.[44]

Amir Timur was furious that some poet so easily would remit his capital Samarkand and one of the finest cities of his kingdom—Bukhara —for mole. So, when Timur captured Shiraz he met Hafez, who looked very poor. It is suggested that before taking a final decision, Timur always listened to his companion. In the case of Hafez he got a repartee from poet and released him with goodies.[45]

Caravan (Episode Twelve) moves into Maghreb. The musical instrument *Qanun* has a beautiful melody. Leitmotif of Timur sounded short and disappeared gradually. Our musical Caravan was "coloured" by the calm leitmotif of Prophet Muhammad. Besides the leitmotifs of Prophet Muhammad and Timur, the composer has used in this episode two musical citations: Arabic melody (rhythm 7/8) and Johann Sebastian Bach's first prelude from the Well-Tempered Clavier (which was the base for *Ave Maria* given in Turkey). The citations came separately first and later mixed with each other (composer's imagination is "East and West are met").

Caravan (Episode Fourteen) focuses on Maghreb where Christianity and Islam met together and moved back to Turan. The Stars (leitmotif of Stars is played by Flute) sanctify the Caravan road and drop-down melody on *Qanun* symbolises the homecoming of travellers. Caravan has come closer to Turan and leitmotif (image) of Amir Timur has become stronger.

Episode Fifteen is "Saga about Amir Timur" (*Skazaniye ob Amire Timure*) is filled with local traditional rhythm and image of the *bakhshi* (storyteller), war and battle, etc. National musical instruments *Karnay*[46] and *Naghora*,[47] both are commonly used in the field of war and during pompous meetings and symbolise legacy of power and kingship. Thus, the image of the *bakhshi* and sounds of his musical instrument *dombra* (stringed musical instrument), *karnay* and *naghora* are created in the musical compositions of the composer. Leitmotif of Prophet Muhammad performed by musical instrument *Ud* and leitmotif of Stars (space) indicate the destination of Amir Timur. Amir Timur's legacy was a mixed one, but his military talents were unique. Amir Timur is given a dual image by the composer—he is both kind and cruel. The piano is the main instrument through which the composer has characterised Amir Timur and his inner world. Amir Timur has played a great role for the prosperity of *Mavera-un-Nahr* (Transoxiania). His outstanding contribution in the governance of the state, its education and culture and general development of his state are reflected in the compositions of Bafoev. The grand celebrations dedicated to Amir Timur take place in independent Uzbekistan, where he is officially recognised as the icon of performing arts. The ballet-show *Buyuk Ipak Yo'li* was staged at the time of the celebration of 660 years of Amir Timur. Thus the last episode, i.e., Episode Sixteen is named "The Grand Celebration" (*Prazdnovaniye*). This is a very pompous musical episode, where the composer has used local traditional music *Gardun* and *Tasnif*[48] from *maqam* (mode) *Buzruk*.[49] With the help of music and musical instruments like *Karnay* and *Naghora* the composer has presented the grandiose picture of mass street celebrations with *Masharaboz* (the local term for comic actor).

Conclusion

The *Buyuk Ipak Yo'li* is a grandiose composition which is based on improvisation and the composer's imagination. This ballet show has several symbols. The musical Caravan passes through seven countries, beginning with China and moves on to India, Tibet, Turkey, Iran, Maghreb and Turan. Very significantly, Bafoev has selected countries and their symbols: Tibet—"Temple of Thousands Bells," India—"The Dream of the Holy Cow," Turkey— "*Aya Sofiya*" and so on. This symbolic number *seven* is very popular among all countries. We have already referred to the conception of *Haft Iqlim* (*Seven Climates*). The number *three* is also symbolic in Bafoev's composition. There are three Great personalities—Alexander the Great, Prophet Muhammad and Amir Timur. There are three sounds in leitmotif of Space-Stars. Here one can mention the symbol of peace in *Tamga* of Amir Timur—where the three circles-in-one and the words "The power in Truth" symbolise the past, present and future—i.e., in Eternity.[50] Amir Timur relied on Islamic symbols and language, referring to himself as the *Sword of Islam.* The *Ave Maria* by Bach/Gounod and prelude by Bach are presented as symbols of Christianity in the composer's imagination. The Great personalities also had inter-regional exchanges and contacts as well as trade between East and West. But the main hero of the ballet show is Amir Timur. Under his time the Silk Road began to pass through *Mavera-un-Nahr* and became very popular too. His legacy spread across time and space—as he built the *caravanserais* all along the Silk Road. The Turan became a place where a great amalgamation of different traditions, especially art and craft, took place.

The music of the *Buyuk Ipak Yo'li* is amazingly well suited to stage performance, with special effects, and at the same time it is very popular. Traditional musical instruments, which were used by composers for every country, are loved by the audience in general. Bafoev has used the intonations, modes and musical instruments which are characteristic of every chosen country. Thus, he showed how the changing of geographical and cultural zones influenced the change of musical instruments. It is necessary to note, that a few decades before, listening to the traditional music of neighbouring countries was very difficult. But in the modern age of globalisation learning the musical culture of Eastern countries has become very simple. Contemporary musical critics have observed the contributions of Mustafo Bafoev as a unique specimen. His brilliant understanding of orchestration and familiarity with different musical styles has given him a special place in the contemporary music scenario.

Notes

1. Also famous as Sutra-Dharmaratna route. Prominent archaeologist from Uzbekistan, E. Rtveladze recently has published *Velikiy Indiyskiy Put,* a monograph dedicated to Great Indian way, which was (as author argued) much older tread way which connected Asia with Europe.
2. Alexander III the Great (356 BC-323 BC) the king of Macedonia and conqueror of the Persian Empire is considered one of the greatest military geniuses of all times. His campaigns greatly increased contacts and trade between East and West, and vast areas to the east were significantly exposed to Greek civilisation and influence. Alexander the Great's accomplishments and legacy have been depicted in many cultures. Alexander has figured in both high and popular culture beginning in his own era to the present day. Firdausi's *Shahnamah* ("The Book of Kings") includes Alexander in a line of legitimate Iranian shahs, a mythical figure who explored the far reaches of the world in search of the Fountain of Youth.
3. Prophet Muhammad (570-632) is a man from Mecca, a messenger and prophet of God, who unified Arabia into a single religious polity under Islam.
4. Tamerlane (Amir Timur, Temur the Great) (1336-1405) was a Turko-Mongol ruler of Barlas. He conquered West, South and Central Asia and founded the Timurid dynasty with the centre in Samarkand. More information at http://www.orexca.com/p_tamerlane.shtml
5. Ballet show *Buyuk Ipak yo'li* was also performed in Marigny Theatre (Paris, 1997), First *Sharq Taronalari* Festival (Samarkand, Registan, 1997), Theatre named after Hamid Olimdjon (Samarkand, 1998).
6. Uzbek Drama Theatre named after Abror Hidoyatov (*Abror Hidoyatov nomidagi o`zbek davlat drama teatri*) was founded on October 26, 1968. It is named after one of the talented actors of Uzbekistan, Abror Hidoyatov (1900-1958).
7. The international music festival *Sharq Taronalari* has been held since 1997 on the initiative of the President of the Republic of Uzbekistan, Islam Karimov, and under the patronage of UNESCO. *Sharq Taronalari* takes place every two years and includes a contest of traditional music performers from different countries, and a scientific and practical conference with musicologists, composers and performers. More information at http://en.sharqtaronalari.uz/
8. He trained at the Tashkent Conservatory as a performer in Uzbek instruments during 1964-1969 and as a composer and has completed a post-graduate course under Boris Giyenko's guidance. He has taught at Bukhara Pedagogical Institute during 1969-1972, has conducted the Uzbek national (reconstructed) instruments orchestra

for the Uzbek TV and Radio company (1980-86) and in 1986 was appointed artistic director of this orchestra. His works have a broad appeal and are heard in festivals and competitions as well as local celebrations; they are rooted in Uzbek folk traditions. Bafoev has received numerous awards, including the Abdul Qadiri State Premium (1997) and the title of Meritorious Worker of Arts of Uzbekistan (1995).

9. Boris Fedorovich Giyenko (b. 1917 Ordjenikidze, Osetiya-d. 2000 Tashkent, Uzbekistan) is a composer, professor/lecturer and teacher in Uzbekistan. Since 1935 he has stayed in Tashkent. He became one of the first students of Tashkent Conservatory in the year 1936 when it was founded. Since 1938 he has started teaching. He is the author of songs, romances, symphonies, music for stage performances, etc. He has received several awards like *Zaslujenniy deyatel iskusstv* (1968), medals like *Trudovogo krasnogo Zanmeni, Znak pochyota, Za trudovoye otlihiye*, etc.
10. Opera: *Umar Khayyam* (libretto by O. Uzakov, 1994), TV-opera *Bukhoro-i Sharif* (1998, new edition 2012), opera-extravaganza *Lison-ut-Tayr* (based on Alisher Navai's poem, 2000), *Al-Farghoni* (libr. by Dj. Djabbarov, 1998), opera-ballet *Sevgim samosi* (libr. by Dj. Djabbarov, 2008), *Shaykh-ur-Rais ibni Sino* (libr. by K. Olimov, 2011, was staged at Dushanbe's opera and ballet theatre named after S. Ayni, Tajikistan), *Borbad* (libr. by N. Qosim, 2013, Dushanbe, Tajikistan).
11. Ballet: TV-ballet *Nodira* (1992), TV-ballet *Ulughbek burji* (1994), TV-ballet *Moziydan nur* (1995), *Buyuk Ipak Yo'li* (1996), oratory-ballet *Zardushtiylar marosimi*, Choreographic miniature *Zvezda al-Khorazmi* (1982), concert-ballet for symphonic orchestra *Khoja Nasriddin va Karmensita Bukhoroda* (2002), etc.
12. Music for stage performance/musical drama: *Yettinchi jin* (I. Babkhanov, 1983), *Uzilgan torlar* (K. Amirov, 1984), comedy *Zo'ldir* (A. Ibrohimov, 1985), *Raja* (Rabindranath Tagore, 1987), *Prometey* (Yu. Martcinkyavichus, 1987), *Toshkentda tuman* (I. To'xtaev, 1988), *Faridun* (A. Firdousi, 1992), *Yorqinoy* (Cho'lpon, 1993), *Sevgi Nidosi* (F. Djoraev, 1994), *Cho'lpon* (T. Nizom, 1997), *Pari qishloq afsonasi* (Gh. Shermuhammedov, 2005), *To'maris* (Kh. Khursandov, 2011), etc.
13. Symphonies and symphonic poems: Symphony no. 1 *Ghazal* (1979), Symphony no. 2 *Ibn Sino* (1986), Symphony no. 3 *Hamza* (1987), Symphony no. 4 *Movarounnahr* (1991), Symphony no. 5 *Holot-i Alisher Navoi* (1991), symphonic poem *Yil fasllari (Bahor, yoz, kuz, qish), Soghd Lavhalari* (2009, *Sogdiana,* RAUM KLANG LC 5068 RK 9505 GEMA compact disc, Made in Germany), symphonic poem *Shiroq dostoni* (1974), etc.
14. Oratory: *Roksananing ko'z yoshlari* (1987), *Hajnoma* (1995), *Zafarnoma,* oratory-ballet *Zardushtiylar marosimi* (1999), *etc.*
15. Vocal compositions: *Hazrat Bahouddin Naqshbandga madhiya,* poem-cantata *Alloma* (1984), poem *Otzvuki makoma* (1986), *Bahoriya* (1987), *Zikr-i al-Haq* (for voice, piano, string and percussion musical instruments, 2000), *Tahsinnoma*

(for soloist, chorus and symphonic orchestra, 2001), *Dedication to Rabindranath Tagore* (for vocal, piano and Uzbek national musical instruments, 2007), Poem *Samarqandnoma* (for vocal soloist and group, 2007), etc.; author of several hundred songs and romances.

16. *Silk Route in my imagination* (2000, for chamber orchestra), *Samo' ohanglari* (2006, for percussion instruments), *Fantasy* for piano (2006), *Ashrohub* (2013), etc.; Instrumental compositions for orchestra of national (folk) musical instruments: *Poem* for *Qashghar rubab* and orchestra, Concert, Concert-poem for *Dutar* and orchestra, *Poem* for Ud and orchestra, *Bukhorcha concert* (2000), *Sayqal* (2005), *Abadiyot* (2007), etc.
17. *Maqamat* is a plural from *Maqam*. Term *Maqam* (ماقم from Arabic: place, staying) means a musical mode, musical tone, the separate place for tone on musical instrument, a musical composition. *Maqam* phenomenon is widely cultivated in a vast area stretching from countries of North Africa (*maqam, nuba*), the near East (in Turkey called *makam*, in Azerbaijan *mugam*, in Iran *dastgah*) to Central Asia (in Uzbekistan and Tajikistan—*Shashmaqom*, in Western China—*mukam*, in Kashmir—*makam* or *Sufiyana Kalam*).
18. Regional and local communities from more than 55 countries are involved in this collective endeavour. To learn more, see UNESCO's online initiative, the Silk Road online platform at http://en.unesco.org/silkroad/
19. Reviving the Historic Silk Roads: UNESCO's new Online Platform at http://www.unesco.org/new/en/culture/themes/dialogue/routes-of-dialogue/silk-road/
20. Tanglewood is a music venue in Lenox and Stockbridge, Massachusetts. Besides classical music, Tanglewood hosts the Festival of Contemporary Music, Jazz Festival of popular artists, concerts, etc. More information at http://en.wikipedia.org/wiki/Tanglewood
21. The Silk Road Project Workshop Reading—Part I (CD 1 of 2) 5:00 p.m., Saturday, July 8, 2000, Chamber Music Hall, Tanglewood-Lenox, MA; Mustafah Bafoev. (Uzbekistan) "Bukhara concert" (19:09).
22. The *Silk Road Ensemble* is a musical collective. The ensemble is not a fixed group of musicians, but rather a loose collective of as many as 59 musicians, composers, arrangers, visual artists and storytellers. The Silk Road Ensemble, founded in 1998 by cellist Yo-Yo Ma, is a loose collective of musicians from around the world. The Silk Road Ensemble has recorded five albums and performed to critical acclaim throughout Asia, Europe, and North America.
23. See at http://en.wikipedia.org/wiki/Silk_Road_Project#cite_note-1 (last modified on February 12, 2014).
24. Theodore Craig Levin is an American ethnomusicologist and is the author of *The Hundred Thousand Fools of God. The Musical Travels in Central Asia,* Bloomington: Indiana University Press, 1999.

25. Later on it was formed composition *Al-Haq,* which was performed in festival "Ilxom-20" at Tashkent in 2001.
26. Alisher Djuraevich Latif-zade (b. June 2, 1962, Dushanbe) is a Tajik composer. Since 2004 is a citizen of USA. Source: ru.wikipedia.org/ wiki/Латиф-Заде._Алишер#cite_note-1
27. The Centre of Silk Road studies in Samarkand and organising the conferences and publications.
28. The ballet show was performed by: Adiba Sharipova (piano), Murod Fayziev (flute), Komil Shermatov (qonun), Rustam Karimov (ud), Nasridiin Roziev (chang-qobuz), Alisher Ikramov (sintezator-orchestra), producer of the sound Nabi Hasanov (Radio committee of Uzbekistan).
29. The musical analysis of ballet show is not the subject of this article.
30. Tritone is a musical term, an interval, which requires you to place two notes six half-steps apart, which means an augmented fourth, for example, sounds F-B.
31. *Gardun* is a musical term related to musical form in the instrumental part of *Shashmaqom.*
32. *Shashmaqom* means in Persian and Tajik languages "six *maqams.*" These six modes are *Rost, Buzruk, Navo, Dugoh, Segoh* and *Iraq.* The *maqam* cycles are each divided into two main sections: instrumental (*mushkilot*, from Arabic "difficulties"; in Khorezm named *chertim yoli*) and vocal (*Nasr*, Persian "prose"; in Khwarezm named *aytim yoli*).
33. A Pentatonic scale is a musical scale or mode with five notes per octave. This scale is very common. The major pentatonic scale is the basic scale of the music of China and Mongolia.
34. The interrelations between Indian and Central Asian music go back to ancient times. In the twentieth century the composers of Uzbekistan realised the Image of India in different musical genres, such as music for stage performances (musical dramas, etc.), ballet, cantata, chamber instrumental music, romances, songs and music for films. Mustafo Bafoev has written about the music of the stage performance of Tagore's *Raja* which was composed in 1986-87. Later on, on the request of the pianist Adiba Sharipova, he composed "Dedication to Tagore."
35. At the time of composing this episode the composer has in his mind Uzbek musicians Ilyas Mallaev, who can play on Sitar and this instrument was presented to him by famous Indian actor Raj Kapoor.
36. *Tamga* or *Tamgha* is an abstract seal or stamp used by Turkic and some other nations of Eurasia. As a rule it was the emblem of a particular tribe, clan or family and the air of a certain clan is kept it or changed according to his test.
37. Shambhala is a mythological and secret place in Inner Asia, according to Tibetan Buddhist and Hindu-Buddhist traditions. This place was mentioned in various ancient texts, such as *Kalachakra Tantra*, *Zhang Zhung*, *Vishnu Purana*, etc. In

modern times often mentioned by Theosophical Society and particularly by Nicholas and Helena Roerich.

38. Hagia Sophia is one of the important historical buildings of Istanbul. It was: Roman Catholic Cathedral (1204-1261), Eastern Orthodox Cathedral (1261-1453), Imperial Mosque (1453-1931), and Museum (1935 to the present).
39. The *Ave Maria* (Latin) is traditional Christian prayer asking for the intercession of the Virgin Mary. Ave Maria in Latin has been set to music by several composers. M. Bafoev has used one of the most famous settings, the version by Charles Gounod (1859), who added melody and words to Johann Sebastian Bach's first prelude from the Well-Tempered Clavier.
40. Maualana Abul Kalam Azad has mentioned it in *Ghubar-i Khatir.*
41. Charles VI of France and Henry IV of England believed that Amir Timur has saved Christianity from the Turkish Empire in the Middle East.
42. A Persian poet Khwaja Shams-ud-Din Muhammad Hafez-i Shirazi (b.1325/1326–d.1389/1390) is well-known by his pen-name Hafez. He is one of the most popular Persian poets in Iran, Afghanistan, Pakistan, Central Asia and India.
43. Zoroastrianism is an ancient Iranian religion and a religious philosophy which was followed by inhabitants of the vast territory. It was once the state religion of the Achaemenid, Parthian and Sasanian empires. The religious philosopher Zoroaster's ideas led to a formal religion bearing his name, and they have influenced other later religions.
44. English translation is given from: en.wikipedia.org/wiki/Hafez
45. The legend has been mentioned in several historical and literary sources. One of them is *Tamburlaine: Shadow of God*, a BBC Radio 3 play by John Fletcher, broadcast 2008, it is a fictitious account of an encounter between Tamburlaine, Ibn Khaldun, and Hafez.
46. The Karnay is a long trumpet with a mouthpiece. It is used in the music of Iran, Tajikistan and Uzbekistan.
47. Naghora is a kind of drum. It is used in vast territories of Asia and differs by size and pronunciation.
48. *Tasnif* is a musical term related to musical form of the Instrumental section of *Shashmaqom.*
49. *Buzruk* (*Buzurg*) گرزب (Persian, *Buzurg*, Great, large; a saint; name of a note in music), means great, grand *maqam*. Even in *Shashmaqom* the *maqam Buzruk* (local pronunciation) has a lot of instrumental and vocal pieces.
50. This symbol was seen in many religious relics through the ages. Nicolas Roerich has chosen this symbol at the end of the nineteenth century and said that it is "Religion, Knowledge and Art in the circle of Culture."

12. Northern Eurasia in the Era of Climate Change: Rhetoric and Reality of the Northern Sea Route

Sanjay Chaturvedi

> There have been definitive changes in the conditions of access. What has not changed is the predominance of the problems of access. Where the geopolitics of the pre-modern period was more circumscribed by anti-routes, modern geopolitics has been both freed and obsessed by routes. The creation of new avenues of access has not removed or, in some cases, even greatly reduced the strategic dilemmas of the past. (Mahnaz Z. Ispahani, 1989: 227)

> These changes are already opening the way for a new geostrategy that has its roots in the geopolitical thinking of the twentieth century but addresses the changes that are turning the Arctic from an afterthought to a central front in the new geopolitical view of the world. In this new geostrategy, Russia assumes a role as one of the maritime powers of the "Rimland," and the Russian Arctic becomes a new geographical pivot among the great powers. Decades will pass before Russia can fully make the shift from Eurasian heartland to Arctic coastal state, but it is already integrating policies toward this end into the strategies of international security council and federal ministries, and it shows every indication of expecting to seize its future seat among the major maritime states of the world. (Caitlyn L. Antrim, 2010: 16)

It is a truism that Arctic is already "hot" not only due to global warming but also due to its enhanced multifaceted salience on the agendas of state actors (Arctic and non-Arctic), major corporations and international climate diplomacy.[1] The physical-material geographies of what British geographer Halford J. Mackinder had graphically pinpointed, more than a century ago, on the globe as the "Geographical Pivot of History," later designated by him as the "Heartland,"[2] are "leaking," especially in the Russian Arctic spaces. One wonders how this astute observer of "geographic causation in history" would have reacted to the manner in which both the physical and ideational impact of highly dynamic and confused (muddled as well as fused) geographies of climate change are slowly but surely turning the northern-most frozen land-sea margins of a gigantic "natural fortress" into a global centre of geo-economic, geopolitical and ecological attention. While most of the studies eulogising Mackinder's relevance in globalising international geopolitical economy have focused on post-Soviet spaces and societies in Central Asia, some analysts (see the epigraph above) have started talking about the Russian Arctic as the "next geographical pivot."[3]

Climate change in the Circumpolar Arctic—a region warming at a rate almost twice the global average—continues to simultaneously invoke both geo-economic hopes and geopolitical fears among various "Arctic" and "non-Arctic" actors and agencies.[4] Some of the most "exciting" geo-economic scripts that focus the image of retreating Arctic sea ice relate to the opening up of Arctic shipping routes, especially the "Northeast Passage" or the "Northern Sea Route" (cited hereafter as NSR) hugging the long Russian coastline. Against the backdrop of steadily increasing volume of overwhelmingly seaborne global trade, the NSR (extending over *approximately* 4,800 km or 3,000 miles, since the *actual voyage* length will vary depending upon variants such as the route selected, ice conditions and the draft of the transiting vessel) promises to deliver considerable geo-economic dividends to all stakeholders due to significantly reduced geographical distance and shipping costs in comparison to routes elsewhere. On the other hand, injecting fear and cartographic anxieties are various geopolitical narratives related to acquisition and denial of access to Arctic Sea Routes. Who gets what, when, where and how from fast changing, more accessible Arctic shipping routes appear to be the proverbial billion dollar questions with no easy or straightforward answers.

I would like to acknowledge at the outset that, as far as theoretical moorings are concerned, this chapter is inspired by the writings of Mahnaz Z. Ispahani[5] and Matthew Sparke.[6] I draw upon the insights offered by these two scholars for the purposes of examining the geo-economics and the geopolitics of the NSR in the era of climate change. Ispahani has provided a fascinating account of the "political uses of access to the borderlands of Asia" through a critical engagement with the concepts of "routes" and "anti-routes." She shows how a "route is both a geographical and political idea, both an end and a means" and how as "physical facts they [routes] can 'map' history—provide an X-ray of political-geographic changes—as well as move it along."[7] Whereas Matthew Sparke has persuasively questioned the thesis that announces the demise of the logic of geopolitics (space-enclosing) as a discourse in International Relations and the arrival of the logic of geo-economics (space-opening) as the dominant signature of contemporary market-led globalisation. According to Sparke, rather than treating geopolitics and geo-economics as two disconnected sets of reasonings marked by distinct socio-historical epochs, the two should be seen as "entangled and affect-laden relays of ongoing uneven development."[8] The outcome of this entangled relationship between geo-economics and geopolitics is what Sparke describes as a "double vision": a double vision that "repeatedly divides the world into distinct zones—zones of geopolitical conflict on the one side and spaces of geo-economic peace on the other—rather than coming to terms with the global ties between the two."[9] I will be returning to the insights offered by the two scholars at some length in the sections to follow.

My overall argument in this chapter is twofold. First, the Circumpolar Arctic—the most graphic and dramatic physical embodiment today of a rather abstract, incremental climate change[10] is deeply implicated in the "double vision"[11] of neoliberal globalisation, shaped by an entangled relationship between geo-economic narratives of hope and geopolitical scripts of fear. Consequently, there is much more to a more "accessible" Arctic than simply the vision of retreating sea ice cover and the opening of new sea routes. Second, is the NSR; a multidimensional coastal of Northern Eurasia where this "double vision," riding simultaneously on de-territorialising and re-territorialising imperatives of neo-liberal globalisation, is becoming most pronounced. The NSR is intriguingly implicated in a whirlpool of space-liberating and space-closing reasonings!

Mapping "Routes" and "Anti-routes": Some Theoretical Reflections

Even though the specific focus of this chapter is on the NSR, some general discussion on the notion of routes is called for and might offer some valuable insights on the geographical politics of access. It is useful to be reminded at the outset that the "written" geographies of various routes—both on land and at sea—are as significant and compelling as the "given" geographies. Equally important is to note that there is not one but several sites where the "strategic value" of various routes are being assessed and canvassed by various actors and agencies (both state and non-state) from the vantage point of their own perceptions, priorities and capacities.

According to Mahnaz Z. Ispahani, "a route is both a geographical and political idea, both an end and a means." It is a geographical idea also in the sense that it involves the notion of a "distance to cover," both on land and at sea, marked in turn by various geographical, geological and ecological features. And it is a political idea in the sense that "routes" connect not just two locations but also various social-cultural spaces, which might be familiar (We) or strange (Them). The nature and role of various routes thus depend on the dynamic and complex interplay between the given geographical proximity/distance and the imagined geopolitical proximity/distance. Furthermore, what gives a geopolitical complexion to routes is the fact that a route might create access rhetorically, which may or may not translate into open and unconditional access. In most cases, as Jean Gottman once observed, access has been a "central problem" in human history, partly political and partly geographical. According to Gottman access in space has been "organised at all times in history to serve political ends, and one of the major aims of politics is to regulate the conditions of access." Gottmann further argued that routes also provide "the means for the movement of ideas, the dominant culture and ideology of the political centre, to its peripheries."[12] But not without inviting friction and resistance! As pointed out by Ispahani, "opposing the route" is what she describes as "*anti-route*—any natural or artificial constraint on access." Furthermore,

> Anti-routes may serve the same human purposes as routes. But anti-routes create pressure against movement—they limit, restrain, or "channel" it—where routes facilitate broader movement. Mountains and deserts (polar sea ice, icebergs, lower visibility caused by blowing snow), legal boundaries and tariffs that raise the cost of crossing them—all are forms of the anti-route ... What routes move, and what anti-routes prevent from moving, are peoples and goods across frontiers. Routes are the means for the centralisation of the state, for the distribution of resources, and for the conduct of war. Transport infrastructure is critical to the definition of the modern state. Routes are also the means for the movement of ideas, transmitting what has been called the "iconography" of the state, the dominant culture and ideology of the political centre to its peripheries.[13]

Ispahani reminds us that routes, both as "natural geographical features" and "physical constructs of men," can take many forms; criss-crossing land, sea and air. She further points out that, "whatever its form, a route is a function of the characteristics of its environment and of technological advances in the modes of transportation and communication."[14] In her view routes, and the access they create, may be systematically conceptualised, as have five dimensions: geographical, political, economic, military and ideational. What is conspicuous by its absence on this list is the ecological-environmental dimension, which acquires critical importance in the case of polar routes such as the NSR.

Geographically, as noted above, the story of a route (including that of the NSR) revolves around the notion of "vanquishing distance" both in spatial and temporal terms. As we would observe in the analysis to follow, what gives the NSR a set of unique features is the manner in which incremental but enhanced global warming is changing the notions of distance, access and mobility in the Arctic Ocean. What Ispahani has to say in the context of borderlands of Asia, as we will observe shortly, resonates well (but not without important qualifications) in the case of the Arctic shipping routes.

> Vanquishing distance is fundamental both to history and to geography—there can be no differentiation of space without movement along defined paths. As paths spread, so does the extent of geographical knowledge. Physical distance is conquered by routes, which overcome natural barriers and topographical constraints; it is conquered, that is to say, in direct relation to advances in the technology of transport and communications and to the sheer will of state-builders. Increased technological prowess leads to increased mobility and carrying capacity and lower costs.[15]

As far as their political dimensions are concerned, routes are intricately intertwined with the projects of national identity building as the key markers of state manipulation of access vis-à-vis the "outsiders."[16] This is where the perceived geopolitical worth of routes is reinforced at times by the strategic deployment of anti-routes.

Matthew Sparke has argued that "as contrasting geostrategic discourses, geopolitics and geo-economics reflect the tensions of uneven development but in ways that tend to abstract particular territorial problems or ideals out of the processes of historical-geographical transformation that produce them."[17] There is no dearth of geopolitical narratives invoking the spectre of "coming anarchy" and holding a particular "arc of instability" or "disputed border" responsible for political unrest. On the other hand, points out Sparke, a "free trade region" or "free zone" is idealised as ushering in geo-economic interdependence, peace and prosperity for all.

Climate Change and the NSR: Impacts and Implications

It is now well established by the earth climate science, uncertainties regarding the pace and pattern notwithstanding, that the Arctic sea ice has been shrinking as well as thinning over the last few decades. The scenario chosen preferred by the Arctic Climate Impact Assessment

(ACIA) in 2004, predicted a largely ice-free Arctic Ocean in late summers in 100 years.[18] According to more recent and less conservative scenarios the Arctic Ocean might become ice free in summers already in 30-50 years. "Under the 100-year scenario, ACIA figures indicate that the NSR sailing season will be prolonged from the current 20-30 days to around 120 days. New generations of larger, stronger, ice-strengthened cargo vessels might however be able to operate unescorted for longer than that, and for such vessels, ACIA predicts an average sailing season in 100 years of up to 170 days. Actually, the sailing season might be even longer, as the ice would also be thinner than today and there would be less risk of encountering hard multi-year ice."[19]

According to IPCC 5th Assessment Report (AR 5), Working Group II (Chapter 28 on "Polar Regions") the evidence for "Polar Amplification" is now well established, graphically proven and hence beyond any doubt.[20] The zonal mean surface temperature warming at high latitudes exceeds global average temperature change. It is said with "very high confidence" that the Arctic region is projected to warm most and with "high confidence" that permafrost temperatures have increased in most regions since the early 1980s. In parts of Northern Alaska it is as high as 3°C and nearly 2°C in parts of the Russian European North. As a result permafrost thickness has reduced and the southern boundary of permafrost regions is fast moving northward. According to the IPCC (AR 5), "The Arctic has been warming since the 1980s at approximately twice the global rate demonstrating the strongest temperature changes (~1°C per decade) in winter and spring, and smallest in autumn. Sea ice declined at an average rate of 13% per decade; the Arctic Ocean is projected to become nearly ice-free in summer within this century. The duration of snow cover extent and snow depth are decreasing in North-America while increasing in Eurasia. Since late 1970s permafrost temperatures have increased between 0.5 to 2°C."[21]

What and Where Is the Northern Sea Route?

It is important to recall, as Claes Lykke Ragner points out, that in Europe "the term *Northeast Passage* has for centuries nurtured visions—that have never complexly died out—of an adventurous short cut that may bring about a revolution in sea trade between Europe and East Asia."[22] Whereas in Russia the term Northern Sea Route holds different connotations, and evokes visions of a grand national transport corridor, created by the efforts of the Russian people, and mainly used for bringing natural resources out, and for bringing deliveries into the many settlements in the Russian Arctic. Since Soviet times, the country has built up an Arctic shipping infrastructure—including most notably the fleet of powerful ice-breakers—and claims jurisdiction over the route.

As noted by David Fairhall, when Russians talk of the NSR today, it is "both more and less than the North-East Passage" of the European geo-historical imaginations.[23] Hence, points out Fairhall, "baffling statistics" prevail about the route. To quote Fairhall:

> The Northern Sea Route's present administrative definition excludes the busiest section of the passage, the Barents Sea. It only starts at the entrance to the Kara Sea, and stretches eastward through the Laptev and East Siberian seas to the Bering Strait. Confusingly therefore, much of the shipping traffic actually plying the Arctic does not appear in official NSR statistics. The authorities have proposed extending the definition, and some of the relevant jurisdiction, westwards as far as Murmansk, but this has so far been resisted by oil and gas interests in the region. For the time being, when Russians are referring to the whole passage, including the Barents Sea and beyond, they tend to use some broader term like "maritime transport corridor."[24]

The NSR also has an important domestic North-South dimension that sometimes is eclipsed in more popular narratives focusing international shipping route dimension. The NSR is integral to the vast river transport network "penetrating the Siberian taiga east of the Urals, most notably along the Ob, the Yenisei, the Lena and their innumerable tributaries."[25] And since railways and all-weather roads are scarce as well as expensive to both build and maintain in these remote areas, especially due to melting permafrost in a warming climate, river transport system becomes critically important. Given that Novey Port on the Ob and Igarka port on the Yenisei are located about 400 miles deep inland, the seagoing ships can and do enter deep inland from the open sea to the north. As Fairhall puts it succinctly:

> The NSR definition which makes most sense in modern economic terms is therefore the broadest—a transport corridor running from the Atlantic to the Pacific, opening up Russia's northern industrial centres—and especially the oil and gas fields around the Barents Sea—to Western markets and foreign investment. The limited official definition harks back to the early Stalinist period, when *Glavsevmorput* was created not just to operate ships, but to administer the region's forcible industrialisation—literally so in the sense that forced labour was so often used. The bloated Communist organisation was disbanded in 1964. Traces of the old bureaucracy may admittedly survive (the re-establishment of a new independent agency to manage the route was announced in 2009) but in a new form and devoted to quite different ends.[26]

It is this Janus faced inside-outside character of the NSR—implicated further in a rather entangled geopolitical and geo-economic interface—that gives this sea route a complex and compelling persona; one that defies unambiguous, uncontested legal-political definition. Richard Sale and Eugene Potapov would argue that behind the legal positions adopted by Russia is a particular notion of a "border," which differs from Western understandings. "In the latter it is a line, while in Russia it is a zone, a ribbon of variable width."[27] Today, Russians claim their formal jurisdiction over the NSR in reference to Article 234 of the UNCLOS, which grants coastal states the right to unilaterally adopt and enforce non-discriminatory laws and environmental regulations in their exclusive economic zones.

Behind the assertions of legal geographies is a rather complex assemblage of both physical and political geographies, which has been graphically captured in an outstanding study on the NSR by The Fridtjof Nansen Institute.[28] It is important to note that the "NSR plays a different role for the different regions along the route."[29] The dependency graph has an east-west dimension. For the settlements in the easternmost region of Chukotka A. O. the dependence on the NSR is critically important. Whereas other parts of the NSR, such as Sakha, are relatively much less dependent "because of alternative import/export routes by river, with Krasnoyarsk Kray being able to use the NSR for export of non-ferrous metals and potentially as an alternative to the Trans-Siberian Railway, and the westernmost regions being able to use the NSR to develop oil and gas reserves which would else not have been commercially recoverable."[30] In other words, while assessing the role of the NSR as a vehicle "to promote the economic development of the northern part of Asian Russia, focus has to be on the western part, where large volumes of hydrocarbons, non-ferrous metals and possibly timber will be exported westwards. This also implies that NSR operations can be carried out on a more-or-less commercial basis in the western part of the NSR area, while NSR operations in the eastern part cannot become profitable in itself, but must rely on the authorities' capability and will to subsidise the supplying of local settlements."[31]

The notion of "vanquishing distance" acquires considerable ambiguity as well as complexity in the case of NSR. Approached as international shipping passage, the NSR, from the west to the east, passes through Russian Arctic seas—the Barents Sea, the Kara Sea, the Laptev Sea, the East Siberian Sea and the Chukchi Sea. At the westernmost end of the route is Murmansk, and the Bering Strait or Provideniya on the coast of the Bering Sea mark the easternmost end. It is important to bear in mind that depending mainly on the transient ice conditions prevailing at a given time, several variations of the NSR can be identified.[32] The most conventional one is the coastal route, which links main Russian Arctic ports and is mostly used for cabotage (port to port along the coast) shipping. The routes far away from the Arctic coast, which are more appropriate for transit shipping, are shorter but the ice conditions there are more severe. The route over the North Pole is the shortest transit way, its economically feasibility remains rather doubtful in the near future.[33] Moreover, with the exception of Murmansk, "only a few along the route are fully geared for providing bunkering, repair facilities, and rest and recuperation for the crew."[34] Open water depths for the NSR also vary from between 20m to 200m. "Different route options require transiting one or more of the many straits along the route."[35]

A number of so called "choke points" have also been identified on the NSR:[36] the Kara Strait (the Kara Gate) between the Novaya Zemlya and the Vaygach Island, the Vilkitsky Strait between the Severnaya Zemlya and the Taymyr Peninsula, the Sannikov Strait traversing the New Siberian Islands, the Longa Strait between the Wrangel Island and Siberian mainland, and the Bering Strait between Asia and North America.

Geo-Historical Perspectives on the Northern Sea Route (*Sevmorput*): Development, Security, and Identity

In sixteenth century Europe, the "discovery of the horn of a unicorn on the shores of the Kara Sea caused great excitement" and thus began the early attempts by the Dutch and the British to find a North-East passage, based on the calculation that "if unicorn horns had been washed up by the Kara Sea, then a sea route eastward clearly existed."[37] Whereas Richard Chancellor could not make it to Kholmogori (which later became Arkhangelsk–Archangel) in 1553, Willem Barents's very best stopped at the Kara Sea in 1594. The anti-route effects induced by the unpredictable and deadly sea ice were too formidable to be overcome by the "existing seafaring technologies and global warming was still centuries away." Whereas the frontiers of the west-east axis of the route could not be pushed any further, the push came from south-north axis in "the wake of the conquest of Siberia" as "Russians explored the northern mainland coast, Dezhnev sailing through the Bering Strait in 1648 and the explorations of the Great Northern Expedition successfully mapping the northern mainland coast."[38] That the Russians knew their northern coast well is revealed by the fact that "as early as 1619 the Tsar ordered that anyone disclosing information on the route from the Kara Sea to the Ob River would be executed, so important was it for the fur trade, and, consequently, the Tsar's coffers."[39]

It was the Finnish-Swedish explorer Adolf Erik Nordenskiöld who reached the Bering Strait in 1879 after traversing a full passage from Europe, braving one winter along the way.[40] No doubt prior to this expedition, the Arctic shores of Northern Eurasia had already been subjected to mapping by Russian expeditions—that entered the Arctic Sea by descending the great Siberian rivers such as the Ob, Yenisei, Lena and Kolyma—but their motives were different.[41] These were driven largely by the desire to extend Russian sovereignty further to the east and north, and to further push the frontiers of profitable fur trade with the native populations: the so-called Small Peoples of the North. By no means a small feat, Nordenskiöld's passage through the "North East Passage" failed to have impact on world trade patterns. The anti-route effects of Arctic ice conditions once again seriously undermined the prospects of sustaining commercial transit passages.[42] It was in the early 1900s that ice-breakers started sailing through the NSR, and *Sibiryakov* would become the first ice-breaker to make the first single-year transit in 1932.[43]

In the wake of the 1917 Russian Revolution, the relevance of the NEP as an international sea route further declined and for all practical practices it became "out of bounds" for non-Soviet vessels. Over the next decade and more the Soviet Union aimed at developing the NSR as an internal Russian waterway integrated to overall Arctic infrastructure. The key drivers were overwhelmingly geo-economic and, using forced labour, ports were constructed and industries were established in areas such as Igarka, Norilsk, and Khatanga. The key uses of NSR included "deliveries to the many indigenous, industrial, military and scientific settlements in the Arctic, as well as an export route for timber, ores and other products."[44]

John McCannon has described how during the First Five-Year Plan (1932 and 1939), a major shift in the USSR's attitude and approach towards its Arctic territories was noticeable with the creation of the Main Administration of the Northern Sea Route (*Glavsevmorput* or GUSMP).[45] The task of the exploration and development of its Arctic territories, marked by a harsh challenging natural environment, was perceived as better served through a strategy of "hyper-centralisation"; replacing a number of agencies by a single agency endowed with nearly complete authority over the Soviet Arctic.[46] According to McCannon:

> The state's priorities in the North included the firming up of its political authority there, both in terms of domestic governance and international recognition; the Sovietisation of Siberia's indigenous ethnicities, or "small peoples of the North"; and, most important, economic exploitation. The possible military usefulness of the Northern Sea Route was not lost upon the Soviet leadership, but efforts to develop its strategic potential took a back seat to the aforementioned goals until the eve of World War II and were mainly concentrated in the northwest, outside GUSMP's purview. Indispensable to all this were two things: a better scientific understanding of the Arctic's geography and meteorology, and a heightened ability simply to move in the North, whether at sea, on the rivers, or in the air.[47]

GUSMP no doubt had a number of successes to its credit, "including several high-profile polar exploits that won international renown, but, in the end, was unable to satisfy the dictates of the state, especially with respect to economic development."[48] What it did manage to deliver was a northern coastal infrastructure that was good enough to provide sufficient support to the USSR's military needs by the time war came in 1941.

Since the 1970s, the NSR has also acted as an important supply line for the development of the oil and gas industry in northwest Siberia. Soviet traffic on the NSR reached its peak in 1987—when 6.6 million tons of cargo was transported on the route[49]—and then experienced a steep decline, caused largely due to fast deteriorating infrastructure.[50] On October 1, 1987, against the backdrop of the disintegration of the USSR—and the infrastructural-logistical wherewithal needed to sustain the functioning of the route—the then Soviet President Gorbachev proposed in his famous Murmansk speech that the NSR should be thrown open to non-Soviet vessels, an initiative which was followed up by the formal opening of the NSR to foreign vessels on July 1, 1991.

Geo-economics of the Northern Sea Route: Scripts of Hope

Maritime traffic in the Arctic is already considerable and nearly 6,000 vessels were in operation during 2009,[51] with a vast majority providing point-to-point services to coastal communities and installations. As the traffic increases, the challenges related to coastguard, search and rescue and hydrographic services too would multiply. The International Maritime Organisation (IMO) is currently working on a compulsory Polar Code based on the guidelines already in place for ships operating in Arctic waters. During the five-month long opening in 2011, as many as 34 vessels transported a total of 820,789 metric tons through the Northern Sea Route. As of October 2012 (the season is not yet over), 35 vessels have already transported a total of 1,022,577 tons of different goods between Europe and Asia.[52] The estimated annual capacity of the Northern Sea Route is estimated to be about 50 million metric tons of cargo.

Given such unprecedented retreat of Arctic sea ice, the prospects of a commercially viable Northern Sea Route providing the shortest link between Northern Europe and the Far East have improved rather dramatically.[53] There is a reduction of about 3,900 miles in the trip from Rotterdam in the Netherlands to Yokohama in Japan in comparison to voyages through the Indian Ocean shipping lanes. Between London and Yokohama, the distance on the NSR is 7,474 nautical miles compared to 11,447 nautical miles on the Suez-Malacca route or 12,581 nautical miles via the Panama Canal.[54] No doubt the hopes of saving 33 to 20 shipping days, achieving enhanced fuel efficiency and substantially reduced costs, are galvanising enough for the fast-growing Asian economies, especially China.

A combination of exploitation of energy and mineral resources in the Barents Sea and longer navigational seasons in the summer, has resulted in expansion of the traffic on the NSR in recent years from a mere 4 ships in 2010 to 71 in 2013.[55] However, only 20 out of the 71 made the trip between Europe and Asia (or vice versa).[56] Moreover, "these figures pale into insignificance compared with other maritime passages: in 2013, 16,596 ships sailed through the Suez Canal, 12,045 through the Panama Canal, and 77,972 through the Strait of Malacca."[57] The fact also remains that:

> While traffic volume on the NSR is expected to increase over the next few decades, for a number of reasons few observers expect that it will

> grow to rival established maritime trade routes. First, upgrading the NSR's physical infrastructure (which atrophied after the dissolution of the Soviet Union in 1991) and improving navigational, meteorological, and search-and-rescue services will require investment on a massive scale. Russia does not possess enough resources.[58]

In May 2014, President Vladimir Putin and Chinese President Xi Jinping signed a joint statement outlining a comprehensive partnership and strategic cooperation between the two countries. According to the joint statement, Russia will facilitate China's goods shipment using its railway networks, ports and the Northern Sea Route. Till the last week of May 2014, the Moscow based Northern Sea Route Administration had received 90 applications requesting the use of the route for the current 2014 season and "none of the registered vessels are carrying Chinese flag."[59] According to data from the Northern Sea Route Administration, four vessels used the route in 2010, 34 used it in 2011, 46 used it in 2012 and 71 used it in 2013. It is useful to note in passing that whereas the number of ships in the region and along the NSR is growing, it still miniscule in comparison to nearly 17,000 vessels using the Suez Canal in 2013.[60]

Even though no Chinese vessels sailed the Northern Sea Route during the 2013 season, five of the vessels sailing the route last year had ports in China as port of destination or port of departure.[61] A year earlier the first ever Chinese vessel to sail all along the NSR into the Barents Sea (and following a straight line from Iceland to the Bering Strait via the North Pole for its return journey) was the ice-breaker "Xue Long" (Snow Dragon). South Korea, having some of the largest shipbuilding yards in the world, and Norway, home to many of the world's largest shipping companies, have been jointly planning, at the highest political level, to exploit the opportunities arising out of shorter transpolar shipping routes.[62]

The geo-economics of the NSR is also anchored in the resource geopolitics of the Circumpolar Arctic.[63] It is useful to note that oil and gas deposits are unevenly distributed in the Circumpolar Arctic. For example, whereas the offshore areas of Norway, USA, and Greenland are richer in terms of oil, the Russian Arctic is much better endowed with gas resources in comparison to others. According to current estimates there are some 30 billion barrels of oil in the Beaufort and Chukchi seas. Looking ahead, the Arctic is going to attract large investments from a number of non-Arctic states, especially China, in the following four key sectors: mineral resources (oil, gas, and mining), fisheries, logistics (including shipping), and Arctic tourism. Combined together they "could generate investment reaching $100 bn or more in the Arctic region over the next decade, mostly in the minerals sector."[64] Most of this investment is likely to be in the Barents Sea area, north of Norway and Russia, and in northern Alaska and we could "expect smaller investments, but with major local and international consequences, could occur in Greenland, Canada, and elsewhere in the Arctic."[65] Other parts of the Arctic could witness a range of other economic activities such as biological prospecting and exploiting Arctic hydropower. It is forgotten at times that despite significant regional and global ecological linkages (for example, organic pollutants from the industrialised South undermining Arctic ecosystems), the Circumpolar North remains geographically remote in many parts and the current capacity of existing infrastructure and technology to deal with a spill in some parts of the Arctic leaves much to be desired. With much less fanfare than their counterparts in oil and gas sectors, mining companies too have increased their investment in the Arctic despite obvious risks like water and air pollution and the controversies that have erupted from time to time. In the Russian Arctic there are 25 mines in full swing, including the mining operations of the largest Russian nickel producer in the world, namely Norlisk Nickel.[66]

Alaska has 75 mineral prospects and "in Southeast [Alaska], gold ore from Kensington Mine helped boost the state's exports to China by $92 million" in 2011.[67] The Red Dog mine, located in northwest Alaska and the world's largest lead–zinc mines in the world, contributed significantly to the earnings from exports of zinc, lead, gold, and copper, to the tune of $1.3 bn—nearly 36.8 per cent of total export earnings.[68] A number of mines can be found in Greenland, and as the impacts of climate change visibly unfold and the coastal areas are subjected to development planning, "a range of other projects including gold, platinum and rare earth metals with high-technology applications at the Kvanefjeld deposit"[69] are likely to materialise. North of Yellowknife in Canada, diamond mining has expanded at a fast pace. Between 2003 and 2008, total spending at a single mine, the Diavik diamond mine, amounted to $4 bn, of which a substantial share was with local businesses. The Mary River iron ore project on Baffin Island in Canada's Nunavut territory is due to enter development in 2013 and will require an estimated $4.1 bn of direct investment up to 2040.[70]

The Asian Access to the Arctic Routes and Resources: Geo-economic Hopes and Geopolitical Fears

It is useful to acknowledge, as pointed out by Margaret Blunden, that, "Historically, alterations in transport routes have been associated with radical shifts in the balance of economic and political power."[71]

> The pioneer oceanic voyages of the Portuguese and the Spanish during the "Age of Discovery" from the fifteenth to the seventeenth centuries, in search of new trade routes to the Indies, shifted the balance of power away from the Mediterranean, both reflecting and accelerating the gradual decline of Venice and the dramatic rise in the wealth and power of the Iberian countries. The pioneers of the new routes, followed closely by French, English and Dutch seamen, created new economic and political opportunities "which allowed Europeans in due course to acquire the greatest concentration of wealth and power in human history." It may not be entirely fanciful to compare the potential significance of a new Arctic sea lane, in economic, geopolitical and security terms, with that of the opening of the new sea routes to the Indies during the Age of Discovery.[72]

It is a truism that the rising Asian powers will redraw the global geo-economic map of growth and development throughout the present century and even beyond. In a recent study on the rise of Asia by a Danish diplomat and economist, Jørgen Ørstrøm Møller has argued that the good news for Asia is that even though it is "still in catch-up phase with regard to technology, innovation, invention and science,"[73] a number of assets remain at the disposal of its policymakers to assist economic growth.

It is Asia where global savings take place and will continue to be the place, "offering it the pleasant policy dilemma of how to use the money available, rather than pondering where to get the money from. Not only will Asia be the world's creditor, but Asia will take over a large part of global economic activity… Most of the new multinationals entering the list of the world's largest and most important enterprises will grow out of Asia."[74]

With Asia acquiring a greater say in how the global financial system should run and, correspondingly, on how global investment patterns are to be shaped,[75] the world view of its key movers and shakers (i.e., China, Japan, India, South Korea) will increasingly become Arctic-centric. Such a prospect is closely tied of course to the scale and pace of climate change induced transformations with regard to energy resources, trade-transportation routes, fishing, tourism and sovereignty polemics.[76]

In 2008, the National Intelligence Council in the US published a study titled, "Global Trends: A Transformed World."[77] The study concluded that in 2025, the current US-dominated global system will be replaced by a multipolar world with China and India demanding and exercising decisive influence on global geopolitics. The West-centric geometry of the old world order, it acknowledged, would be challenged by the economic and political geographies of the transformed world. Commenting on the Arctic, the report pointed out that "The greatest strategic consequence over the next couple of decades may be that relatively large, resource-deficient trading states such as China, Japan, and Korea will benefit from increased energy resources provided by any Arctic opening and shorter shipping distances."[78]

The rise of China—at a double-digit rate since 2002—continues to evoke wide-ranging responses from analysts and policymakers the world over.[79] Located at the heart of China's world view and self-image appears to be the proposition that as a rising power, China has compelling reasons to register its authoritative presence in the frontier domains of oceans, outer space and the polar regions, and actively shape their future governance. According to Guo Peiqing of the Ocean University of China, "any country that lacks comprehensive research on Polar politics will be excluded from being a decisive power in the management of the Arctic and therefore be forced into a passive position."[80]

While the growing polar discourse in China underscores the value of international cooperation in the Arctic, it is at the same time alert to the possibility of climate change-induced melting of the Arctic ice. The subsequent geo-economic, geopolitical, and strategic transformation in Northern Eurasia has put additional strain on China relations.[81] Furthermore:

> To date China has adopted a wait-and-see approach to Arctic developments, wary that active overtures would cause alarm in other countries due to China's size and status as a rising global power. Chinese officials are therefore very cautious when formulating their views on China's interests in the Arctic. They stress that China's Arctic research activities remain primarily focused on the climatic and environmental consequences of the ice melting in the Arctic. However, in recent years Chinese officials and researchers have started to also assess the commercial, political and security implications for China of a seasonally ice-free Arctic region.[82]

China has been responding warmly to friendly gestures made by Norway (considerably strengthened in turn by cooperation in deep-sea drilling projects between the Chinese and Norwegian companies), and appears particularly determined to cultivate strong, friendly relations with the Nordic countries, especially Iceland. According to a recent story published in the *Daily Mail*, "A Chinese tycoon has sparked fears that his country has a covert plan to dominate new Arctic shipping lanes after buying up a huge chunk of frozen wilderness in Iceland. Former Communist Party official Huang Nubo has offered £100 million to turn a barren stretch of northeast Iceland into an eco-tourism resort. But observers fear his proposals for the bleak area are a way for China to exploit commercial and military shipping lanes in the Arctic when melting ice makes it possible to sail through the North Pole region."[83]

Be that as it may, China, fully conscious of its enviable status as a major export country (with half of its GDP dependent on shipping in one way or the other), is steadily augmenting its polar exploration and research capacity and also aiming to strengthen Chinese shipping companies.[84] Both the Chinese analysts and the government seem fully conscious of the threats and opportunities that a more accessible Arctic and its shipping routes will provide to China. The opportunities offered by reduced logistic costs of shipping companies, economic rejuvenation of Asia's high latitude ports, tourism potential and shifting global trade and shipping patterns in favour of China, however, may be seriously challenged by the deficit of trust and cooperation among the major Arctic coastal states themselves and the cut-throat competition posed by others to Chinese shipping companies and the decline in importance of Chinese ports located in lower latitudes.[85] China also remains deeply conscious of the fact that contemporary international law is least helpful to China's shipping interests.[86] Some Chinese academics have expressed the view that China could consider the option of questioning the Canadian and the Russian official positions on the status on North-West Passage and Northern Sea Route, respectively, under the law of the sea (Blunden, 2012). In April 2012 the first ever visit by the Chinese Premier Wen Jiabao, accompanied by a high-power delegation, to Iceland was widely perceived and reported by media in terms of Iceland turning into "a new regional hub" on new maritime transport route between Europe and Asia.[87] China will soon become the second country after Russia to issue an official guide containing "practical, comprehensive and authoritative information" for Chinese cargo ships wanting to take the polar short cut to Europe.[88]

According to Shyam Saran, former foreign secretary of India, climate change induced transformations in the ecologically pristine Arctic are likely to have a major impact on India and the world.[89] He does raise a number of interesting questions carrying geopolitical connotations:

> Should five countries, which, as an accident of geography, form the Arctic rim, have the right to play with the world's ecological future in pursuit of their economic interests? If there are significant shifts in the world's shipping and, therefore, trade patterns, what will this mean for countries like India? Will the exploitation of energy resources in

> the Arctic improve India's energy security or complicate it even more than currently is the case? There is currently a shift in the centre of gravity of the global economy from the trans-Atlantic to Asia-Pacific. Will there be a reversal of this shift back to the trans-Atlantic via the Northern Tier? Will Russia re-emerge as a major power?[90]

Shyam Saran strongly disagrees with the contention that India should follow China in seeking a pie in the Arctic resource bonanza in pursuit of her energy security and describes the ongoing politicking as "short-sighted" and highly damaging to Arctic ecology. Instead, Saran argues that both Antarctica and the Arctic Ocean are "global commons" and share a "common heritage and mankind," and India, along with other Arctic states, should assert a role in Arctic governance, which in his view cannot be "exclusive privilege of the Arctic littoral countries."

South Korea's interest in the Arctic is also prompted by the titillating prospects of the distance between Korea and Europe becoming much shorter.[91] During 2007 one ship successfully shuttled between Ulsan, Korea and Rotterdam through the Northern Sea Routes. Singapore may not welcome this development, as China, Japan and Korea may ultimately decide to skip its port for most of their international shipments. Sensing the heated competition early on, countries with a stake have decided to form an intergovernmental forum to coordinate their activities and manage the race to the North Pole.

Japan, another Asian economic giant in the grip of energy insecurity and related cartographic anxieties, is observing climate change-induced physical transformations in the Arctic Ocean and emerging geopolitical discourses *in* and *about* the Arctic with a great deal of concern. Such concerns are being increasingly shared and articulated in Japan by media, academia and the public at large. Besides environmental concerns associated with the threats induced by climate change, there is a growing focus on the opportunities related to navigation in an ice-free Arctic Ocean. The distance between Yokohama and Hamburg is expected to be reduced by nearly 62 per cent in comparison to the distance via the Suez Canal. According to Hidehisa Horinouchi, the Deputy Director-General of International Legal Affairs Bureau, Ministry of Foreign Affairs of

Japan, "Japan's position is that the legal issues related to the Arctic Ocean should be addressed within the existing legal framework."[92]

Mitsui O.S.K Lines of Japan has recently announced that it will start transporting LNG on a regular basis from Yamal, Russia via the Northern Sea Route from 2018. The first ever regular service to North East Asia, using NSR, will be operating from June to October. It is expected that Yamal project will produce 16,500,000 tons of LNG, which will amount to nearly 20% of the current level of import of LNG to Japan. Mitsui O.S.K. Lines and China Shipping will co-own an ice-breaker/LNG tanker. The tankers, costing roughly ¥100 billion, will be owned and operated jointly in partnership with a Chinese shipping firm. China's Offshore Oil Engineering Co. Ltd. recently signed a contract for the Yamal project. They are expected to transport about 3 million tons of LNG a year. The gas produced at the Yamal Peninsula will reach Northeast Asia, including Japan, through NSR in about 18 days.

Mapping Anti-Routes in the NSR

Recalling some of the insights offered by Ispahani, discussed earlier in the chapter, this section intends to map out briefly some of the major anti-route factors and forces that are likely to hamper the flows of various kinds through the NSR. There are a number of factors that might act as anti-routes and seriously undermine the feasibility and viability of such titillating future prospects of shorter and cheaper NSR. As pointed out in a recent report published by Lloyd's and Chatham House, "Distance is important, but it is not the only consideration in determining how fast the Northern Sea Route, or other trans-Arctic shipping routes, will develop. Navigation or particular routes in terms of sea-depth, knowledge of the seabed, availability of suitable ships and the risks associated with Arctic shipping are all factors."[93]

The Arctic Sea Ice: Reassessing the Retreat

It is so obvious that the Arctic sea ice, having acted as a formidable anti-route for so long, is retreating. The Arctic witnessed a record reduction of 3.41 million square kilometres (1.32 million square miles) in September 2012, amounting to almost half of the 1979 to 2000 average.[94] All that is left now in the Arctic is the year-old ice, which melts during the summer season. The extent to which the Arctic sea ice has lost its anti-route effects needs a closer scrutiny. According to some of the leading experts of Arctic shipping, "As receding ice exposes larger areas of open water and wind fetch, storm surges will present an increasing environmental hazard, particularly to container vessels carrying above-deck stacked cargoes. Even in low concentrations, ice can cause significant hull damage. Ships navigating in mostly open water are especially vulnerable to "growlers" (small blocks of hard MYI) as these ships are likely to be operating at higher speeds."[95] More recently it has been found out by Jim Thomson, a researcher from University of Washington that as the Arctic sea ice retreats and results in a season of increasingly open water—which is likely to extend across the whole Arctic Ocean before the middle of twenty-first century—"a new and unpredictable dimension" is going to be introduced by the storms that could create Arctic swell of huge waves.[96]

Sometimes it is forgotten that there is a rather complex economic geography to Arctic sea ice. Here are a few examples from the Russian Arctic that are directly relevant to the NSR. One finds a rather uneven distribution of ice along the NSR due to the prevalence of distinct climatic regions in the Russian Arctic coastal seas. In the west, the marine climatic conditions in the Barents and western Kara Seas are tempered with relatively warm current from the Atlantic Ocean. This intervention has facilitated a continuous year-round transport of nickel from Dudinka to Murmansk since 1979. Thanks to significant run-off from the Yenisei and Ob rivers, the process of ice disappearance in the Kara Sea is hastened by over two weeks near river mouths. In the case of the Chukchi Sea, at the eastern terminus of the NSR, the north Pacific current passing through Bering Strait exerts a similar marine climate influence. In contrast:

> The climate of the "interior" region encompassing the eastern Kara, Laptev, and East Siberian Seas is much colder, dominated by continental air masses and the adjacent Arctic Ocean. While the Kara Sea is often sheltered from heavy ice to the north by the Novaya Zemlya

and Franz Josef Land archipelagos, the interior seas receive significant ice transport from the central Arctic Ocean, including some MYI floes. Historically, the navigation season has been limited to approximately July through October in every region east of the port of Dikson, and the East Siberian Sea has rarely been more than 50% ice-free in a typical year.[97]

According to a recent comprehensive study, whereas there is little doubt that "the NSR is emerging as a seasonal trade route for shipping Arctic natural resources to global markets,"[98] yet "All shipping in the NSR is constrained to some degree today by sea ice and bathymetry."[99] The following factors need to be taken into account while critically examining the geopolitical issue of access and the expected geo-economic benefits for various stakeholders:

1. Arctic sea ice in the Russian maritime Arctic remains a key constraint to the operation of non-ice-strengthened or open water ships during the period of study, 2013-2027. There remains limited accessibility for non-ice-strengthened ships in select coastal seas from July to October, if the Russian authorities even allow seasonal navigation of such ships east of Vilkitsky Strait.
2. Ships may operate in the western NSR for substantially longer seasons, including year-round navigation (with appropriate ice-class vessels), compared with more limited accessibility remaining in the eastern NSR (Laptev, East Siberian and Chukchi seas).
3. While PC3 vessels may technically navigate along the NSR in winter for short periods, marine access is highly variable leading to large uncertainties in the plausibility of year-round operation across the whole of the NSR.
4. Bathymetry around the New Siberian Islands presents a significant constraint for deeper draft vessels, forcing ships northward into more challenging sea ice for PC ships.[100]

Technological Gaps and Knowledge Deficit

Another important anti-route pertains to persisting gaps on technological and scientific know-how. Despite such obvious geophysical transformations in the Arctic Ocean, the lack of technology in various crucial domains such as infrastructure and transportation remains a major barrier to Arctic access.[101] The prospects of acquiring technological capabilities that would allow year-round recovery of Arctic resources remain remote, at least in the short term. Given the huge distances to cover, it is far from certain whether the project of building pipelines and putting in place complex liquefaction infrastructure would be cost-effective.[102] Ice-breakers, many nuclear powered, are necessary for not only geopolitical influence and power projection in the region year-round but also for facilitating geo-economic goals. Ice-breakers are expensive but without escort provided by them, commercial vessels face much higher risks. In this respect the capacity profile of the Arctic rim states is quite asymmetrical. As pointed out by Charles K. Ebinger and Evie Zambetakis:

> The various Arctic nations have widely divergent capabilities. For example, Russia has 20 ice-breakers; Canada has 12, and is working on budgeting for 8 more; the US has, to all intents and purposes, just one functional ice-breaker. These ships take eight to ten years to build, and cost approximately $1 billion each. The global economic crisis has, however, put a strain on budgets, and ice-breaker fleets are unlikely to expand rapidly in the short term. Nonetheless, even if the US started building tomorrow it would long remain far behind other Arctic states such as Russia and Canada, taking decades and at least $20 billion to catch up.[103]

There are other critically important maritime domains where anti-routes are quite obvious. Navigating the Arctic seas without sufficient hydrographic data and adequate satellite communications (which enable real-time high resolution images) amounts to very high risks. As pointed out by Vijay Sakhuja, "The ships would also require special navigation and communications instruments. It is important to note that satellite communications poses a challenge in the higher latitudes. Meanwhile, Russia has put into orbit three Meridian-series communications satellites, which can serve both military and civilian users. These are capable of supporting communication between ships, aircraft and the shore stations. Russia plans to expand this communications network to other regions along the NSR including northern Siberia and the Far East."[104]

Strategic Distrust

According to Kenneth Lieberthal and Wang Jisi[105] "strategic distrust" implies "mutual trust of long intentions." They further point out that "Distrust is itself corrosive, producing attitudes and actions that themselves contribute to greater distrust." There are two levels at which the notion of "strategic distrust" as a major anti-route factor could be applied in the Arctic context. Firstly at the level of eight Arctic rim states themselves. Secondly, with regard to the growing interest and involvement of Asian states in Arctic affairs including governance issues.

The geostrategic-military fallout of the Ukraine crisis reminds us of the "double vision" argument made by Matthew Sparke. As far as the rhetoric and reality of the NSR are concerned, the Ukraine crisis seems to unravel the entangled relationship between developmental imperatives demanding access to resources and/or markets through friction-free spaces and conventional "national security" concerns imposing barriers and enclosures. Some Arctic observers are quite right in pointing out that, "The Ukrainian crisis has rekindled doubts and reopened old insecurities among the Nordic nations as to whether Russia's military intervention could sour years of bridge-building and cooperation in the High North and wider Arctic regions."[106] The following recent statements made by Sergei Markov, personal envoy of President Putin, might have added to the growing cartographic anxieties in Finland and other Nordic countries. Markov is reported to have said: "Anti-Semitism started World War II, Russophobia could start the third. Finland is one of the most Russophobian countries in Europe, together with Sweden and the Baltic states ... Russia recommends Finland not to join NATO. That military alliance has lost its aim and goal and is therefore looking for new tasks. If Finland joins NATO it would weaken the security in Europe, not strengthen it."[107] That ten nuclear submarines are under construction in Russia too has not gone unnoticed.

The uneven geographies of development in the era of neoliberal globalisation are also visible in the Russian Arctic. The Russian Arctic region is steadily accumulating debt as spending increases. Murmansk, for example, "in the first half of 2014 had a budget deficit close to 20 per cent."[108] The phenomenon of melting permafrost with wide-ranging implications for coastal erosion, waterfront infrastructure and pipelines connected to offshore regions is going to add extra financial burden to agencies concerned.

A remarkable feature of contemporary Arctic geopolitics, in the context of climate change, is the assertion and counter-assertion of classical notions of sovereignty and territoriality.[109] According to Klaus Dodds, the manner in which the Arctic coastal states have pressed their claims to outer/extended continental shelves should compel us "to reflect on how Arctic territories are being made legible and re-legible for the purpose of intervention and/or management."[110] The planting of the Russian flag at the bottom of the Arctic Ocean in August 2007 (by a private Russian expedition in two mini-submarines lead by Duma and United Russia party member and polar explorer Arthur Chilingarov) and its underlying geopolitical symbolism has generated considerable cartographic anxieties around the Arctic rim and even beyond. According to Valur Ingimundarson:

> While the Russian act of planting a flag at the North Pole seabed was designed to remind the whole world that Russia was a great polar and scientific power, it mostly served internal political aims within the context of Russia's presidential succession after Putin and parliamentary elections in 2007. Yet, geopolitical realities can be created wholly irrespective of whether they correspond to internal or scientific realities. The flag planting episode had deep impact on other Arctic stakeholders.[111]

There also appears to be a growing trend among some of the analysts to frame complex and dynamic India-China interactions in highly reductionist and sensational terms of a "New Great Game"[112] especially in view of the expanding economies of the two Asian civilisations and their voracious appetite for energy resources. The alarmist narratives of the New Great Game[113] and "Climate Wars"[114] can also be found in some recent studies of Arctic geopolitics.[115]

Yet another Arctic paradox appears to be as follows: Whereas the rhetoric and reality of "Asian Century" are among the key drivers behind the "opening up" of the Arctic and its routes, fears associated with the "rise" of China and India are also generating some anti-route factors. I have argued elsewhere that it is simply unrealistic to ignore the emerging contours of a new geopolitical landscape marked by Asia's geo-economic ascendance. China and India as the two "planetary powers" (so called by some in view of the global ecological impact and fallout of their fast-growing economies) look able and determined to act as mapmakers.[116]

According to the 2008 Scenario Narratives Report entitled "The Future of Arctic Marine Navigation in Mid-Century" (Arctic Marine Shipping Assessment of the Arctic Council's Protection of the Arctic Marine Environmental Working Group: 8):

> By 2025, China and India were developing navies that could guard their network of secure maritime transport routes from energy states to their ports of Hong Kong, Shanghai, Calcutta, and Mumbai. China managed to sign an energy deal with Russia, one that included significant reductions in the amount of gas and oil that Russia would export to the EU. Russian-Chinese trade increased, with both countries making use of the Northern Sea Route with well-publicised "demonstration voyages." Norway, nervous about future Russian plans, reluctantly decided to invest in more naval forces to protect its own Arctic interests. Japan did the same. Mariners began calling the Bering Strait the "Bering Gate," with US and Russian patrols on continuous deployment.[117]

I have argued elsewhere recently that "there is no convincing reason that the leading Asian economies, entangled as they are in a web of capital flows, supplier-consumer interdependencies, and international regulatory mechanisms, institutions, and norms, would undermine the mandate and mission of the Arctic Council and thereby destabilise the region."[118] All said and done, at the Arctic Council Ministerial Meeting held in Kirunaon May 15, 2013, it was decided to grant observer status to China, India, Japan, South Korea, Singapore, and Italy.

Concluding Reflections

The route-anti-route interplay in the Russian maritime Arctic is likely to acquire unprecedented complexity in the months to follow in view of the stand-off between the "West" and Russia over the Ukraine issue. Having noted that one could argue that alternative scenarios, far more benign and cooperative in nature, cannot (and should not) be ruled out for Circumpolar Arctic. It is not inevitable that the NSR will become a site of strategic mistrust and militarisation and not a site of cooperation and burden sharing between the Arctic States and Asian stakeholders. No doubt the imaginative geographies of the Arctic have historically varied[119] and the circumpolar landscapes still bear the imprints of military-strategic and geopolitical contestations of the Cold War era.[120] Also, at a time when both the physicality and the ideational aspects of the Arctic, including the Russian Arctic, are in a state of flux, what is being forgotten at times is the long-standing history of ecological degradation, even destruction, all along the NSR, along with the fact that, howsoever small in number, there are indigenous peoples with their Arctic homelands who also have a stake in ecologically sustainable development of the NSR.

What distinguishes the NSR from other sea routes in the non-Arctic parts of the globe (e.g., Straits of Malacca, Straits of Hormuz and the Suez Canal) is also the fact that it is physically located and anchored in the Circumpolar Arctic. In other words, neither the Russian Arctic nor the NSR can be divorced from the Circumpolarity and all that it implies. As rightly pointed out by some keen analysts of the Circumpolar North:

> The Arctic has never fit well within the spatial template of the state system, which is based on a foundational, permanent distinction between enclosable land and free-flowing water. Today, climate change is

> bringing this divergence, which long had been at the margins of political consciousness to the core, in the Arctic states and beyond. On the one hand, climate change is opening opportunities in the Arctic, giving states new incentive to clearly define the region within the spatial ontology of the state system, whether as developable space that can be enclosed within territories or as transit space that is exempt from state power. On the other hand, these same geophysical changes that are spurring increased interest in the region are making it all the more difficult for the Arctic stakeholders to designate specific points in Arctic space as either definitively "inside" or "outside" the state territory.[121]

The process of the "opening" of the Arctic shipping routes in general and the NSR in particular is also taking place in the context of what Karen T. Litfin has described as "planetary politics," the key dynamics of which are "well illustrated in the case of ozone depletion and climate change, namely the complexity of local-global linkages; the importance of science and global civil society; the necessity and inherent difficulty of North-South cooperation; intergenerational time horizons and a holistic perspective; and the problematic nature of sovereignty as a framework for addressing problems of global ecology."[122]

As Adriana Craciun points out so thoughtfully, "Circumpolarity [which currently appears to be under threat] should be orienting principle for our current discussion of the planetary."[123] Moreover:

> The Circumpolar Arctic, defined from both within and without, using both indigenous and alien knowledge, sustains a power incarnation of the planetary, one that reaches out beyond territoriality in ways uniquely possible in a polar world encircling an ocean ... The Arctic invites us beyond the terrestrial "global human ideal" on which current "planetary longings" typically depend, offering allegiances with non-anthropogenic alterity on an extreme scale ... a circumpolar orientation is also significant, with asymmetrical configurations, for current formulations of the "Global South," its Southern Ocean, mythic Great Southern Continent, and post-colonial struggles in the looming "Question of Antarctica."[124]

From one important perspective, the scale at which we should be approaching the NSR context of planetary politics is the unorthodox scale of the new geological period called "Anthropocene" by Paul Crutzen.[125] As Simon Dalby puts it so thoughtfully, "the sheer scale of human activities means that we are living in increasingly artificial circumstances in a biosphere that we are changing."[126] A radical revision of the conventional state-centric understandings of sovereignty and security in an increasingly warming world is overdue and the NSR provides an excellent interdisciplinary laboratory to revisit and rethink the concepts of scale, space and power in the era of profound flows, transformations and transitions.

Arctic Shipping Routes (Please refer colour map on page 250).

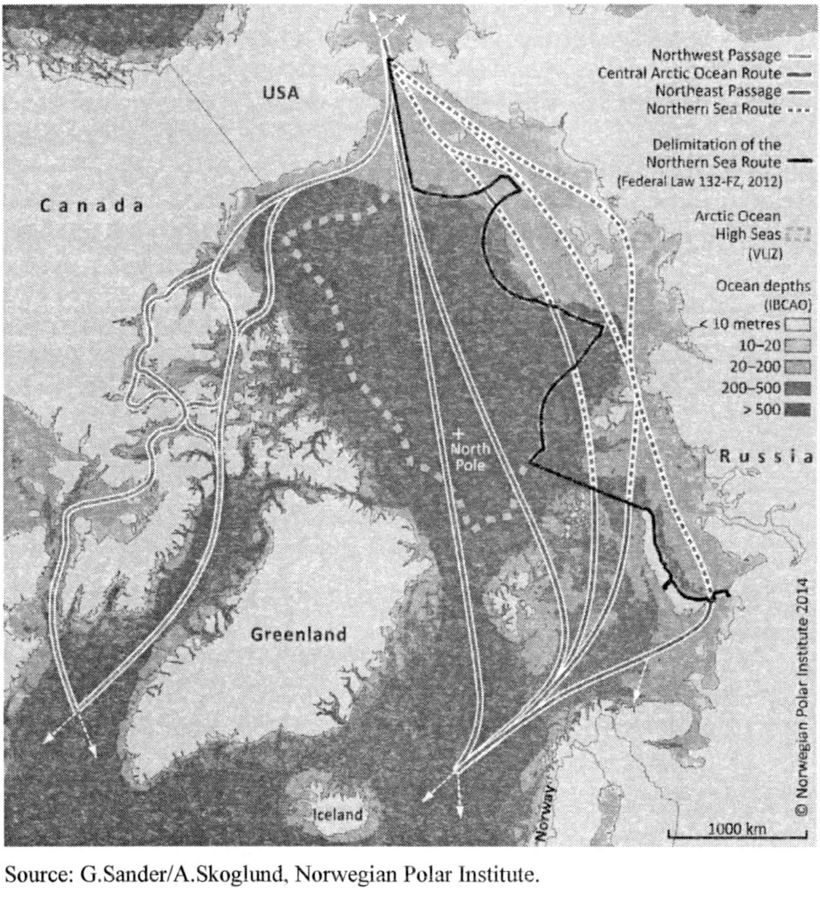

Source: G.Sander/A.Skoglund, Norwegian Polar Institute.

Notes

1. See O. Young, "Building an international regime complex for the Arctic: current status and next steps," *The Polar Journal*, vol. 2, no. 2, 2012: 391-407.
2. Those who are interested in the geopolitics of Heartland may turn to the following outstanding study: A. Sengupta, *Heartlands of Eurasia: The Geopolitics of Political Space* (Lanham, Md.: Lexington Books, 2009); N. Megoran and S. Sharapova (eds.), *Central Asia in International Relations: The Legacies of Halford Mackinder* (New York: Columbia University Press, 2013).
3. Caitlyn L. Antrim, "The Next Geographical Pivot: The Russian Arctic in the 21st Century," *Naval War College Review*, vol. 63, no. 3, 2010: 15-37.
4. See Alun Anderson, *After the Ice: Life, Death and Geopolitics in the New Arctic* (New York: Smithsonian Books, 2009); Michael Byers, *Who owns the Arctic? Understanding sovereignty disputes in the North* (Vancouver: Douglas and McIntyre, 2009); Charles Emmerson, *The future history of the Arctic* (London: The Bodley Head, 2010); David Fairhall, *Cold Front: Conflict ahead in Arctic Waters* (London and New York: I. B. Tauris, 2010); Shelagh D. Grant, *Polar Imperative: a History of Arctic Sovereignty in North America* (Vancouver: Douglas and McIntyre, 2010); Roger Howard, *The Arctic Gold Rush: the New Race for Tomorrow's Natural Resources* (London and New York: Continuum, 2009); Richard Sale and Eugene Potapov, *The Scramble for the Arctic: Ownership, Exploitation and Conflict in the Far North* (London: Frances Lincoln, 2010).
5. Mahnaz Z. Ispahani, *Roads and Rivals: The Political Uses of Access in the Borderlands of Asia* (Ithaca and London: Cornell University Press, 1989).
6. Matthew Sparke, *Introducing Globalization: Ties, Tensions and Uneven Integration* (Chichester: Wiley Blackwell, 2013).
7. Ispahani, *Roads and Rivals*, 214.
8. Sparke, *Introducing Globalization.*
9. Sparke, *Introducing Globalization.*
10. Sanjay Chaturvedi, "(De) Securitizing the Ice: Circumpolar Arctic in 'Global' Climate Change," in Pami Aalto, Vilho Harle and Sami Moisio (eds.), *Global and Regional Problems: Towards an Interdisciplinary Study* (Ashgate: Farnham, 2012), 171-98.
11. Sparke, *Introducing Globalization.*
12. Jean Gottmann, "The Political Partitioning of Our World: An Attempt at Analysis," *World Politics*, vol. 4, July 1952: 515.
13. Ispahani, *Roads and Rivals*, 2-3.
14. Ispahani, *Roads and Rivals*, 3.
15. Ispahani, *Roads and Rivals*, 7.
16. Ispahani, *Roads and Rivals.*
17. Sparke, *Introducing Globalization.*

18. This is the English translation of a chapter originally published in Swedish in the Norden Association's Yearbook for 2008. Claes Lykke Ragner, "Den norra sjövägen," in Torsten Hallberg (ed.), *Barents—ett gränsland i Norden* (Stockholm: Arena Norden, 2008), 120. www.norden.se
19. Ragner, "Den norra sjövägen."
20. IPCC, Working Group II, AR 5, "Polar Regions," chapter 28, 2014. http://ipcc-wg2.gov/AR5/images/uploads/WGIIAR5-Chap28_FGDall.pdf
21. IPCC, Working Group II, AR 5, "Polar Regions," 4.
22. Ragner, "Den norra sjövägen," 114-27.
23. David Fairhall, *Cold Front: Conflict Ahead in Arctic Waters* (Berkeley: Counterpoint, 2010).
24. Fairhall, *Cold Front*, 144.
25. Fairhall, *Cold Front*.
26. Fairhall, *Cold Front*.
27. Sale and Potapov, *The Scramble for the Arctic*, 155.
28. Claes Lykke Ragner, "Northern Sea Route Cargo Flows and Infrastructure Present State and Future Potential," The Fridtjof Nansen Institute Report 13, 2000. Available online at: http://www.fni.no/doc&pdf/FNI-R1300.pdf
29. Ragner, "Northern Sea Route Cargo Flows."
30. Ragner, "Northern Sea Route Cargo Flows."
31. Ragner, "Northern Sea Route Cargo Flows."
32. Hua Xu , Zhifang Yin, Dashan Jia, Fengjun Jin and Hua Ouyang, "The potential seasonal alternative of Asia-Europe container service via Northern sea route under the Arctic sea ice retreat," *Maritime Policy & Management: The flagship journal of International Shipping and Port Research*, vol. 38, no. 5, 2011: 541-60.
33. Xu et al., "The potential seasonal alternative of Asia-Europe container service," 543.
34. Vijay Sakhuja, "Sailing through the Northern Sea Route: Opportunities and Challenges," *Strategic Analysis*, vol. 37, no. 4, 2013: 495.
35. The water depths in the straits are as follows: Kara Strait (in the fairway part)–50m; Matisena and Lenina–not less than 20 to 25m; Vilkitskogo–50 to 250m; Shokalskogo–200 to 250m; Yugorskiy Shar–13m; Sannikova–13 to 15m; Dmitriya Lapteva–8 to 9m; Bering–30 to 50m. See American Bureau of Shipping, "Navigating the Northern Sea Route: Status and Guidance," 2014. http://www.eagle.org/eagleExternalPortalWEB/ShowProperty/BEA%20 Repository/References/Capability%20Brochures/NSR_Advisory
36. Xu et al., "The potential seasonal alternative of Asia-Europe container service," 543.
37. Sale and Potapov, *The Scramble for the Arctic*.

38. Sale and Potapov, *The Scramble for the Arctic*.
39. Sale and Potapov, *The Scramble for the Arctic*.
40. For a detailed historical account of the NSR see for example Willy Østreng, "Historical and Geopolitical Context of the Northern Sea Route," in W. Østreng (ed.), *The Natural and Societal Challenges of the Northern Sea Route. A Reference Work* (Dordrecht/Boston/London: Kluwer Academic Publishers, 1999).
41. Ragner, "Northern Sea Route Cargo Flows," 2-3.
42. Ragner, "Northern Sea Route Cargo Flows."
43. Sale and Potapov, *The Scramble for the Arctic*, 155.
44. Sale and Potapov, *The Scramble for the Arctic*.
45. John McCannon, "The Commissariat of Ice: The Main Administration of the Northern Sea Route (GUSMP) and Stalinist Exploitation of the Arctic, 1932-1939," *The Journal of Slavic Military Studies*, vol. 20, no. 3, 2007: 393-419.
46. McCannon, "The Commissariat of Ice."
47. McCannon, "The Commissariat of Ice," 395.
48. McCannon, "The Commissariat of Ice," 393.
49. McCannon, "The Commissariat of Ice," 393.
50. Margaret Blunden, "Geopolitics and the Northern Sea Route," *International Affairs*, vol. 88, no. 1, 2012: 115.
51. AMSA Report, Arctic Council, "Arctic Marine Shipping Assessment Report," 2009. http://www.pame.is/images/stories/PDF_Files/AMSA_2009_Report_2nd_print.pdf (accessed July 27, 2014).
52. AMSA Report, "Arctic Marine Shipping Assessment Report."
53. AMSA Report, "Arctic Marine Shipping Assessment Report."
54. Ian Storey, "The Arctic Novice: Singapore and the High North," *Asia Policy*, vol. 18, 2014: 66-72.
55. Storey, "The Arctic Novice," 70.
56. Storey, "The Arctic Novice," 70.
57. Storey, "The Arctic Novice," 70.
58. Storey, "The Arctic Novice," 70.
59. Trude Pettersen, "Russia will facilitate China's shipments of goods using its railway networks, ports and the Northern Sea Route, a statement from Presidents Putin's visit to Shanghai says," May 21, 2014. http://barentsobserver.com/en/arctic/2014/05/china-get-better-terms-northern-sea-route-21-05
60. Pettersen, "Russia will facilitate China's shipments of goods."
61. Pettersen, "Russia will facilitate China's shipments of goods." For up-to-date information on the NSR see the website of the Northern Sea Route Administration, Federal State Institution: http://asmp.morflot.ru/en/perechen_zayavlenii/
62. Thomas Nilsen, "South Korea ties up with Norway on Arctic Shipping," *Barents*

Observer, September 12, 2012. http://barentsobserver.com/en/arctic/south-korea-ties-norway-arctic-shipping-12-09

63. This section draws extensively on the data I have used on Arctic resources in my article, "China and India in the 'Receding' Arctic: Rhetoric, Routes and Resources," *Jadavpur Journal of International Relations*, vol. 17, no. 1, 2013: 41-68.
64. Charles Emerson and Glada Lahn, *Arctic Opening: Opportunity and Risk in the High North*, Chatham House-Lloyd's, 2012. http://www.chathamhouse.org/sites/default/files/public/Research/Energy,%20 Environment%20and%20Development/0412arctic.pdf .
65. Emerson and Lahn, *Arctic Opening.*
66. Emerson and Lahn, *Arctic Opening.*
67. Alex DeMarban, "New Interactive Map Portrays Mining Boom across Alaska," *Alaska Dispatch*, 2012. Available at http://www.alaskadispatch.com/m/node/218416 (accessed on October 20, 2012).
68. DeMarban, "New Interactive Map."
69. Emerson and Lahn, *Arctic Opening*, 26.
70. Emerson and Lahn, *Arctic Opening.*
71. Margaret Blunden, "Geopolitics of the Northern Sea Route," *International Affairs*, vol. 88, no. 1, 2012: 117.
72. Blunden, "Geopolitics of the Northern Sea Route."
73. Jørgen Ørstrøm Møller, *How Asia Can Shape the World: From the Era of Plenty to the Era of Scarcities* (Singapore: Institute of South East Asian Studies, 2011).
74. Møller, *How Asia Can Shape the World.*
75. Møller, *How Asia Can Shape the World.*
76. Anneta Lytvynenko, "Arctic Sovereignty Policy Review," 2011. www4.carleton.ca/cifp/app/serve.php/1355.pdf (accessed August 17, 2011).
77. National Intelligence Council, "Global Trends 2025: A Transformed World," Government Printing Office, 2008.
78. National Intelligence Council, "Global Trends 2025," 53.
79. Harsh V. Pant, *The China Syndrome: Grappling with an Uneasy Relationship* (New Delhi: HarperCollins Publishers, India Today Group, 2010), 186.
80. Cited in Linda Jakobson, "China Prepares for an Ice-free Arctic," *SIPRI Insights on Peace and Security*, no. 2, 2010. http://books.sipri.org/files/insight/SIPRIInsight1002.pdf (accessed July 27, 2014).
81. Jakobson, "China Prepares for an Ice-free Arctic."
82. Jakobson, "China Prepares for an Ice-free Arctic."
83. Simon Parry, "Fears over China's Arctic ambitions as tycoon makes £100 million move on Iceland," 2011. http://www.dailymail.co.uk/news/article-2033509/Fears-China-s-Arctic-ambitions-tycoon-makes-100-million-Iceland.html#ixzz1qCnLKLFZ (accessed October 15, 2011).

84. Jakobson, "China Prepares for an Ice-free Arctic."
85. Jakobson, "China Prepares for an Ice-free Arctic."
86. Jakobson, "China Prepares for an Ice-free Arctic."
87. Atle Staalesen, "China Strengthens Arctic Cooperation with Iceland," *Barents Observer*, April 24, 2012.http://barentsobserver.com/en/arctic/china-strengthens-arctic-cooperation-iceland
88. Trude Pettersen, "China to Release Guide Book on Arctic Shipping," *Barents Observer*, June 20, 2014. http://barentsobserver.com/en/arctic/2014/06/china-release-guidebook-arctic-shipping-20-06
89. Shyam Saran, "Why the Arctic Ocean is important to India? Developments in the Arctic Ocean will redraw the geopolitical map of the world," *Business Standard*, June 12, 2011. See also Shyam Saran, "India's Stake in the Cold War," *The Hindu,* New Delhi, February 1, 2012.
90. Shyam Saran, "Why the Arctic Ocean is important to India? Developments in the Arctic Ocean will redraw the geopolitical map of the world."
91. Charles K. Ebinger and Evie Zambetakis, "The geopolitics of Arctic melt," *International Affairs*, vol. 85, no. 6, 2009: 1215-32.
92. Hidehisa Horinouchi, "Japan and the Arctic," 2010. http://www.norway.or.jp/PageFiles/395907/JAPAN_AND_THE_ARCTIC.pdf (accessed July 27, 2014).
93. Emerson and Lahn, *Arctic Opening*.
94. RIA Novosti, "Arctic Sea Route to Open Year-Round in 2013," *Scientists*, October 17, 2012.
95. Scott R. Stephenson, Lawson W. Brigham and Laurence C. Smith, "Marine accessibility along Russia's Northern Sea Route," *Polar Geography*, vol. 37, no. 2, 2014: 111-33, see 127. Note: "MYI" stands for Multi-Year Ice.
96. W. Erick Rogers, "Huge Waves Measured for First Time in Arctic Ocean," *MarineLink.com*, July 29, 2014. http://www.marinelink.com/news/measured-arctic-first373890.aspx
97. Stephenson et al., "Marine accessibility," 114.
98. Stephenson et al., "Marine accessibility," 128-29.
99. Stephenson et al., "Marine accessibility," 113.
100. Stephenson et al., "Marine accessibility," 129.
101. Stephenson et al., "Marine accessibility," 129.
102. Stephenson et al., "Marine accessibility."
103. Ebinger and Zambetakis, "The Geopolitics of Arctic Melt," 1220.
104. Vijay Sakhuja, "Sailing through the Northern Sea Route: Opportunities and Challenges," *Strategic Analysis*, vol. 37, no. 4, 2013: 497.
105. Kenneth Lieberthal and Wang Jisi, "Addressing US-China Strategic Distrust," John L. Thornton China Centre Monograph Series, no. 4, The John L. Thornton China Centre, Brookings Institute, March 2012.

106. Gerard O'Dwyer, "Nordic Cooperative Stance Bolstered by Ukraine Crisis," *Defense News*, June 10, 2014.
http://www.defensenews.com/article/20140610/DEFREG01/306100029/Nordic-Cooperative-Stance-Bolstered-by-Ukraine-Crisis
107. Thomas Nilsen, "Putin envoy warns Finland against joining NATO," *Barents Observer*, June 9, 2014.
http://barentsobserver.com/en/security/2014/06/putin-envoy-warns-finland-against-joining-nato-09-06
108. Atle Staalesen, "The Russian Arctic region is accumulating debts as spending increases. At the same time, Moscow ups pressure on regional economies," 2014. http://barentsobserver.com/en/business/2014/07/murmansk-growing-budget-deficit-29-07
109. Chaturvedi, "De(securitizing) the Ice."
110. Klaus Dodds, "A Polar Mediterranean? Accessibility, Resources and Sovereignty in the Arctic Ocean," *Global Policy*, vol. 1, no. 3, 2010: 303-11.
111. Valur Ingimundarson, *The Geopolitics of Arctic Natural Resources*, Brussels: The European Parliament, 2010.
112. David Scott, "The Great Power 'Great Game' Between India and China: 'The Logic of Geography,'" *Geopolitics*, vol. 42, no. 1, 2008: 1-26.
113. Guy Killaby, "Great game in a cold climate: Canadian Arctic Sovereignty in Question," *Canadian Military Journal*, 2005-6: 31-40.
114. Benedikt Korf, "The Imaginative Geographies of Climate Wars," *Procedia—Social and Behavioral Sciences*, vol. 14, 2011: 35-39.
115. Scott G. Borgerson, "The Great Game Moves North," *Foreign Affairs*, March/April 2009. http://www.foreignaffairs.com/articles/64905/scott-g-borgerson/the-great-game-moves-north
116. Kishore Mahbubani, *The New Asian Hemisphere: The Irresistible Shift of Global Power to East* (Public Affairs: New York, 2008).
117. Scenario Narratives Report, "The Future of Arctic Marine Navigation in Mid-Century," Arctic Marine Shipping Assessment of the Arctic Council's Protection of the Arctic Marine Environmental Working Group: 8, 2008.
118. Sanjay Chaturvedi, "India's Arctic Engagement: Challenges and Opportunities," *Asia Policy*, vol. 18, 2014: 73-79.
119. David D. Caron, "Climate Change and Arctic Governance: Three Images of a Changing Arctic," in Davor Vidas and Peter Johan Schei (eds.), *Climate Change and Arctic Governance: Three Images of a Changing Arctic* (Leiden/Boston: Martinus Nijhoff Publishers/Brill, 2011), 155-63.
120. Younkyoo Kim and Stephen Blank, "The Arctic: A New Issue on Asia's Security Agenda," *The Korean Journal of Defense Analysis*, vol. 23, no. 3, 2011: 303-20.
121. Hannes Gerhardt, Philip E. Steinberg, Jeremy Tasch, Sandra J. Fabiano and Rob

Shields, "Contested Sovereignty in a Changing Arctic," *Annals of the Association of American Geographers*, vol. 100, no. 4, 2010: 992-1002.

122. Karen T. Liftin, "Planetary Politics," in John Agnew, Katharyne Mitchell and Gerard Toal (eds.), *A Companion to Political Geography* (London: Blackwell Publishing, 2007), 476.
123. Adriana Cracium, "The Scramble for the Arctic," *Interventions*, vol. 11, no. 1, 2009: 109.
124. Cracium, "The Scramble for the Arctic," 113.
125. Paul Crutzen, "Geology of Mankind," *Nature*, vol. 415, 2002: 23.
126. Simon Dalby, *Security and Environmental Change* (Polity Press: Cambridge, 2009), 199.

Appendix A
Railroad Tracks of Northern Russia, USSR

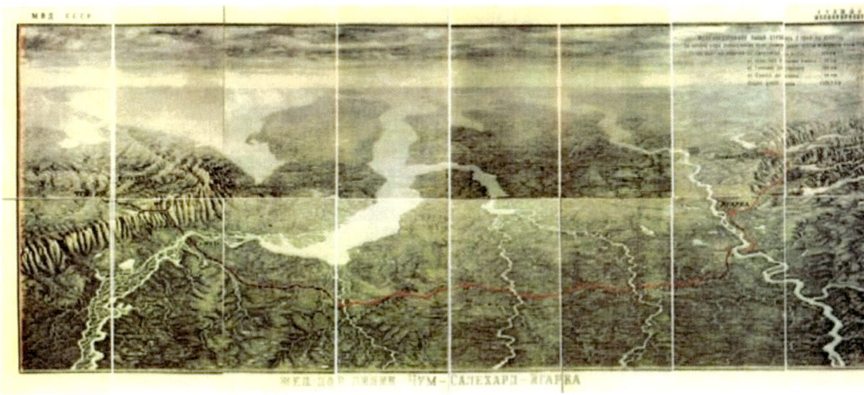

Figure 1. The railway line Chum-Salekhard-Igarka // V. Lamin, V. Plenkin, V. Tkachenko. Global track. The development of the transport system in the east of the country. Schematic maps of the construction of railways USSR.Yekaterinburg, 1999. No. 5.

Figure 2. The railway line Yakutsk-Chukotka // V. Lamin, V. Plenkin, V. Tkachenko. Global track. The development of the transport system in the east of the country. Schematic maps of the construction of railways USSR.Yekaterinburg, 1999. No. 6.

Appendix B
Arctic Shipping Routes

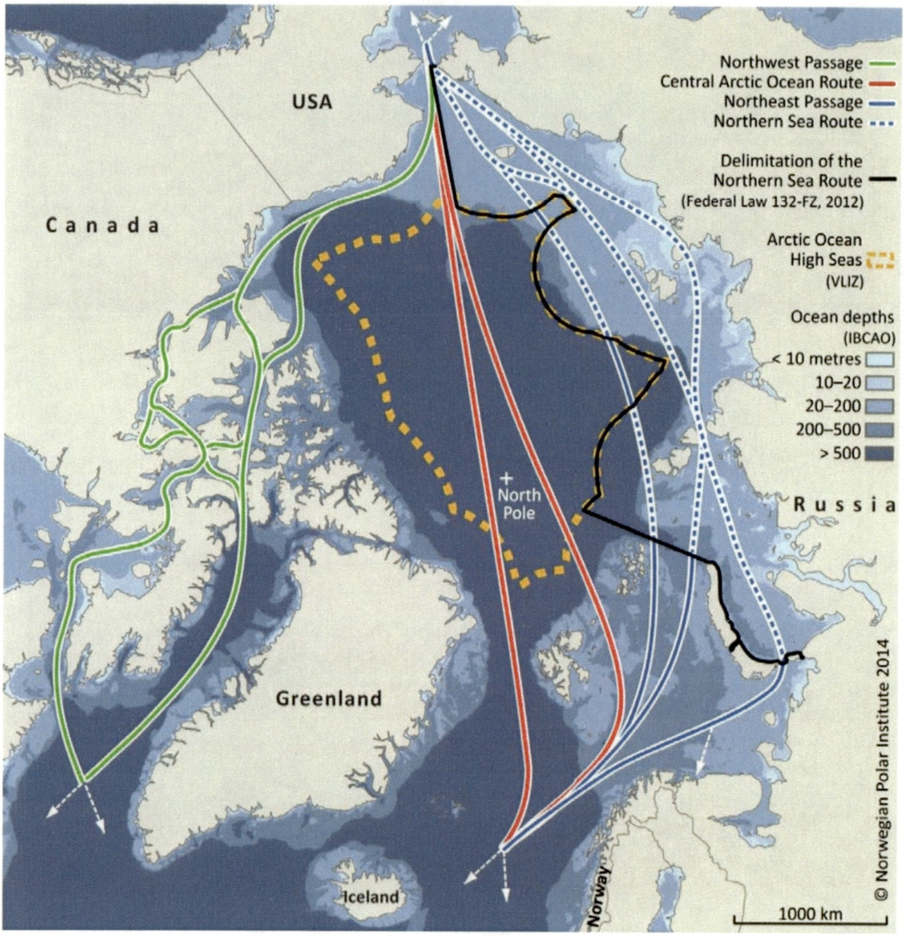

Source: G.Sander/A.Skoglund, Norwegian Polar Institute.

INDEX